Money Matters

Sir Alan Walters

Money Matters

Essays in Honour of Alan Walters

Edited by Patrick Minford
Professor of Economics
Cardiff Business School
Cardiff University, UK

Edward Elgar
Cheltenham, UK Northampton, MA, USA

Published by
Edward Elgar Publishing Limited
Glensanda House
Montpellier Parade
Cheltenham
Glos GL50 1UA
UK

Edward Elgar Publishing, Inc.
136 West Street
Suite 202
Northampton
Massachusetts 01060
USA

A catalogue record for this book
is available from the British Library

Library of Congress Cataloguing in Publication Data
European Monetary Forum Conference on Money in Honour of Sir Alan Walters (2002 : Cardiff, Wales)
Money matters : essays in honour of Alan Walters / edited by Patrick Minford.
p. cm.
This book is the revised and edited proceedings of a European Monetary Forum conference held in Cardiff in May 2002.
1. Monetary policy—Congresses. 2. Monetary unions—Congresses. 3. Monetary policy—Great Britain—Congresses. 4. Monetary unions—Great Britain—Congresses. I. Walters, A. A. (Alan Arthur) , 1926– II. Minford, Patrick. III. Title.
HG205.E87 2002
339.5′3—dc22

2003068786

ISBN 1 84376 443 1

Printed and bound in Great Britain by MPG Books Ltd, Bodmin. Cornwall

Contents

Contributors

Rouben V. Atoian, University of North Carolina
Michael Beenstock, Hebrew University of Jerusalem
Matthew B. Canzoneri, Georgetown University
Jagjit S. Chadha, Clare College, Cambridge
Bernard Connolly, AIG Trading Ltd.
Robert E. Cumby, Georgetown University
Harris Dellas, University of Bern, CEPR and IMOP
Behzad T. Diba, Georgetown University
Michele Fratianni, Indiana University
Gregory E. Givens, University of North Carolina
Jürgen von Hagen, Center for European Integration Studies, University of Bonn, Indiana University and CEPR
Dale Henderson, Federal Reserve Board, Washington DC
Andrew Hughes Hallett, Cardiff Business School, Cardiff University
Juha Kilponen, Bank of Finland
Kent Matthews, Cardiff Business School, Cardiff University
Bennett T. McCallum, Carnegie Mellon University and NBER
Jacques Melitz, University of Strathclyde
Edward Nelson, Federal Reserve Bank of St. Louis
Charles Nolan, University of Durham
Ivan Paya, Cardiff Business School, Cardiff University
David A. Peel, Cardiff Business School, Cardiff University
Gordon Pepper, Cass Business School, City of London
Michael K. Salemi, University of North Carolina
Mark Salmon, Cass Business School, City of London
Jan Frederik Slijkerman, Erasmus University Rotterdam and Tinbergen Institute
David J.C. Smant, Erasmus University Rotterdam and Tinbergen Institute
Casper G. de Vries, Erasmus University Rotterdam and Tinbergen Institute
Sir Alan Walters, AIG Trading Ltd, and Emeritus Professor, Johns Hopkins University, Baltimore

Diana N. Weymark, Vanderbilt University
Jizhong Zhou, Center for European Integration Studies, University of Bonn

Preface and Acknowledgments

This book is the revised and edited proceedings of a European Monetary Forum conference held in Cardiff in May 2002. The European Monetary Forum is a group of academic monetary economists mainly based in northern Europe which meets every nine months or so. This conference was made possible by support from several people and bodies to whom I extend my warmest thanks. Sir Julian Hodge provided the funding through the Carlyle Trust to set up the Julian Hodge Institute in Applied Macroeconomics within Cardiff Business School and Cardiff University; the conference was organised under its auspices. Cardiff County Council, its leader Russell Goodway and chief executive Byron Davies kindly sponsored the opening policy panel and dinner, and made available the Council's meeting facilities for the conference sessions and Jeff Andrews, the Council's chief officer for European Affairs, ensured their smooth functioning. Sir Rocco Forte and the St. David's Hotel sponsored the conference dinner. The Centre for European Integration Studies at the University of Bonn and its Director of Economic Studies, Jürgen von Hagen, supported the travel expenses of a number of transatlantic participants. Details of the conference and its participants can be found in the Conference Appendix at the end of the book.

The book was typeset by Bruce Webb, my Business School colleague, in LaTeX; I am most grateful to him and also to Edward Elgar, Luke Adams and the other staff of Edward Elgar Publishing for their help in realising this project.

Introduction

I organized the conference, of which this volume is the product, to pay tribute to someone — my old mentor at the LSE — who was not only an important UK academic economist but also a major influence on the policy thinking of a whole generation of UK economists and politicians. Alan Walters was an innovative academic economist and an exciting teacher of micro and monetary economics; and then as a policy adviser in the 1970s and 1980s he also helped Margaret Thatcher change the course of British history. This volume is devoted particularly to monetary economics which was the main strand in this revolution.

Kent Matthews writes an introduction to Alan's academic work in the following chapter — as he says, it had an astonishingly wide span, from the Econometrica article on cost functions all the way to the first macroeconomic application of rational expectations in a 1970 Economic Journal article. Though Alan was well-known as a policy adviser, even notorious in some circles especially over the issue of the European Exchange Rate Mechanism (ERM), his crucial role in establishing the success of the 1980s monetary policy revolution has not perhaps been widely appreciated. When he arrived to be Thatcher's personal economic adviser in very early 1981 Britain was in the grip of a severe recession; the 'wide money' targets were being greatly overshot, yet short- and long-run interest rates were in middle to high double digits and there was talk of raising the fiscal deficit above 6 per cent of GDP to counteract their strongly restrictionary effect. He diagnosed the problem as one of lack of confidence combined with a technically over-restrictive monetary policy as indicated by the collapse in narrow money growth. His suggested policy cure was radical in terms of macroeconomic thinking of the time: the budget deficit must be cut sharply to revive confidence that money supply growth would be permanently curbed and at the same time money conditions must be loosened. The logic was that of rational expectations: inflation expectations could not be brought down without confidence in the new policies' permanency, being undermined by fears of a policy U-turn fed by the poor fiscal situation, itself aggravated by the monetary squeeze which had already had its effect in cutting inflation sharply.

He managed to explain the logic to Margaret Thatcher who forced it on her reluctant Treasury and Chancellor, not to speak of other ministers, the famous 'wets'. The Budget of 1981 which brought the deficit down sharply can now be seen as a turning point at which Thatcher's policies began to achieve credibility and the economy to revive into a strong seven-year expansion. Inflation expectations came down rapidly, bringing down long-term interest rates with them; inflation fell into a range of 3–5 per cent. Monetary targeting for interest-rate setting was re-orientated around narrow money, M0; budgetary discipline was restored, as part of the monetary plan to maintain confidence in the continuity of monetary control.

What struck me about Alan's effectiveness as a policy adviser was his ability to integrate a variety of potentially conflicting strands of monetary thought into a working policy framework. As is well known, Thatcher and her ministerial team brought into government in 1979 a monetarist programme of some eclecticism; there were 'gradualist' monetary targets courtesy of Milton Friedman and adaptive expectations, but they were for '£M3' courtesy of the Treasury and Bank of England view that narrow money could or should not be controlled but that interest rate policy could restrain broader money and credit aggregates. In addition there was the 'fiscalist back-up agenda' which was strongly proposed by Alan Budd and Terry Burns at the London Business School, and supported by our rational expectations group at Liverpool University. Plainly in practice these elements could come into conflict and by late 1980 they were in full battle (as a reading of the evidence to the Treasury and Civil Service Committee's 1980 Report on Monetary Policy clearly shows); there was a severe squeeze in progress, it was certainly hitting inflation hard but there was political trouble with rising unemployment and there was a strong risk that this would cause the policies' abandonment. Finding the necessary prioritisation of the elements so that the policies could proceed was vital. Basically, Alan managed to formulate this and unite most of the conflicting elements in such a way that Thatcher could also provide clear leadership. It can be said without any exaggeration that he saved Thatcherism — Thatcher went on to win the inflation battle, stabilise the fiscal situation and so to proceed to the later vital micro, supply-side, reforms.

At the heart of this excellent policy advice lay Alan's instinctive understanding of monetary economics. So it is appropriate that in this volume we bring together many distinguished monetary economists to write about money. The essays were not commissioned to follow any particular monetary topic; rather the authors were asked to write about whatever they felt was important. They cover a wide set of issues and provoked wide-ranging discussion, theoretical, empirical and policy-related, in which Alan joined continuously. The participants and I are very pleased to offer this record to him in his honour.

Kent Matthews opens the book with a thematic summary of Alan Walters' career as a professional economist: 'Taking on the Economics Establishment: An Appreciation of Alan Walters the Political Economist'. Three themes emerge from an examination of his academic and policy-type publications: the recurring critiques of government policy; liberal market economics; and respect for sound money. His influence on economic policy during the 1980s led to the general acceptance of sensible macroeconomic policy and liberal supply-side policy within the UK. This chapter lays out many of the topics that form the basis of work in this book.

The next chapter, 'Consistent Expectations, Rational Expectations, Multiple-Solution Indeterminacies, and Least-Squares Learnability', by Bennett McCallum, considers a central methodological issue underlying monetary policy analysis. McCallum takes up the perennial topic of indeterminacy in rational expectations (RE) models which one way or another today form the centrepiece of monetary analysis; Alan Walters' 1970 article in the Economic Journal was in fact the first published contribution to this macroeconomics literature. After some historical discussion of the rational expectations (RE) solution procedures of John Muth, Alan Walters, and Robert Lucas, this paper considers the relevance for actual economies of issues stemming from the existence of multiple RE equilibria. In all linear models, the minimum state variable (MSV) solution — as defined by McCallum (*JME*, 1983) — is unique by construction. While it might be argued that the MSV solution warrants special status as the bubble-free solution, the focus in this paper is on its adaptive, least-squares learnability by individual agents, as discussed extensively in important recent publications by George Evans and Seppo Honkapohja.

Although the MSV solution is learnable and the main alternatives are not, in most standard models, Evans and Honkapohja have stressed an example in which the opposite is true. McCallum's paper shows, however, that parameter values yielding that result are such that the model is not well formulated, in a specified sense (one that avoids implausible discontinuities). More generally, analysis of a pair of prominent univariate specifications, featured by Evans and Honkapohja, shows that the MSV solution is invariably learnable in these structures, if they are well formulated.

McCallum's search for a new basis for 'sensible' solutions of rational expectations models, which notoriously have multiple solutions, is interesting and potentially important. Whether 'learnability' turns out to be such a basis remains to be seen; the difficulty is that the concept is slippery and silly solutions might turn out to be 'learnable', while sane ones might turn out not to be. The previous literature stressed the need for appropriate terminal or transversality conditions to ensure sensible solutions — implicitly the justification was that such conditions ensured optimality for the relevant agents (including the government.) One is tempted to assert that if a solution is optimal, then it is in everyone's interests that it be learned and such an incentive should be effective in the end — notably for the government. However, this still leaves open the question of what happens if governments fail in this respect (as has, it might seem, the Japanese government in preventing deflation) — presumably a period of confusion as people wander between available equilibria. In practice, learning as in McCallum must play a role in digging economies out of such holes.

The following four chapters deal with monetary regimes, including exchange rate mechanisms, an area in which Alan Walters was heavily involved, particularly over the question of whether Britain should join the Exchange Rate Mechanism of the European Monetary System (EMS). He was of course a notorious sceptic on this matter; and his views on joining the Euro and related matters are to be found in the later panel chapter. The modern literature, exemplified in what follows, tends to support his insight that monetary policy generally operates best when unfettered by fixed exchange rates. The exceptions, as illustrated by some Mercosur and transitional economies below, may occur when the domestic monetary policy-making capacity is weak or the country is very open like Hong Kong.

In the first of these chapters, 'The Efficacy of Monetary Policy in a Multi Sector, Two Country Model', Matthew B. Canzoneri, Robert E. Cumby and Behzad T. Diba discuss how a new generation of models — based on optimizing agents, monopolistic wage and price setting, and nominal rigidities — is being used to assess the efficacy of monetary policy. King and Wolman (1999) suggested that monetary policy can be very effective: price stability (if achievable) replicates the optimal flexible price solution in their model. However, their result has been shown to depend on symmetries in nominal inertia, productivity, and policy decision making. In this paper, the authors ask which of these asymmetries are important empirically. Is it asymmetries in nominal inertia? Asymmetries in sectoral productivity? Or the lack of a common goal in international decision making? Canzoneri, Cumby and Diba

(2002b) developed a tractable multi sector framework for the analysis of asymmetries in nominal rigidity and productivity in a closed economy; Canzoneri, Cumby and Diba (2002a) developed a rather simple model of international policy coordination. Here, they combine these modelling efforts to develop a general two country, multi sector framework that can be used to assess the quantitative importance of all three asymmetries

In 'Model Misspecification, Robustness and Monetary Policy' Juha Kilponen and Mark Salmon provide an introductory discussion of several issues relating to robust policy design. They apply $\mathcal{H}_\infty$ methods to a standard empirical New Keynesian model of inflation and output gap and derive optimal LQG and $\mathcal{H}_\infty$ interest rate policy rules and compare them with the historical record in the UK over 1988–2001. Both optimal rules are substantially more active than the historical policy record. Kilponen and Salmon also investigate the importance of measurement errors on the output gap and inflation forecast. It is clear that implementing the most robust rule does not make sense but more robust rules than the LQG rule seem to coincide well with actually policy over the period when the MPC has been in place. However there is still a question as to why actual monetary policy has been less responsive than these optimal rules suggest and whether any preference for robustness is explicit within the MPC.

In 'The Case for Monetary Union in Mercosur' Michele Fratianni argues that Mercosur countries have to pursue monetary integration if they want to save their customs union and deepen economic integration. Monetary integration is a catalyst of other forms of integration. As to the type of monetary union (MU), these countries have two options: a unilateral form, whereby each country either pegs to the US dollar or dollarises outright; or a multilateral form with its own currency, its own central bank, and the adoption of common minimum financial standards. A multilateral MU is preferable to a unilateral one, although it is more complex and involves significant institution building. Under ideal conditions, a multilateral MU should be preceded by a transition period long enough to allow member countries to give independence to their national central banks and pursue inflation targeting, while adjusting to idiosyncratic shocks. However, Argentina now is in no condition to put in place a credible inflation-targeting strategy. Thus, Fratianni recommends that the process of monetary unification be jump-started with an immediate "realisation" (i.e., the adoption of the Brazilian currency) of the Argentine economy, to be followed by institution building in Mercosur.

'De Facto Exchange Rate Regimes in Transition Economies: Identification and Determination' by Jürgen von Hagen and Jizhong Zhou reminds us of the long-running debates on the choice of an exchange rate regime and in particular Alan Walters' famous critique of the EMS, emphasising the trade-off between exchange-rate stability and price stability. In this paper the authors extend this discussion to the transition economies and investigate the factors determining the actual de facto (as opposed to the announced or 'official') exchange rate regime in the 1990s. They apply cluster analyses to classify de facto exchange rate regimes according to the behaviour of exchange rates and international reserves. They construct a trichotomous choice structure, with fixed, intermediate, and flexible de facto regimes, and use an ordered-probit model for the empirical work. The results suggest that the choice of official exchange rate regimes, especially that of a fixed-rate regimes, constrains to some extent the choice of de facto exchange rate regimes. While high inflation rates, strong exchange-rate pass-through, better financial institutions, and large current account deficits make a de facto fixed exchange rate regime a more likely choice, heavy burden of non-performing loans, large fiscal deficits, and fast monetary expansion all raise the chances of a more flexible de facto exchange rate regime. They also find that the CIS countries, although still officially favouring more flexible regimes, are not statistically different from the others when choosing their de facto exchange rate regimes.

The book continues with five chapters on issues concerning the demand for money and the appropriate conduct of monetary policy. All revisit old controversies in monetary policy from a present-day perspective. In 'News-Magazine Monetarism' Edward Nelson examines some recent monetary policy debates, in light of commentary on those issues contained in some of the work of Milton Friedman. The specific aspect of Friedman's work considered here is the commentary on monetary policy in his Newsweek magazine columns from 1966 to 1984. His conclusions from this examination include: (1) In contrast to claims made in the VAR literature, the analysis of monetary policy and the business cycle by Friedman and other critics of monetary policy in the 1960s and 1970s did not assume that the money supply was exogenous, or contend that monetary policy shocks were the dominant source of cyclical fluctuations. Rather, the criticism was of the destabilising tendency of the monetary policy feedback rule followed in those decades. (2) There is support for the argument of Orphanides (2000a) that many monetary policy prescriptions by commentators in the 1970s were based on over-optimistic estimates of the growth rate of productive potential. Friedman's Newsweek discussions, like his other work, were unusual for not making policy prescriptions based on output gap estimates.

'Alan Walters and the Demand for Money: An Empirical Retrospective' by Kent Matthews, Ivan Paya, and David Peel notes that the work by Alan Walters and his colleagues on the demand for money was the beginning of applied monetary economics in the UK. Up until that time, there was little interest in applied monetary economics in academic circles and no interest on the role of money in policy circles. Their paper revisits the work of Kavanagh and Walters. It uses the same data base to re-estimate the main demand for money functions reported in their paper with the aid of the modern econometric technology of cointegration and equilibrium-correction. It reports the results of estimated short-run dynamic money demand functions and asks the question, what remains of the original Kavanagh and Walters' results? Our results show that modern econometric techniques have little to add to the long-run estimates produced by Walters in 1966. The value added of modern techniques is to confirm that the results found in 1966 were valid but also to show that the dynamic adjustment was of a non-linear error correction type that could not have been foreseen by Walters in 1966.

In 'The Interaction of Monetary and Fiscal Policy: Solvency and Stabilisation Issues' Jagjit S. Chadha and Charles Nolan explore two key topics on the interaction of monetary and fiscal policy. First, they discuss the concerns forcefully exposited by Sargent and Wallace (1981). Naturally one way to avoid unpleasant fiscal effects on the conduct of monetary policy is to pass conduct of the latter to a credible, independent institution. However, such a reform questions the proper role of monetary and fiscal policy at the business cycle frequencies. Chadha and Nolan therefore develop a simple dynamic stochastic general equilibrium model to examine this issue and study the properties of simple constrained rules for monetary and fiscal policy. In both topics they find that the heart of the tension between monetary and fiscal policy is the determination of the interest rate.

'Monetary Policy under Banking Oligopoly' by Michael Beenstock discusses how monetary policy is transmitted in Israel. If the banking system is oligopolistic the volume of credit, the quantity of money and the general level of prices are less than when the banking system is competitive. Beenstock shows that as the banking system becomes more competitive repressed inflation is released, but the central bank's interest rate policy becomes more effective in controlling inflation. Oligopoly power in the market for bank credit is assumed to depend upon the degree of conjectural variation conjectured by each bank. This implies that oligopoly power may be independent of the number of rival banks. The arguments of the paper are illustrated empirically for Israel. It is shown that increased competition in the banking sector requires the central bank to raise interest rates to prevent repressed inflation from taking effect.

'Money Targeting' by Harris Dellas uses the New Neoclassical Synthesis (NNS) model to compare the properties of two monetary policy rules: monetary targeting; and a standard Taylor rule. There exists a strong presumption in the literature that monetary targeting does not produce satisfactory results when money demand in unstable. Dellas finds that while a Taylor rule does indeed produce more stable output and inflation in the face of money demand shocks it is still welfare inferior to money targeting in spite of this. Moreover, monetary targeting delivers greater inflation stability and also higher welfare in the face of supply and fiscal shocks.

The book's next three chapters consider issues of institutional design. 'Credit Value-at-Risk Constraints, Credit Rationing and Monetary Policy' by Jan Frederik Slijkerman, David J.C. Smant and Casper G. de Vries considers the effect of the new 'Credit Value-at-Risk' (CVaR) regulation of banks. Banks provide risky loans to firms which have superior information regarding the quality of their projects. Due to asymmetric information the banks face the risk of adverse selection. CVaR regulation counters the problem of low quality, i.e. high risk, loans and therefore reduces the risk of the bank loan portfolio. However CVaR regulation distorts the operation of credit markets. The authors show that a binding CVaR constraint introduces credit rationing. CVaR regulation also affects the operation of monetary policy. In 'Policy Games and the Optimal Design of Central Banks' Andrew Hughes Hallett and Diana N. Weymark investigate the impact, on economic performance, of the timing of the moves in a policy game between governments and central banks. It is assumed that the government will have both stabilisation and redistribution objectives. They show that both inflation and income inequality are reduced without sacrificing growth if governments assume a leadership role — compared to monetary leadership, or a regime in which monetary and fiscal policies are determined individually but separately. In particular government leadership benefits both the fiscal and monetary authorities, provided that fiscal policies can be precommitted. This result is consistent with the common presumption that fiscal policy should determine the general policy stance, and monetary policy supply the stabilisation role. The explanation is that allowing the government to set the inflation target in return for committing its fiscal policies, imposes an element of coordination not seen in the other solutions. They point out the implications for a country deciding whether to join a monetary union.

'Policy Evaluation with a Forward-Looking Model' by Rouben V. Atoian, Gregory E. Givens and Michael K. Salemi follows the standard two-step approach to policy evaluation. They set out a small structural model and obtain estimates of its parameters, and then evaluate the performance of alternative policy rules while treating estimates of the structural parameters as fixed and known. They break with standard practice in an interesting way. On the assumption that structural-error covariances are fixed and known, they compare the performance of fixed coefficient rules that condition on past state variables, current state variables, and expectations of future state variables. They also compare fixed-coefficient rules to optimal commitment and discretion. Our paper provides evidence on the practical importance to a central bank of obtaining a commitment mechanism and on the loss in performance when the commitment mechanism takes the form of a simple fixed-coefficient policy rule.

The book's final chapter brings together policy discussions culled from the conference's two panels. The first panel addressed the question of whether Britain should join the euro; I edited the transcript to capture its key themes. The conclusion was euro-sceptical, partly on standard optimal currency area grounds, partly on concerns about the political agendas being pursued on the continent using the euro as an instrument. This ground has by now been very well trodden in the UK in the course of the British Treasury's voluminous examination of the 'Five Tests' and the accompanying debate. This panel's discussions favour the Treasury's ultimate conclusion that the UK should not join at this stage.

The second panel was on 'What should monetary policy be targeting?' It consisted almost entirely of invited contributions which the authors were invited to revise for the book's final section. Dale Henderson presents a carefully-argued personal view of the need for 'rule-informed discretion' in place of either intermediate targets or any explicit rules; effectively the authorities should forecast likely outcomes for output and inflation compared with their targets (potential output and a low inflation rate), then set interest rates to minimise their loss function. He also argues that, because of the zero bound constraint on nominal interest rates, the inflation target should depend on the environment (for example, the lower the normal real interest rate and the less responsive aggregate demand is to real interest rates, the higher it should be).

Bennett McCallum assesses monetary policy in the last two decades in three major economies — the US, the UK and Japan. His method is to compare actual growth in the monetary base with the growth mandated by rules that would have hit a number of widely-used target- inflation, nominal GDP, or a combination of inflation and output as in the Taylor Rule. Generally all three rules give similar assessments of whether monetary policy was too loose or too tight, which suggests that Henderson's 'rule-informed discretion' may not in practice be too different from behaviour driven by a variety of practical rules, provided they are focused on domestic needs. The rules motivated by exchange rate considerations stand out as exceptions: for the UK this is illustrated by the 'Dm-shadowing' period of 1986–1988 when money was on all measures too loose.

Michael Beenstock focuses on the case of Israel where for a long time from the early 1980s exchange rate targets were used to bring down inflation and then hold it down. The policy failed to get it below 12 per cent, and under pressure from Israeli monetarists it was switched in 1994 to the setting of base money to hit a low inflation target under a floating exchange rate.

Gordon Pepper reviews the way in which the wide variety of money supply measures in the UK required constant adjustment for the effects (mainly) of financial deregulation. He argues that, provided such 'distortions' were removed, the money figures gave suitable warnings of emerging problems. In particular he argues that paying attention to these would have helped temper the asset price 'bubble' of the late 1980s. In this he is consistent with McCallum's assessment of Dm-shadowing: it is not clear that the epsiode justifies any direct attention to 'bubbles'.

Finally, Alan Walters discusses the role of fiscal policy in gaining the confidence of financial markets — essentially an implication of rational expectations. This picks up a theme running through many of the earlier chapters: the importance of fiscal policy in providing a constraining and therefore stable environment for monetary policy. He reviews the 1981 experience of the UK where budgetary consolidation caused a sharp improvement in inflation expectations and a revival in growth. He suggests that there is a parallel with Japan today and its high fiscal deficits. Instead of endless 'packages', Japan should consolidate its finances; this in turn could restore private confidence. Koizumi seems to share the Walters view but vested interests prevent implementation, just as they nearly did in the UK in 1981.

Much has changed in the institutional environment over the course of Alan Walters' career to date as a monetary economist. Most notably there is great freedom of intermediation whereas in the early post-war period controls on both credit and foreign exchange were the rule. This change has forced modern monetary analysis to adapt. However, this book reveals that money still matters and has to be controlled in a way that would not surprise a monetarist of long standing.

Patrick Minford

1 Taking on the Economics Establishment: An Appreciation of Alan Walters the Political Economist

Kent Matthews

The very first time I came across Alan Walters was in 1972. He was debating with one of the senior figures of the economics establishment Nicholas Kaldor, on 'Monetarism versus Keynesianism'. What I witnessed was a single link in a continuous chain throughout Alan's professional career — taking on the economics establishment. Being in my first year as an undergraduate at the London School of Economics, I had some understanding of Keynesian economics and I knew about the Quantity Theory of Money. I had even heard of Kaldor but I had never associated Walters, who was a Professor at the LSE at the time, with Monetarism. Indeed my student reading of Walters was his work on road pricing [4]. But what I saw was a slightly apologetic individual taking on a rather superior sounding Cambridge academic. I was unaware that this was a debate that had been raging in the academic journals and what I was listening to was a repeat of Walters' rebuttal of Kaldor's critique of monetarism. However, in my opinion Alan won the debate, not because of the force of his argument or the eloquence of his delivery but because of the dismissive air of superiority projected by Professor Kaldor. Kaldor represented the voice of the establishment, the voice of reason, and the voice of authority. Monetarism was the cry of the unreasonable, the crank, and the cult sect. My sympathies instinctively went out to the Monetarists.

My appreciation of Alan's applied monetary work came much later while in my last year at the NIESR, where in their opinion I had been irredeemably corrupted by Patrick Minford (who was editor of the Review for a short period), when they let me work on St. Louis-type monetary models. However, it was only during the period of notoriety as Mrs Thatcher's personal economic advisor that I really began to appreciate the breadth and depth of Alan Walters' contribution to economic policy.

While most modern economists are content to specialise in a single field, Alan Walters' interest and contribution to economics has been astonishingly wide. His work has spanned transport, econometrics, welfare, development, monetary, macro and international economics. But the common thread throughout was policy and it was here that he usually found himself up against the establishment. Even in his occasional forays into theory, the implications for economic policy were drawn. Frequently, the policy maker was presented with the full costs and implications of ill thought out policies.

This volume is in honour of Alan's contribution to monetary economics but it was as an applied microeconomist that he began his career as a political economist. His first major contribution was in the area of transport economics. The paper that was actually written in 1952 was possibly the first to advocate the use of short run marginal cost for road pricing [1]. A policy implication that has a contemporary resonance is that the paper advocated a 'London licence' for vehicles travelling into central London.[1]

Walters continued to work and publish in the area of transport economics[2] and road pricing. But the two most influential contributions were a paper on road pricing [4] and his book The Economics of Road User Charges [14]. Walters was the first to use data collected by traffic surveys to estimate the elasticity of marginal private cost so as to estimate the best congestion tax.

It was natural for Walters to extend the expertise he had developed as an applied transport economist to wider problems of econometric estimation of cost and production functions. There followed a number of papers on applied econometrics [2], [3], [5], a textbook [17] and a survey article on production and cost functions published in Econometrica [6]. While these studies were not directly policy related, they laid the foundations for his important applied work in monetary economics and macroeconomic policy.

Walters' work in monetary economics followed three stages. We can think of the first as empirical, dealing broadly with the demand for

[1]The adoption of a road-pricing scheme to deal with congestion in downtown Singapore in 1975 was based on this model.

[2]Walters applied marginal cost pricing to transport matters in general. In 1968 he was appointed to the Roskill Commission to conduct a cost–benefit study of the third London Airport.

money and the monetary multiplier [9], [10], [11]. The second was about money and the business cycle [20], [26], [27]. The third and more recent, were about monetary policy in general and the supply side [28], [29], [30], [31], [32].

In the 1960s, the monetarist counter-revolution was in full swing across the Atlantic. Walters' work on the demand for money and the monetary multiplier was a turning point for British monetarism. The dominant view was Keynesian. Government intervention and discretionary policy was the accepted norm. Since Monetarism was for cranks, argument alone would not have won against the economic establishment. It was important that empirical evidence support the monetarist camp.[3] Spurred on by the work of Friedman and others, Walters and his team in Birmingham produced empirical studies of the monetary multipliers and the long-run demand for money. The monetarist case rested on the proposition that there exists a stable long-run demand for money. Walters and his co-researchers demonstrated this.

However, Walters was disarmingly honest about the statistical properties of his estimates. He recognised the dangers of spurious correlation, trended data, autocorrelation in the residuals and so on. But even with the problems of estimation, the results are relevant and remain of interest. This early work which has been confirmed by numerous studies, has been re-tested in this volume by Matthews, Paya and Peel. They ask the question would Walters have come up with the same answers had the modern technology of econometric estimation existed in 1966? Not only do they confirm Alan's long run results; their value-added is to identify a non-linear disequilibrium adjustment mechanism, which they are confident, would meet with his approval.

But Walters was well aware of the difficulties of econometrically testing the 'money matters' hypothesis. The money multiplier analysis found a lag in effect for output of 9 months and for inflation of about 2 years. But taking the Friedman line, he argued that money could not be used as an instrument for 'fine tuning' the economy.

The difficulties of fine-tuning were a constant theme in his writings about money and the business cycle. The inflationary dangers of lax monetary policy were announced time and again, only to be ignored. In the first edition of his Hobart Paper,[4] Walters pointed to the rapid growth in M3 in 1967–68 at an annual rate of 11.5 per cent and warned

---

[3] In Walters [33] he reveals that he applied to the Bank of England for a modest grant to construct a historical data series on money. His request was refused on the grounds that the quantity of money was irrelevant and that there was little interest in such statistics.

[4] [18] but the first edition was published in 1969 and written in November 1968.

that by 1970–71 the rate of inflation would be 8–10 per cent. By the time the third edition was written (July 1971), inflation had risen to 8.5 per cent in 1970 and was 10 per cent in the first quarter of 1971.

In the second half of 1971, the conservative government, in pursuit of the elusive goal of 'full employment', generated a massive expansion in demand in which the growth rate of money reached over 20 per cent per year. In June 1972, Walters wrote a paper which warned of the coming inflation catastrophe. The paper entitled 'Inflation and More Inflation and then ... Devaluation'[5] was forwarded to Edward Heath, the Prime Minister, and in Walters' words 'everything then hit the fan'.[6] Walters predicted that inflation would rise to between 10 and 15 per cent over the next two years and that any attempt to curb inflation through statutory prices and incomes policies would only make matters worse than they would otherwise be.[7] This was the first major monetarist critique of government policy and the economic orthodoxy in the UK. The predictions were borne out by the facts leading to much soul-searching by the leading Keynesian econometric model builders and the greater acceptance of the monetarist approach [26].

The Hobart Paper also has a revealing statement regarding the effects of the monetary expansion of 1967–68 on inflation and interest rates;

> ...a high rate of expansion of money itself generates an expectation of price increases (especially among the influential bankers and financial press) which, ceteris paribus, will push up the nominal interest rate

This theme was taken up in Walters' 1971 paper on 'Consistent Expectations' [21]. In this paper Walters asked the question 'why do people continue to ignore the increase in the quantity of money when they formulate their expectations?' This was the great unfinished paper that, if the full implications had been fully explored, could have scooped Lucas (1972) and the genesis of the rational expectations revolution may have been shared with the LSE rather than Chicago and Minnesota.

Much of Walters' writings on the political economy were during the 1970s but a lot more was to come in the 1980s. It was no accident that this latter burst of activity coincided with the decade of the Thatcher government. Up until the election of the Conservative government in June 1979, the economic establishment regarded Walters as part of a

[5] Seebag Review, Gilt Edged News Letter, 23 June 1972.

[6] Personal correspondence.

[7] Inflation actually rose 9, 16, and 25 per cent in the years 1973–75.

cranky monetarist sect, many of whom had fled the country during the Wilson–Callaghan period. They were to be respectfully ignored on all things to do with macroeconomic policy. The close political relationship Walters had forged with the Prime Minister, Mrs Thatcher changed all that.

In his challenge to the Keynesian establishment, Walters criticised government policy during the late 1970s, focussing on what governments cannot deliver [26]. Walters laid bare the exaggerated claims produced by economists and their macroeconomic models.[8] In the eighth Wincott Memorial Lecture to the Institute of Economic Affairs, Walters stated that 'change is in the air...that the theory of the nicely managed growth economy died in the 1970s'.[9] Two years later a radical new government came to power which swept away the fine tuning methods of the past and announced monetary targeting and a 'medium-term financial strategy'.

To loud protests from the Economics establishment in the UK, Alan Walters was appointed Personal Economic Advisor to Mrs Thatcher. In his own words 'I had the best job anyone could devise. Since I soon earned Mrs. Thatcher's trust, I acquired a considerable influence on economic policy'.[10] Walters advocated accompanying a drastically tightened monetary environment in 1980–81 with the tightest budgetary squeeze in post-war history, over-riding the usual Keynesian stabilisers. The severe contractionary output effects of such a policy prompted the infamous 364 economist's letter of protest to the Times. But it is also clear that this 'sudden death' approach had the effect of knocking long term inflation expectations on the head and reinforcing the credibility of the anti-inflationary programme. The recession that was expected by the economics establishment to last much longer, ended with the recovery in the second half of 1981. Without a tight fiscal policy, scepticism about the political willingness to follow through with the Thatcher programme would have quickly emerged, followed by a financial crisis that would have blown the whole strategy off course (see [31]).

Perhaps the most influential of recent statements by Alan Walters was what has come to be known as the 'Walters critique' [34], [36]. Walters argues that if a high inflation country joins a low inflation country in a pegged exchange rate system, the common interest rate will be too low for the high inflation country, creating more inflationary pressure,

---

[8] This was the theme of a more developed critique of economic methodology and economists by Bauer and Walters [25]. The main aim of their critique was the failure to use microeconomic theory to underpin macroeconomics.

[9] [27] p31.

[10] Walters [33].

and too high for the low inflation country, creating deflationary pressure. The divergence in inflation will lead to realignment of the exchange rate, or interest rates in both countries will have to move in opposite directions to compensate for the expected devaluation. Thus contrary to its aims, the Exchange Rate Mechanism (ERM) of the European Monetary System would result in oscillating interest rates and diverging inflation rates. Walters' influence was the main reason why Mrs Thatcher resisted entry of the UK into the ERM. But it was also the cause of a major political crisis culminating in the resignation of the Chancellor of the Exchequer — Nigel Lawson in October 1989[11] and Walters resigning his post as personal economic adviser to the Prime Minister.

Walters' time as Personal Economic Adviser to Mrs Thatcher was anything but uneventful. But there was always the danger of 'bureaucratic capture' once an economist gets too close to the levers of power. In his essay on the political economy of the Thatcher programme [28], Walters outlined the difficulties of implementing the radical agenda of the Thatcher programme — 'Policies must be vote catchers'.[12] The gradual change in public perception and attitudes to unemployment, welfare and trade unions was traced alongside the successes and failures of government policy in the first few years of the MTFS. Public expenditure, tax and (by implication supply side policy) was to be approached gradually not precipitously — politics, after all, is the art of the possible! It was also on political grounds that Walters did not press for money base control following the failure of M3 to signal the state of monetary policy in the first few years of the MTFS.

The transitory uncertainties of a jump to MBC would have been 'too great and too dangerous politically'.[13] The combined force of the Treasury and the Bank of England remained unconvinced by the operational viability of MBC. Walters felt that it would have been foolhardy to press the venture, 'No battles had been won by generals leading defeatist troops' but 'MBC should remain our long-term goal'.[14] Twenty years later, MBC is not even on the agenda. But we should not be too harsh in our judgement. With the operational independence of the Bank of England and the success of inflation targeting, MBC is no longer an issue and can safely remain on the back-burner.

Alan Walters probably did not anticipate becoming one of the most

---

[11] N. Lawson, The View from No 11: Memoirs of a Tory Radical, London: Corgi, 1992, p964.

[12] [28] p296.

[13] [28] p309.

[14] [28] p310–311.

influential UK political economists of his generation. But each step that took him up against the economics establishment brought him closer to this position. If it is possible to provide a thematic summary of Alan's career, three immediately spring to mind. First, would be the implication of poorly thought-out government policy. Second, the application of liberal market economics and third, the respect for sound money. His influence on economic policy during the 1980s led to the general acceptance of sensible macroeconomic policy and liberal supply-side policy within the UK.

Most economists would be content to be recognised for their academic work, be respected by their peers, and wield influence through the papers they publish, the policy makers they advise and the students they teach. Very few of us can say we really make a difference, but by taking on the economics establishment, Alan Walters did just that!

Bibliography of Alan Walters work

[1] "Track Costs and Motor Taxation", *Journal of Industrial Economics*, 2, April, 1954, pp 135–146

[2] "Expectations and the Regression Fallacy in Estimating Cost Functions", *Review of Economics and Statistics*, 42, 1960, pp 210–215

[3] "The Allocation of Joint Costs with Demands as Probability Distributions", *American Economic Review*, 50, 1960, pp 419–432

[4] "The Theory and Measurement of Private and Social Cost of Highway Congestion", *Econometrica*, 29, 1961, pp 679–699

[5] "A Note on Economies of Scale", *Review of Economics and Statistics*, 45(4), November, 1963, pp 425–427

[6] "Production and Cost Functions: An Econometric Survey", *Econometrica*, 31, 1963, pp 1–66

[7] "Professor Friedman on the Demand for Money", *Journal of Political Economy*, 123, 1965, pp 545–551

[8] "The Revival of the Quantity Theory of Money", *Malayan Economic Review*, October, 1965, pp 1–6

[9] "Demand for Money in the UK, 1877–1961: Some Preliminary Findings" (with N J Kavanagh), *Bulletin of the Oxford Institute of Economics and Statistics*, 28, 1966, pp 93–116

[10] "The Stability of Keynesian and Monetary Multipliers in the United Kingdom" (with C R Barrett), *Review of Economics and Statistics*, 48(4), November, 1966, pp 395–405

[11] "Monetary Multipliers in the UK 1880–1962", *Oxford Economic Papers*, 18, 1966, pp 270–283

[12] "The Demand for Money — The Dynamic Properties of the Multiplier", *Journal of Political Economy*, 75, June, 1967, pp 293–298

[13] "Lags and the Demand for Money", *Journal of Economic Studies*, 2, 1967, pp 3–22

[14] The Economics of Road User Charges, *World Bank Staff Occasional Papers*, No 5, IBRD, 1968

[15] "The Demand for Money, Expectations and Short and Long Rates" in *Value, Capital and Growth*, Papers in honour of Sir John Hicks, J N Wolfe (ed.), Edinburgh University Press: Edinburgh, 1968, pp 505–529

[16] "A Development Model of Transport", *American Economic Review*, 58, 1968, pp 360–377

[17] *An Introduction to Econometrics*, Norton, 1969

[18] "The Radcliffe Report — Ten Years After: A Survey of Empirical Evidence" in *Money and Britain 1959–1969*, D R Croome and H G Johnson (eds.), Oxford University Press: Oxford, 1970, pp 39–68

[19] "Kaldor on Monetarism", *The Banker*, 120, pp 1052–1060, 1970

[20] Money in Boom and Slump, *IEA Hobart Paper*, No 44, 3rd Edition, Institute of Economic Affairs, 1971

[21] "Consistent Expectations, Distributed Lags and the Quantity Theory", *Economic Journal*, 81, 1971, pp 273–281

[22] "Real Balances and Output: A Productivity Model of a Monetary Economy" (with L McGregor), in *Econometric Studies of Macro and Monetary Relations: Papers Presented at the second Australian Conference of Econometricians*, A A Powell and R A Williams (eds.), Monash University, August, North Holland: Amsterdam, 1971, pp 233–259

[23] "A Note on Rules Authorities and Information", *Journal of Political Economy*, 80, 1, 1972, pp 176–178

[24] Money and Banking, *Penguin Modern Economics Readings*, Penguin Books, 1973

[25] "The State of Economics" (with P T Bauer), *Journal of Law and Economics*, XVIII, 1, 1975, pp 1–23

[26] "Macroeconomic Models and Policy in Britain", in *Frontiers of Econometrics*, M Intriligator (ed.), North Holland: Amsterdam, 1977, pp 809–819

[27] Economists and the British Economy, *IEA Occasional Paper 54*, Institute of Economic Affairs, 1978

[28] "The United Kingdom: Political Economy and Macroeconomics" in *Essays on Macroeconomic Implications of Financial and Labor Markets and Political Processes*, Karl Brunner and Alan Meltzer (eds.), Carnegie-Rochester Conference Series on Public Policy, 21, 1984, pp 259–279

[29] "Consumption, Savings and the Multiplier" in *Keynes 'General Theory' Fifty Years on, Its relevance and irrelevance to modern times*, J Burton et al. (eds.), IEA, 1986, pp 89–100

[30] *Britain's Economic Renaissance: Margaret Thatcher's Reforms 1979–1984*, Oxford University Press: Oxford

[31] "Monetary and Fiscal Policy in the UK", in *Keynes and Economic Policy*, W Eltis and P Sinclair (eds.), Macmillan/NEDO, 1988, pp 271–294

[32] "Supply Side Policies: The Lessons from the UK" in *A Supply Side Agenda for Germany: Sparks from the United States — Great Britain European Integration*, G Fels and G M Von Furstenberg (eds.), Springer: New York, 1989, pp 185–214

[33] "A Life Philosophy", *American Economist*, Fall, 1989, pp 18–24

[34] *Sterling in Danger: The Economic Consequences of Pegged Exchange Rates*, Fontana/Collins/Institute of Economic Affairs: London, 1990

[35] "Currency Boards", *New Palgrave Dictionary of Economics*, Vol. 1 A–D, J Eatwell, M Milgate and P Newman (eds.), Macmillan, 1991, pp 740–742

[36] "Walters Critique", *New Palgrave Dictionary of Money and Finance*, Vol. 3 N–Z, P Newman, M Milgate and J Eatwell (eds.), Macmillan, 1994, pp 781–783

[37] "Money, Narrow or Broad", *The Review of Policy Issues*, 5, Autumn, 1995, pp 29–34

2 Consistent Expectations, Rational Expectations, Multiple-Solution Indeterminacies, and Least-Squares Learnability

Bennett T. McCallum[1]

1 INTRODUCTION

It is not widely known, I believe, that the first publication to present a rational expectations analysis of a complete macroeconomic/monetary model was authored by A. A. Walters (1971). This paper, "Consistent Expectations, Distributed Lags, and the Quantity Theory," appeared somewhat earlier in the year than Thomas Sargent's (1971) justly influential "A Note on the Accelerationist Controversy" and, furthermore, the latter did not feature the explicit solution of a full macroeconomic model.[2] Robert Lucas's first two money/macro papers with rational expectations (1972a, 1972b) had been presented at conferences in 1970–71 but had not yet appeared in print.

Of course Walters termed his expectational hypothesis "consistent expectations," rather than rational expectations (RE), and refers to John Muth's (1961) seminal paper only briefly, in a footnote.[3] But that does not diminish the insightfulness of Walters's analysis. Indeed, this reader is left with the feeling that his expectational hypothesis and method

[1] I am indebted to Huberto Ennis, Andreas Hornstein, Andrew Levin, and Edward Nelson for helpful discussions.

[2] Sargent's paper, like Walters's, emphasizes that fixed distributed-lag formulas for expectations can be consistently incorrect, since they fail to reflect policy processes.

[3] There Muth is given his brother's first name, Richard. Incredibly, the same mistake appears over 20 years later in Krugman (1994, p. 49).

of analysis were worked out independently of previous writings, with knowledge of Muth's paper perhaps arriving rather late in the publication process.

In the 30-plus years since 1971 a lot of activity has taken place in the area of RE money/macro analysis, to put it mildly. Consequently, I have no intention of trying to survey the many developments that have taken place. But I would like to take up some particular issues concerning solution concepts and the problem of "indeterminacy," or multiple solutions, in RE models. I will begin in Section 2 by outlining Walters's solution procedure and contrasting it with the one used by Muth (1961). Then, in Section 3, I will outline Lucas's (1972b) procedure and turn to the topic of multiple solutions, which has been active for many years and recently has become increasingly prominent. My own "minimum-state-variable" interpretation and extension of Lucas's procedure, developed in McCallum (1983), is also discussed and the dependence of several recent controversies on the solution concept is emphasized. Next, Section 4 describes an approach to selection among multiple solutions, based on the criteria of E-stability and adaptive learnability, that was initiated in the 1980s by George Evans and recently treated comprehensively in major publications by Evans and Honkapohja (1999, 2001). Section 5 examines an example featured by those authors in which their criterion conflicts with my own, and argues that this conflict occurs only with parameter values that make the model economically implausible. That argument is rather ad hoc in nature, however, so Section 6 proposes some general requirements for a model to be regarded as plausible or "well formulated." The papers main result is in Section 7, which shows that for an important class of well formulated models, the unique MSV solution is invariably learnable. Finally, Section 8 provides a brief summary and conclusion.

2 Consistent and Rational Expectations

Walters (1971) analyzed price level behavior in a model that is fairly similar to the standard workhorse for monetary RE analysis, which includes the Cagan (1956) money demand function and a policy process represented in terms of money supply. Walters's money-demand equation is written as

$$p_t = \alpha m_{t-1} + \beta(p_t^e - p_{t-1}) + \varepsilon_t \tag{1}$$

with $\alpha > 0$ and $0 < \beta < 1$. Here the dating of variables differs from the version that has become standard and, for some reason, p_t and m_t represent the price level and the money stock, rather than their logarithms.

The expectational variable is p_t^e, the expectation of p_t formed at time $t-1$. The shock term ε_t is taken to be purely random (i.e., white noise) so its expectation at $t-1$ is zero and thus we have $p_t^e = \alpha m_{t-1} + \beta(p_t^e - p_{t-1})$. Consequently, we can solve out p_t^e and obtain the solution expression

$$p_t = [\alpha/(1-\beta)]\, m_{t-1} - [\beta/(1-\beta)]\, p_{t-1} + \varepsilon_t \tag{2}$$

It will be noted that the foregoing solution procedure — of taking expectations, solving for p_t^e, and substituting out the latter — cannot be used when p_{t+1}^e enters the system.

Walters (1971) considers the implied paths of p_t, and representations of p_t^e, for three different money supply processes. The paper's main message is that the p_t^e representations usually do not satisfy the adaptive expectations formula, $p_t^e = (1-\lambda)\left[p_{t-1} + \lambda p_{t-2} + \lambda^2 p_{t-3} + \ldots\right]$, that was very widely used at the time. Indeed, any fixed distributed-lag formula for expectations will be systematically incorrect unless it happens to reflect the money supply process. This important conclusion, which was also the main message of Sargent (1971), is a precursor of the famed Lucas (1976) critique. Two limitations of Walters's analysis are that (i) the effect of shocks to the money supply is not considered and (ii) the model is not extended to include structural equations of a more standard macroeconomic system with sluggish price adjustments of the expectational Phillips-curve type.

Walters (1971, p. 273; 1988, p. 290) has expressed the view that the term "consistent expectations" is preferable to rational expectations, and I would not strongly disagree. I would argue, however, that the related term "model-consistent expectations" is somewhat undesirable.[4] The reason is that it leads easily into an anti-RE argument such as "it is implausible that all of an economy's agents would believe in the particular model of the economy being used by the researcher."[5] My objection (McCallum, 1999b) is that this statement does not represent the assumption that is actually required for the basic version of RE. The proper assumption is that agents form expectations so as to avoid systematic expectational errors in actuality, which implies that each agent behaves as if he knew the structure of the actual economy. Then expectations will agree with the researcher's model, but the reason is that the latter is by design his best attempt to depict the true structure of the

[4]This term has been used by many writers including Brayton et al. (1997) and Isard, Laxton, and Eliasson (1999).

[5]A variant is the claim that it is implausible that all agents would believe in the same model of the economy. But, first, this is an objection to macroeconomics, not rational expectations, and second, there are some RE models in which agents' expectations are not all alike.

actual economy — for if it were not, he would adopt a different model. There is no assumption that agents consciously create explicit models at all, only that they manage their own private affairs so as to avoid systematic expectational errors in actuality.

From here on I will use $E_t z_{t+j}$ to denote $E(z_{t+j}|\Omega_t)$, where Ω_t is the information set at t, typically (but not necessarily) taken to include all variables dated t and earlier. Using this notation, the first of Muth's (1961) two models can be written as

$$-\beta p_t = \gamma E_{t-1} p_t + u_t \tag{3}$$

where p_t is a market price and u_t is a random shock term. If the latter is white noise, the same solution procedure as Walters's could be used, but Muth generalises to permit $u_t = \sum_{i=0}^{\infty} w_i \varepsilon_{t-i}$ where ε_t is white noise. Then to obtain a solution he essentially applies an undetermined coefficient approach to the moving-average solution form

$$p_t = \sum_{i=0}^{\infty} W_i \varepsilon_{t-i} \tag{4}$$

in order to evaluate the W_is in terms of β, γ, and the w_is. That same strategy is adequate, and is used, with Muth's second and more complex model. The latter, which recognizes inventory speculation, can be expressed as

$$-\beta p_t + I_t = \gamma E_{t-1} p_t + u_t + I_{t-1} \tag{5}$$

$$I_t = \alpha(E_t p_{t+1} - p_t) \tag{6}$$

where I_t is inventory holdings at the end of t, $-\beta p_t$ is consumption demand in t, and $\gamma E_{t-1} p_t + u_t$ is production. Substituting (6) into (5), one obtains an equation involving p_t, $E_{t-1}p_t$, $E_t p_{t+1}$, and p_{t-1} as well as u_t. Again the solution procedure of undetermined coefficients (henceforth, UC) in terms of the moving average representation of the solution (i.e., in terms of $\varepsilon_t, \varepsilon_{t-1}, \ldots$) is applicable, but now it leads to a quadratic characteristic equation. Muth selects between the two roots on the grounds of boundness — i.e., non-explosiveness or dynamic stability — of the resulting solution. This same procedure could be applied if additional exogenous shocks were included in the model, so we see that Muth's (1961) paper developed a solution procedure — and an implicit solution concept — for a rather wide class of linear models.[6]

[6] To me, writing without the benefit of inside information, it seems possible that his recognition of the extent of Muth's achievement may have provided a major reason for Walters to have abstained from additional research in the area during the 1970s. Matthews (1998) suggests that the dominant reason was the attitude taken by the Economic Journal's editor, David Champernowne, who was not favorably inclined toward the hypothesis of consistent or rational expectations.

3 Multiple Solutions and the MSV Concept

Lucas (1972a, 1972b) provided the next — enormously influential — publications with RE in money/macro models. The former was the greater piece of work, of course, but for present purposes it will be useful to focus on the simplified linear model in the second. There Lucas's aggregate demand–supply system includes a Phillips-type supply function and a logarithmic nominal income identity, plus a policy rule assumed for simplicity to pertain directly to nominal income. I will not now discuss the model itself, since it includes some questionable features, but will go immediately to the relevant point. This is that Lucas's solution procedure involves a UC calculation not in terms of moving average parameters, but with respect to the parameters (coefficients) of a conjectured solution form that includes only the variables and shocks recognized to be relevant to the current state of the system, i.e., the relevant state variables.

The importance of this step can be illustrated simply in terms of the following basic, non-specific, model:

$$y_t = \alpha + aE_t y_{t+1} + u_t \tag{7}$$

$$u_t = \rho u_{t-1} + \varepsilon_t \tag{8}$$

Here $|\rho| < 1$ and ε_t is white noise. Since there are no relevant state variables in sight except u_t,[7] it is natural to conjecture a solution of the form

$$y_t = \phi_0 + \phi_1 u_t \tag{9}$$

and then solve for the coefficients ϕ_0 and ϕ_1. Since (9) implies $E_t y_{t+1} = \phi_0 + \phi_1 \rho u_t$, substitution into (7) gives $\phi_0 + \phi_1 u_t = \alpha + a(\phi_0 + \phi_1 \rho u_t) + u_t$, which implies

$$\phi_0 = \alpha + a\phi_0 \tag{10a}$$

$$\phi_1 = a\rho\phi_1 + 1 \tag{10b}$$

Thus we have $\phi_1 = 1/(1 - a\rho)$ and $\phi_0 = \alpha/(1-a)$, the unique solution that is of form (9).

But there are more solutions. Suppose that one enters the apparently extraneous variables y_{t-1} and u_{t-1} into the following candidate solution expression that might be considered instead of (9):

$$y_t = \phi_0 + \phi_1 y_{t-1} + \phi_2 u_t + \phi_3 u_{t-1} \tag{11}$$

[7] One could proceed equivalently in terms of u_{t-1} and ε_t, since u_t is AR(1).

Then proceeding as before leads to the UC equalities

$$\phi_0 = \alpha + a\phi_0 + a\phi_1\phi_0 \tag{12a}$$

$$\phi_1 = a\phi_1^2 \tag{12b}$$

$$\phi_2 = a\phi_1\phi_2 + a\rho\phi_2 + 1 \tag{12c}$$

$$\phi_3 = a\phi_1\phi_3 \tag{12d}$$

The second of these is satisfied by $\phi_1^{(-)} = 0$ or by $\phi_1^{(+)} = 1/a$. The first of these roots implies a solution equivalent to the one given previously, but the second leads to the solution

$$y_t = -(\alpha/a) + (1/a)y_{t-1} - (1/a\rho)u_t + \phi_3 u_{t-1} \tag{13}$$

which is consistent with all of the model's equations for any value of ϕ_3. Thus there is an infinity of solutions, if ones of form (11) are considered. In some models based firmly on full optimizing analysis, there will be transversality conditions that exclude explosive solutions, which would eliminate this infinity if $|a| < 1$, as would usually be the case. But there are several notable examples in the literature in which relations such as (13) qualify as solutions under stringent optimizing assumptions.

To many workers, Lucas's procedure of restricting attention to solutions of a form such as (9) will be attractive, since it is capable of generating solutions that are based only on fundamentals — thereby excluding "bubble" components that involve variables that do not enter the model and therefore can appear in the solution only because they are (arbitrarily) expected (by the model's agents) to be relevant. This elimination of bubble solutions does not occur if one adopts a moving average formulation, in the fashion preferred by Muth (1961). Partly for this reason, perhaps, Lucas's approach rapidly gained popularity during the 1970s.

An issue arises, however, in models that include lagged values of endogenous variables. Suppose that the relevant model includes

$$y_t = \alpha + aE_t y_{t+1} + cy_{t-1} + u_t \tag{14}$$

rather than (7), in addition to (8). Then the solution clearly must include y_{t-1} as well as u_t as a relevant state variable. And then if one searches for a solution of the form

$$y_t = \phi_0 + \phi_1 y_{t-1} + \phi_2 u_t \tag{15}$$

it will be found that $E_t y_{t+1} = \phi_0 + \phi_1(\phi_0 + \phi_1 y_{t-1} + \phi_2 u_t) + \phi_2 \rho u_t$ and the UC equations become

$$\phi_0 \quad = \quad \alpha + a\phi_0 + a\phi_1\phi_0 \tag{16a}$$

$$\phi_1 = a\phi_1^2 + c \tag{16b}$$
$$\phi_2 = a\phi_1\phi_2 + a\rho\phi_2 + 1 \tag{16c}$$

In this case there are two solutions, one based on

$$\phi_1^{(-)} = \frac{1 - \sqrt{1 - 4ac}}{2a} \tag{17}$$

and the other on

$$\phi_1^{(+)} = \frac{1 + \sqrt{1 - 4ac}}{2a} \tag{18}$$

where we use the convention that $\sqrt{z}$ is positive for all $z > 0$. Of course, we shall require that ϕ_1 be real-valued, since complex solutions make no sense for prices or quantities. But whenever there is a real solution there seem to be two — which will often have very different properties — even if we follow the Lucas (1972b) procedure.

A solution concept that provides uniqueness was proposed, however, by McCallum (1983). Clearly, the two expressions (17) and (18) define two different functions and therefore two quite distinct solutions to the model (14)(8). Consequently, consider the special case of (14) in which $c = 0$. In this case y_{t-1} does not enter the model and thus could be considered to be an extraneous state variable, which should not appear in the solution, if it is to include only relevant state variables. Accordingly, McCallum (1981, 1983) proposed that since $\phi_1^{(-)}$ equals 0 in this special case, and $\phi_1^{(+)}$ does not, then the solution based on $\phi_1^{(-)}$ should be regarded as the relevant solution. His (1983) paper develops a rather general procedure for finding this "bubble-free" solution, which is unique by construction in linear models.[8] This procedure was given the name "minimum state variable" (MSV) solution by Evans (1986), who referred to the step of choosing between the two roots in the last example as constituting a "subsidiary principle." In what follows it will be important to be unambiguous about the concept of a MSV solution. Throughout I will be using that term to designate the unique solution — unique by construction — described in McCallum (1983, 1999). This is the way that the term was used by Evans (1986, 1989) and by Evans and Honkapohja (1992), but differs from the terminology in the latter's more recent publications (1999, p. 496; 2001, p. 194), where their convention permits multiple solutions to be given the MSV adjective. Either terminology could be used, of course, but the one adopted here is more appropriate for the issues at hand.

---

[8]The MSV solution is required, by definition, to be linear. For a discussion of this and several other points, see McCallum (1999).

Recently, the possible occurrence of multiple solutions has assumed new prominence in the area of monetary economics under the heading of "indeterminacies." Notable topics in which indeterminacy is central to policy issues include (i) inflation forecast targeting [e.g., Woodford (1994), Bernanke and Woodford (1997), King (2000)], (ii) the Taylor Principle [Woodford (2001), King (2000), Clarida, Gali, and Gertler (1997, 1999)], (iii) the zero-lower-bound deflation trap [Benhabib, Schmitt-Grohe, and Uribe (2001), Schmitt-Grohe and Uribe (2000), McCallum (2002), Alstadheim and Henderson (2002)], and (iv) the fiscal theory of the price level [Woodford (1995), Sims (1994), Cochrane (1998), McCallum (2001), Kocherlakota and Phelan (1999)].

In this context it is important to recognize that the type of indeterminacy present in all of these cases involves multiple RE solutions and accordingly is quite different from the "price level indeterminacy" problem that was discussed extensively in the monetary literature of the 1940s and 1950s by Lange (1942), Patinkin (1949, 1961, 1965), Gurley and Shaw (1960), and Johnson (1962). In particular, the former involves multiple time paths for real variables even with some nominal variable fixed (as a consequence of dynamic expectational behavior) whereas the latter involves the model's failure to determine any nominal variable despite unique paths for all real variables (occurring as a consequence of the absence of any nominal anchor, a static concept). I have suggested several times that a more constructive terminology would refer to "multiple solutions" and "nominal indeterminacy," respectively, but thus far have made little headway.

In any event, one's position on policy issues relating to the four topics (i)–(iv) logically depends on his beliefs concerning the status of multiple RE solutions. Are such multiplicities relevant in principle and empirically for actual economies, or are they theoretical curiosa with little or no relevance to actual economies? The following sections present the outline of an argument in favor of the latter position.

4 E-Stability and Learnability

In a series of articles appearing in the 1980s, George Evans (1985, 1986, 1989) proposed an alternative criterion for designation or "selection" of the economically relevant RE solution in cases in which multiplicity obtains. His initial criterion, now known as iterative E-stability, can be briefly reviewed. The basic presumption is that individual economic agents will not be endowed with perfect knowledge of the economic system's structure, so it is natural to consider whether plausible error-correction mechanisms are convergent to particular solutions. This can be determined for each of the multiple RE solutions, and the presence or absence of such mechanisms may yield a criterion for selection of one solution as economically relevant. For an illustration, consider again the model (14)(8), which we rewrite for convenience:

$$y_t = \alpha + aE_t y_{t+1} + cy_{t-1} + u_t \tag{14}$$
$$u_t = \rho u_{t-1} + \varepsilon_t \tag{8}$$

Suppose that the economy's individuals believe that the actual behavior of y_t can be expressed by an equation that includes the same variables as (15), but that they do not know the exact values of the parameters. If at time t the typical agent's belief is that these values are $\phi_0(n)$, $\phi_1(n)$, and $\phi_2(n)$, then the system's perceived law of motion (PLM) will be[9]

$$y_t = \phi_0(n) + \phi_1(n)y_{t-1} + \phi_2(n)u_t \tag{19}$$

In this case the implied expectation at t of y_{t+1} will be

$$\phi_0(n) + \phi_1(n)y_t + \phi_2(n)\rho u_t \tag{20}$$

Using that expression in place of $E_t y_{t+1}$ in (14) — which implies that we are temporarily abandoning RE — gives

$$y_t = \alpha + a\left[\phi_0(n) + \phi_1(n)y_t + \phi_2(n)\rho u_t\right] + cy_{t-1} + u_t \tag{21}$$

or, rearranging,

$$y_t = \left[1 - a\phi_1(n)\right]^{-1}\left[\alpha + a\phi_0(n) + a\phi_2(n)\rho u_t + cy_{t-1} + u_t\right] \tag{22}$$

as the system's actual law of motion (ALM). Now imagine a sequence of iterations from the PLM to the ALM. Writing the left-hand side of (22) in the form (19), but for iteration $n+1$, gives $\phi_0(n+1) + \phi_1(n+1)y_{t-1} + \phi_2(n+1)u_t = [1 - a\phi_1(n)]^{-1}[\alpha + a\phi_0(n) + a\phi_2(n)\rho u_t + cy_{t-1} + u_t]$ and therefore implies that

$$\phi_0(n+1) = [1 - a\phi_1(n)]^{-1}[\alpha + a\phi_0(n)] \tag{23a}$$
$$\phi_1(n+1) = [1 - a\phi_1(n)]^{-1}c \tag{23b}$$
$$\phi_2(n+1) = [1 - a\phi_1(n)]^{-1}[a\phi_2(n)\rho + 1] \tag{23c}$$

The issue, then, is whether iterations defined by (23) are such that the $\phi_j(n)$ converge to the ϕ_j values in (15) as n increases without bound. If

[9] Here n is being used to index iterations in an eductive process of learning that takes place in meta-time.

they do, then the solution (15) is said to be iteratively E-stable. Evans (1986) found that in several prominent and controversial models the MSV solution is iteratively E-stable.

On the basis of results by Marcet and Sargent (1989), Evans (1989) switched his attention to E-stability without the "iterative" qualification, defined as follows. Conversion of equations (23) to the continuous form, appropriate as the iteration interval approaches zero, yields

$$d\phi_0(n)/dn = [1 - a\phi_1(n)]^{-1}[\alpha + a\phi_0(n)] - \phi_0(n) \quad \text{(24a)}$$
$$d\phi_1(n)/dn = [1 - a\phi_1(n)]^{-1}c - \phi_1(n) \quad \text{(24b)}$$
$$d\phi_2(n)/dn = [1 - a\phi_1(n)]^{-1}[a\phi_2(n)\rho + 1] - \phi_2(n) \quad \text{(24c)}$$

If the differential equation system (24) has $\phi_j(n) \longrightarrow \phi_j$ for all j, the solution (15) is E-stable. An important feature of this continuous version of the iterative process is that it is intimately related to an adaptive learning process that is modeled as taking place in real time.[10] For most non-explosive models, that is, values of parameters analogous to the ϕ_j in (15), which are estimated by least squares (LS) regressions on the basis of data from periods $t-1, t-2, \ldots, 1$ and used to form expectations in period t, will converge to the actual values in (15) as time passes if and only if equations (24) converge to those values. Thus E-stability and LS learnability typically go hand in hand.[11] This result, which is discussed extensively by Evans and Honkapohja (1999, 2001), is useful because it is technically much easier, in most cases, to establish E-stability than to establish LS learnability.[12]

5 Questionable Example

As mentioned above, Evans's early work indicated that the E-stability/learnability principle often supports the MSV criterion. More recently, however, the implied message has been quite different. Thus in various places Evans and Honkapohja (E&H) have argued that MSV solutions may or may not have the property of E-stability (and LS learnability). It

[10]The E-stability process itself is conceived of as taking place in notional time (meta-time). For the sake of brevity, the present account omits discussion of several important papers on learning; for many references, see Evans and Honkapohja (1999, 2001).

[11]It is interesting to note that a modeling strategy closely related to LS learning is explicitly mentioned by Walters (1971, p. 281).

[12]For a notable recent application to monetary policy analysis, see Bullard and Mitra (2000).

is my belief, however, that this recent message is misleading; that in all or almost all sensible models the MSV solution does possess E-stability. Thus the agenda of this section is to discuss and reconsider the main example put forth by E&H (1992, pp. 9–10; 1999, pp. 496–7; 2001, p. 197) as representing a case in which the MSV solution is not E-stable.

Following E&H (1992), the relevant model's reduced form can be written as

$$y_t = \alpha + \gamma E_{t-1} y_t + \zeta E_{t-1} y_{t+1} + \delta y_{t-1} + \varepsilon_t \tag{25}$$

with $\delta \neq 0$, $\zeta \neq 0$, and ε_t white noise. The MSV solution will be of the form

$$y_t = \phi_0 + \phi_1 y_{t-1} + \phi_2 \varepsilon_t \tag{26}$$

and ϕ_1 will be determined by a quadratic equation with the MSV solution given by the ϕ_1 root that equals zero when $\delta = 0$. The other root gives a bubble solution and there are also bubble solutions of a form that includes additional terms involving y_{t-2} and ε_{t-1} on the right-hand side of (26).

Necessary conditions for E-stability of a solution of the form (26) are (E&H, 1992, p. 6)

$$\gamma + \zeta - 1 + \zeta\phi_1 < 0 \text{ and } \gamma - 1 + 2\zeta\phi_1 < 0 \tag{27}$$

On the basis of these, E&H show on their pp. 9–10 that the non-MSV solution of form (26) is E-stable, and the MSV solution is E-unstable, when $\gamma = -\zeta > 1$ and $\delta > 0$. Also, on p. 5 they show that the bubble solutions are E-stable if $\gamma > 1$, $\delta\zeta > 0$, and $\zeta < 0$. If such parameter values were economically sensible, these results would constitute explicit counter-examples to my suggestion that MSV solutions are invariably E-stable.

Let us, however, reconsider the economic model that E&H (1992) use to motivate the reduced form equation (25). It is a log-linear "model of aggregate demand and supply with wealth effects in aggregate demand, money demand, and aggregate supply" (1992, p. 9). Letting y_t, m_t, and p_t be the logs of output, money, and the price level, with it a nominal interest rate, they write:[13]

$$\begin{aligned} y_t &= g_1 (i_t - E_{t-1}(p_{t+1} - p_t)) + g_2 (m_t - p_t) + v_{1t} && \text{(28a)} \\ y_t &= f(m_t - p_t) + v_{2t} && \text{(28b)} \\ m_t - p_t &= y_t - a_1 i_t + a_2 (m_t - p_t) + v_{3t} && \text{(28c)} \end{aligned}$$

[13] Here (28b) is aggregate supply and (28c) is money demand. It is my distinct impression that E&H intend for all parameters to be interpreted as non-negative.

$$m_t \quad = \quad dp_{t-1} + v_{4t} \tag{28d}$$

The fourth equation "is a monetary policy reaction function" (1992, p. 9). Solving these four equations for a reduced form expression for p_t gives

$$p_t = dp_{t-1} + hE_{t-1}(p_t - p_{t+1}) + u_t \tag{29}$$

with $h = g_1[f - g_2 + g_1(a_2 + f - 1)a_1^{-1}]^{-1}$ and where u_t is a linear combination of the (white noise) v_{it} terms. Consequently, the model is of form (25) with y_t in the latter representing p_t in the model and with $\gamma = h$, $\zeta = -h$, and $\delta = d$.

It follows, then, that the condition $\gamma = -\zeta > 1$ requires $h > 1$. In that regard, note first that if real-balance terms are excluded, i.e., if $g_2 = f = a_2 = 0$, then $h = -a_1$ is negative. Thus sizeable real-balance effects are needed. Second, note that a_2 should probably be specified as negative, not positive, since the latter would imply a money-demand function with income elasticity greater than 1.0, in contrast with most empirical estimates. But with $a_2 < 0$, the parameter f would have to be quite large to generate $h > 1$. In other words, real money balances would have to enter strongly in the production function for output. Thus $h > 1$ seems highly improbable in the context of the IS-LM model of the type utilized.

In addition, the condition $\delta > 0$ implies $d > 0$ in (28d), implying that the money supply is increased by the monetary authority when the price level is higher than average in the previous period. That represents, arguably, a somewhat perverse form of policy behavior.

An alternative way of interpreting the reduced-form equation (25), not mentioned by E&H, is as a microeconomic supply–demand model. Suppose we have demand and supply functions

$$q_t \quad = \quad \beta_0 + \beta_1 p_t + \beta_2 E_{t-1}(p_{t+1} - p_t) + v_{1t} \tag{30a}$$

$$q_t \quad = \quad \alpha_0 + \alpha_1 p_t + \alpha_2 E_{t-1} p_t + v_{2t} \tag{30b}$$

where the disturbance terms include effects of exogenous variables such as demanders' income and the price of inputs to production. Here we would hypothesize that $\beta_1 < 0$ and $\beta_2 > 0$, to reflect downward sloping demand with respect to the current price and a speculative demand motive. Also, let $\alpha_1 \geq 0$ and $\alpha_2 \geq 0$ to reflect upward sloping supply with respective to relevant prices. Then the reduced form is

$$p_t = (\alpha_1 - \beta_1)^{-1}[(\beta_0 - \alpha_0) + \beta_2 E_{t-1} p_{t+1} - (\alpha_2 + \beta_2)E_{t-1} p_t + v_{1t} - v_{2t}] \tag{31}$$

In terms of equation (25), this specification suggests $\zeta > 0$, $\gamma < 0$, and $\delta = 0$. But the first two of these are just opposite in sign to the requirements for the E&H example. Furthermore, it is plausible that p_{t-1} might appear instead of $E_{t-1}p_t$ in the supply equation (as in the cobweb model). But then its coefficient in the reduced form would be negative, and therefore inconsistent with the $d > 0$ assumption in the E&H case under discussion.

In sum, I would argue that the specification used most prominently by E&H, to provide an example featuring the absence of E-stability for the MSV solution, is highly unappealing in terms of basic economic theory. It must be admitted, however, that this argument is quite specific and rather ad hoc in nature. Accordingly, I will now turn to a more general line of argument.

6 Well-Formulated Models

In this section I propose conditions necessary for important classes of linear models to be "well formulated." Consider again the single-variable specification (14), which is reproduced once more for convenience:

$$y_t = \alpha + aE_t y_{t+1} + cy_{t-1} + u_t \tag{32}$$

with $u_t = \rho u_{t-1} + \varepsilon_t$. With ε_t white noise, u_t is an exogenous forcing variable with an unconditional mean of zero. Applying the unconditional expectation operator to (32) yields

$$Ey_t = \alpha + aEy_{t+1} + cEy_{t-1} + 0 \tag{33}$$

But if y_t is covariance stationary, we then have[14]

$$Ey_t = \alpha / \left[1 - (a + c)\right] \tag{34}$$

From the latter, it is clear that as $a + c$ approaches 1.0 from above, the unconditional mean of y_t approaches $-\infty$ (assuming that $\alpha > 0$), whereas if $a + c$ approaches 1.0 from below, the unconditional mean approaches $+\infty$. Thus there is an infinite discontinuity at $a + c = 1.0$. This implies that a tiny change in $a + c$ could alter the average (i.e., steady state) value of y_t from an arbitrarily large positive number to an

[14] Note that it is not being assumed that y_t is necessarily covariance stationary. Instead, an implication that would hold, if it were, is being used to motivate the assumption that will be made subsequently.

arbitrarily large negative number. Such a property is highly implausible and therefore, I suggest, unacceptable for a well-formulated model.

In light of the preceding discussion, my argument is that, to be considered well formulated, the model at hand needs to include a restriction on its admissible parameter values, a restriction that rules out $a+c=1$ and yet admits a large open set of values that includes $(a,c) = (0,0)$. In the case at hand, the appropriate restriction is $a+c<1$. Of course, $a+c>1$ would serve just as well mathematically to avoid the infinite discontinuity, but it is clear that $a+c<1$ is vastly more appropriate from an economic perspective since it includes the region around $(0,0)$. Note that the oft-seen condition $a+c \neq 1$ does not eliminate the unacceptable property. It should be clear, in addition, that the foregoing argument could be easily modified to apply to y_t processes that are trend stationary, rather than strictly (covariance) stationary.[15]

Now let us consider a second model specification that, like (32), is emphasized by E&H (1999, 2001). It can be written as

$$y_t = \alpha + \beta_0 E_{t-1}y_t + \beta_1 E_{t-1}y_{t+1} + \delta y_{t-1} + u_t \tag{35}$$

with $u_t = \rho u_{t-1} + \varepsilon_t$ as before. For this case, consider the conditional expectation, $E_{t-1}y_t$:

$$E_{t-1}y_t = (1-\beta_0)^{-1}[\alpha + \beta_1 E_{t-1}y_{t+1} + \delta y_{t-1} + \rho u_{t-1}] \tag{36}$$

Here it is clear that, for given values of $E_{t-1}y_{t+1}$, y_{t-1}, and u_{t-1}, $E_{t-1}y_t$ will pass through an infinite discontinuity at $\beta_0 = 1$. Consequently, for basically the same reason as before, $\beta_0 < 1$ is necessary for the model to be well formulated. In addition, $\beta_0 + \beta_1 + \delta < 1$ continues to apply.[16]

An application of these criteria to the questionable example of E&H (1992), featured above in Section 5, is immediate. That example's result, of a MSV solution that is not E-stable, requires $\gamma = h > 1$. But in the notation of (35), that condition is $\beta_0 > 1$, which is incompatible with our requirement for models of form (35) to be well formulated. Thus the questionable example is discredited on general grounds, in addition to the specific reasons described in Section 5.

---

[15] Generalizing, suppose that y_t in (32) is a $m \times 1$ vector of endogenous variables, so that α is $m \times 1$ while a and c are $m \times m$ matrices. Then the counterpart of $1-(a+c)>0$ is that the eigenvalues of $[I-(a+c)]$ all have positive real parts, i.e., that the eigenvalues of $[a+c]$ all have real parts less than 1.0. That requirement is necessary for the multivariate version of (32) to be well formulated.

[16] The multivariate extension for the case in which y_t is a vector yields the requirements that the eigenvalues of $[I-\beta_0]$ and $[I-(\beta_0+\beta 1+\delta)]$ all have positive real parts.

7 Main Results

We are now prepared to develop a more general version of the foregoing argument. In particular, it will be shown that being well formulated (henceforth, WF) is a sufficient condition for the MSV solution to be E-stable in univariate models of classes (32) and (35). Let us begin with (35), but assuming that $\delta = 0$ since that case has been emphasized by E&H. For this model, conditions for E-stability can be found by reference to Figure 1, which is adapted from the diagram of E&H (1999, p. 492; 2001, p. 191). In the cited references, it is derived and reported that the MSV solution is E-stable in regions I, V, and VI but E-unstable in regions II, III, and IV. In regions I and VI, moreover, the MSV solution is reported to be strongly E-stable whereas in V it is weakly E-stable.[17] Reference to our conditions for model (35) to be well formulated (with $\delta = 0$) shows immediately that the condition obtains only for regions I and VI. Thus in this particular but prominent case, the MSV solution is strongly E-stable if the parameter values are such that the model is well formulated.

Next consider the more difficult and important model of equation (32). The issue at hand is whether the MSV solution possesses E-stability, i.e., whether the differential equations (24) are locally stable at the MSV values for the ϕ_j. Necessary and sufficient conditions for this to be true are given by Evans and Honkapohja (2001, p. 202) as follows: $a\,(1 - a\phi_1)^{-1} < 1$, $ca\,(1 - a\phi_1)^{-2} < 1$, $\rho a\,(1 - a\phi_1)^{-1} < 1$. These will be utilized below, but first it will be useful to examine Figure 2, which again is adapted from E&H (2001, p. 203). There E-stability regions are shown under the assumption $0 \leq \rho < 1$. In this case, the results reported by E&H indicate that the MSV solution is E-stable in regions I and VII but E-unstable in region IV, while "both solutions [i.e., from both roots of (16b)] are explosive or nonreal" elsewhere (E&H, 2001, p. 203).[18] Specifically, solutions for ϕ_1 are complex-valued in regions III and VI, and both solutions feature explosive behavior in regions II and V. As indicated above, the MSV solution is well formulated in regions I, V, and VII (being complex in VI). Thus for regions I and VII, the E&H version of Figure 2 supports the hypothesis that the MSV solution is E-stable in all well-formulated models of form (32). But what about

[17] Strong E-stability occurs in cases in which local convergence to the MSV parameter values occurs even when the function considered includes additional variables (excluded from the MSV specification). This implies that certain other solutions are not E-stable.

[18] Note that the MSV solution is the AR(1) solution that E&H (2001) refer to as "the $\bar{b}$_solution."

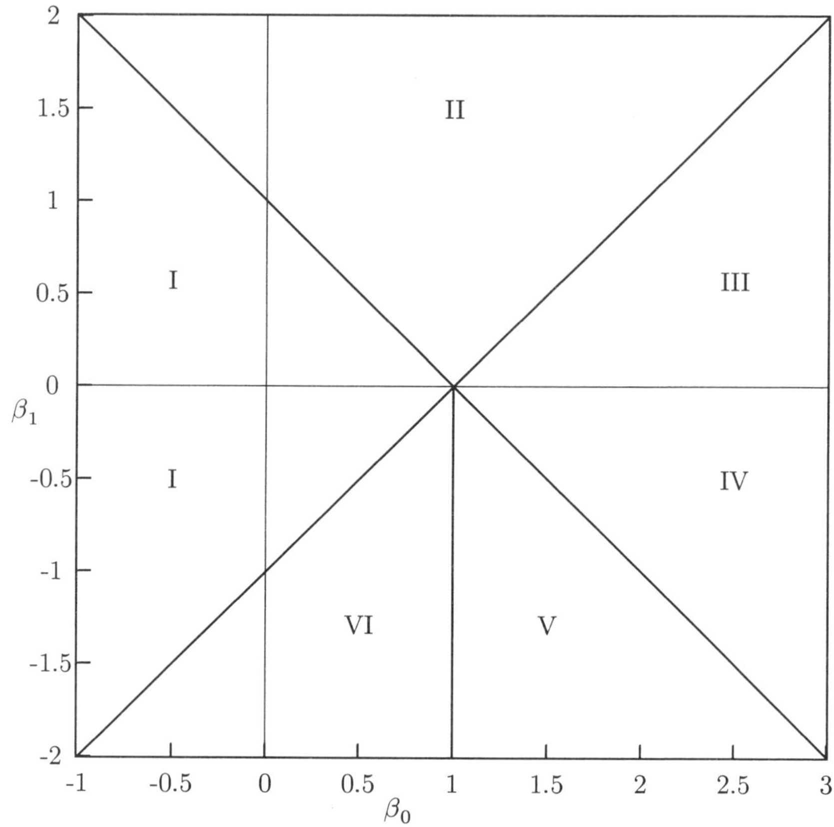

Figure 1: E-Stability Regions for Eq. 35

region V? There the E-stability conditions are in fact met (E&H, 2001, p. 202). In the E&H graphical summary this region is not distinguished from VI because in V the solutions are both dynamically unstable (explosive). But there is no compelling reason to ignore the MSV solution simply because it is explosive; it may be accurately indicating what would happen if (e.g.) extremely unwise policy behavior were imposed on the system.[19] For a discussion and rationalization of this position, with a closely related example, see McCallum (1999). In any case we see that this specification, too, conforms to the proposition that MSV

[19]The same statement does not apply to region II, where the MSV solution is E-stable but explosive, because there the model is not well formulated. This region illustrates that, though sufficient, the WF condition is not necessary for E-stability.

solutions are E-stable in all well-formulated models.[20]

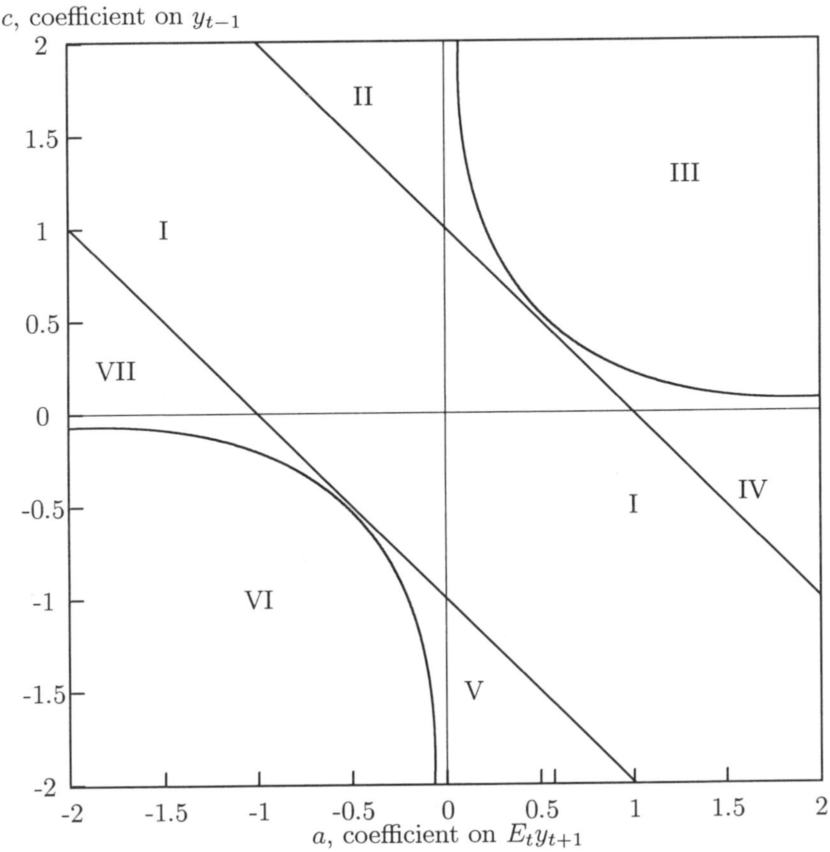

Figure 2: E-Stability Regions for Eq. 32

We wish to have results for the more general case with $|\rho| < 1$, permitting negative values, but let us proceed by first demonstrating algebraically that the E-stability conditions are satisfied by the MSV solution to model (32) when $0 \leq \rho < 1$ and the WF restriction $a + c < 1$ is imposed. Afterwards we can go on to the case with $-1 < \rho < 0$ permitted. The main task, then, is to show that if $1 - (a + c) > 0$,

[20]The usual presumption that E-stability implies LS learnability does not carry over automatically in cases of dynamic instability (explosive solutions). E&H (2001, pp. 219–220) indicate, however, that learnability will prevail in the current case if an adjustment is made to the model to permit the shock variance to grow along with the y_t values (and u_t is white noise).

then $(1 - a\phi_1)^{-1}a < 1$ where $\phi_1 = (1 - d)/2a$ with $d = \sqrt{1 - 4ac}$. Note first that $1 - a\phi_1 = (1 + d)/2$ so $(1 - a\phi_1)^{-1}a = 2a/(1 + d)$. Then for a proof by contradiction, suppose that $2a/(1 + d) > 1$. Then $a > 0$ and $2a - 1 > d$. Since both of its sides are positive, the latter implies $4a^2 - 4a + 1 > d^2 = 1 - 4ac$. But with $a > 0$ the last inequality reduces to $a - 1 > -c$ or $0 > 1 - (a + c)$, which is the contradiction that proves $(1 - a\phi_1)^{-1}a < 1$. The latter is the first of the three E-stability conditions listed in the previous paragraph. The second results from writing $(1 - a\phi_1)^{-2}ac = (1 - a\phi_1)^{-1}a\phi_1$, which follows because $(1 - a\phi_1)^{-1}c = \phi_1$.[21] Since $(1 - a\phi_1)^{-1}a\phi_1 = (1 - d)/(1 + d)$, which is smaller than 1 for all $d > 0$, we have the desired inequality. Finally, with $(1 - a\phi_1)^{-1}a < 1$ and ρ non-negative, the third condition also holds.

If ρ can be negative, which is plausible, it is possible that a sufficiently large negative ρ together with $(1 - a\phi_1)^{-1}a < 1$ could lead to failure of the last condition. This possibility can be eliminated, however, by adding a second WF requirement to rule out a different type of infinite discontinuity. This type pertains to the dynamic response of y_t to the exogenous forcing variable u_t. The response coefficient is $\phi_2 = (1 - a\phi_1 - a\rho)^{-1}$ so to avoid an infinite discontinuity we require that $1 - a\phi_1 - a\rho > 0$ or $1 - a\phi_1 > a\rho$. To see that this condition is sufficient for our purposes, note that with the MSV solution, $1 - a\phi_1 = (1 + d)/2$ is unambiguously positive. Consequently, the WF condition $1 - a\phi_1 > a\rho$ implies that $1 > (1 - a\phi_1)^{-1}a\rho$, which is identical to the E-stability condition under discussion. Thus we have shown that in model (32) with $|\rho| < 1$, the MSV solution is E-stable for all parameter values satisfying our two WF conditions.[22,23]

What about possible E-stability of the non-MSV solutions? A recent analysis that recognizes not just solutions such as (15) with root (18), but also ones involving "ARMA-type stationary sunspot" phenomena, has recently been conducted by Evans and McGough (2002). Their finding is that such solutions can be E-stable only in regions equivalent to IV and VII.[24] Whether their results are consistent with the position that non-MSV solutions are not E-stable or least-squares learnable in model (32)(8) if its parameters satisfy both of our conditions for being well

[21] The last expression is just a rearrangement of (16b).

[22] A closely related result, more general in some respects but without inclusion of the u_t shock term, has been developed by Gauthier (2003). Also see Wenzelburger (2002), who suggests that some extension to nonlinear models may be possible.

[23] A stronger condition than our second WF requirement, process consistency, is considered in the Appendix.

[24] Evans and McGough (2002) do not, however, consider the explosive regions II and V.

formulated is unclear. Other relevant results have been provided by Desgranges and Gauthier (2002).

Clearly, the main weakness of the foregoing argument is that the results pertain only to univariate models. It is my conjecture that the results can be extended to rather general multivariate linear formulations, but this extension has not yet been verified.

8 Conclusions

Let us conclude with a brief restatement of the results. After some historical discussion of the RE solution procedures of Walters (1971), Muth (1961), and Lucas (1972b), this paper considers the relevance for actual economies of issues stemming from the existence of multiple RE equilibria. In all linear models, the minimum state variable (MSV) solution — as defined by McCallum (1983, 1999) — is unique by construction. While it might be argued that the MSV solution warrants special status as the (unique) bubble-free solution, the focus in the present paper is on its adaptive, least-squares learnability by individuals not initially endowed with full knowledge of the economy's parameters, as discussed in important recent publications by Evans and Honkapohja (1999, 2001).

Although the MSV solution is learnable and the main alternatives are not learnable in most standard models, Evans and Honkapohja (1992, 1999, 2001) have stressed an example in which the opposite is true. The present paper shows, however, that parameter values yielding that result are such that the model is not well formulated, in a specified sense (one that avoids implausible discontinuities). More generally, analysis of a pair of prominent univariate specifications, featured by Evans and Honkapohja, shows that the MSV solution is invariably learnable in these structures, if they are well formulated.

Appendix

Because of the possibility that $-1 < \rho < 0$, we have ruled out a second type of infinite discontinuity, pertaining to the dynamic response of y_t to the exogenous forcing variable u_t, by requiring that $1 - a\phi_1 - a\rho > 0$. For the MSV solution, $1 - a\phi_1 = (1 + d)/2$ so we need

$$1 + d - 2a\rho > 0, \text{ or } d > 2a\rho - 1$$

to avoid the discontinuity. Clearly there is no problem unless $2a\rho > 1$ (so $a < 0$). If it is, the relevant condition may be written (since $d =$

$\sqrt{1-4ac}$) as $1 - 4ac > 1 - 4a\rho + 4a^2\rho^2$ or $-4ac > -4a\rho + 4a^2\rho^2$ or, with $a < 0$, $-c < a\rho^2 - \rho$. Now for the latter to hold for all ρ such that $-1 < \rho < 0$, it is necessary and sufficient that $a + c > -1$. That requirement is stronger, however, than the one adopted in this paper.

For the stronger condition, an alternative and more general argument can be based on the concept of "process consistency," discussed by Flood and Garber (1980), McCallum (1983, pp. 159–160), and Evans and Honkapohja (1992, pp. 10–12). A model fails to be process consistent when solving out expectational variables, by iteration into the infinite future, is illegitimate because the implied infinite series does not converge.[25] For model (32)(8) to be process consistent, then, it must be the case that at least one of the roots to (16b) exceeds 1.0 in absolute value. Thus process consistency obtains in region V of Figure 2, but not in region VII, according to the root properties reported by E&H (2001, p. 203). Requiring process consistency is therefore consistent with our main result but rules out some MSV solutions that are E-stable and permitted by the weaker condition adopted in Section 7.

BIBLIOGRAPHY

[1] Alstadheim, Ragna, and Dale W. Henderson, "Price-Level Determinacy, the Zero Lower Bound on the Interest Rate, and the Liquidity Trap," Working Paper, May 2002.

[2] Benhabib, Jess, Stephanie Schmitt-Grohe, and Martin Uribe, "The Perils of Taylor Rules," Journal of Economic Theory 96 (January/February 2001), 40–69.

[3] Bernanke, Ben S., and Michael Woodford, "Inflation Forecasts and Monetary Policy," Journal of Money, Credit, & Banking 29(4) (November 1997), 653–684.

[4] Brayton, Flint, Andrew Levin, Ralph W. Tryon, and John C. Williams, "The Evolution of Macro Models at the Federal Reserve Board," Carnegie-Rochester Conference Series in Public Policy 47 (December 1997), 115–167.

[5] Bullard, James, and Kaushik Mitra, "Learning About Monetary Policy Rules," W.P. 2000-001B (July 2000), Federal Reserve Bank of St. Louis.

[25] An extensive discussion of related issues is given by Sargent (1987, pp. 176–204 and 305–308).

[6] Cagan, Phillip, "The Monetary Dynamics of Hyperinflation," in Studies in the Quantity Theory of Money, M. Friedman. ed. University of Chicago Press, 1956.

[7] Clarida, Richard, Jordi Gali, and Mark Gertler, "The Science of Monetary Policy: A New Keynesian Perspective," Journal of Economic Literature 37 (December 1999), 1661–1707.

[8] Clarida, Richard, Jordi Gali, and Mark Gertler, "Monetary Policy Rules and Macroeconomic Stability: Evidence and Some Theory," NBER W.P. 6442, 1997.

[9] Cochrane, John H., "A Frictionless View of U.S. Inflation," NBER Macroeconomics Annual 1998. MIT Press, 1998.

[10] Desgranges, Gabriel and Stephane Gauthier, "Uniqueness of Bubble-Free Solution in Linear Rational Expectations Models," Macroeconomic Dynamics, 7 (April 2003), 171–191.

[11] Evans, George W., "Expectational Stability and the Multiple Equilibrium Problem in Linear Rational Expectations Models," Quarterly Journal of Economics 100 (November 1985), 1217–1233.

[12] Evans, George W., "Selection Criteria for Models with Non-Uniqueness," Journal of Monetary Economics 18 (September 1986), 147–157.

[13] Evans, George W., "The Fragility of Sunspots and Bubbles," Journal of Monetary Economics 23 (1989), 297–317.

[14] Evans, George W., and Seppo Honkapohja, "On the Robustness of Bubbles in Linear RE Models," International Economic Review 33 (February 1992), 1–14.

[15] Evans, George W., and Seppo Honkapohja, "Learning Dynamics," in Handbook of Macroeconomics, J.B. Taylor and M. Woodford, eds. North-Holland, 1999.

[16] Evans, George W., and Seppo Honkapohja, Learning and Expectations in Macroeconomics, Princeton University Press, 2001.

[17] Evans, George W., and Bruce McGough, "Stable Sunspot Solutions in Models with Predetermined Variables," Working Paper, University of Oregon, April 2002.

[18] Flood, Robert P., and Peter M. Garber, "An Economic Theory of Monetary Reform," Journal of Political Economy 88 (February 1980), 24–58.

[19] Gauthier, Stéphane, "On the Dynamic Equivalence Principle in Linear Rational Expectations Models, Macroeconomic Dynamics 7 (January 2003), 63–88.

[20] Gurley, John G., and Edward S. Shaw, Money in a Theory of Finance, Brookings Institution, 1960.

[21] Isard, Peter, Douglas Laxton, and Ann-Charlotte Eliasson, "Simple Monetary Policy Rules Under Model Uncertainty," International Tax and Public Finance 6 (November 1999a), 537–577. Also in International Finance and Financial Crises: Essays in Honor of Robert P. Flood, Jr., P. Isard, A. Razin, and A.K. Rose, eds. Kluwer Academic Publishing, 1999.

[22] Johnson, Harry G., "Monetary Theory and Policy," American Economic Review 52 (June 1962), 325–384.

[23] King, Robert G., "The New IS-LM Model: Language, Logic, and Limits," Federal Reserve Bank of Richmond Economic Quarterly 86 (Summer 2000), 45–103.

[24] Kocherlakota, Narayana, and Christopher Phelan, "Explaining the Fiscal Theory of the Price Level," Federal Reserve Bank of Minnesota Quarterly Review 23 (Fall 1999), 14-23.

[25] Krugman, Paul, Peddling Prosperity. W.W. Norton, 1994.

[26] Lange, Oscar, "Say's Law: A Restatement and Criticism," in Studies in Mathematical Economics and Econometrics, O. Lange, F. McIntyre, and T.O. Yntema, eds. Chicago, 1942.

[27] Lucas, Robert E., Jr., "Expectations and the Neutrality of Money," Journal of Economic Theory 4 (April 1972a), 103–124.

[28] Lucas, Robert E., Jr., "Econometric Testing of the Natural Rate Hypothesis," in Econometrics of Price Determination, O. Eckstein, ed. Board of Governors of the Federal Reserve System, 1972b.

[29] Lucas, Robert E., Jr., "Econometric Policy Evaluation: a Critique." in The Phillips Curve and Labor Markets, K. Brunner and A.H. Meltzer, eds. Amsterdam: North Holland, 19–46, 1976

[30] Marcet, Albert, and Thomas J. Sargent, "Convergence of Least Squares Learning Mechanisms in Self-Referential Linear Stochastic Models," Journal of Economic Theory 48 (April 1989), 337–368.

[31] Matthews, Kent, "Introduction," in The Economics and Politics of Money: The Selected Essays of Alan Walters, K. Matthews, ed. Edward Elgar Publishing, 1998.

[32] McCallum, Bennctt T., "Pricc Lcvcl Determinacy with an Interest Rate Policy Rule and Rational Expectations," Journal of Monetary Economics 8 (November 1981), 319–329.

[33] McCallum, Bennett T., "On Non-Uniqueness in Rational Expectations Models: An Attempt at Perspective," Journal of Monetary Economics 11 (March 1983), 139–168.

[34] McCallum, Bennett T, "Role of the Minimal State Variable Criterion in Rational Expectations Models," in International Tax and Public Finance 6 (November 1999a), 621–639. Also in International Finance and Financial Crises: Essays in Honor of Robert P. Flood, Jr., P. Isard, A. Razin, and A.K. Rose, eds. Kluwer Academic Publishing, 1999b.

[35] McCallum, Bennett T., "Indeterminacy, Bubbles, and the Fiscal Theory of the Price Level," Journal of Monetary Economics 47 (February 2001), 19–30.

[36] McCallum, Bennett T., "Inflation Targeting and the Liquidity Trap," in Inflation Targeting: Design, Performance, Challenges, N. Loyaza and R. Soto, eds. Central Bank of Chile, 2002.

[37] Muth, John F., "Rational Expectations and the Theory of Price Movements," Econometrica 29 (June 1961), 315–335.

[38] Patinkin, Don, "The Indeterminacy of Absolute Prices in Classical Economic Theory," Econometrica 17 (January 1949), 1–27.

[39] Patinkin, Don, "Financial Intermediaries and the Logical Structure of Monetary Theory: A Review Article," American Economic Review 51 (March 1961), 95–116.

[40] Patinkin, Don, Money, Interest, and Prices, 2nd ed. Harper and Row, 1965.

[41] Sargent, Thomas J., "A Note on the Accelerationist Controversy," Journal of Money, Credit, & Banking 3 (August 1971), 721–725.

[42] Sargent, Thomas J., Macroeconomic Theory, 2nd ed. Academic Press, 1987.

[43] Schmitt-Grohe, Stephanie, and Martin Uribe, "Liquidity Traps with Global Taylor Rules," Working Paper, July 2000.

[44] Sims, Christopher A., "A Simple Model for the Study of the Determination of the Price Level and the Interaction of Monetary and Fiscal Policy," Economic Theory 4 (1994), 381–399.

[45] Walters, Alan A., "Consistent Expectations, Distributed Lags, and the Quantity Theory," Economic Journal 81 (June 1971), 273–281.

[46] Walters, Alan A., "Monetary and Fiscal Policy in the UK," in Keynes and Economic Policy, W. Eltis and P. Sinclair, eds. Macmillan, 1988.

[47] Wenzelburger, Jan, "Learning in Linear Models with Expectational Leads," Working Paper, University of Bielefeld, January 2002.

[48] Woodford, Michael, "Nonstandard Indicators for Monetary Policy: Can Their Usefulness Be Judged From Forecasting Regressions?," in Monetary Policy, G.N. Mankiw, ed. University of Chicago Press for NBER, 1994.

[49] Woodford, Michael, "Price-Level Determinacy Without Control of a Monetary Aggregate,"Carnegie-Rochester Conference Series on Public Policy 43 (December 1995), 1–46.

[50] Woodford, Michael, "Price Level Determination Under Interest Rate Rules," Ch. 2 of Interest and Prices, Manuscript, 2001.

3 The Efficacy of Monetary Policy in a Multi Sector, Two Country Model

Matthew B. Canzoneri, Robert E. Cumby and Behzad T. Diba

1 Introduction

How effective is monetary policy in macroeconomic stabilization? A new generation of policy evaluation models — based on optimizing agents, monopolistic wage and price setting, and nominal rigidities — is being used to address this age old question.[1] Initial results by King and Wolman (1999) and others suggested that monetary policy could be very effective: monetary policy could replicate the flexible price solution in a model with staggered price setting, thereby maximizing the expected utility of the representative household. However, this result was later shown to depend on symmetries in nominal inertia, productivity, and monetary policy decision making. Erceg, Henderson and Levin (2000) added nominal wage rigidities; Benigno (2001) introduced regional differences in price rigidity; Canzoneri, Cumby and Diba (2002a,b) allowed asymmetries in sectoral productivity; and Obstfeld and Rogoff (2002) and Corsetti and Pesenti (2001a) studied the gains from policy coordination in a multi country setting. These studies showed that each of these asymmetries make monetary policy less effective.

This paper asks which of the asymmetries is important empirically.[2]

[1] These models — often portrayed as the "new neoclassical synthesis" — grew out of the real business cycle literature. Goodfriend and King (1997) describe this synthesis and cite a number of early references. Ongoing work includes draft chapters of Michael Woodford's *Interest and Prices*, which are currently available on his web page.

[2] Some would argue that the costs of the business cycle are small, and that therefore

Is it asymmetries in nominal inertia? Asymmetries in sectoral productivity? Or the lack of a common goal in international decision making. In Canzoneri, Cumby and Diba (2002b), we developed a tractable multi sector framework for the analysis of asymmetries in nominal rigidity and productivity in a closed economy; in Canzoneri, Cumby and Diba (2002a) we developed a rather simple model of international policy coordination.[3] In Section 2, we combine these modeling efforts to develop a general two country, multi sector framework that can be used to assess all three asymmetries. Readers who are familiar with our earlier papers can proceed directly to Section 3. In Section 3, we discuss the difference between Nash and cooperative solutions in the paradigm, and in Section 4, we show how the model can be calibrated to assess the relative importance of the three asymmetries. Data limitations are severe, and we view the results we present here as suggestive. In the concluding section, we discuss directions for future work.

2 A Two Country Model with Multiple Sectors and Nominal Inertia

In this section, we generalize the models developed in Canzoneri, Cumby and Diba (2002a,b). In both of these modeling efforts, a judicious choice of functional forms — logarithmic utility for consumption, and a Cobb–Douglas aggregator for the consumption good — allowed us to aggregate sectors easily.[4] This in turn allows us to develop a general analytical framework that is easy to calibrate for specific applications. We can, for example, let some industries (or countries) exhibit more wage rigidity than others, or we can let some industries (or countries) exhibit different stochastic processes for productivity. In Section 2.1, we outline our framework for sectors and industries. In Section 2.2, we describe the behavior of households and firms in a given sector. In Section 2.3, we show how the sectors are aggregated into closed form equilibrium solutions.

none of these asymmetries is very important to the representative household's utility. We do not take on this larger question here.

[3] Actually, the model followed closely the path breaking work of Obstfeld and Rogoff (2000) and Corsetti and Pesenti (2001a).

[4] In Canzoneri, Cumby and Diba (2002a), we also showed that this choice of functional forms is not entirely innocuous. It produces a macroeconomic interdependence between the two countries that is highly stylized.

2.1 Sectors and Industries

Our two country model consists of $2K$ sectors. Sectors are defined by their supply side characteristics — the goods they produce and the nominal rigidities they exhibit — and by their country of origin. Sectors $k \in F = \{1, 2, ..., K\}$ are located in the home country, while sectors $k \in F^* = \{K + 1, K + 2, ..., 2K\}$ are in the foreign country. We can partition the home and foreign economies, F and F^*, into industry subsets. Following the Balassa–Samuelson literature, we allow differences in productivity across traded and non-traded goods. Following Corsetti and Dedola (2002), we will also distinguish between tradable goods that are sold at home and tradable goods that are sold abroad, since transportation costs and distribution networks may differ across domestic and foreign markets. In the home economy, N is the subset of sectors — or industry — producing non-tradable goods; E is the subset producing tradable goods that are exported, and T is the subset producing tradable goods that are sold at home. The set of foreign sectors, F^*, is similarly partitioned into industries N^*, E^*, and T^*. Sectors (even within a given industry) can exhibit different kinds of nominal rigidity. W is the set of sectors — home and foreign — with wage stickiness, and P is the set of sectors — home and foreign — with price stickiness.[5] A superscript "c" denotes the complement of a set. So, for example, $N \cap W \cap P$ is the set of home sectors that produce non-tradable goods and have sticky wages and sticky prices; $N^* \cap W^c \cap P^c$ is the set of foreign sectors that produce non-tradable goods and have flexible wages and prices.

Each sector has a continuum of firms. Home firms are indexed by $f \in [1, ..., K)$; foreign firms are indexed by $f \in [K, 2K)$. Firms in $[0, 1)$ are in sector $k = 1$, firms in $[1, 2)$ are in sector $k = 2$, and so on. Each firm has a continuum of wage setting households working for it. Home households are indexed by $(h, f) \in [0, 1] \otimes [0, K)$; foreign households are indexed by $(h, f) \in [0, 1] \otimes [K, 2K)$. The mass of households working at each firm is equal to one, and the mass of firms in each sector is also equal to one.

We let $\lambda(\cdot)$ be the number of sectors in a set. So, $\lambda(F) = K$ is the number of sectors in the home economy, and also the mass of firms in the home economy; it is a natural measure of the size of the home economy. $\lambda(F \cap W \cap P)$ is the number of home sectors that have sticky wages and sticky prices; it is a measure of the nominal inertia in the home economy. $\lambda(F * \cap W^c \cap P^c)$ is the number of foreign sectors that have flexible wages

[5] We will assume that households and firms set their wages and prices in terms of their own home currency. That is, we do not consider "pricing to market."

and prices; it is a measure of the flexibility of the foreign economy.

2.2 Households and Firms

At time t, the utility of home household (h, f), employed in sector k, is given by

$$U_t(h,f) = E_t \sum_{\tau=t}^{\infty} \beta^{\tau-t} [\ln(C_{H,\tau}(h,f)) - AN_{k,\tau}(h,f)) \\ + v(M_\tau(h,f)/P_{H,\tau})] \quad (1)$$

where $C_{H,\tau}(h, f)$ is the household's consumption of a composite good (defined below), and $P_{H,\tau}$ is its price in domestic currency. $N_{k,\tau}(h, f)$ is the household's work effort, and $M_\tau(h, f)$ is its domestic currency holdings.[6]

The household's optimization problem can be divided into an intratemporal cost minimization problem — which determines demand for the components of composite goods — and an intertemporal utility maximization problem — which determines savings behavior. The basic elements of the household's intratemporal problem are well known; we just summarize them here.[7] Each firm f in sector k produces a differentiated product; the sector k good, $Y_{k,t}$, is a composite of its firms' products,

$$Y_{k,t} \equiv \left[\int_{k-1}^{k} Y_{k,t}(f)^{(\theta-1)/\theta} df \right]^{\theta/(\theta-1)} \quad (2a)$$

where $\theta > 1$ is the elasticity of substitution; the price of the sector k good is

$$P_{k,t} = \left[\int_{k-1}^{k} P_{k,t}(f)^{1-\theta} df \right]^{1/(1-\theta)} \quad (2b)$$

where $P_{k,t}(f)$ is the price set by the firm. Demand for the output of an individual firm f is

$$Y_{k,t}^{d}(f) = \left(\frac{P_{k,t}}{P_{k,t}(f)} \right)^{\theta} Y_{k,t} \quad (2c)$$

---

[6] The linearity of the disutility of work is an innocent assumption, but the log utility of consumption is not, as we shall see. The utility of money, $v(\cdot)$, can take any standard form.

[7] See for example Blanchard and Fischer (1989, Ch. 8) and Frenkel and Razin (1987, Ch. 6). In Canzoneri, Cumby and Diba (2002b), we present a detailed description of the intratemporal problem.

The final consumption good is a composite of all the goods that the household consumes. A home household consumes the goods produced by the firms in $H = N \cup T \cup E^*$, while a foreign household consumes the goods of firms in $H^* = N^* \cup T^* \cup E$. For simplicity, we have already assumed that the number of home sectors is equal to the number of foreign sectors; that is, $\lambda(F) = \lambda(F^*) = K$. We will also assume that the number of sectors in home industries is the same as the number of sectors in the corresponding foreign industries; that is, $\lambda(N) = \lambda(N^*), \lambda(E) = \lambda(E^*)$, and $\lambda(T) = \lambda(T^*)$. These assumptions taken together imply that $\lambda(H) = \lambda(H^*) = K$. The final consumption good of a home household is

$$Y_{H,t} = \Pi_{k \in H} Y_{k,t}^{1/K} \tag{3a}$$

and its price is

$$P_{H,t} = K \Pi_{k \in H} P_{k,t}^{1/K} \tag{3b}$$

Demand for the sector k good is

$$Y_{k,t}^{d} = (1/K)\left(P_{H,t}/P_{k,t}\right) Y_{H,t} \tag{3c}$$

for $k \in H$. The final consumption good of a foreign household is defined in an analogous manner, with H^*replacing H. Note that the elasticity of substitution across sectoral goods is equal to one; this restriction — first introduced by Corsetti and Pesenti (2001a) — greatly simplifies the model, but we shall see that it is not entirely innocent. In any case, this completes the description of the household's intratemporal problem.

Firms also have an intratemporal optimization problem. Recall that each firm has a continuum of workers. Each household associated with the firm f supplies a differentiated labor input, $N_{k,t}(h, f)$, at a wage, $W_{k,t}(h, f)$. The firm uses a composite labor input

$$N_{k,t}(f) \equiv \left[\int_0^1 N_{k,t}(h, f)^{(\phi-1)/\phi} dh\right]^{\phi/(\phi-1)} \tag{4a}$$

where $\phi > 1$, to produce

$$Y_{k,t}(f) = Z_{k,t} N_{k,t}(f) \tag{4b}$$

where $Z_{k,t}$ is a sector wide productivity shock. The wage the firm pays for the composite input is

$$W_{k,t}(f) = \left[\int_0^1 W_{k,t}(h, f)^{1-\phi} dh\right]^{1/(1-\phi)} \tag{4c}$$

and the demand for the labor of household (h, f) is

$$N^d_{k,t}(h,f) = (W_{k,t}(f)/W_{k,t}(h,f))^{\phi} N_{k,t}(f)$$

Turning now to the intertemporal optimization problems, the flow budget constraint of home household (h, f), employed in sector k, at time τ is

$$\begin{aligned} M_\tau(h,f) + E_\tau[\delta_{\tau,\tau+1} B_{\tau+1}(h,f)] + P_{H,\tau} C_{H,\tau}(h,f) + T_\tau \\ = W_{k,\tau}(h,f) N^d_{k,\tau}(h,f) + M_{\tau-1}(h,f) + B_\tau(h,f) + D_\tau(h,f) \end{aligned} \quad (5)$$

where $B_{\tau+1}(h, f)$ is a state contingent claim on other households, and $\delta_{\tau,\tau+1}$ is the stochastic discount factor.[8] $D_\tau(h, f)$ are the household's dividends, and T_τ is a lump sum tax (which the government uses to balance its budget each period).[9]

Household (h, f)'s intertemporal optimization problem is to choose $B_{t+1}(h, f)$, $C_{H,t}(h, f)$, $M_t(h, f)$, and $W_{k,t}(h, f)$ to maximize (1) subject to (4d) and (5). Differentiation with respect to the first three variables produces standard first order conditions that do not depend upon where the household works or assumptions about nominal rigidities:

$$\delta_{t,t+1} = \beta \alpha_{t+1}(h,f)/\alpha_t(h,f) \quad (6)$$

$$\alpha_t(h,f) = 1/P_{H,t} C_{H,t}(h,f) \quad (7)$$

$$v'(\cdot) = [1/C_{H,t}(h,f)][1 - E_t(\delta_{t,t+1})] \quad (8)$$

where $\alpha_t(h, f)$ is the household's marginal utility of wealth, measured in units of domestic currency.

In an equilibrium in which all home households have the same initial wealth, the Euler equation (6) implies that the marginal utility of wealth equalizes across home households, and (7) implies that consumption equalizes as well, even though labor incomes, work efforts and dividends may not. So, in what follows, we set $C_{H,t}(h, f) = C_{H,t}$. Equation

[8] The parsimonious notation for contingent claims in (5) comes from Woodford (1997). Cochrane (2001, Ch. 3) introduces contingent claims in the following way: let $p(B) = \sum_\sigma pc(\sigma)B(\sigma)$ be the price of a portfolio B of contingent claims; the σ's denote states of nature, $pc(\sigma)$ is the price of a claim on one dollar received in $\tau+1$ contingent on the state σ occurring, and $B(\sigma)$ is the number of such claims in portfolio B. Letting $\pi(\sigma)$ be the probability of state σ, $p(B) = \sum_\sigma \pi(\sigma)[pc(\sigma)/\pi(\sigma)]B(\sigma) = E[\delta(\sigma)B(\sigma)]$, where $\delta(\sigma) \equiv pc(\sigma)/\pi(\sigma)$ is called the "stochastic discount factor". $B_{\tau+1}(h, f)$ and $\delta_{\tau,\tau+1}$ in (5) correspond to $B(\sigma)$ and $\delta(\sigma)$. All households face the same asset prices and have the same subjective probabilities; so, all households face the same discount factor, $\delta_{\tau,\tau+1}$, in (5).

[9] We assume that each household owns a representative share in all of the firms. We have suppressed the buying and selling of shares since, as explained below, state contingent claims make the distribution of dividends irrelevant in this model.

(8) gives the household's demand for real money balances. Consider a "risk free" bond that costs 1 dollar (or one unit of home currency) in period t and pays I_t dollars in period $t+1$ for all states of nature; $1 = E_t[\delta_{t,t+1} I_t]$ or $I_t^{-1} = E_t[\delta_{t,t+1}]$. So, equation (8) relates the demand for real money balances to the level of consumption and the gross nominal interest rate, I_t.

The last first order condition — from the derivative with respect to $W_{k,t}(h,f)$ — describes the household's wage setting behavior. If the household works in a sector with flexible wages ($k \in F \cap W^c$), then optimal wage setting requires

$$A = (1/\mu_w)[W_{k,t}(h,f)/P_{H,t}](1/C_{H,t}) \tag{9a}$$

where $\mu_w \equiv \phi/(\phi-1) > 1$ is a "markup factor." To get (9a), we used equation (7), and we set $W_{k,t}(h,f) = W_{k,t}(f)$ and $N_{k,t}(h,f) = N_{k,t}(f)$, in the first order condition for $W_{k,t}(h,f)$.[10] The left hand side of (9a) is the disutility of working one more hour; the right hand side is the utility of spending the proceeds, $(1/\mu_w)(W_{k,t}(h,f)/P_{H,t})$. The proceeds are less than the original real wage, $W_{k,t}(h,f)/P_{H,t}$, because the household faces a downward sloping demand curve, (4d); it has to lower its wage to induce the extra hour of work. If the household works in a sector with fixed wages ($k \in F \cap W$), then $W_{k,t}(h,f)$ is set at the end of period $t-1$, with the information available at that time; optimal wage setting requires

$$E_{t-1}[N_{k,t}(h,f)A_t] = (1/\mu_w)E_{t-1}[N_{k,t}(h,f)W_{k,t}(h,f)/P_{H,t}C_{H,t}] \quad \text{(9a)}$$

Once again, we used (7), and the fact that $W_{k,t}(h,f) = W_{k,t}(f)$, and $N_{k,t}(h,f) = N_{k,t}(f)$, in the first order condition for $W_{k,t}(h,f)$.

Firms also have an intertemporal optimization problem. The market value of firm f is

$$MV_t(f) = E_t \sum_{\tau=t}^{\infty} \delta_{t,\tau} R_\tau(f) \tag{10}$$

where $\delta_{t,\tau}$ is the stochastic discount factor (representing the current price of a nominal claim in a particular state in period τ, and $R_\tau(f) \equiv P_{k,\tau}(f)Y_{k,\tau}(f) - W_{k,\tau}(f)N_{k,\tau}(f)$ is net revenue. Firm f sets $P_{k,t}(f)$

[10] Since all the workers employed by the same firm face the same optimization problem, they all set the same wage and end up working the same number of hours in equilibrium. And since the measure of workers employed by each firm is one, (4a) and (4c) imply $N_{k,t}(h,f) = N_{k,t}(f)$ and $W_{k,t}(h,f) = W_{k,t}(f)$.

to maximize (10) subject to its demand curve, (2c), and its production technology, (4b).

If firm f is in a sector with flexible prices ($k \in F \cap P^c$), then it sets

$$P_{k,t}(f) = \mu_p[W_{k,t}(f)/Z_{k,t}] \tag{11a}$$

where $\mu_p \equiv \theta/(\theta - 1) > 1$; price is set at a constant markup, μ_p, over marginal cost. To get (11a), we have set $P_{k,t}(f) = P_{k,t}$ and $Y_{k,t}(f) = Y_{k,t}$ in the firm's first order condition.[11] Note that (11a) applies to firms with either flexible wages or sticky wages — firms take the wage rate (flexible or sticky) as given in calculating their marginal cost. If firm f is in a sector with sticky prices ($k \in F \cap P$), then it sets its price at the end of period $t-1$, and

$$P_{k,t}(f) = \mu_p E_{t-1} \frac{[Y_{k,t}(f)/P_{H,t}C_{H,t}]\,[(W_{k,t}(f)/Z_{k,t})]}{E_{t-1}[Y_{k,t}(f)/P_{H,t}C_{H,t}]} \tag{11b}$$

To get (11b), we have used the Euler equation (6) to eliminate $\delta_{t-1,t}$ and equation (7) to eliminate α_t, and we have set $P_{k,t}(f) = P_{k,t}$ and $Y_{k,t}(f) = Y_{k,t}$. Once again, it does not matter whether wages are sticky or flexible.

Throughout this paper, we assume "producer currency pricing." Home firms set prices in units of the home currency, and foreign firms set prices in units of the foreign currency.[12] We will denote foreign currency prices by a star. So, home exporters ($k \in E$) sell their products to foreign consumers at the price $P^*_{k,t}(f) = P_{k,t}(f)/S_t$, where the exchange rate, S_t, is the home currency price of foreign exchange; similarly, foreign exporters ($k \in E^*$) sell their product to home consumers at the price $P^*_{k,t}(f) = S_t P^*_{k,t}(f)$.

2.3 Equilibrium in the Two Country Model

It is well known that there is no international borrowing or lending in models like this; the current account is always balanced in equilibrium. The key assumptions that shut down the current account are the log utility of consumption and the Cobb–Douglas aggregator for the final

[11] Since all the firms in a given sector face the same optimization problem, they all set the same price and end up producing the same amount of output in equilibrium. And since the measure of firms in each sector is one, (2a) and (2b) imply $P_{k,t}(f) = P_{k,t}$ and $Y_{k,t}(f) = Y_{k,t}$.

[12] There is a growing literature comparing "producer currency pricing" with "consumer currency pricing"; with the latter, exporters set prices in terms of their consumers' currency. See, for example, Corsetti and Pesenti (2001b, 2002) and Devereux and Engel (2000).

consumption good. The result was highlighted by Corsetti and Pesenti (2001a), and we discussed it in some detail in Canzoneri, Cumby and Diba (2002a). In this paper, we will take the result as given.

Since there are no interesting dynamics to be analyzed, we can simplify the notation by dropping the time subscripts. Moreover, the first order conditions for households and firms in a given sector are identical; so, we can simplify our discussion by aggregating sectoral variables. As already noted in a series of footnotes, $N_k(h,f) = N_k(f) = N_k$, $W_k(h,f) = W_k(f) = W_k$ and $P_k(f) = P_k$. In equilibrium, sectoral consumption is equal to output:

$$\int_0^K \left[\int_0^1 C_k(h,f)dh\right] df = KC_k(h,f) \equiv KC_k = Y_k = Y_k(f)$$
$$\equiv \left[\int_{k-1}^{k} Y_k(f)^{(\theta-1)/\theta} df\right]^{\theta/(\theta-1)}$$

For $k \in N \cup T$, consumption is aggregated over the K home households; for $k \in E$, consumption is aggregated over the K foreign households. Analogous statements hold for sectors in the foreign country.

The Cobb–Douglas aggregator for the final consumption good implies that a fixed share of expenditure goes to each sectoral good; that is, (3c) and its foreign country counterpart imply

$$(1/K)P_H C_H = P_k C_k \text{ for } k \in H \equiv N \cup T \cup E^* \tag{12a}$$
$$(1/K)P^*_{H^*} C_{H^*} = P^*_k C_k \text{ for } k \in H^* \equiv N^* \cup T^* \cup E \tag{12b}$$

In this setting, it is natural to take nominal expenditure as the instrument of monetary policy,

$$\Omega = P_H C_H \tag{13a}$$
$$\Omega^* = P^*_{H^*} C_{H^*} \tag{13b}$$

The home policy instrument, Ω, controls nominal expenditure in all sectors producing for the home market; the foreign policy instrument, Ω^*, controls nominal expenditure in all sectors producing for the foreign market.[13]

As noted in Canzoneri, Cumby and Diba (2002a), current account balance and constant expenditure shares imply a particularly simple the-

[13] In a cash-in-advance model, Ω and Ω^* would be the home and foreign money supplies. In our money-in-the-utility-function model, Corsetti and Pesenti (2001a,b) have identified Ω and Ω^* with the home and foreign interest rates, via the Euler equations.

ory of exchange rate determination. Trade balance implies

$$\sum_{k\in E} P_k C_k = S \sum_{k\in E^*} P_k^* C_k \tag{14}$$

and, since $\lambda(E) = \lambda(E^*)$, (12a,b) and (13a,b) imply

$$S = \Omega/\Omega^* \tag{15}$$

The equilibrium exchange rate is the ratio of nominal expenditure in the two countries, and therefore the ratio of the instruments of monetary policy.

2.3.1 Equilibrium in sectors with no nominal rigidities

First, we derive the employment and output levels in sectors that have flexible wages and flexible prices. It is important to understand what happens in these sectors, since we will see that they provide a normative benchmark for sectors that do have some form of nominal inertia.

Consider a home sector k with flexible wages and flexible prices. In equilibrium, the wage and price setting equations, (9a) and (11a) take the form

$$A = (1/\mu_w)W_k/P_H C_H \text{ for } k \in F \cap W^c \cap P^c \tag{16a}$$

$$P_k = \mu_p W_k/Z_k \text{ for } k \in F \cap W^c \cap P^c \tag{16b}$$

Recalling that $P_H C_H = K P_k C_k = P_k Y_k$, these equations can be combined to show that[14]

$$Y_k = Z_k/A\mu \text{ for } k \in F \cap W^c \cap P^c \tag{17a}$$

where $\mu \equiv \mu_w \mu_p$ is the combined monopolistic markup; and since $N_k = Y_k/Z_k$,

$$N_k = 1/A\mu \text{ for } k \in F \cap W^c \cap P^c \tag{17b}$$

Analogous results hold for sectors in the foreign country.

In sectors with flexible wages and prices, employment is constant, and productivity shocks pass directly to the level of output and consumption. This particular outcome is due to the log specification of the utility of consumption. We will see that the flexible wage/price solution is a (constrained) optimum for monetary policy. So, (17a) and (17b) give the responses that a benevolent policy maker would like to replicate in sectors with nominal rigidities.

---

[14] The algebra is straightforward for $k \in N \cup T$. There are some extra steps for $k \in E$, since exports are consumed by foreign households. (16a) implies $A\mu_w = W_k/P_k Y_k = W_k/\Omega$. Using this to eliminate W_k in (16b), $P_k = A\Omega\mu/Z_k$. Since $S = \Omega/\Omega^*$, $P_k^* = P_k/S = P_k\Omega^*/\Omega = A\mu\Omega^*/Z_k = A\mu P_k^* Y_k/Z_k$. Cancelling the P_k^*, we get (17a) for these export sectors as well.

2.3.2 *Equilibrium in sectors with fixed prices (and fixed or flexible wages)*

Consider a home sector k with fixed prices (and fixed or flexible wages). In equilibrium, the preset prices can be found by substituting (13a) into the equilibrium version of (11b). However, the details of that are not of much concern to us here;[15] we simply need to keep track of which prices are preset, and the currency in which they are set.

From (12a) and (13a),

$$\Omega = P_H C_H = K P_k C_k \text{ for } k \in (N \cup T) \cap P \tag{18a}$$

For these sectors, P_k is fixed, and the levels of consumption and output are determined by aggregate demand, or Ω. If Ω is held constant, output will not fluctuate with changes in productivity, Z_k; the work effort will absorb changes in productivity. If the central bank wants to replicate the flexible wage/price solution in this sector, it has to let Ω accommodate changes in productivity. Of course, if productivity shocks differ across fixed price sectors, then monetary policy can not achieve the flexible wage/price solution economy wide. Asymmetries in productivity create sectoral tradeoffs for monetary policy.

For sectors in the home export industry, (12b) and (13b) imply $\Omega^* = K P_k^* C_k$, but recall that home exporters set prices in terms of the home currency, and that the foreign currency price P_k^* is equal to P_k/S. So, $\Omega^* = K P_k^* C_k = K(P_k/S) C_k$, and since $S = \Omega/\Omega^*$, an increase in Ω^* simply produces a proportionate increase in the foreign currency price, leaving consumption and output unchanged. Foreign consumption of the home export is instead determined by home monetary policy,

$$\Omega = K P_k C_k \text{ for } k \in E \cap P \tag{18b}$$

Note that it does not matter whether the wage rate is fixed or flexible in sectors with fixed prices. Output and employment are demand determined in the manner described above. The wage rate determines the distribution of receipts between labor income and profits, but with complete contingent claims markets, this does not matter.

Analogous results hold for sectors in the foreign country. In summary, home monetary policy sets the level of output in all of the home sectors, and foreign monetary policy sets the level of output in all of the foreign sectors. The supply sides of the economies are, in this sense, insulated from one another. This does not mean, however, that households are indifferent about monetary policy in the other country. Home

[15] See Canzoneri, Cumby and Diba (2002b) for a fuller discussion.

consumption of foreign exports is determined by foreign monetary policy, and foreign consumption of home exports is determined by home monetary policy.

The model is nicely log linear. Letting the productivity shocks be log normally distributed, the equilibrium versions of (9a) (or (9b)) and (11b) can be solved for the expected (logs of the) levels of home consumption of sectoral goods,

$$E(c_k) = E(\hat{y}_k) - \frac{1}{2}\text{VAR}[\omega - z_k] - \log(K) \quad \text{for } k \in (N \cup T) \cap P \quad (19a)$$

$$E(c_k) = E(\hat{y}_k) - \frac{1}{2}\text{VAR}[\omega * - z_k] - \log(K) \text{ for } k \in E^* \cap P \quad (19b)$$

where small letters represent the logs of capital letters, a "^" denotes a flexible wage/price outcome, and $E[\cdot]$ and $\text{VAR}[\cdot]$ denote expectations and variances conditional on beginning of period information.[16] The home central bank has to set $\omega = z_k$ to bring expected (and actual) home consumption to its flexible wage/price level in home sectors selling to the home market; the foreign central bank has to set $\omega^* = z_k$ to bring expected (and actual) home consumption to its flexible wage/price level in foreign sectors exporting to the home market. With our postulated utility functions, the expected work effort of home households is fixed, and independent of monetary policy,[17]

$$E(n_k) = -\log(A\mu) \text{ for } k \in (N \cup T \cup E) \cap P \quad (20)$$

Analogous results hold for expected foreign consumption and for the expected foreign work effort.

2.3.3 Equilibrium in sectors with fixed wages and flexible prices

Consider a home sector k with fixed wages and flexible prices. In equilibrium, the preset wages can be found by substituting (13a) into the equilibrium version of (9b); once again, the details of that are not of much concern to us here. From (12a), (13a), and the equilibrium version of (11a),

$$\Omega = KP_kC_k = K(\mu_p W_k/Z_k)C_k \text{ for } k \in (N \cup T) \cap W \quad (21a)$$

[16] See Canzoneri, Cumby and Diba (2002a,b) for a more detailed discussion.

[17] This result depends on both the log utility of consumption and the linear disutility of work; see Canzoneri, Cumby and Diba (2002b).

For these sectors, W_t is fixed, and the levels of consumption and output are determined by aggregate demand, or Ω, and sectoral productivity, Z_k. If the central bank wants to replicate the flexible wage/price solution in these sectors, it should hold Ω constant. Note that the central bank can not simultaneously replicate the flexible wage/price solution in fixed wage sectors and fixed price sectors, it would have to hold demand constant, while in the fixed price sectors, it would have to repond to the productivity shocks. Asymmetries in normal inertia create tradeoffs for monetary policy.[18]

For sectors in the home export industry, (12b), (13b), and an equilibrium version of (11a) imply

$$\Omega^* = KP_k^*C_k = K(P_k/S)C_k = K(\mu_p W_k/Z_k)(1/S)C_k$$

where W_k is once again fixed. Since $S = \Omega/\Omega^*$, an increase in Ω^* produces a proportionate increase in the foreign currency price, leaving consumption and output unchanged. Foreign consumption of the home export is once again determined by home monetary policy, and of course sectoral productivity,

$$\Omega = K(\mu_p W_k/Z_k)C_k \text{ for } k \in E \cap W \tag{21b}$$

Analogous results hold for sectors in the foreign country. Once again, home monetary policy (and productivity) sets the level of output in all of the home sectors, while foreign monetary policy (and productivity) sets the level of output in all of the foreign sectors. The supply sides of the economies are insulated, but home consumption of foreign exports is affected by foreign monetary policy, and foreign consumption of home exports is affected by home monetary policy.

Assuming the productivity shocks are log normally distributed, the equilibrium versions of (9b) and (11a) can be solved for the expected (logs of the) levels of home consumption of sectoral goods,[19]

$$E(c_k) = E(\hat{y}_k) - \frac{1}{2}\text{VAR}[\omega] - \log(K) \text{ for } k \in (N \cup T) \cap W \tag{22a}$$

$$E(c_k) = E(\hat{y}_k) - \frac{1}{2}\text{VAR}[\omega^*] - \log(K) \text{ for } k \in E^* \cap W \tag{22b}$$

The home central bank has to hold ω fixed to bring expected (and actual) home consumption to its flexible wage/price level in home sectors selling to the home market; the foreign central bank has to hold ω^*

[18] Erceg, Henderson and Levin (2000) made this point in a closed economy model with staggered wage and price setting.

[19] See Canzoneri, Cumby and Diba (2002a,b) for a more detailed discussion.

fixed to bring expected (and actual) home consumption to its flexible wage/price level in foreign sectors exporting to the home market. Once again, the expected work effort is fixed,[20]

$$E(n_k) = -\log(A\mu) \text{ for } k \in (N \cup T \cup E) \cap W \qquad (23)$$

Analogous results hold for expected foreign consumption and for the expected foreign work effort.

In what follows, we will assume that the productivity shocks of all sectors in a given industry are the same. So, $z_k = z_N$ for $k \epsilon N$, $z_k = z_T$ for $k \epsilon T$, and so on.

3 Nash and Cooperative Solutions

3.1 Central Bank Objective Functions

The utility of the representative household is a natural measure of national welfare. We will however follow the literature in assuming that the utility of real money balances is small and can be neglected; national welfare consists of the first two terms in the household utility functions. We will also assume that central banks commit to monetary policy rules relating their instruments, Ω and Ω^*, to the productivity shocks in an attempt to maximize the expected value of national welfare.[21]

Since the expected work effort is fixed, and not influenced by monetary policy, and since monetary policy does not affect sectors with flexible wages and prices, the home country's objective reduces to maximizing the expected value of the log of consumption in sectors with some form of nominal rigidity. More specifically, using (19a,b), (22a,b) and their foreign country counterparts, and recalling that the number of sectors in a set of sectors is measured by $\lambda(\cdot)$, the home central bank's objective is to maximize

$$J \equiv \sum_{k \in H \cap (P \cup W)} E[c_k] = \lambda\left((N \cup T) \cap W \cap P^c\right) \left\{ E(\hat{y}_k) - \frac{1}{2}\text{VAR}[\omega] \right\}$$
$$+ \lambda(E^* \cap W \cap P^c) \left\{ E(\hat{y}_k) - \frac{1}{2}\text{VAR}[\omega^*] \right\}$$

---

[20] This strong result depends on both the log utility of consumption and the linear disutility of work; see Canzoneri, Cumby and Diba (2002b).

[21] Monopolistic competition leads to inefficiently low levels of employment and output. Central banks could raise national welfare by creating surprise expansions; pre-commitment to policy rules excludes this possibility. See Canzoneri, Cumby and Diba (2002b) for a fuller discussion of the specification of central bank objectives.

$$+\lambda(N \cap P)\left\{E(\hat{y}_k) - \frac{1}{2}\text{VAR}[\omega - z_N]\right\}$$
$$+\lambda(T \cap P)\left\{E(\hat{y}_k) - \frac{1}{2}\text{VAR}[\omega - z_T]\right\}$$
$$+\lambda(E^* \cap P)\left\{E(\hat{y}_k) - \frac{1}{2}\text{VAR}[\omega^* - z_{E^*}]\right\}$$
$$+\text{constant} \quad (24a)$$

The first $\lambda(\cdot)$ is the number of sectors in the non-traded goods industry and the traded goods industry selling to home consumers that have sticky wages and flexible prices; the second $\lambda(\cdot)$ is the number of foreign export sectors with fixed wages and flexible prices; the third $\lambda(\cdot)$ is the number of sectors in the non-traded goods industry that have fixed prices (and fixed or flexible wages); and so on. Similarly, the foreign central bank's objective is to maximize

$$J^* = \lambda((N^* \cup T^*) \cap W \cap P^c)\left\{E(\hat{y}_k) - \frac{1}{2}\text{VAR}[\omega *]\right\}$$
$$+\lambda(E \cap W \cap P^c)\left\{E(\hat{y}_k) - \frac{1}{2}\text{VAR}[\omega]\right\}$$
$$+\lambda(N^* \cap P)\left\{E(\hat{y}_k) - \frac{1}{2}\text{VAR}[\omega^* - z_{N^*}]\right\}$$
$$+\lambda(T^* \cap P)\left\{E(\hat{y}_k) - \frac{1}{2}\text{VAR}[\omega^* - z_{T^*}]\right\}$$
$$+\lambda(E \cap P)\left\{E(\hat{y}_k) - \frac{1}{2}\text{VAR}[\omega - z_E]\right\} \quad (24b)$$

It is clear from (24a,b) that the best monetary policy can do is to make sectors with nominal inertia replicate the flexible wage/price solution; the flexible wage/price solution is in this sense a constrained optimum.

3.2 Nash and Cooperative Solutions

In a Nash solution, the home central bank chooses a rule for Ω that maximizes J taking the foreign central bank's rule as given, and the foreign central bank chooses a rule for Ω^* that maximizes J^* taking the home central bank's rule as given. In a cooperative solution, the central banks choose policy rules for Ω and Ω^* that maximize the sum of their national welfares, $J + J^*$. Equal weights on J and J^* might not make sense if there were significant asymmetries across the home and foreign countries. However, we have already imposed a symmetric sectoral structure on the two countries, and in the next section, data limitations will lead us to impose symmetry on the productivity processes in the home and foreign countries.

To simplify notation, let $\lambda_1 \equiv \lambda(N \cap P) = \lambda(N^* \cap P)$, $\lambda_2 \equiv \lambda(T \cap P) = \lambda(T^* \cap P)$, $\lambda_3 \equiv \lambda(E \cap P) = \lambda(E^* \cap P)$, $\lambda_4 \equiv \lambda((N \cup T) \cap W \cap P^c) = \lambda((N^* \cup T^*) \cap W \cap P^c)$, and $\lambda_5 \equiv \lambda(E \cap W \cap P^c) = \lambda(E^* \cap W \cap P^c)$. Then, we have:

Proposition 1: The Nash and Cooperative Monetary Policies.

A. The Nash policies are

$$\omega = \bar{\omega} + \frac{\lambda_1 z_N + \lambda_2 z_T}{\lambda_1 + \lambda_2 + \lambda_4} \text{ and } \omega^* = \bar{\omega}^* + \frac{\lambda_1 z_{N^*} + \lambda_2 z_{T^*}}{\lambda_1 + \lambda_2 + \lambda_4}$$

where $\bar{\omega}$ and $\bar{\omega}^*$are arbitrary, non-stochastic intercept terms.

B. The cooperative policies are

$$\omega = \bar{\omega} + \frac{\lambda_1 z_N + \lambda_2 z_T + \lambda_3 z_E}{\lambda_1 + \lambda_2 + \lambda_3 + \lambda_4 + \lambda_5}$$

and

$$\omega^* = \bar{\omega}^* + \frac{\lambda_1 z_{N^*} + \lambda_2 z_{T^*} + \lambda_3 z_{E*}}{\lambda_1 + \lambda_2 + \lambda_3 + \lambda_4 + \lambda_5}$$

where $\bar{\omega}$ and $\bar{\omega}^*$are once again arbitrary, non-stochastic intercept terms.

Proof:

Decompose the expression for J in (24a) into a variance term that depends on ω, a term that depends on ω^*, and terms that are independent of policy (labeled t.i.p.).

$$\begin{aligned}
2J = & -\lambda_4 \text{VAR}[\omega] - \lambda_5 \text{VAR}[\omega^*] - \lambda_1 \text{VAR}[\omega - z_N] - \lambda_2 \text{VAR}[\omega - z_T] \\
& - \lambda_3 \text{VAR}[\omega^* - z_{E^*}] + \text{t.i.p.} \\
= & -(\lambda_1 + \lambda_2 + \lambda_4)\text{VAR}[\omega] + 2\{\lambda_1 \text{COV}[\omega, z_N] + \lambda_2 \text{COV}[\omega, z_T]\} \\
& - \lambda_3 \text{VAR}[\omega^* - z_{E^*}] - \lambda_5 \text{VAR}[\omega^*] + \text{t.i.p.} \\
= & -(\lambda_1 + \lambda_2 + \lambda_4)\text{VAR}[\omega] + 2\{\text{COV}[\omega, \lambda_1 z_N + \lambda_2 z_T]\} \\
& - \lambda_3 \text{VAR}[\omega^* - z_{E^*}] - \lambda_5 \text{VAR}[\omega^*] + \text{t.i.p.} \\
= & -(\lambda_1 + \lambda_2 + \lambda_4)\text{VAR}[\omega - (\lambda_1 + \lambda_2 + \lambda_4)^{-1}(\lambda_1 z_N + \lambda_2 z_T)] \\
& - \lambda_3 \text{VAR}[\omega^* - z_{E^*}] - \lambda_5 \text{VAR}[\omega^*] + \text{t.i.p.}
\end{aligned}$$

Similarly,

$$\begin{aligned}
2J^* = & -(\lambda_1 + \lambda_2 + \lambda_4)\text{VAR}[\omega^* - (\lambda_1 + \lambda_2 + \lambda_4)^{-1}(\lambda_1 z_{N^*} + \lambda_2 z_{T^*})] \\
& -\lambda_3 \text{VAR}[\omega - z_E] - \lambda_5 \text{VAR}[\omega] + \text{t.i.p.}
\end{aligned}$$

In the Nash equilibrium, the home (foreign) central bank maximizes J (J^*) by choosing ω (ω^*) that sets the first variance term in J (J^*)

equal to zero. This establishes Part A. Part B is established in a similar manner by decomposing $J + J^*$ into a variance term that depends on ω, a variance term that depends on ω^*, and terms that are independent of policy.

In the flexible wage/price solution (which is the constrained optimum), the household's work effort remains constant while its consumption of the sectoral goods fluctuates with the sectoral productivity shocks. To replicate this outcome, the central bank would have to make nominal expenditure fluctuate with productivity in sectors with fixed prices, and it would have to hold nominal expenditure constant in sectors with fixed wages (and flexible prices).[22] In an economy where productivity shocks and/or the type of nominal rigidity vary across sectors, the central bank can not replicate the flexible wage/price solution economy wide; it faces sectoral tradeoffs.

In the Nash solution, central banks react to a weighted average of the productivity shocks in sectors with fixed prices, with weights that reflect their numbers (λ_1 and λ_2); they intervene less aggressively if the number (λ_4) of fixed wage/flexible price sectors is large. In the Nash solution, central banks do not care about consumption in the other country. In the cooperative solution, central banks do care about foreign consumption of their exports; so, they react to the productivity shock in their fixed price export sectors, with a weight that once again reflects their number (λ_3).

Monetary policy can be very effective if there are no asymmetries in productivity or nominal inertia. If for example there are no fixed wage sectors (strictly speaking, if $\lambda_4 = 0$), and if traded good productivity is perfectly correlated with non-traded good productivity ($z_N = z_T = z_E \equiv z$ and $z_{N^*} = z_{T^*} = z_{E^*} \equiv z^*$), then monetary policy can replicate the flexible wage/price solution in each country by simply reacting to its own productivity shock ($\omega = z$ and $\omega^* = z^*$); there are no sectoral tradeoffs. This is essentially the result of King and Wolman (1999).[23] Moreover, there is no need for policy coordination. This was noted by Obstfeld and Rogoff (2002) and Corsetti and Pesenti (2001b). Canzoneri, Cumby and Diba (2002a,b) showed that sectoral tradeoffs would exist if there were asymmetries in productivity, and Erceg, Henderson and Levin (2000) showed policy tradeoffs would exist if there were asymmetries in nominal inertia.[24] And when there are tradeoffs for national monetary policy,

---

[22] These optimal monetary responses were discussed at the end of the last section.

[23] King and Wolman (1999) demonstrated their result in a closed economy model with staggered price setting.

[24] Erceg, Henderson and Levin (2000) demonstrated their result in a closed economy

there is a potential for gains from international policy coordination. In the next section, we show how our model can be calibrated to gauge the relative importance of these asymmetries, and the efficacy of monetary policy in general.

4 Estimates of the Gain From Monetary Stabilization

In this section we present some rough estimates of the extent to which active monetary policies described in the previous section — either the Nash or cooperative policies — succeed in offsetting the welfare costs of nominal rigidities. We begin by describing how we obtain estimates of the values necessary to compute the welfare measures — the covariance matrix of innovations to sectoral productivity, the numbers of sectors with rigid prices (λ_1, λ_2, and λ_3), and the numbers of sectors with flexible prices but rigid wages (λ_3 and λ_4). We then turn to our baseline calculations of the welfare effects of passive monetary policy and optimal Nash and cooperative monetary policies under alternative assumptions about price and wage rigidity. Finally, we explore the robustness of those baseline calculations.

4.1 Calibrating the Model

We measure sectoral productivity as real value added per worker using data from the OECD STAN database. We classify sectors into tradable and non-tradable aggregates for both the United States and the Euro area.[25] The tradable-goods industry consists of manufacturing and agricultural sectors. The non-tradable-goods industry is made up of service producing sectors.[26] We compute the innovations to productivity by es-

---

model with staggered wage and price setting. Their setup differs from ours in some interesting ways, but we think our model captures their basic insight.

[25] Our Euro area aggregate consists of Austria, Belgium, Finland, France, Italy, Portugal, and Spain. We excluded Germany and the Netherlands from the aggregate because missing data limited us to fewer than 10 years of German data and only 14 years of Dutch data.

[26] When possible, we measure employment as the number of full-time-equivalents. Services include wholesale and retail trade; restaurants and hotels; transportation; communications; finance, insurance and real estate; business services; and community, social, and private services. Construction, utilities, and mining are not included in our classification so that our total value added from the two sectors differs from aggregate value added computed by the OECD.

timating a vector autoregression with all four productivity series (tradables and non-tradables in both the United States and the Euro area) and use the covariance matrix of the residuals. We make two assumptions that are more restrictive than are those in the model we present above. First, because we do not have data that distinguishes the labor employed in producing tradables that are exported from those that are consumed domestically, we assume $z_N = z_E$ and $z_{N^*} = z_{E^*}$. Second, so as not to push cross-country differences in the estimates too hard, we impose symmetry by averaging the estimated U.S. and Euro area variances of the innovations to tradables and non-tradables productivity as well as the two covariances between the sectoral productivity innovations. This gives us estimates of VAR$[z_T]$ =VAR$[z_{T^*}]$ =VAR$[z_E]$ =VAR$[z_{E^*}]$, VAR$[z_N]$ =VAR$[z_{N^*}]$, and COV(z_T, z_N) =COV(z_{T^*}, z_{N^*}) that we need to compute the welfare measures.

In our model, λ_1 is the number of sectors producing non-tradables in which prices are rigid. We normalize the number of sectors, K, in each economy to be one and estimate λ_1 by taking the share of non-tradables value added in overall value added and multiplying by an estimate of the fraction of non-tradable goods with rigid prices. We compute the shares by dividing non-tradables value added by the sum of tradables and non-tradables value added. The non-tradables shares for both the United States and the Euro area turn out to be around 75 per cent.[27] For our baseline estimates we assume that 80 per cent of goods in the service sector have rigid prices. This value is roughly consistent with a large number of studies that have investigated price stickiness.[28] We therefore set $\lambda_1 = 0.6 (= 0.75 \times 0.8)$ in our baseline calculation.

We estimate λ_2 and λ_3 in a similar way. The estimates in Bils and Klenow (2002) suggest that firms in manufacturing sectors are somewhat more likely than firms in services sectors to change prices in any given month. Based on their estimates we pair our assumption that 80 per cent of nontradables have rigid prices with an assumption that 70 per cent of tradables sectors have rigid prices. We thus take $\lambda_2 = 0.07 (= 0.1 \times 0.7)$ and $\lambda_3 = 0.105 (= 0.15 \times 0.7)$ in our baseline calculations.

As we discuss above, the presence of wage rigidity only matters when prices are flexible. To compute λ_4 and λ_5 we assume that 75 per cent of workers in firms with flexible prices have rigid wages. We combine this with the assumptions about price flexibility above and set the share of

[27] We divide the remaining 25 per cent share between the T and E sectors by assuming both imports and exports make up roughly 15 per cent of overall value added.

[28] See, for example, Gali and Gertler (1999) and their discussion of previous work.

value added accounted for by firms with flexible prices but rigid wages as follows. For firms in N and T (N^* and T^*), we set $\lambda_4 = 0.10125(= 0.75[(1-0.8) \times 0.75 + (1-0.7) \times 0.1])$. Similarly, for firms in E (E^*), we set $\lambda_5 = 0.0253(= 0.75(1-0.7)0.15)$.

4.2 Which Asymmetries Matter Most?

Given these baseline values for the parameters of the model, we can compute the welfare measures, J and J^* under three assumptions about monetary policy. First we assume that monetary policy is passive — that it does not react to productivity shocks. Next we assume that the monetary authority in each country maximizes domestic welfare and implements the optimal Nash policy. Finally, we assume that the two monetary authorities jointly maximize the sum of their welfares and implement the optimal cooperative policy.

In Table 1, we report our calculations using the baseline parameter values. For ease of interpretation, we report the fraction of the welfare loss under passive monetary policy that is eliminated by each of the two optimal monetary policies in the first two rows.[29] In addition, we report the incremental gain achieved by moving from the optimal Nash policy to the optimal cooperative policy in the third row and the ratio of this incremental gain to the gain from moving from passive policy to the optimal Nash policy in the fourth row.[30]

We begin with our full set of baseline parameter values, so that there are both asymmetries in productivity shocks ($\text{VAR}(z_N) \neq \text{VAR}(z_T)$) and asymmetries in nominal rigidities ($\lambda_4 \neq 0$, $\lambda_5 \neq 0$). These two asymmetries limit the ability of the monetary authorities to offset the welfare costs of nominal rigidities. As we report in column 4 of Table 1, the optimal Nash policy manages to offset just over 45 per cent of the welfare loss that arises when monetary policy is passive. The additional gain from the optimal cooperative policy is quite small, amounting to just seven per cent of the gain from moving from passive policy to the optimal Nash policy.

Next we consider some counterfactuals in order to determine which of the asymmetries is most important in limiting the ability of the monetary authorities to offset the welfare costs of nominal rigidities. In the first of these we assume each economy is subject to a single aggregate

---

[29] Cedric Tille suggested this way of presenting the welfare results.

[30] We refer to this last measure as the "R-ratio" in Canzoneri, Cumby and Diba (2002a).

productivity shock ($z_N = z_T$) and wages are flexible ($\lambda_4 = \lambda_5 = 0$).[31] The results are in the first column of Table 1. As we show in the previous section, the monetary authorities set $\omega = z_N = z_T = z_E$ and $\omega^* = z_{N^*} = z_{T^*} = z_{E^*}$ and can fully offset the effects of price rigidity. Nash policy replicates the equilibrium with flexible prices and wages.

Next we consider the case where wages are flexible but tradables and nontradables are subject to different productivity shocks. In marked contrast to the previous case, the optimal Nash policy is able to eliminate only slightly more than half of the welfare loss experienced under passive monetary policy. This suggests that the asymmetries in productivity considered in Canzoneri, Cumby and Diba (2002a,b), taken by themselves, are quantitatively important. The optimal cooperative policy is only slightly better than the optimal Nash policy, eliminating only an additional 3.6 per cent of the welfare loss under passive policy. The additional welfare gain from moving from the optimal Nash policy to the optimal cooperative policy amounts to just under seven per cent of the gain from moving from a passive monetary policy to the optimal Nash policy.

Next we consider the case in which there is a common productivity shock to the two sectors but wages are rigid (λ_4 and λ_5 are set to the values discussed above). As in Erceg, Henderson and Levin (2000), optimal monetary policy is unable fully to offset the effect of nominal rigidities and cannot achieve full stabilization. With this set of parameter values, the importance of asymmetric productivity shocks is considerably greater than the importance of asymmetries in nominal rigidities. The optimal Nash policy is able to get fairly close to full stabilization, eliminating 86 per cent of the welfare loss under passive policy. And moving from the optimal Nash policy to the optimal cooperative policy results in no additional gain in welfare.

In all of these calculations, we confirm the conclusions reached in an earlier literature on policy coordination (Canzoneri and Minford (1988), Canzoneri and Edison (1990), and McKibbin (1997), for example). In McKibbin's words, "the largest gains for the world economy are to be realized from some form of policy optimization at the individual economy level or the sensible choice of a policy regime given the nature of shocks expected to impinge on the world economy. Any additional gains from coordination of policies between economies have been found to be dwarfed by the potential gains from individual countries adjusting poli-

[31] In order to make the welfare measures comparable to those we compute when the productivity shocks in tradables and non-tradables are not perfectly correlated, we set the variance of the common shock equal to the variance of the sum of the two sectoral shocks.

	One Shock	Two Shocks	One Shock	Two Shocks
Achieved by:	Flexible Wages		Rigid Wages	
Nash	100.0%	53.2%	86.0%	45.6%
Cooperative	100.0%	56.8%	86.0%	48.8%
Cooperative − Nash	0.0%	3.6%	0.0%	3.2%
$\frac{\text{Cooperative} - \text{Nash}}{\text{Nash}}$	0.0%	6.9%	0.0%	7.0%

Table 1: The Gains From Active Monetary Policy (Expressed as Per Cent of Welfare Loss Under Passive Policy)

cies in a sensible manner."

4.3 Robustness

Next we examine the robustness of the conclusions that we have drawn from the calculations summarized in Table 1 by making two sets of changes. First, the evidence presented in Bils and Klenow suggests that prices are more flexible in the U.S. economy than is suggested by previous studies. We therefore cut our estimates of the fraction of firms in each sector with rigid prices in half. Because we assume that 75 per cent of firms with flexible prices have rigid wages, reducing the degree of price rigidity will raise the degree to which wage rigidity matters. The first three columns of Table 2 therefore consider the welfare effects of the two optimal monetary policies when price rigidity plays a smaller role than in Table 1 but wage rigidity plays a larger role. Second, we consider the effects of reducing the share of non-tradables in value added. We have two reasons for doing so. Our classification of all services as nontradable clearly understates the extent to which services currently enter into international trade. In addition, the volume of international trade has been growing more rapidly than has GDP, so that in the future we might expect the share of nontradables in value added to shrink. In the last column of Table 2 we set the non-tradables share to 50 per cent and raise the shares of domestically consumed tradables and exports correspondingly.

The first three columns of Table 2 report the welfare calculations assuming less price rigidity than in Table 1. When wages are flexible, the results are identical to those reported in Table 1.[32] As can be seen

[32] This is trivially true when we assume there is a common productivity shock because the monetary authorities are able fully to offset the effects of nominal rigidities. As a result we do not report the results of these calculations.

from Proposition 1, the optimal monetary policies depend on weighted averages of the shocks. When wages are flexible, a proportional scaling of λ_1, λ_2, and λ_3 will leave the weights unchanged. As a result, the optimal monetary policy will be unchanged as will the variance terms in J and J^* (equations 24a and 24b). And because λ_1, λ_2, and λ_3 are all changed in the same proportion, each of the welfare measures will change in that same proportion (see 24a and 24b). The relative welfare gains that we report in Table 1 and Table 2 are therefore unaffected.

The results do change, however, when we add wage rigidity. Increasing the importance of wage rigidity increases the importance of asymmetries in nominal rigidities and significantly reduces the ability of monetary policy to replicate the flexible wage/price solution. When the productivity shocks in tradables and non-tradables are perfectly correlated, the optimal Nash policy now eliminates only slightly more than half of the welfare loss experienced under passive policy. The impact of asymmetries in nominal rigidities is now roughly comparable to the impact of asymmetries in productivity shocks. And when we combine the two asymmetries, the optimal Nash policy is able to eliminate less than 30 per cent of the welfare loss experienced under passive monetary policy. Reducing the degree of price rigidity and raising the degree of wage rigidity has no measurable impact on the welfare effect of moving from the optimal Nash policy to the optimal cooperative policy.

Reducing the non-tradables share does, however, raise the incremental effect of cooperative monetary policies. Changing the nontradables share has little impact on the gain from the optimal Nash policy. In Table 1, it offsets roughly 45 per cent of the welfare loss from passive policy. In Table 2, the offset is roughly 40 per cent. The incremental gain from adopting cooperative policies doubles when we compare Tables 1 and 2. In Table 2, the gain from moving from Nash to cooperative policies is nearly 16 per cent of the gain from moving from passive policy to the optimal Nash policy. Although this gain is much larger than the gains found in Table 1, it is still consistent with the conclusions that we drew from that table. The additional gains from coordination of policies appear to be much smaller than the potential gains from each county reacting to shocks using the optimal Nash policy.

5 Summary and Conclusions

King and Wolman (1999) and others have shown that monetary policy can replicate the flexible price solution in a closed economy with sticky prices. However, subsequent work has shown that asymmetries in nom-

	Less Price Rigidity			Larger Non-tradable Share
	Two Shocks	One Shock	Two Shocks	Two Shocks
Achieved by :	Flexible Wages	Rigid Wages		Rigid Wages
Nash	53.2%	52.9%	28.1%	40.5%
Cooperative	56.8%	0.0%	30.1%	46.9%
Cooperative − Nash	3.6%	0.0%	2.0%	6.4%
$\frac{\text{Cooperative} - \text{Nash}}{\text{Nash}}$	6.9%	0.0%	7.0%	15.7%

Table 2: Robustness of The Gains From Active Monetary Policy (Per Cent of Gain From Passive Policy to Full Stabilization)

inal inertia, asymmetries in sectoral productivity, and asymmetries in decision making (or the lack of policy coordination) can make monetary policy less effective.

In this paper, we have tried to assess the empirical importance of these asymmetries. We develop a two country, multi sector model, and calibrate it using US and European data. In our baseline model — with separate productivity shocks for the traded and non-traded goods sectors, with both wage and price rigidity, and with decentralized (or Nash) decision making — monetary policy is far less effective than the results in King and Wolman (1999) would suggest. Monetary policy is able to close only about 45 per cent of the utility gap between the no-response solution and the flexible wage/price solution. Policy coordination only closes the utility gap by another 3 per cent. Our baseline model suggests that asymmetries in nominal inertia and asymmetries in sectoral productivity greatly limit the effectiveness of monetary policy, and that eliminating asymmetries in decision making (through policy coordination) does not alter that basic conclusion.

We also consider the relative importance of the asymmetries in nominal inertia and sectoral productivity. First, we assume that productivity shocks are perfectly correlated across sectors, and analyze a hypothetical economy with asymmetric nominal inertia and Nash decision making. Monetary policy is much more effective; it is able to close about 85 per cent of the utility gap. Then, we eliminate wage rigidity, and analyze a hypothetical economy with asymmetric productivity shocks, sticky prices and Nash decision making. Monetary policy is able to close only about 50 per cent of the utility gap. We conclude that while both of the asymmetries are important, the asymmetry in sectoral productivity appears to be the more important than the asymmetry in nominal inertia.[33]

Data limitations are severe. We impose cross country symmetry in the stochastic processes driving sectoral productivity; however, there is some indication that the processes might, in fact, be asymmetric. Furthermore, our data does not allow us to make a distinction between traded goods that are sold domestically and traded goods that are exported. In Canzoneri, Cumby and Diba (2002a), we argued that this asymmetry might offer the greatest scope for policy coordination. Further work on the identification and measurement of sectoral productivity is clearly warranted; it may change our assessment of the importance of policy coordination.

Two key modeling assumptions — the log utility of consumption and the Cobb–Douglas aggregator for the final consumption good — may also be a limiting factor. These assumptions produce a very tractable model, but they also close down the current account and cross country risk sharing, and they result in a rather specialized pattern of international macroeconomic inter-dependence. Relaxing these assumptions may also alter our assessment of the importance of policy coordination.

Finally, we should note that we have been analyzing the effectiveness of monetary policy under the assumption of complete information. It is unlikely that central banks have full information about sectoral productivity or the degree of sectoral wage and price rigidity. Future work should also focus on the efficacy of simple rules for monetary policy.

Despite any limitations in data or theoretical modeling, our results about the importance of asymmetries in nominal inertia and sectoral productivity are dramatic enough to warrant serious consideration. Policy studies should take both asymmetries into account.

BIBLIOGRAPHY

[1] Benigno, Pierpaolo, "Optimal Monetary Policy in a Currency Area," mimeo, January, 2001.

[2] Bils, Mark and Peter J. Klenow, "Some Evidence on the Importance of Sticky Prices," NBER working paper #9069, 2002.

[3] Blanchard, Olivier and Stanley Fischer, *Lectures on Macroeconomics*, MIT Press, 1989.

[33] Policy coordination was not important in either of these hypothetical cases.

[4] Canzoneri, Matthew, Robert Cumby and Behzad Diba, "On the Need for International Policy Coordination: What's Old, What's New and What's Yet to Come," NBER working paper #8765, 2002a.

[5] Canzoneri, Matthew, Robert Cumby and Behzad Diba, "Recent Developments in the Macroeconomic Stabilization Literature: Is Price Stability a Good Stabilization Strategy?," in Altug Sumra, Jagjit Chadha and Charles Nolan (eds.), Dynamic Macroeconomic Analysis: Theory and Policy in General Equilibrium, Cambridge University Press, forthcoming., 2002b.

[6] Canzoneri, Matthew and Hali Edison, "A New Interpretation of the Coordination Problem and Its Empirical Significance," in Peter Hooper et al. (eds) *Monetary Aggregates and Financial Sector Behavior in Interdependent Economies*, Board of Governors of the Federal Reserve System, 1990, 299–433.

[7] Canzoneri, Matthew and Patrick Minford, "When International Policy Coordination Matters: an Empirical Analysis," *Applied Economics*, 20, 1988, 1137–1154.

[8] Cochrane, John, *Asset Pricing*, Princeton University Press, 2001.

[9] Corsetti, Giancarlo and Luca Dedola, "Macroeconomics of International Price Discrimination," mimeo, 2002.

[10] Corsetti, Giancarlo and Paolo Pesenti, "Welfare and Macroeconomic Interdependence," *Quarterly Journal of Economics*, 116 (2), May 2001a, 421–446.

[11] Corsetti, Giancarlo and Paolo Pesenti, "International Dimensions of Optimal Monetary Policy," FRBNY Staff Report No. 124, April, 2001b.

[12] Corsetti, Giancarlo and Paolo Pesenti, "Self-validating Optimum Currency Areas," mimeo, 2002.

[13] Devereux, Michael and Charles Engel, "Monetary Policy in the Open Economy Revisited: Price Setting and Exchange Rate Flexibility," NBER working paper #7665, 2000.

[14] Erceg, Christopher, Dale Henderson and Andrew Levin, "Optimal Monetary Policy with Staggered Wage and Price Contracts," *Journal of Monetary Economics*, 46, 2000.

[15] Frenkel, J. and A. Razin, *Fiscal Policies and the World Economy*, MIT Press, 1987.

[16] Gali, Jordi and Mark Gertler, "Inflation Dynamics: A Structural Econometric Analysis," *Journal of Monetary Economics*, 44, 1999, 195–222.

[17] Goodfriend, Marvin and Robert King, "The New Neoclassical Synthesis and the Role of Monetary Policy," *NBER Macroeconomics Annual*, MIT Press, 1997, 223–283.

[18] King, Robert and Alexander Wolman, "What Should the Monetary Authority Do When Prices are Sticky?," in John Taylor (ed.), *Monetary Policy Rules*, Chicago Press, 1999.

[19] McKibbin, Warwick, "Empirical Evidence on International Economic Policy Coordination," Chapter 5 of M. Fratianni, D. Salvatore and J. Von Hagen (eds) Handbook of Comparative Economic Policies volume 5: *Macroeconomic Policy in Open Economies*, Greenwood Press, 1997, 148–176.

[20] Obstfeld, Maurice and Kenneth Rogoff, "New Directions for Stochastic Open Economy Models," *Journal of International Economics*, 50, 2000, 117–153.

[21] Obstfeld, Maurice and Kenneth Rogoff, "Global Implications of Self-Oriented National Monetary Rules," *Quarterly Journal of Economics*, 117 (2), May 2002,503 – 535.

[22] Woodford, Michael, *Interest and Prices*, book in progress, chapters available on his web page.

[23] Woodford, Michael, "Control of Public Debt: A Requirement for Price Stability?,"in Guillermo Calvo and Mervyn King, (eds), *The Debt Burden and Monetary Policy*, Macmillan, 1997.

4 Model Misspecification, Robustness and Monetary Policy

Juha Kilponen and Mark Salmon[1]

1 Introduction

Alan Walters' work on monetary policy explicitly recognised, amongst other issues, the impact of the potential misspecification of the demand for money function in the design of monetary policy. In fact the policy debate at that time, while fundamentally different in many respects from the current debate on inflation targeting, identified exactly the same issues regarding the difficulty of constructing policy when we have a poor understanding of the dynamic responses in the economy. Charles Goodhart (1999) has, for instance recently discussed the impact of both model uncertainty and data uncertainty on the decision making process of the Monetary Policy Committee, and many of these concerns can be seen in Alan Walters' own discussion of the difficulties of getting reliable estimates of monetary multipliers and a stable demand for money function for control of the monetary base, Walters (1966a,b,c). The recognition that the policy maker's empirical model was misspecified argued against using monetary policy as a fine tuning instrument and in favour of a Friedman style constant growth rule. In the absence of an alternative solution to the problems of model and data uncertainty this may be seen as a natural response at the time.

In this paper we describe a new approach to the design of robust policy that could perhaps have helped to shape the monetary policy debate in the 1970s if it had been available and would perhaps have relieved some of Alan Walters' legitimate concerns regarding model misspecification. Instead of assuming that agents and policy makers know the true model up to some additive uncertainty modelled by a stochastic process

[1]We would like to thank Christos Roupakiotis for help and advice on this paper.

whose properties are known, or at least, can be learned from the historical data, we assume that they do not know the model or the form of the uncertainty exactly and design policy by taking this *explicitly* into account.

The standard formal characterisation of policy making using optimal control methods delivers the best performance in the case of no misspecification and invariably a linear model with quadratic preferences. Certainty equivalence then implies we can ignore the impact of uncertainty and continue by assuming the uncertain variables are equal to their expected values. The practical reality of policy making is however far from this simplistic paradigm and involves subjective trade offs between potential risks that are often only barely perceived. Measurement errors in the data, misspecifications in the formulation of the model and in the stochastic process of disturbances are all too well known to the econometrician and policy makers; making the policy process complex and riddled with uncertainty. The best policy making procedures aim to reduce the impact of these uncertainties on outcomes whilst guiding the economy towards a better outcome. The so called robust control approach, which we describe below, was developed by control engineers in the 1980s to achieve this same objective in response to similar difficulties in controlling physical systems in the face of similar uncertainty. These methods show considerable promise for the analysis and design of economic policy; an objective we believe Alan Walters would support given his wide experience, both as an econometrician and policy advisor.

The basic idea in this robust control approach is to search for a "safe" policy, which secures at least a minimum performance in terms of stability given a range of potential realisations of the uncertainty (different model specifications or effectively different probability distributions describing the uncertainty). Zames (1981) recognised that the goal of guaranteeing some minimum performance in the presence of model uncertainty could be formalised simply by switching the norms in the context of optimal control applications. His idea of analysing traditional control problems in the $\mathcal{H}_\infty$ norm, rather than the standard linear quadratic norm, sparked a revolution in control theory. This resulted in what has become known as *robust decision theory.* It was also soon realised how robust decision theory relates to certain stochastic optimisation problems under risk-sensitive preferences in the linear quadratic case (Whittle 1981) leading to decision rules that follow Wald's (1950) min-max type of behaviour. In addition starting from the basic principles, Gilboa and Schmeidler (1989) showed how uncertainty aversion implies a preference ordering which also corresponds to the use of Wald's min-max decision rules.[2]

This paper demonstrates the robust control method by introducing a recognition of misspecification into the central bank's objective function and studies the resulting impact on monetary policy.[3] It derives a robust monetary policy rule when the central bank's model is potentially misspecified and then compares the average performance of robust policy rules to those derived from the standard Bayesian or LQG approach.

The rest of the paper is organised as follows. Section 2 discusses the basic ideas behind robust control and reviews the similarity between robust control and risk sensitivity. Section 3 applies the risk sensitivity criteria to a Barro–Gordon type of policy model and familiarises the reader with the concepts and solution methodology involved in robust control. Section 4 concludes and provides suggestions for further research.

2 Theoretical Preliminaries

Robust decision theory can be best understood when set up as a game between two players; the policy maker who attempts to find stabilising policy rules by minimising his loss and a malevolent virtual second player, often described as nature, who seeks that disturbance within some prespecified range which will maximise the policy maker's loss. Since we can control the range of these potential disturbances, which correspond to potential misspecifications in our model or data or indeed any other aspect of the decision problem, these solutions do not need to be dramatically bad from the policy maker's viewpoint. The range of potential disturbances considered just describes the degree of robustness the policy maker seeks as the resulting policy will be robust to misspec-

[2] Min-max behaviour has also been supported by many experimental studies. Usually these experimental studies stem from the Allais and Ellsberg paradoxes. In particular, the Ellsberg paradox demonstrates that when information on the "likelihoods" of potential events is uncertain, preferences across alternatives cannot be described by an ordinary probability measure. It appears that people prefer acts with a known probability structure or known uncertainty. That is, they take confidence in estimates of subjective probability into account when making choices. Such a pattern is inconsistent with the sure-thing principle of subjective expected utility. The sure-thing principle assumes that a state with a consequence common to all acts is irrelevant in determining preference between the acts.

[3] For applications of robust control to monetary economics see for instance Hansen and Sargent (2001), Tetlow and von zur Muehlen (2001), Onatski (2000), Onatski and Stock (2002), Giannoni (2000), Kasa (2002), Kilponen and Salmon (2001), Jääskelä and Kilponen (2001), and Kilponen (2000).

ifications within the set. The solution is then found by searching for a saddle point of the objective function

$$J(u, v) \tag{1}$$

where u is the choice variable of the policy maker and v is a choice variable of the malevolent opponent. If J is interpreted as a "loss function", we are interested in finding an optimal feedback rule u^* which minimises J and v^* which simultaneously maximises J. In choosing a loss function, it is possible to apply standard equilibrium concepts, notably Nash equilibrium, to the solution of the above game. A quadratic loss function will do, as long as we make sure that the loss function is convex in u and concave in v.

In the robust control problem the policy maker then seeks to minimise a supremum of the closed loop ∞-*norm* with respect to some linear law of motion of the economy. This ∞-*norm* (or $\mathcal{H}_\infty$ norm) is defined as

$$\|\mathcal{S}\|_\infty = \sup_{\|v\|_2 \neq 0} \frac{\|z\|_2}{\|v\|_2} \tag{2}$$

In (2) $\|z\|_2$ and $\|v\|_2$ denote Euclidian vector norms of real valued vectors z and v and sup denotes supremum. Vector z contains a linear (or potentially non-linear) combination of variables that the policy maker seeks to control and depends on the policy maker's decision variables u, and v contains unobservable components of the disturbances. It is important to notice that this norm applies to the *closed loop* gain of the economy under control and the optimal robust policy will be found as that policy that effectively minimises the maximum impact of the disturbances on the output variables in which the policy maker is interested.

The so called robust control, or $\mathcal{H}_\infty$ control problem is then to find a state feedback policy rule, $u = u(z)$, which minimises this ∞-*norm* given some $\gamma > 0$, where γ defines the performance bound or range of potential disturbances the policy maker wishes to be robust against. This (suboptimal or bounded) problem can be stated as

$$\sup_{\|v\|_2 \neq 0} \frac{\|z\|_2}{\|v\|_2} < \gamma \tag{3}$$

Remarkably, as demonstrated first by Glover and Doyle (1988), it turns out that the optimal state-feedback policy rule based on the minimisation of a bounded ∞-*norm* is simply the optimal policy for a risk-sensitive criterion. To see this, the optimal policy must also satisfy the square of (2) i.e.

$$\|\mathcal{S}\|_\infty^2 = \sup_{\|v\|_2 \neq 0} \frac{\|z\|_2^2}{\|v\|_2^2} < \gamma^2$$

Next, we notice that in order for the supremum to satisfy the strict inequality above, the term $\|z\|_2^2 / \|v\|_2^2$ must be bounded away from γ^2 so for some $\varepsilon > 0$ we can write

$$\frac{\|z\|_2^2}{\|v\|_2^2} \leq \gamma^2 \square \varepsilon^2$$

$$\|z\|_2^2 \square \gamma^2 \|v\|_2^2 \leq \square\varepsilon^2 \|v\|_2^2 \tag{4}$$

When this inequality (4) holds, so does the strict equality (2) for all disturbances v and for some $\varepsilon^2 > 0$. Consequently, the left hand side of (4) can be used as an objective function in the dynamic game between the two players,[4]

$$J_\gamma = \|z\|_2^2 \square \gamma^2 \|v\|_2^2 \tag{5}$$

This objective function, then, suggests the alternative interpretation arising from what has been called "risk-sensitive" decision theory, developed and studied in Whittle (1981). γ^2 in (5) describes the policy maker's attitude towards uncertainty or his desire for robustness.[5] It allows an interpretation of the "risk sensitivity" parameter when the policy rule results from a saddle point solution to (5). That is, the optimal feedback policy rule (u^*) and the most destabilising deterministic input (v^*) are solutions to

$$\begin{aligned} u^* &\in \arg\min_u \{J_\gamma(u, v)\} \\ v^* &\in \arg\max_v \{J_\gamma(u, v)\} \end{aligned}$$

In particular, the solution pair (u^*, v^*) is a saddle point when it fulfils the following inequalities

$$J_\gamma(u^*, v) \leq J_\gamma(u^*, v^*) \leq J(u, v^*), \ \forall \ v \in \mathcal{V}, \ u \in \mathcal{U} \tag{6}$$

In other words $J_\gamma(u, v)$ has a minimum with respect to the policy variable u and a maximum with respect to v at the point (u^*, v^*).

All that has changed with respect to the familiar optimisation formulation is that the unobserved disturbance input v is introduced into the objective function directly. This disturbance, v, is treated simply as another control term which is penalised by an uncertainty preference factor

---

[4] See Basar and Bernhard (1995).

[5] Notice that there is a terminological ambiguity here when compared to standard economic theory as the policy maker's familiar risk preferences as opposed to his uncertainty preferences will be captured as usual by the nature of his economic cost or utility function which is implicit in the closed loop transfer function or $\|z\|_2^2$.

$\gamma^2 > 0$.[6] Notice that unlike standard decision making under uncertainty these disturbances are no longer regarded as stochastic but represent the worst case deterministic shocks that could impact on the decision problem. The policy maker now plays a mind game against the virtual opponent, or in the language of Whittle (2002), against "the Phantom other" who opposes with the policy maker: While the policy maker wants to minimise J_γ by choosing some u^* for given v, the phantom wants to find the v^* which maximises J_γ at any given u. The policy rule that results from this policy maker–phantom game, therefore, is equivalent to a min-max policy rule in pure strategies.

3 APPLICATION

3.1 Preliminaries of the Model

In this section, we apply the basic ideas of risk sensitivity/robust control to the familiar theory of monetary policy originally developed in Kydland and Prescott (1977) and Barro and Gordon (1983).[7]

Let the economy evolve[8] according to

$$x = \alpha(\pi - \pi^e) + \epsilon + v \tag{7}$$

which is the Lucas supply function (or expectations augmented Phillips curve), but with an additional disturbance component v, which is of immediate interest in this paper. x is the output gap, α is the slope of the Phillips curve and ϵ is a Gaussian supply shock with zero mean and variance σ_ϵ^2. In this simple model α can also be interpreted as a policy multiplier, similarly to the original Brainard (1967) paper on monetary policy and uncertainty.

The two additive disturbance terms v and ϵ are now treated fundamentally differently. Whilst ϵ is assumed to be a standard Gaussian

---

[6] In practice, nothing prevents $\gamma^2 < 0$. In this case the policy maker would be a risk-lover, or in the language of Whittle (1981) optimistic. In this case, the policy maker would believe that "nature" plays into the "same pocket" as the policy maker. So far the monetary policy literature has concentrated on the risk-sensitive case, although it might be equally interesting to study situations where the policy maker is "optimistic".

[7] Hansen and Sargent (2001) study a similar Phillips curve example in Chapter 5 of their manuscript. Our own original work on this problem (Kilponen, 2000) was carried out independently of Hansen and Sargent's analysis.

[8] Notice that this is a "time-less" game so we have dropped the time subscripts for convenience.

error term with *a priori* known stochastic properties, we assume that the policy maker is *not* able to assign a probability distribution to v. This could be due to the fact that the available data do not allow the identification of a unique probability distribution for v either because we are considering an event that may not have arisen in the past so we have no repeated sampling basis on which to construct a pdf or alternatively we are just uncertain as to which one of many potential pdfs could be correct. In both cases the uncertainty introduced by v is Knightian in nature (c.f. Knight, 1921). In the second case the set of alternative potential pdfs essentially provides one way of describing the range of alternative misspecified models that the policy maker may wish to be robust against but he is either unable or unwilling to use just one of these alternative models. These pdfs could correspond to uncertainty about the multiplier α or an additional unobserved component of the output gap x or misspecification of the functional form of the supply function. According to this interpretation, different values of v represent model perturbations in the sense that the policy maker does not know the position of the Phillips curve in $(x, (\pi - \pi^e))$ space exactly. The basic equation (7) without v and including the stochastic specification of the random disturbances ϵ serves as the nominal or base model against which we consider potential misspecification.

We assume now that the central banker makes a particular subjective assessment of v, based on the robust control approach outlined above. That is, we let the policy maker hedge against the expected loss from the worst-case model governed by γ. In other words, the policy maker finds the worst case $v \neq 0$ for any given π and then designs the corresponding policy rule π which minimises his loss given this v. Subjectivity of the assessment of the worst-case model is parameterised by the risk-sensitivity factor γ, which then determines v uniquely.

We start by transforming a standard quadratic loss function into a risk-sensitive loss function. Formally, let

$$\|z\|_2^2 = E[(x - \hat{x})^2 + \lambda(\pi - \hat{\pi})^2] \tag{8}$$

where x and π are output and inflation, $\hat{x}$ are $\hat{\pi}$ are the output and inflation targets of the policy maker and finally $\lambda > 0$ is the inflation aversion parameter of the central banker as in conventional monetary policy models. In this model, the rate of inflation is set by the central bank and the level of output is determined by an expectations augmented Phillips curve, by the central bank's chosen rate of inflation and the the private sector's expected inflation rate. The key element of this stylised model is the hypothesis that the output level $\hat{x}$, targeted by the policy maker, is above the level that would be determined by the market without policy intervention: discretionary policy making leads to an inflation bias that arises from monetary policy aimed at raising output above its equilibrium level (Kydland and Prescott (1977), Calvo (1978), Barro and Gordon (1983)). In this analysis, however, we assume away this conventional time inconsistency problem and focus solely on the impact of robustness on the basic problem.[9] This can be done by simply assuming that $\hat{x} = 0$. The strategic assumptions we make are that the policy maker (but not the private sector) knows the non-zero realisation of the supply shock, ϵ, prior to selecting its policy and that it takes the private sector's inflation expectations as given in a Nash manner. A range of potential alternative strategic assumptions are clearly possible at this point, some of which are explored in Kilponen and Salmon (2002). Without loss of generality, we also assume that the inflation target ($\hat{\pi}$) is zero.

The robust loss function can now be written as

$$J_\theta = E[x^2 + \lambda\pi^2] - \theta v^2 \tag{9}$$

where $\theta = \gamma^2 > 0$. The design of a robust policy rule now becomes a min-max problem, or in the language of Whittle (1981), an extremisation where optimal level of inflation is found by minimising J_θ, wrt π and with v being chosen to maximise J_θ subject to the linear constraint (7). We seek a solution to the following problem

$$\min_{\pi}\max_{v}\ E[x^2 + \lambda\pi^2] - \theta v^2 \tag{10}$$

subject to

$$x = \alpha(\pi - \pi^e) + \epsilon + v$$

All that has changed with respect to the standard policy optimisation problem is that there is a new unobserved endogenous component v, another control term which is penalised by the subjective risk-preference factor θ. It is perhaps already clear from (9) that letting $\theta \to \infty$ takes us back to the familiar certainty equivalent LQG case which corresponds to a subjective assessment that v is zero. In contrast, a smaller θ means that more weight is given to the disturbance in the loss function as the policy maker fears his model is misspecified with v taking values that are far from zero. If we think of v as representing unstructured model misspecification errors, we have the interpretation that the resulting min-max policy rule is *robust* to arbitrary model uncertainty captured in v. In due course, we will see that θ is always bounded below and that choosing θ arbitrarily close to the neighbourhood of this bound is what is typically done in the $\mathcal{H}_\infty$ control problem.

---

[9] Kilponen and Salmon (2002) consider the time inconsistency problem in detail within the context of robust inflation targeting.

3.2 Discretion Without Time Inconsistency

The solution to the simple extremisation problem given in (10) delivers the robust policy rule and the worst-case shock implicitly in the (v, π) plane as

$$\pi(v) = \alpha\frac{\alpha\pi^{e} - \epsilon - v}{\lambda + \alpha^{2}} \tag{11a}$$

$$v(\pi) = -\frac{\alpha(\pi - \pi^{e}) + \epsilon}{1 - \theta} \tag{11b}$$

In order to solve these equations explicitly, we need to solve for the rational expectation of inflation. Since the private sector do not have prior knowledge of the supply shock their model consistent inflation expectations are zero.[10] Consequently, setting $\pi^{e} = 0$ in the above equations and solving delivers reduced form expressions for the worst-case shock v^{*} and for inflation π^{*}

$$v^{*} = \frac{\lambda}{\lambda(\theta - 1) + \alpha^{2}\theta}\epsilon \tag{12}$$

$$\pi^{*} = -\frac{\theta\alpha}{\lambda(\theta - 1) + \alpha^{2}\theta}\epsilon \tag{13}$$

which implies

$$\pi^{*} = -\frac{\alpha\theta}{\lambda}v^{*} \tag{14}$$

which indicates how policy responds to the worst-case disturbance shaped by θ and the inflation preference parameter λ. Using these equations we can calculate the equilibrium output gap (x^{*}) in the worst case

$$x^{*} = \frac{\lambda\theta}{\lambda(\theta - 1) + \alpha^{2}\theta}\epsilon \tag{15}$$

Furthermore,

$$\pi^{c.e.} = \lim_{\theta\to\infty}\pi^{*} = -\frac{\alpha}{\lambda + \alpha^{2}}\epsilon \tag{16}$$

where *c.e.* denotes certainty equivalent. That is, when the risk sensitivity or robustness preference parameter θ approaches infinity, it is possible to recover the certainty equivalent rule from the extremisation problem.

On the other hand, the more risk-sensitive the policy maker is, *ceteris paribus*, the more "aggressive" the policy maker becomes. In this simple

[10] These model consistent expectations are precisely those discussed by Alan Walters in 1971, prior to Lucas (1972).

model, this shows up as a desire to stabilise inflation more, at any given λ. This tendency becomes even more pronounced as θ becomes smaller. This can be shown easily. First, remember that $\lim_{\theta \to \infty} \pi^* = \pi^{c.e.}$ and then notice from (13) that

$$\left| \frac{\partial^2 \pi^*}{\partial \epsilon \partial \theta} \right| < 0 \tag{17}$$

This is a typical result obtained in many different contexts using robust control theory and in many applications of robust control to monetary policy.[11] It is in sharp contrast to a familiar Brainard (1967) result, according to which the policy maker should act more cautiously under multiplier uncertainty as compared to the certainty equivalent rule.

On the other hand, as the central banker becomes more inflation conservative (λ becomes bigger) and $\theta > 1$, it becomes harder to distinguish whether the central bank's reactions are driven by its concern for model uncertainty or not. At the limit where $\lambda \to \infty$, inflation conservativeness completely over-rides the desire for robustness: the central banker's reactions towards supply shocks are driven purely by his concern for inflation stabilisation.

Finally, the reason why v can be interpreted as characterising "model misspecification errors" becomes clear by considering the worst-case model at any given π and π^e. Substituting (11b) into (7) delivers

$$x^w(\theta) = \frac{\theta}{\theta - 1}\alpha(\pi - \pi^e) + \frac{\theta}{\theta - 1}\epsilon \tag{18}$$

In (18) the single parameter θ parameterises model misspecification at any given policy instrument π, and we can see that as $\theta \to \infty$ we are returned to the standard Lucas supply function. A specific value of θ pins down the worst-case model, against which the policy maker protects himself by choosing the loss minimising policy rule.

3.3 Neurotic Breakdown and Stability

Allowing θ to depart from infinity allows the policy maker to make his policy rule more robust against model misspecification errors, but not by an unlimited amount. There is a minimum for the attainable value of θ where (12) and (13) become infinite. Let us denote this value by $\inf(\theta)$. For values lower than $\inf(\theta)$, no stabilising feedback policy rule exists. The same equations suggest that this lower bound of θ can easily be found by solving the following simple equation with respect to θ

[11] Onatski and Stock (2002), Kilponen and Salmon (2001), Jääskelä and Kilponen (2001), Svensson (1999).

$$\lambda\left(\theta \square 1\right) + \alpha^2\theta = 0 \tag{19}$$

This delivers the lower bound for θ as

$$\inf\left(\theta\right) = \frac{\lambda}{\lambda + \alpha^2} < 1 \; \forall \; \lambda > 0 \tag{20}$$

Choosing θ arbitrarily close to inf (θ) delivers the "optimally robust policy rule". Such a policy rule is optimal in the sense that it stabilises the economy subject to the largest possible perturbations from the nominal model. This is exactly the motivation in the $\mathcal{H}_\infty$ optimal control problem. We can also see that inf (θ) is a function of the structural parameters of the model only, namely, the slope of the Phillips curve (α), and the inflation preference parameter (λ). This lower bound for θ is increasing in λ and decreasing in α.

Finally, the expected worst-case loss $E^*(L)$ under different values of θ for the performance analysis is readily derived as

$$E^*(L) = \|z\|_2^2 = \frac{\lambda\theta^2\left(\lambda + \alpha^2\right)}{\left(\lambda(\theta \square 1) + \alpha^2\theta\right)^2}\sigma_\epsilon^2 \tag{21}$$

It is important to notice from (21) that $\inf(\theta)$ delivers infinite loss $E^*(L)$. It is exactly for this reason that Whittle calls this situation "a neurotic breakdown", or

> ...marks a point at which the optimizer is so pessimistic that his apprehension of uncertainties completely overrides the assurance given by known statistical behaviour. It is not stretching matters to term this point of "neurotic breakdown" [Whittle, 2002, p. 6].

In order to visualise these important properties of robust policy rules, Figure 1 shows expected worst-case loss $E^*(L)$ as a function of the risk-sensitivity parameter θ with two different values of the inflation aversion parameter λ ($\lambda = .5, \lambda = 1.5$) and with $\sigma_\epsilon^2 = 1$ and $\alpha = .5$.

We notice that as the central banker becomes more inflation averse (λ becomes bigger) the breakdown occurs at larger values of θ. This is due to the fact that the worst-case shock (v^*) approaches infinity faster when λ is larger. Figure 1 also illustrates that close to the neighbourhood of $\inf(\theta)$, small changes in the risk sensitivity parameter can have dramatic effects on the expected worst-case loss. As θ departs further from its lowest attainable value, the expected loss settles down to the value which is equal to the certainty equivalent loss.

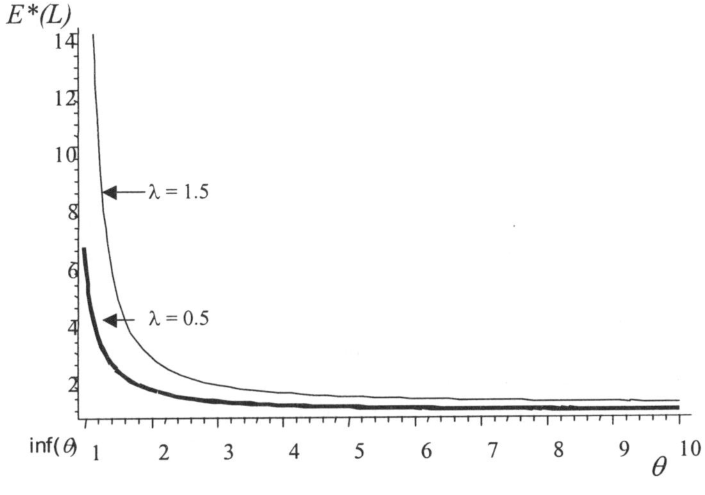

Figure 1: Worst-Case Loss as a Function of Risk Sensitivity Parameter θ

Finally, while $E^*(L)$ is maximised at the point of the neurotic breakdown, $\inf(\theta)$ actually minimises the ∞-*norm*. To see this formally, we just need to use (12) and (21) to find that

$$\frac{\|z\|_2^2}{\|v\|_2^2} = \theta^2 \left(1 + \frac{\alpha^2}{\lambda}\right) \tag{22}$$

The lowest attainable value can be found by replacing θ with $\inf(\theta)$ in (22), delivering

$$\inf \left(\frac{\|z\|_2^2}{\|v\|_2^2}\right) = \frac{\lambda}{\lambda + \alpha^2} = \inf(\theta) \tag{23}$$

While (23) provides a theoretical lower bound for θ, it is worth noting that in order for equilibrium strategies (π^*, v^*) to fulfil the saddle point property, the inequality in (6) must also be fulfilled. It can quite easily be proved that while the first inequality $J_\theta(\pi^*(v), v) \leq J_\theta(\pi^*, v^*)$ holds for all $\theta > \inf(\theta)$, the second inequality $J_\theta(\pi^*, v^*) \leq J_\theta(\pi, v^*(\pi))$ fails to hold at $\inf(\theta) < \theta < 1$. This implies that for $\theta < 1$, it would no longer be optimal for the central bank to follow the equilibrium strategy π^* when given $v^*(\pi)$. We therefore concentrate on those situations where $\theta > 1$.

3.4 Robustness

This robust policy rule is designed to perform reasonably well across a range of alternative models, but it has not been designed to be optimal relative to any particular model. As we have seen in the previous section, a larger degree of uncertainty implies that the policy maker acts more aggressively. This brings better stability but it does not come without costs. Roughly speaking, increasing robustness means that the policy maker needs to pay an insurance (or robustness) premium compared to the standard certainty equivalent rule: concern for robustness brings more aggressive policy responses and generates more volatile movements in the policy instrument, namely inflation, yet it performs better as the model misspecification becomes more serious.

In order to highlight this important property of the robust rules, we compare the robust rules and the certainty equivalent rule under a different range of model misspecifications $|v|$. Effectively, we do this by evaluating the expected loss $E[L(\pi(\theta_c), v(\theta_n))]$ under different values of θ_c and θ_n. θ_c pins down subjective assessment of the uncertainty surrounding the model by the central banker, while $v(\theta_n)$ generates a range of model perturbations $|v|$. Figure 2 plots $E[L(\pi(\theta_c), v(.))]$ with θ_n varying along the ordinate axis and with two different values of θ_c. Smaller values of θ_n imply larger model perturbations $|v|$ as can be seen from (12). Similarly, smaller values of θ_c imply that the central bank believes larger model misspecifications are possible. In Figure 2, the solid line corresponds to the certainty equivalent rule while the dashed and dotted lines correspond to the robust rules with $\theta_c = 1.15$ and $\theta_c = 1.3$ correspondingly. As expected, the certainty equivalent rule with $\theta_c = \infty$ generates the lowest expected loss for the central bank when there are no misspecification errors in the model $(\theta_n \to \infty)$.

However, as the model misspecification error becomes larger, the performance of the certainty equivalent rule deteriorates more rapidly than the robust rule. Finally, as the model misspecification becomes large, the robust rules outperform the certainty equivalent rule.

4 Conclusions

In this paper we have introduced a concern for model misspecification into the monetary policy maker's objective function. We have shown in this simple framework how pessimism towards the accuracy of the underlying model can result in a more aggressive policy response. However, in the absence of inflation bias, it has been shown that such a policy rule is

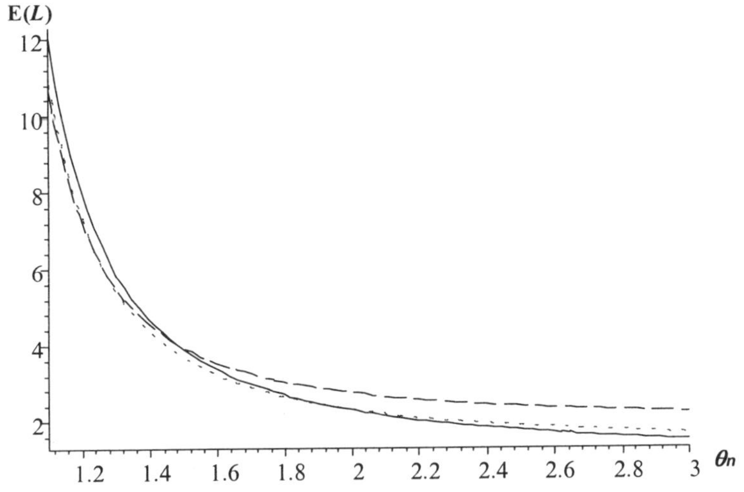

Figure 2: Expected Losses Under Different Rules and Model Misspecification Errors

more robust to model uncertainty than the ordinary certainty equivalent rule. This result is interesting in its own right but needs to be studied in more detail with alternative assumptions on the private sector's expectation formation and the strategic form of the game.[12] Another important observation is that extreme risk sensitivity or in other words, extreme robustness could potentially deliver policy rules that are overly reactive and deflationary. In such policy rules a concern for robustness matters too much and this may actually harm the economy. Consequently, when applying robust decision theory to policy making, one should bear in mind that there is a trade off between robustness properties of the policy rules and average performance.

The money policy debate in which Alan Walters played an important role in the 1970s adopted different solutions to model misspecification to those described here. It is interesting to speculate how events may have unfolded during the 1970s and 1980s if these ideas and techniques had been available then.

Several interesting topics within this conventional framework have been left unexplored. One important direction for research is to ex-

[12] See for instance Kasa (2002), Giannoni (2002), Kilponen and Salmon (2002).

plore time inconsistency in the misspecification environment. The fact that delegation of monetary policy to a risk-sensitive, but conservative central banker partially solves the inflation bias problem, might suggest that Svensson's (1999) inflation targeting regime would completely solve the problem of inflation bias in this environment as well. Furthermore, several interesting issues arise by altering the Lucas supply function. For instance, as shown by Roberts (1995) most of the new-Keynesian models suggest that the Lucas supply function is misspecified and that the forward-looking behaviour of the agents should be included in the aggregate supply function. This implies that the policy maker cannot take inflation expectations as predetermined since the aggregate supply function contains expectations of future inflation. In fact, many of the more practical applications of robust control theory to monetary policy rely on the new-Keynesian type of models.[13]

Bibliography

[1] Barro, R. and Gordon, D. (1983). A Positive Theory of Monetary Policy in a Natural Rate Model. *Journal of Political Economy*, 91, 589–610.

[2] Basar, T. and Bernhard, P. (1995). *H_∞-Optimal Control and Related Minimax Design Problems, A Dynamic Game Approach*, Second edition, Birkhauser.

[3] Calvo, G. (1978). Some Notes on Time Inconsistency and Rawls' Maximin Criterion, *Review of Economic Studies*, 45 (1), 97–102

[4] Brainard, W. (1967). Uncertainty and the Effectiveness of Policy. *American Economic Review, Papers and Proceedings*, 57, 411–425.

[5] Giannoni, M. (2002). Does Model Uncertainty Justify Caution? Robust Optimal Monetary Policy in a Forward-Looking Model. *Macroeconomic Dynamics*, forthcoming.

[6] Gilboa, I. and Schmeidler, D. (1989). Max-min Expected Utility with Non-unique Prior. *Journal of Mathematical Economics*, 18, 141–153.

---

[13] See for instance Onatski and Stock (2002), Hansen and Sargent (2001), Giannoni (2000), and Kilponen and Salmon (2001), (2002).

[7] Glover, D. and Doyle, J. (1988). State-Space Formulae for All Stabilizing Controllers that Satisfy an H_∞-Norm Bound and Relations to Risk Sensitivity, *System and Control Letters,* 11(1), 167–172.

[8] Goodhart, C. (1999). Central Bankers and Uncertainty. *Bank of England Quarterly Bulletin*, February, 102–121.

[9] Hansen, L. and Sargent, T. (2001). Robust Control and Filtering for Macroeconomics, University of Chicago, Stanford University and Hoover Institution, manuscript.

[10] Jääskelä, J. and Kilponen, J. (2001). Risk, Uncertainty and Model Misspecification in a Monetary Policy Game, manuscript.

[11] Kasa, K. (2002). Model Uncertainty, Robust Policies, and the Value of Commitment. *Macroeconomic Dynamics,* 6(1), 145–166.

[12] Kilponen, J. (2001), A Positive Theory of a Risk Sensitive Central Banker, manuscript, Sir John Cass Business School, London.

[13] Kilponen, J. and Salmon, M. (2001). Elements of Robust Control Applied to the U.K. Monetary Policy, manuscript, Sir John Cass Business School, London, submitted for publication.

[14] Kilponen, J. and Salmon, M. (2002), Robust Inflation Targeting, manuscript, Sir John Cass Business School, London, forthcoming in *Robust and Risk Sensitive Decision Theory in Economics and Finance*, Cambridge University Press, M. Salmon (ed.).

[15] Knight, F. (1921). *Risk, Uncertainty and Profit.* Boston, New York, Houghton Mifflin Company.

[16] Kydland, F. and Prescott, E. (1977). Rules Rather than Discretion: The Inconsistency of Optimal Plans. *Journal of Political Economy,* 85(3), 473–91.

[17] Lucas, R.E., (1972). Expectations and the Neutrality of Money, *Journal of Economic Theory*, 4(2), 103–124.

[18] Onatski, A. (1999). Minimax Monetary Policy: Comparison to Bayesian Approach, Worst Cases, and Exact Minimax Rules, *Robust Decision and Risk Sensitive Theory in Economics and Finance*, Cambridge University Press, M. Salmon (ed.)

[19] Onatski, A. (2000). Robust Monetary Policy Under Model Uncertainty: Incorporating Rational Expectations, manuscript, Harvard University.

[20] Onatski, A. and Stock, J. (2002). Robust Monetary Policy under Model Uncertainty in a Small Model of the U.S. Economy. *Macroeconomic Dynamics*, 6(1). 85–110.

[21] Roberts, J. (1995). New Keynesian Economics and the Phillips Curve. *Journal of Money, Credit and Banking*, 27(4), 975–84.

[22] Svensson, L. (1999). Inflation Targeting: Some Extensions. *Scandinavian Journal of Economics*, 101, 337–361.

[23] Swank, O. (1994). Better Monetary Control May Increase the Inflationary Bias of Policy. *Scandinavian Journal of Economics*, 96, 125–131.

[24] Tetlow, R. and von zur Muehlen, P (2001). Robust Monetary Policy with Misspecified Models: Does Model Uncertainty Always Call for Attenuated Policy?, *Journal of Economic Dynamics & Control*, 25 (June 2001), 911–949.

[25] Wald, A. (1950). *Statistical Decision Functions*, John Wiley and Sons, New York.

[26] Walters, A. (1966a). The Stability of Keynesian and Monetary Multipliers in the United Kingdom. (with C.R. Barrett). *Review of Economics and Statistics*, 4, 395–405.

[27] Walters, A. (1966b), Demand for Money in the UK, 1877–1961: Some Preliminary Findings (with N.J. Kavanagh), *Bulletin of the Oxford Institute of Economics and Statistics*, 93–116.

[28] Walters, A.(1966c), Monetary Multipliers in the UK 1880–1962. *Oxford Economic Papers*, 18, 270–283.

[29] Walters A.(1971), Consistent Expectations, Distributed Lags and the Quantity Theory. *Economic Journal*, 81, 273–281.

[30] Whittle, P. (1981). Risk-Sensitive Linear Quadratic Gaussian Control. *Advances in Applied Probability,* 13, 764–777.

[31] Whittle, P. (2002). Risk-Sensitivity — A Strangely Pervasive Concept. *Macroeconomic Dynamics, 6(1), 5–18.*

[32] Zames, G. (1981). Feedback and Optimal Sensitivity: Model Reference Transformations, Multiplicative Seminorms, and Approximate Inverses. *IEEE, Transactions on Automatic Control*, 26, 301–320.

5 The Case for Monetary Union in Mercosur

Michele Fratianni

1 Introduction

The Mercado Común del Sur (Mercosur) is floundering, mostly because of uncoordinated monetary policy. Exchange rate turmoil and competitive devaluations have inflicted economic pain in the region. It is not enough for each of the Mercosur countries to establish a stable monetary environment; as a group they must go a step farther and coordinate their monetary systems with the explicit purpose of deepening integration and boosting their standards of living. In essence, Mercosur needs a strategy of monetary unification, aimed at delivering low and predictable inflation rates in each member country, while simultaneously promoting economic integration in the area.

In the bargaining process over the Maastricht treaty, two opposing views emerged, reminiscent of the controversy of the 1970s between "economists" and "monetarists" (Swann, 1988, pp. 180–82). Germany — with Belgium, Luxembourg, the Netherlands and the United Kingdom — was the leading exponent of the "economic" view of MU, namely that economic convergence must precede monetary union (MU). France — with Italy and the southern countries — was the leading exponent of the "monetarist" view of MU, namely that MU facilitates economic convergence. Germany favored a long transition period and formal convergence criteria before the final stage of MU; France, on the other hand, wanted MU quickly and without strong preconditions. The result was a compromise between the two camps (Garrett, 1993). This debate is as relevant for Mercosur today as it was for EMU. Is economic integration independent of monetary integration? Can monetary integration enhance economic integration?

Before EMU, there was general acceptance that MU would not generate anything comparable to the net benefits of economic integration (Krugman, 1993). Now, we recognize to have underestimated the benefits associated with higher price transparency and lower transaction costs (Frankel and Rose, 1998; Rose, 2000). Before EMU, received wisdom had it that political unification must precede monetary unification. Now, we accept that MU may actually facilitate other forms of integration, in accordance with the principle of the "cumulative logic of integration" (Tsoukalis, 1977).

The paper starts with the basic premise that the Mercosur countries want to deepen integration, beyond customs union; in this scheme, MU would act as a catalyst of further integration and cement what Eichengreen (1998, p. 4) calls "a coherent political economy logic." Without this foundation, the architecture of the proposal would be shaky. The rest of the paper is organized as follows. Section 2 takes up the issues of the link between trade integration and exchange rate regimes and trade integration and business cycles. Section 3 reviews the historical and more recent record of Mercosur with regard to inflation, including Argentina's currency board and Brazil's inflation targeting strategy. Section 4 makes the case for a multilateral MU as opposed to a unilateral one. Section 5 deals with the transition phase and proposes that Argentina, with an immobilized banking system and a collapsing economy, adopt the currency of its large neighbor, the real, and make the initial steps towards MU in Mercosur. Section 6 draws conclusions.

2 Mercosur Integration, Exchange Rate Regimes and Shocks

Mercosur came to life in 1991 when Argentina, Brazil, Paraguay and Uruguay signed the Treaty of Asunción; it graduated to a customs union in 1995; and expanded in 1996 by granting Bolivia and Chile association status. Mercosur has a population of 215 million, a labor force of 96 million, and a per-capita GDP of $4,315; Brazil and Argentina account for 97 per cent of Mercosur GDP (EIU Argentina, 2001, p. 51). Measured in terms of real GDP, Mercosur is approximately one-seventh of NAFTA and one-sixth of the EU (Carrera and Sturzenegger, 2000, Table 1.4). Mercosur countries are much less open to international trade than EU countries. For example, the average of exports and imports of goods and services as a per cent of GDP for the two largest countries of Mercosur is approximately 10 per cent (Figure 1).

Mercosur's total exports of goods rose more rapidly than world exports during the early 1990s, in 1997 and in 2000, but their growth rate

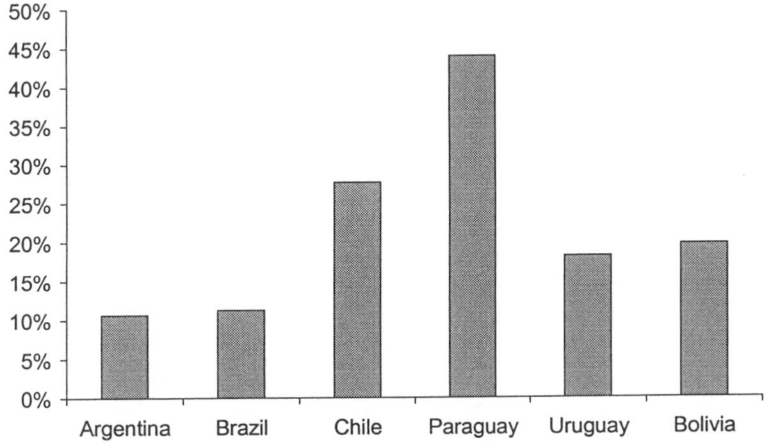

Figure 1: Degree of Openness in Mercosur — 1999

fell relative to world exports in 1995 (the year of the Mexican currency crisis) and in 1999 (the year of the devaluation of the Brazilian real). Intra-regional exports have consistently outpaced extra-regional exports since the inception of Mercosur, except for 1999 (Table 1). The ratio of intra-regional to total exports began at 14.4 in 1991 and peaked at 27.3 in 1998; in 2001 it had fallen to 23.7.

The common external tariff in Mercosur ranges between 0 and 20 per cent, but many categories of goods and services are exempted from it, albeit temporarily. Automobiles and capital goods are the most recurrent exceptions. In 1997, Brazil raised unilaterally tariffs on imports. The devaluation of the real in January of 1999 dealt a severe blow to the customs union, by setting in motion protectionist policies. Rozemberg and Svarzman (2000) offer a detailed account of the impact of the real's devaluation on protectionism in the area. The most intense disputes have involved Argentina and Brazil on poultry, pork, dairy products, shoes, textiles, and iron and steel.

2.1 Integration and Exchange Rate Regimes

The existence of different exchange rate regimes in Mercosur has hampered trade integration. Real exchange rate misalignments in a regional trade agreement (RTA) like Mercosur prompt member countries to push for an upward revision of the common external tariff and/or to adopt non-tariff protection against member countries. Fernández-Aria *et al.* (2002) provide evidence of protectionist backlash in the wake of real exchange rate misalignment, using data from 6 RTAs, including Mercosur. These authors find not only that real exchange rate appreciation impacts negatively on home exports, but that intra-regional misalignment is considerably stronger than extra-regional misalignment. For developing countries, the inter-regional misalignment effect rises, while the extra-regional misalignment effect becomes statistically insignificant. This could be due to a combination of gravity effects and preferential trade treatments in RTAs with a high common external tariff. Quantitatively, the elasticity of domestic exports with respect to intra-regional real exchange rate appreciation in RTAs involving developing countries is in excess of 2. These findings and the sharp depreciation of the Brazilian real are consistent with the 22 percentage drop in intra-Mercosur exports and the zero growth in extra-Mercosur exports in 1999 (Table 1).

	Total exports	Intra-regional	Extra-regional	Ratio intra /total	World exports
1991	−0.5	23.4	−3.6	14.4	2.7
1992	10	33.6	6	17.5	6.4
1993	5	30.4	−0.3	21.7	0.2
1994	17	18.6	16.5	22	13.7
1995	17.6	22	16.4	22.8	19.6
1996	4.2	14.4	1.2	25	4.3
1997	9.7	16.5	7.5	26.6	3.6
1998	−3.4	−0.7	−4.4	27.3	−1.6
1999	−6	−22.2	0.1	22.6	3.4
2000	14	18.6	12.6	23.6	12.5
2001	5.4	−5.4	9.4	23.7	

* Argentina, Brazil, Paraguay, Uruguay, Chile and Bolivia
Source: Inter-American Development Bank, Integration and Trade in the Americas, Periodic Note 2000 and 2001, Washington, D.C. and International Monetary Fund, International Financial Statistics.

Table 1: Exports of Expanded Mercosur* (annual percentage increase, except for ratio intra/total)

Bigger gains in trade integration would be reaped if Mercosur were to become a MU. According to the literature on the "endogeneity of the optimum currency areas," started by Frankel and Rose (1998), monetary unification enhances economic integration, not only through a higher degree of price transparency and lower transaction costs, but also through more predictable costs and product differentiation; more on this below.

As a result, shocks become more symmetric in a monetary union. Hence, the impact of monetary union on trade flows is so much larger than the impact of fixed exchange rates (Rose, 2000).

Quite a controversy has risen around Rose's large empirical effect of MU on trade. The specification of the trade equation is based on an expanded gravity model to include political, cultural, regional trade agreement, exchange rate variability and common currency effects, all of which — except for exchange rate variability — are measured by (0,1) dummy variables. The coefficient of the common currency, γ, ranges from 0.87 in 1970 to 1.51 in 1990 and 1.21 for the pooled regression (Rose, 2000, Table 2). Using the latter and noting that $\exp(1.21) = 3.35$, the implication is that MU can more than treble trade, a large effect that dwarfs the impact of exchange rate variability on trade.[1] One possible criticism of Rose's results is that his sample is restricted to countries that have close trade relations and political affinity to begin with; thus, a selection bias may be in place. Mélitz (2002), using the same data, tries to disentangle regional trade agreement and political union effects from MU effects and arrives at a preferred estimate of γ equal to 0.7: so MU merely doubles trade!

In a recent paper, Rose (2002) replies to his critics by performing a meta-analysis of 18 studies dealing with the impact of MU on trade, six of which are authored or co-authored by Rose himself. The null hypothesis of $\gamma = 0$, obtained from the preferred estimates by each study, is rejected at standard levels of statistical significance. Furthermore, the pooled estimates of γ excluding the six Rose studies are very close to the pooled estimates including them. Finally, two-thirds of the 365 estimates reported by the 18 studies exceed 0.7, the estimate preferred by Mélitz. In sum, available evidence points to a strong economic impact on trade integration, much bigger than that of exchange rate variability. We will have to wait for additional data to sort out whether the most reliable estimate of γ is closer to 0.7 or 1.2, but the importance of MU on trade integration is not in doubt.

2.2 Mercosur and Shocks

Traditional optimum currency area (OCA) criteria tend to be inconclusive (Tavlas, 1994), in the sense that one criterion may point in one direction (e.g., low labor mobility as in Mundell (1961)), while another in the opposite direction (e.g., a high degree of economic openness as

[1] The coefficient of exchange rate variability in the pooled regression was found to be -0.017 and statistically significant. A two standard deviation drop in this variability would boost trade by 24 per cent.

in McKinnon (1963)). More recently, Frankel and Rose (1998) have underscored that the same criteria suffer from the so-called Lucas critique. That is, even abstracting from inconclusiveness, it is not proper to judge whether a group of countries are suited for MU on ex-ante criteria. Monetary unification is an engine of structural change and as such generates endogenous OCA criteria. This is consistent with the "monetarists" position in the alluded debate of the 1970s.

Take, for example, the OCA criterion of shocks to the economy. The benefit of MU depends on participating countries experiencing similar business cycles; there would be more value to an independent, national monetary policy if shocks were idiosyncratic. But how would the creation of MU affect business cycles of the participating countries? Two separate effects need to be distinguished. The first works through trade intensification and the second through a common monetary policy. Trade intensification can occur either through deeper industry specialization — as predicted by theories of comparative advantage — or through deeper product differentiation. With deeper industry specialization, regions or countries become more dissimilar and become more prone to industry-specific shocks; monetary unification would exacerbate asymmetric shocks. With deeper product differentiation, regions and countries would trade in the same industries with products differentiated along the dimension of either variety or quality; monetary unification would enhance symmetric shocks. A diversified economy would have a high proportion of intra-industry trade in total trade and would suffer from asymmetric shocks less than a specialized economy (Kenen, 1969). In sum, the effect of MU on business cycles depends on the relative strength of product specialization and diversification.

Frankel and Rose (1998) test the two opposing trade forces by regressing correlations of bilateral economic activity on bilateral trade intensity and a proxy of monetary policy coordination for a group of 21 industrial countries (14 of which belong to the European Union), each with four distinct observations. The critical finding is that trade intensity exerts a positive and statistically significant impact on the proxy for shock correlation: that is, trade intensity brings about more shock symmetry. This result is consistent with a rise of intra-industry trade as a proportion of total trade as trade intensifies in a monetary union.

Earlier, Bayoumi and Eichengreen (1993) had presented evidence of a two-speed Europe, divided between a core — consisting of Germany, France, Denmark, Belgium and the Netherlands — sharing similar shocks and a periphery facing asymmetric shocks relative to the core. The core countries had the more diversified economic structure and enjoyed the highest ratios of intra-industry trade in total EU trade, whereas the periphery countries tended to be more specialized in inter-industry trade.[2] But the interesting question is whether monetary policy coordination, first, and MU, later, are bringing about a convergence of the periphery to the core. Fontagné and Freudenberg (1999, Table 8) gather detailed evidence that dispersion of specialization has decreased among EU countries from the 1980s to the 1990s.[3] Monetary policy coordination in the EU has been accompanied by a convergence process of the member countries' economic structure, a finding that is consistent with the hypothesis that the degree of symmetry shocks is endogenous to the process of monetary unification.[4]

Studies on Mercosur conclude, as one would expect, that shocks in this area are less symmetric than in either the EU or NAFTA and that their sizes are substantially larger in either of the two other economic areas. In his PhD dissertation, Licandro Ferrando (2000, ch. 1) finds that Mercosur, over the period 1975–1996, has faced a mixture of symmetric and asymmetric shocks, with neither prevailing over the other. The shock correlations of real GDP between Argentina and Brazil, Argentina and Uruguay, and Brazil and Uruguay were statistically not significant from zero.[5] However, when the estimates were conditioned on countries simultaneously undertaking exchange-rate-based stabilization programs, supply shock correlations became positive and statistically significant; contrarily, shock correlations turned negative when stabilization programs were not synchronized across member countries. Furthermore, the average size of the supply shocks in Mercosur was several times that of supply shocks in the EU.[6] These results highlight the importance of monetary policy coordination in dampening asymmetric shocks. They also suggest that exchange rate variability may be more damaging to

[2] Based on 1994 data, Fontagné and Freudenberg (1999, Table 6) compute that intra-industry trade as a proportion of total intra-EU trade was close to 70 per cent for France, Germany, and Belgium-Luxembourg, whereas for Spain and Italy it was close to 50 per cent and for Greece 14 per cent.

[3] The data consist of 10,000 products, which are subsequently aggregated in 14 industries. The authors define products as horizontally differentiated (significant overlap and small degree of price differences), vertically differentiated (significant overlap and small degree of price differences) and inter-industry trade (no overlap). Values of the dispersion coefficients are reported for 1980, 1987 and 1994. There is a decline in 31 out of the 42 coefficients. Only two industries have bucked the trend of declining specialization: agriculture and automobiles.

[4] Corsetti and Pesenti (2002) develop a theoretical justification why the endogenous output correlations are higher under MU than under the alternative of an optimal float. This effect works independently of intra-industry trade intensification.

[5] Regional VAR equations were used for the identification of shocks.

[6] This is also confirmed by Bayoumi and Eichengreen (1994).

Mercosur than to the EU.

Returning to the issue of whether economic integration fosters shock symmetry, Licandro Ferrando finds an increase in the estimated values of shock correlations between Brazil and Uruguay and between Argentina and Uruguay after 1990, with only the latter pair being statistically different from zero. The increased "coherence" between the Argentine and the Uruguayan business cycles can also be observed from Figure 2, showing the annual growth rates of real GDP in the 3 Mercosur countries. These results were accompanied by a rise in the ratio of intra-industry to total trade in Mercosur. For Licandro Ferrando (p. 27), "Intra industry is the main explanation of trade between Uruguay and Argentina " The phenomenon is much less present in trade between Argentina and Brazil, two economies with diverse economic structures. Yet, even for them intra-industry trade has been rising for quite some time.

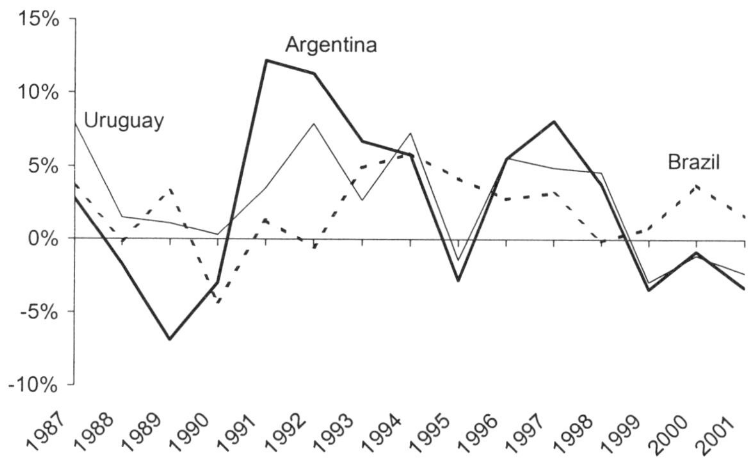

Figure 2: Real GDP Growth in 3 Mercosur Countries

In sum, the evidence from Mercosur is far from the quality and quantity available in the EU. The link between trade intensity and shock symmetry cannot be disentangled as easily as in the EU from the link between monetary policy coordination and shock symmetry. The positive result is that it is clear that exchange rate shocks like the real's depreciation of 1999 have severely damaged trade flows in Mercosur.

3 Mercosur and Inflation

High and variable rates of inflation and currency depreciation are the distinctive feature of the economic history of Latin America. Figure 3 plots pairs of the annual average of these two variables for the periods 1951–1970, 1971–1990 and 1991–2001 for the 6 countries of the expanded Mercosur. What emerges is a vicious circle, where high inflation rates spark currency depreciations and the latter, in turn, validate the former. Numerous stabilization plans have come and gone over the years, jolting the variance of the inflation rate while leaving the mean relatively unaffected.

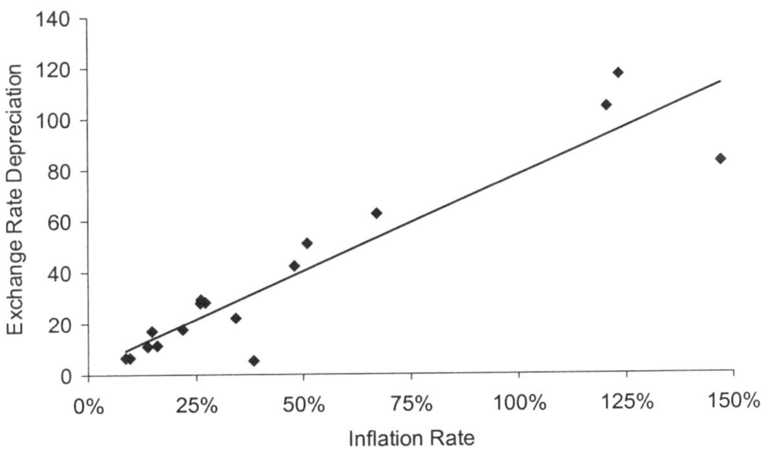

Figure 3: Inflation and Depreciation in Mercosur: 1951–2001

But a new regime, or better new regimes, emerged in the 1990s to interrupt the vicious circle between inflation and currency depreciation. The equally weighted average inflation rate in the 6 countries fell from 66 per cent in 1991 to 3.5 per cent in 2001 (Figure 4); the dispersion of inflation rates, measured by the standard deviation, fell almost in perfect sympathy with the decline in the average inflation rate. Argentina established a currency board in 1991, which lasted until early this year; more on this below. Brazil adopted inflation targeting following the real's depreciation of 1999; more on this below. Chile was one of the earliest converts to inflation targeting; it started at the very beginning of the 1990s and has had a low and stable inflation rate ever since (IMF, 2001, p. 142).

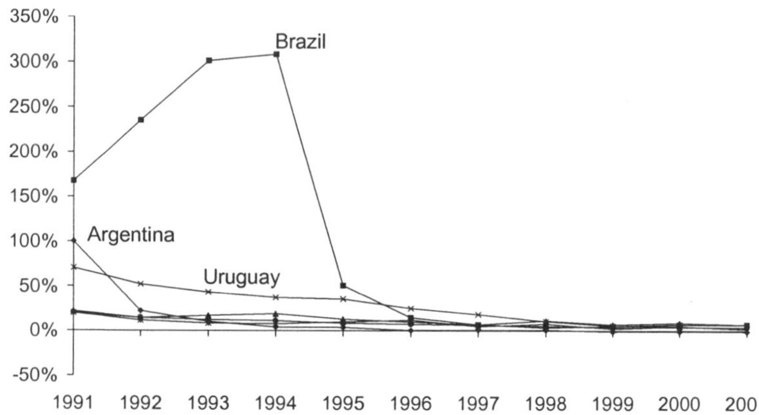

Figure 4: Inflation Rates in Expanded Mercosur, 1991–2001

3.1 Argentina

The Convertibility Law of 1991, which set the peso equal to the U.S. dollar and in fact established a currency board, was the big innovation of the 1990s in Mercosur. It lasted until early in 2002, when the peso was allowed to float.

In its pure form, a currency board requires that liquid international reserves or backing assets be at least equal to the monetary base. In Argentina, these were defined as gold and foreign reserves.[7] The excess of international reserves over the monetary base becomes eligible for lending to the banking system. For example, in October 2001, the Argentine central bank had international reserves of 27.3 billion pesos against a monetary base of 16 billion pesos, leaving 11 billion pesos as potential lender-of-last-resort funds.[8]

Legally, a currency board guarantees the convertibility of its liabilities (the monetary base), but not that of bank deposits (Ho, 2002). For the latter to be converted into the backing asset they must be first transformed into currency. As of October 2001 peso bank deposits

[7] The convertibility law actually set backing assets at 0.8 of the monetary base (Carrera, 2002).

[8] Central Bank of Argentina, Department of Financial Analysis and Information, October 2001 (www.bcra.gov.ar).

were 22.9 billion and foreign-currency bank deposits 50 billion dollars (www.bcra.gov.ar). While Argentina had also \$6.5 billion of contingent credit lines negotiated with international banks and the World Bank (EUI Argentina, 2001, p. 8), it did not have enough to prevent an implosion of the banking system sparked by a massive deposit withdrawal. This, in turn, led to a freeze of bank deposits and ultimately to the demise of the currency board.

Argentina was (and is) also extensively dollarized, with approximately 70 per cent of domestic bank deposits denominated in U.S. dollars. This figure understates the true degree of dollarization by the unknown amount of dollar currency in circulation in Argentina and dollar bank deposits owned by Argentine residents abroad. At the end of October 2001, peso time deposits had an average yield of 44.23 per cent and dollar time deposits 16.72 per cent. Given that the risk of bankruptcy is independent of the denomination of the deposit, deposit owners were expecting a 27 per cent devaluation of the peso in relation to the dollar.[9] In fact, the high degree of currency substitution led to currency mismatches and raised the risk of a bank run.[10]

Under a currency board, government budget deficits cannot be monetized. This, in itself, suggests an incentive for more fiscal discipline. To shore up confidence in the currency board, the Argentine federal government passed a balanced-budget law that kicked in July 2001. But the province of Buenos Aires responded by relaxing the monetization constraint by paying salaries with promissory notes, so-called *patacones*,

[9] The expected size of the peso depreciation had been rising in the last two years.

[10] Let $L(i)$ indicate the value of bank loans in pesos, with $L'(i) < 0$; $L^*(i^*)$ the value of loans in dollars, with $L^{*\prime}(i_*) < 0$; e be the peso price of one U.S. dollar; D and D^* the value of peso and dollar deposits; r the reserve requirement per unit of deposits; and E the mathematical expectations. Deposits will run on banks if:

$$E\left[L\left(i\right)-D\left(1-r\right)\right]/e < E\left[D^*\left(1-r\right)-L^*\left(i^*\right)\right]$$

A bank run is more likely the greater the currency mismatch, reaching its peak when liabilities are exclusively in U.S. dollars and assets in pesos. A currency depreciation would affect bank assets as follows:

$$-E\left[L\left(i\right)-D\left(1-r\right)\right]/e^2+\left(\partial EL/\partial i\right)\left(\partial i/\partial e\right)/e$$

The first term of the last expression represents the direct impact of the depreciation on balance-sheet values: it is negative if banks have net positive domestic assets. This is clearly the case for Argentina at the end of October 2001: $L = 33.3$ billion, $D = 22.9$, and $r = 0.2$. The second term shows the impact of the depreciation on the value of peso loans. This effect is positive if the new convertibility ratio is believed to be credible by the market. In this case, the new convertibility ratio brings about a drop in i, and a drop in i in turn raises the value of peso bank loans. The total impact can be either positive or negative, but it is more likely to be negative the higher the initial value of the net domestic assets.

that in fact became legal tender money in August 2001.[11] The national government as well issued money-like bonds, *lecop*, and so did other provinces.[12] The hard budget constraint was gone.

There is no consensus on the break-down of the currency board in Argentina. I consider three possible and partially overlapping explanations: the external shock, fiscal profligacy and monetary mismanagement. According to the first explanation, the root cause of the problem was "a combination of tight monetary policy from the US, plus a steady risk premia of 2%–4% [percentage] points above the US Treasury rates on Argentine debt, and a rising dollar exchange rates vs. the rest of the world ..." (Hughes Hallett, 2002, p. 3). Such events led to a decline in national output, rising budget deficits and government debt, and further rises in country risk premia. In essence, Argentina was caught in a vicious circle unleashed by events outside its control. Fiscal austerity was introduced by the Argentine government at the end of 2000 and again in 2001, partly to reduce the rise of government debt, most of which was in foreign hands, and partly to meet the requirements of IMF loans. But fiscal discipline, argues Hughes Hallett, was the wrong medicine because it could not reverse the negative debt dynamics. The solution to the problem required a boost to economic growth. The obvious question is why did the Argentine authorities decide to simultaneously default on debt and loosen the straight jacket of the currency board. If fiscal discipline was not able to solve the exploding debt dynamics, why not default on debt but save the board?

The second explanation puts the onus of the problem on the endogenous fiscal response to a currency board. Conventional wisdom ascribes to a tough exchange rate commitment with positive spill-over effects on public finances: fiscal discipline results from the inability to monetize budget deficits and the greater transparency of these deficits. In other words, a currency board creates an environment of monetary dominance. The alternative hypothesis is that a hard monetary regime cannot discipline fiscal policy makers (Fratianni and Spinelli, 2001).[13] In the specific case of Argentina, the high reputation of its currency board allowed government to finance deficits through foreign borrowing without facing immediate costs (Carrera, 2002, p. 11). The result was excessive bor-

---

[11] The notes were accepted for tax payments and are making inroads into retailing.

[12] A fairly up to date list of Argentina's quasi currencies has been published by the Financial Times (April 11, 2002).

[13] In his empirical investigation, Edwards (2001, Tables 2 and 3) finds that dollarized economies perform better than non-dollarized economies in terms of inflation but not in terms of fiscal discipline.

rowing and ultimately the undoing of the board itself. Under flexible exchange rate — the argument goes — the market would have reacted quickly to budget deficits with a depreciation of the domestic currency, and the government would have behaved more responsibly. The obvious question here is: why is the signal from currency depreciation louder than the signal from a rising country risk premium.

The third explanation focuses on monetary mismanagement as the source of the break-down of the currency board. Cavallo implemented inconsistent policies, swinging between fiscal rectitude and the desire to re-ignite the economy through lower interest rates (Carrera, 2002, p. 4). The change of the reference basket of the currency board from one dollar to 50 per cent dollar and 50 per cent euro (subject to the euro reaching parity with the dollar), the removal of the governor of the central bank, the export subsidy and import tariffs induced peso holders to wonder about the integrity of the currency board. Bank depositors switched on the margin from peso to dollar deposits and then tried to cash them in. The threat of implosion of the banking system led to the bank deposit freeze.

The three explanations have in common one or another inadequacy of the currency board. In the external shock hypothesis, the inadequacy is the board's inflexibility to absorb shocks. In the fiscal hypothesis, the inadequacy is that its rigid money-changing rule is not capable to discipline fiscal authorities; to obtain the necessary discipline the board would have to be accompanied by a fiscal rule, as is present in the EMU. In the monetary mismanagement hypothesis, the inadequacy is that it is not sufficiently independent from government. These inadequacies, as I argue below, are not present to the same extent in a multilateral MU.

3.2 Brazil

The credibility of the Brazilian central bank as an inflation fighter has much improved in the wake of the 1999 devaluation of the real. In June of that year, Brazil adopted inflation targeting and entrusted the National Monetary Council — composed of the Governor and Deputy Governors of the central bank — to set inflation rate targets and tolerance intervals on the basis of a proposal by the Finance Minister (Bogdanski *et al.*, 2000). The central bank has full responsibility to meet the targets, reports quarterly on performance (http://www.bcb.gov.br), and must justify its failure to meet the targets with a public letter addressed to the Minister of Finance. The target for 1999 was set at 8 per cent of the cumulative yearly change of a broad consumer price index; for 2000 at 6 per cent and for 2001 at 4 per cent; tolerance intervals at ± 2 per cent. Actual inflation rates for 1999 and 2000 were very close to target rates; in 2001 the outcome was 7.4 per cent and exceeded the target rate plus the 2 per cent tolerance interval. The global slowdown in economic activity and the turbulence in Argentina are mitigating factors of the 2001 performance. The central bank of Brazil forecasts inflation rate to decline to 3.7 per cent by the end of 2002 and 2.5 per cent by the end of 2003 (http://www.bcb.gov.br, Inflation Report, December 2001). The appreciation of the real with respect to the U.S. dollar in the latter part of 2001 is in sympathy with the forecast of the central bank. In sum, Brazil appears determined to implement a credible inflation-targeting strategy aimed at price stability.

4 The Multilateral MU

Many of the proposals to dollarize Argentina and other parts of Latin America have been inspired, in part, by the benefits of a stable monetary regime, but did not address the larger issue of how to create a low-inflation MU in Mercosur. One way to achieve it would be for all participating countries to adopt the dollar as their currency. Call this the unilateral MU, although there is an element of coordination. The alternative form of MU is the multilateral one, whereby participating countries adopt a single central bank, a common currency, and common financial regulation; in other words the EMU model.

The multilateral MU is much more complex than a unilateral MU. It requires a strong motivation on the part of the prospective member countries to integrate institutions, laws, regulations, and practices; in essence, the infrastructure for economics and finance. This desire need not be strong at the start of the process; it develops as cooperation in one field opens possibilities for cooperation elsewhere (Tsoukalis, 1977). Integration has its own internal dynamics and its full benefits are perceived as time goes on, in a sort of learning-by-doing process. Unlike unilateral MUs, multilateral unions make large investments in institution building.

4.1 Multilateral vs. Unilateral MU

Dollarization or unilateral MU differs from multilateral MU in four fundamental aspects (Fratianni and Hauskrecht, 2002). The first is that, in the absence of an explicit agreement, dollarization, unlike a multilateral MU, implies a loss of seigniorage, lender-of-last-resort facility, and no voice in the running of the monetary policy of the adopted-currency country. Argentina, in its plan to dollarize, made proposals to the US government to share seigniorage, have access to the Federal discount window, and cooperate on bank supervision. The "International Monetary Stability Act of 1999" (the Act) is the closest official position of the United States on the subject.[14]

The Act states unequivocally that "the Federal Reserve System has no obligation to act as a lender of last resort to the financial systems of dollarized countries; no obligation to consider the economic conditions of dollarized countries when formulating or implementing monetary policy; and the supervision of financial institutions in dollarized countries remains the responsibility of those countries" (Section 2, part (b)). The Act allows for the US Treasury to rebate 85 per cent of the seigniorage resulting from currency flows after "official" dollarization; there is no rebate on the stock of currency before official dollarization. To enjoy the rebate on the new currency flows, dollarized countries would have to surrender US Treasury securities and receive in exchange an equal amount of US currency and interest-bearing US consols or perpetuities. The Act states that coupon payment on these perpetuities "is rendered null and void upon a United States declaration of war on the country or a publicly issued statement by the Secretary [of the Treasury] that the country is no longer officially dollarized " (Section 6).

The declaration-of-war clause underscores the nexus between money and power. Countries that are considering the adoption of the dollar as their legal tender cannot ignore the possibility that their monetary systems may be disrupted by the United States in times of conflict. It happened to Noriega's Panama in March of 1998, when the US government put a payment squeeze on the country. Banks were closed for two months and Panamanian real GDP suffered a sharp drop (Moreno-Villalaz, 1999). These factors may explain why fully "dollarized" economies tend to be small.[15] It is far fetched that a country of

---

[14] The Act was introduced by Senator Connie Mack in the U.S. Senate (S. 1879) on November 8, 1999 and by Representative Paul Ryan in the House of Representatives (H.R. 3493) on November 18, 1999. Hearings were held on the Act, but legislation was not enacted (Schuler and Stein, 2000, p. 2).

[15] Schuler and Stein (2000, Table 1) list 31 "dollarized" countries, dependencies and territories; all of them are very small. The U.S. dollar has been adopted in East Timor, Marshall Islands, Micronesia, Palau, Panama, Pitcairn Island, Turks and Caicos Islands, British Virgin Islands, Guam, Northern Mariana Islands, Puerto Rico, American Samoa, U.S. Virgin Islands; the French franc in Andorra and Monaco; the UK pound in Saint Helena; the German mark in Kosovo; the Italian lira in the Vatican and San Marino; the Swiss franc in Liechtenstein; the Australian dollar in Kiribati, Nauru, Tuvalu, Cocos Islands, Norfolk Island; the New Zealand dollar in Cook Islands, Niue and Tokelau; the Spanish peseta in Andorra; the Danish krone in Greenland; and the Turkish lira in Northern Cyprus. As of 2002, the euro is replacing the French franc, the German mark, the Italian lira and the Spanish peseta.

the size of Brazil would acquiesce politically to a clause or the implied threat that its monetary system would be under potential threat of a foreign government.

The second difference is that in a multilateral union a positive interaction takes place between the efficiency and reputation of the common currency and financial depth (Rey, 1997; Fratianni *et al.*, 1998). The source of the efficiency gain resides in the degree of competitiveness and completeness of financial markets. MU promotes financial integration, and as regional markets replace national markets, depth and liquidity improve. More intense competition reduces bid and ask spreads on asset prices, making it more attractive for global investors to transact in assets denominated in the new currency. To what extent the new currency becomes also an international currency depends critically on the quality of monetary policy of the multilateral union. The reputation of the common central bank and common currency depends on a low-inflation record and an independent central bank. In turn, a more reputable currency promotes additional financial integration. Under dollarization, the gains of financial integration accrue largely to the external currency. Should that currency become mismanaged, MU will suffer from it. Under a multilateral union, the gains of financial integration accrue largely to the union's currency.[16]

The third difference is that a multilateral MU has incentives to absorb the effects of common or union-wide shocks, leaving each member to deal with their own idiosyncratic disturbances. Being unsystematic, these country disturbances can be diversified away within the union (von Furstenberg, 2002). Under dollarization, in contrast, monetary policy is more likely to be targeted to shocks affecting the home-currency country than shocks affecting the entire dollar area. This basic public-choice principle is clearly expressed in the referred International Monetary Stability Act of 1999.[17]

Finally, a multilateral MU spurs additional forms of cooperation, from common financial standards to tax-based insurance arrangements. The cumulative principle of cooperation suggests that successful cooperation in some areas creates opportunities and incentives for cooperation in other areas (Tsoukalis, 1977). Take, for example, the issue of the union adjusting to a persistent current-account deficit under the assumption that the union's monetary policy aims at maintaining a low rate of infla-

[16]The use of largely is justified by the fact that financial integration and monetary union generate positive externalities for other countries.

[17]The exact phrase is "... no obligation to consider the economic conditions of dollarized countries when formulating or implementing monetary policy."

tion while fiscal policy remains under the control of each member government. In the absence of a specified rule, what member country might want to undertake a reduction in its own budget deficit for the benefit of the union as a whole? The obvious lesson is that the creation of a multilateral MU opens the issue and creates an opportunity to establish a more complex mechanism of coordinated fiscal policies. This leads to some form of fiscal insurance through rules of tax sharing collected at the center or through transfers across regions (Kenen, 1969).

4.2 Financial Standards

With integrated financial markets, national differences in regulation create more opportunities for regulation avoidance and risk of erosion of regulatory standards. The approach adopted by the EMU (and the EU more broadly) is that national regulators retain the right and obligations of financial regulation and that national financial standards are mutually recognized subject to common floor requirements. The alternative is for the centralized MU to have a common regulatory framework. The difference between the two approaches has more to do with transition strategies than ultimate objectives. Agreements on minimum common standards are easier to obtain than agreements about a uniform standard. Once regulatory competition among member states reduces drastically differences in national standards, the transition from the principle of mutual recognition to a uniform standard becomes relatively easy to effect.

At the moment, the EMU has centralized the responsibility of monetary policy and the regulation and supervision of the euro payments system; has left to member states other regulations; and left others ambiguous. As a result, the system suffers from unnecessary uncertainty. The application of the lender of last resort is a good example of this uncertainty: there is no script about the respective roles of the European Central Bank, national central banks, and national regulators and supervisors with respect to this function (Goodhart, 2000). The lesson for other multilateral MUs is that a uniform financial standard may be more suitable than the heterogeneous approach adopted by the EMU. This is the point made in the Lamfalussy Report (2000). On the other hand, a uniform standard is more costly to obtain.

In sum, a multilateral MU goes way beyond the dollarization of the economies. It requires building shared institutions and formulating policies that are "owned" by the member countries. This ownership permits the internalization of many of the benefits of a common money, common monetary policy and common financial standards. Furthermore, a multilateral MU promotes additional forms of cooperation.

5 The Path to a Multilateral MU

Having argued that a multilateral MU is preferable to a unilateral one, let's see how this goal could be achieved. Transition strategies, regardless of their complexities, can be grouped under the rubric of either "fast" or "slow." A fast strategy, such as a currency reform, has the advantage of giving no time to lobby against it and no time to economic operators to make adjustments that would undermine MU. Politicians could not renege on MU without incurring the extremely high cost of a monetary secession and the significant burden of reintroducing the national currency. Thus, intra-regional currency risk would disappear; interest rates within MU would only differ by differences in national country risk premia. The most obvious criticism of a sudden monetary reform is that it is politically very costly. Even if the political will existed, it would take months and perhaps years to ratify an agreement of this importance; and even if this political will existed, it would take months to overcome the technical and legal obstacles of replacing old currencies with the new one. In fact, a sudden multilateral MU is not realistic.

The advantage of a slow strategy is that it would give individuals and institutions time to amortize the adjustment costs over the transition phase. On the other hand, a slow strategy is less credible than a fast strategy; hence, there is a trade-off between credibility and adjustment costs (Fratianni and von Hagen, 1992, ch. 9). To boost credibility, governments can find ways to signal the seriousness of their commitment to a centralized MU. Consider two possible slow strategies: an exchange-rate arrangement similar to the European EMS, and an approach based on independent central banks and inflation targeting. In the European experience the credibility of the exchange-rate regime was relatively low because of the possibility of parity realignments; interest rate differentials embedded sizable currency risk (country risk was not much of a problem in the EMS). If realignments had been ruled out, the market would have shifted its attention to the credibility of the no-realignment provision. Realignments become more likely as individual member countries face idiosyncratic shocks and domestic goals come into conflict with the maintenance of the fixed exchange rate regime. It is not obvious that fixing exchange rates during the transition phase raises the quality of the signal. Fixing the exchange rate prematurely may actually deliver the opposite outcome: as long as inflation rates have not fully converged, the fixed rate imposes continuous changes in real exchange rates and, consequently, changes in competitiveness. Since such an environment is not sustainable in the long run, the public will expect a break-down of the fixed exchange rate.

The credibility problem stems from monetary authorities pursuing objectives other than long-run price stability. The signal can be strengthened by restricting the ability of the central bank to trade off long-run price stability for other objectives. This entails, as in the third scenario, giving independence (from government) to national central banks and rewarding them for delivering long-run price stability. Central bank independence must be buttressed by fiscal rules; persistent and large budget deficits lead inexorably to fiscal dominance and the undoing of central bank independence.

Central bank independence is preferable to a rigid monetary rule because the bank retains enough policy discretion to respond flexibly to real economic shocks. The conservative German Bundesbank, before and during the EMS, was keenly aware of its role of stabilizing short-run output fluctuations without losing sight of long-run price stability (Neumann and von Hagen, 1992). National idiosyncratic shocks will peter out as the member countries integrate and their inflation rates converge.

In sum, there are two credible strategies to consummate a multilateral MU: the fast launch of a common currency and a common central bank, or the slow transition to give time to member countries to build independent national central banks dedicated to the pursuit of price level stability, while adjusting to idiosyncratic shocks. A multilateral MU would come about when economic and financial integration would have made shocks sufficiently symmetric in the region and inflation rates would have converged.[18]

The merit of a gradualist strategy is to allow institutions to adjust slowly to the new regime; but this requires that these institutions be sufficiently sturdy to converge to the targeted regime. This premise, unfortunately, appears patently unrealistic for Argentina that has defaulted on its massive debt, put an end to its currency board and is letting the peso float in the exchange markets, and has declared, on April 22, 2002, an indefinite bank holiday. Weak institutions and a fragile democracy do not augur well for a gradualist solution. Without a significant reduction in the budget deficits of the central and provincial governments, money growth in Argentina will be propelled by the monetization of those deficits and the country will be pulled back to its long history of

[18]For Eichengreen (1998, pp. 26–28), the transition path would have to be sufficiently long for aspirants to achieve also wage and price flexibility, a stronger financial sector, and higher exit costs.

inflationary policies. Under these conditions, it is wishful to think that the Argentine government may grant its central bank full independence and give it a mandate to pursue a low inflation rate policy.

The better course of action for Argentina is to quickly adopt the Brazilian real as its currency and consummate an early MU with its most important trading partner. A "realization" of the Argentine economy not only would deepen Mercosur, but would stabilize the purchasing power of money in Argentina relative to the alternative of a float in a regime of fiscal dominance.

"Realization" would involve more than the replacement of pesos with reals. Argentina and Brazil would have to negotiate a sharing of seigniorage, lending-of-last-resort facility, and ultimately agree on the "voice" Argentina would have in the running of the common monetary policy. Shared decision-making, however, should be made conditional on the adoption and implementation of good rules of behavior such as the Maastricht parameters for fiscal policy.

The "realization" of Argentina would also strengthen the Brazilian central bank as an institution seeking more independence from its government and as an inflation fighter. The regional importance of both features would make it easier to overcome whatever resistance remains at home against them. The "realization" of Argentina would have to be followed by institution building in Mercosur. While politically unpalatable, the adoption of the real as the Mercosur currency and the evolution of the Brazilian central bank into a common central bank have lower cost than the creation of a new common currency and a new common central bank. It is true that the EMU could have opted for the low-cost strategy of adopting the German mark as its common currency and the Bundesbank as its common central bank. But history — national division and literally centuries of warfare — was a big factor in Europe, for which EMU had to pay the added cost of building institutions de-novo. There is no reason for that experience to be repeated in Mercosur. The relative fragility of democracy and institutions in Mercosur argue in favor of consolidating and strengthening older institutions rather than putting in place new ones.

6 Conclusions

To resuscitate its customs union Mercosur needs a long-term monetary strategy. A multilateral monetary union may be the answer to both the historic propensity to inflate and the requirement to enhance economic integration in the region. A multilateral MU is a complex undertaking that cannot be built overnight, as the European experience illustrates. The dollarization alternative is inferior to a multilateral MU in providing the flexibility of counteracting union-wide shocks and in empowering member countries in the conduct of a common monetary policy; yet, it is no less difficult to bring about politically.

Ideally, the creation of a multilateral MU should be preceded by a transition long enough to give member countries the time to give independence to their national central banks and pursue inflation targeting, while adjusting to idiosyncratic shocks. The final phase would be consummated when economic and financial integration would have made shocks sufficiently symmetric in the region and inflation rates would have converged. However, the economic and political conditions of Argentina are so weak to make the adoption of a credible inflation-targeting strategy purely wishful thinking. Desperate conditions create opportunities that are easily discarded under normal circumstances. Argentina could solve her monetary problems and help launch the future multilateral MU of Mercosur by an immediate "realization" of its economy.

Like most radical proposals, this one may suffer from touches of unrealism and be overly ambitious. One can think of many reasons why this proposal has no chance to see the light of day. Let us consider three. The first and most serious is that Mercosur countries have weak institutions and democracies. Governments, unstable at home, may find it difficult to embark on a big project like a multilateral MU. Can political leaders in Argentina recognize and accept that, given the country's long history of monetary mismanagement, it is better to entrust monetary policy to its bigger neighbor than to continue on the present course? Will Brazilian inflation-targeting strategy meet the test of time? Are Mercosur governments ready to grant independence to their central banks? Will they behave responsibly on the fiscal side and thus facilitate the job of their central bankers to focus on reducing and maintaining low inflation rates? We do not know; but few knew in 1969 — when the EU leaders met in the Hague and signaled their intention to create a monetary union in the region — that EMU would have become a reality in 1999. Who would have thought in the 1980s that Italy would have joined a stable MU? The answer to this important question lies in one big unknown: leadership. Leadership is required to pull this off, and one is not sure whether it exists now in the region.

The second objection is that Mercosur is not an optimal currency area and that the search for monetary unification puts the cart before the horse. However, history is replete with MUs being created despite the fact that they did not meet the ex-ante canons of optimal currency areas. This paper has argued that a monetary union can be the horse, or at least one of the horses, of the integration cart.

The third objection is that a dollarization of Mercosur would be a superior strategy to the "realization" of Mercosur because the real is a local currency. Even if adopted by Mercosur, this currency could not compete with the US dollar and the euro. The competitive disadvantage of the real may well lead to a consolidation of the regional trade arrangements in the North and the South, and presage a grand monetary union of the Americas. For that to occur, not only the smaller countries but the United States as well will have to accept that shared monetary sovereignty is better than national monetary independence, if independence implies an unwelcome hegemon over a large monetary area.

BIBLIOGRAPHY

[1] Bayoumi, T. and B. Eichengreen (1993), 'Shocking Aspects of European Monetary Unification', in F. Torres and F. Giavazzi (eds.), *Adjustment and Growth in the European Monetary Union*, Cambridge: Cambridge University Press.

[2] Bayoumi, T. and B. Eichengreen (1994), 'One Money or Many? Analyzing the Prospects for Monetary Unification in Various Parts of the World', Princeton Studies in International Finance N. 76, Princeton, NJ: Princeton University Press.

[3] Bogdanski, J., A. A. Tombini and S. R. da Costa Werlang (2000), 'Implementing Inflation Targeting in Brazil', Banco Central do Brasil.

[4] Carrera, J. (2002), 'Is the Currency Board an Exportable Model for Monetary Unions? The Argentinean Experience', Paper presented at the Conference on "Euro and Dollarization: Forms of Monetary Union in Integrated Regions," Fordham University and CEPR, New York, April 5–6, 2002.

[5] Carrera, J. and F. Sturzenegger (2000), *Coordinación de Políticas Macroeconómicas en el Mercosur*, Buenos Aires: Fundación Gobierno y Sociedad.

[6] Commission of the European Communities (cited as the Lamfalussy Report) (2001), *Final Report of the Committee of Wise Men on the Regulation of European Securities Markets*, Brussels.

[7] Corsetti, G. and P. Pesenti (2002), 'Self-validating Optimum Currency Areas', Paper presented at the Conference on "Euro and Dollarization: Forms of Monetary Union in Integrated Regions," Fordham University and CEPR, New York, April 5–6, 2002.

[8] Economist Intelligence Unit (cited as EIU) (2001), *Argentina: Country Profile 2001*, London.

[9] Edwards, S. (2001), 'Dollarization and Economic Performance: an Empirical Investigation', NBER working paper n. 8274.

[10] Eichengreen, B. (1998), 'Does Mercosur Need a Single Currency?', NBER working paper n. 6821.

[11] Fernández-Aria, E., U. Panizza and E. Stein (2002), 'Trade Agreement, Exchange Rate Disagreements', Paper presented at the Conference on "Euro and Dollarization: Forms of Monetary Union in Integrated Regions," Fordham University and CEPR, New York, April 5–6, 2002.

[12] Financial Times (2002), 'Argentines snowed under by paper IOU's', April 11, p. 4.

[13] Fontagné, L. and M. Freudenberg (1999), 'Endogenous Symmetry of Shocks in a Monetary Union', *Open Economies Review 1999*, 10: 263–287.

[14] Frankel, J. A. and A. K. Rose (1998), 'The Endogeneity of the Optimum Currency Area', *The Economic Journal,* 108: 1009–25.

[15] Fratianni, M. and F. Spinelli (2001), 'Fiscal Dominance and Money Growth in Italy: the Long Record', *Explorations in Economic History*, 38: 252–272.

[16] Fratianni, M. and A. Hauskrecht (2002), 'A Centralized Monetary Union for Mercosur: Lessons from EMU', Paper presented at the Conference on "Euro and Dollarization: Forms of Monetary Union in Integrated Regions," Fordham University and CEPR, New York, April 5–6, 2002.

[17] Fratianni, M., A. Hauskrecht and A. Maccario (1998), 'Dominant Currencies and the Future of the Euro', *Open Economies Review*, 9 (Supplement): 97–121.

[18] Fratianni, M. and J. von Hagen (1992), *The European Monetary System and European Monetary Union*, Boulder, CO: Westview.

[19] Garrett, G. (1993), 'The Politics of Maastricht', *Economics and Politics,* 5, 2: 105–123.

[20] Goodhart, Ch. A. E. (ed.) (2000), *Which Lender of Last Resort for Europe?*, London: Central Banking Publications.

[21] Ho, C. (2002), 'A Survey of the Institutional and Operational Aspects of Modern-day Currency Boards', BIS Working Paper N. 110, Basel: Bank for International Settlements.

[22] Hughes Hallett, A. (2002), 'Could Fiscal Austerity Have Saved the Argentine Economy?', Paper presented at the Conference on "Euro and Dollarization: Forms of Monetary Union in Integrated Regions," Fordham University and CEPR, New York, April 5–6, 2002.

[23] Inter-American Development Bank (periodic), *Integration and Trade in the Americas*, Washington, D.C.

[24] International Monetary Fund (CD-ROM), *International Financial Statistics.*

[25] International Monetary Fund (2001), World Economic Outlook — May 2001, Washington, D.C., International Monetary Fund.

[26] Kenen, P. B. (1969), 'The Theory of Optimal Currency Areas: an Eclectic View', in R. A. Mundell and A. K. Swoboda (eds.), *Monetary Problems of the International Economy*, Chicago: Chicago University Press, 41–60.

[27] Krugman, P. (1993), 'What Do We Need to Know About the International Monetary System?', Essays in International Finance n. 190, Princeton, NJ: Princeton University Press.

[28] Licandro Ferrando, G. M. (2000), *Monetary Policy Coordination, Monetary Integration and Other Essays*, PhD Dissertation at the University of California, Los Angeles.

[29] McKinnon, R.I. (1963), 'Optimum Currency Areas', *American Economic Review*, 52, September: 615–623.

[30] Mélitz, J. (2002), 'Georgraphy, Trade and Currency Union', Paper presented at the Conference on "Euro and Dollarization: Forms of Monetary Union in Integrated Regions," Fordham University and CEPR, New York, April 5–6, 2002.

[31] Moreno-Villalaz, J. L. (1999), 'Lessons from the Monetary Experience of Panama: a Dollar Economy with Financial Integration', *The Cato Journal*, 18, 3: 421–439.

[32] Mundell, R. A. (1961), 'A Theory of Optimal Currency Areas', *American Economic Review*, 51, September: 657–665.

[33] Neumann, M. and J. von Hagen (1992), 'Monetary policy in Germany', in M. Fratianni and D. Salvatore (eds.), *Handbook of Monetary Policy in Industrial Countries*, Wesport, CT: Greenwood Press.

[34] Rey, H. (1997), 'International Trade and Currency Exchange', Centre for Economic Performance, London School of Economics.

[35] Rose, A. K. (2002), 'The Effect of Common Currencies on International Trade: a Meta-analysis,' Paper presented at the Conference on "Euro and Dollarization: Forms of Monetary Union in Integrated Regions," Fordham University and CEPR, New York, April 5–6, 2002.

[36] Rose, A. K. (2000), 'One Money, One Market: the Effects of Common Currency on Trade', *Economic Policy*, 30, April: 9–45.

[37] Rozemberg, R. and G. Svarzman (2000), *Report Mercosur: 1999–2000*, Intal Mercosur Report N. 6, Buenos Aires: Inter-American Development Bank and INTAL.

[38] Schuler, K. and R. Stein (2000), 'The Mack Dollarization Plan: an Analysis', Paper presented at the Conference on "Dollarization: A Common Currency for the Americas," Federal Reserve Bank of Dallas, March 6, 2000.

[39] Swann, D. (1988), *The Economics of the Common Market*, London: Penguin Books, 6th edition.

[40] Tavlas, G. (1994), 'The Theory of Monetary Integration', *Open Economies Review*, 5: 211–230.

[41] Tsoukalis, L. (1977), *The Politics and Economics of European Monetary Integration*, London: George Allen and Unwin.

[42] von Furstenberg, G. M. (2002), 'Income Insurance Aspects of Monetary Union', Paper presented at the Conference on "Euro and Dollarization: Forms of Monetary Union in Integrated Regions," Fordham University and CEPR, New York, April 5–6, 2002.

6 De Facto Exchange Rate Regimes in Transition Economies: Identification and Determination

Jürgen von Hagen and Jizhong Zhou

1 Introduction

The choice of an exchange rate regime has long been a topic vividly debated in international finance. Sir Alan Walters makes his contribution to this topic through his famous critique on the EMS, which emphasizes the trade-off between exchange-rate stability and price stability. The vast theoretical literature on the choice of an exchange rate regime relates this issue to the management of other macroeconomic issues, including balance-of-payment adjustment, output and price stabilization, and prevention of currency crises.[1] The empirical studies on exchange rate regime choices that emerged after the collapse of the Bretton Woods system examine the validity of various theoretical arguments pertaining to the choice of an exchange rate regime.[2] The results of these studies are generally consistent with the theoretical expectations, though the robustness of the empirical findings is still debatable.[3]

A prominent feature of the existing literature, however, is the negligence of the difference between official and de facto exchange rate regimes. *Official* exchange rate regimes are those formally announced exchange arrangements reported to and classified by the International Monetary Fund (IMF). The *de facto* exchange rate regime is the actual framework for daily exchange-rate management, for which there still

[1] See von Hagen and Zhou (2002a) for a brief review.

[2] See, among others, Heller (1978), Melvin (1985), Savvides (1990), Edwards (1996), and Poirson (2001).

[3] Juhn and Mauro (2002).

lacks a consensus on the appropriate way of identification. Theoretical studies implicitly assume that they are the same. In reality, however, de facto exchange rate policies can deviate from the official frameworks to a substantial extent. As documented by Ghosh *et al.* (1997), many countries with formally pegged exchange rates adjust central parities (in case of single-currency pegs) or currency weights (in case of composite-currency pegs) very frequently, making the "pegged" exchange rates behave like floating ones, while other countries with officially floating rate regimes manage their exchange rates so tightly that they are hardly distinguishable from fixed rate pegs.[4] Despite the observed regime discrepancies, however, most empirical studies treat the official regimes as "the" exchange rate regimes in place, and works on the determination of de facto exchange rate policies are much rarer, which is probably due to the lack of an easy and clear identification scheme of de facto exchange rate regimes.[5]

In this paper we focus on the de facto exchange rate policies in a group of 25 transition economies in Central and Eastern Europe and the Former Soviet Union in the 1990s. This is an interesting sample because, despite a common background of central planning and similar tasks in economic transition, these countries show a large variety in their exchange rate policies, not only across countries but over time as well. In trying to understand these varieties, we argue that de facto exchange rate policies are to some extent constrained by the official exchange rate arrangement, especially when a formal peg is adopted, as deviation from such a regime reveals weak commitment of the authority and may result in damages to the reputation of the government. De facto exchange rate policies are also influenced by other macroeconomic factors, such as inflation, balance of payment difficulties, fiscal dominance, and financial fragility. Our empirical study provides some support to these arguments.

The rest of the paper is organized as follows. Section 2 reviews different methods for the identification of de facto exchange rate policies. In Section 3 we discuss the possible determinants of de facto exchange rate policies, their potential roles, and their empirical proxies. Section 4 presents the model and discusses the empirical results. Some concluding remarks are collected in Section 5.

---

[4] The latter case is dubbed by Calvo and Reinhart (2000) as "fear of floating." Inspired by this phrasing, von Hagen and Zhou (2002b) dubbed the former case as "fear of pegging."

[5] An early exception is Holden *et al.* (1979), who construct a continuous-valued index of (de facto) exchange rate flexibility. Poirson (2001) devises a similar flexibility index. Bénassy-Quéré and Coeuré (2002) as well as Juhn and Mauro (2002) use discrete-valued classification for de facto exchange rate regimes.

2 Identification of De Facto Exchange Rate Regimes

2.1 Two Identification Approaches

There are two approaches to the identification of de facto exchange rate regimes. The first is basically a descriptive one, which is based on the IMF's classification of official exchange rate regimes, with necessary reclassifications when the observed policy behavior deviates sufficiently from the official framework, or with refinements of the official labels when more disaggregated regime categories can be identified.[6] Information for these revisions usually comes from consultations with the member governments by the IMF officials, press reports, news articles, and other relevant sources. Sometimes descriptive statistical analyses of the behavior of exchange rates are also used as a supplement.[7]

The second approach is a statistical one based on the analysis of the observed movements of the exchange rate and the international reserves. The rationale underlying this approach is that, under fixed rate regimes, the volatility of the exchange rate should be low but that of reserves should be high due to interventions to stabilize the exchange rate. Under floating rate regimes the opposite should be true, since the exchange rate is typically volatile but foreign exchange interventions are rare. One application of this approach is to construct an index to measure de facto exchange rate flexibility, which is defined as the ratio of the volatility of the exchange rate to that of international reserves.[8] This index is continuous-valued and increases in the flexibility of the de facto exchange rate policy. A different application of this approach applies cluster analysis to the data containing observations on the volatility of exchange rates and of international reserves. The idea is to sort countries into several "clusters," which are then labeled as a particular de facto regime according to the characteristics of that cluster. Since the observations are relatively homogeneous within the same cluster but rather heterogeneous across clusters, cluster analysis produces a set of discrete, qualitative classifications of de facto exchange rate regimes.[9]

---

[6] Ghosh *et al.* (1997) and Bubula and Ötker-Robe (2002).

[7] Bubula and Ötker-Robe (2002).

[8] Holden et al. (1979) and Poirson (2001).

[9] Levy-Yeyati and Sturzenegger (2000).

2.2 De Facto Exchange Rate Regimes in Transition Economies

We follow the statistical approach to identify de facto exchange rate regimes in transition economies. We believe that, since the descriptive approach relies heavily on official policy announcements, the result is still a classification of official exchange rate regimes, though on a much finer scale. In contrast, the statistical approach does not require any information on official regime announcements, it identifies de facto exchange rate policies based solely on observed behavior of exchange rates and international reserves. This conforms better to the idea that the de facto exchange rate regime is one that is actually adopted and can be verified by the movement of the exchange rate.

We follow the methodology used by Levy-Yeyati and Sturzenegger (2000) and run the cluster analysis on a data set for 25 transition economies during the 1990s. We have a total of 149 country-year observations on all of the following three volatility variables: (1) volatility of the exchange rate ($\sigma(e)$), defined as the average absolute monthly percentage change of the exchange rate during a given year, (2) volatility of the change of the exchange rate ($\sigma(\Delta e)$), defined as the standard deviation of the monthly percentage change of the exchange rate during a given year, and (3) volatility of reserves ($\sigma(r)$), defined as the average absolute monthly changes of the non-gold international reserves (normalized by the monetary base in the previous month) in a given year. Those observations with low $\sigma(e)$ and $\sigma(\Delta e)$ but high $\sigma(r)$ are classified as fixed regimes, those with high $\sigma(e)$ and $\sigma(\Delta e)$ but low $\sigma(r)$ are classified as flexible regimes, and those with intermediate values on all three dimensions are classified as intermediate regimes.[10] Table 1 reports the distribution of the volatility measures across three de facto exchange rate regimes. We have another 54 country-year observations with data available only for the first two volatility variables, which are assigned to the regime whose centroid is the closest to the data point. This gives us a trichotomous classification of 203 de facto exchange rate regimes.[11] In

[10] See von Hagen and Zhou (2002b) for a detailed explanation of the definitions of the variables, data sources, and the procedures of the cluster analysis. In actual classification there is a fourth cluster with low volatility on all dimensions, which is labeled "inconclusive regimes," since we are not sure whether the stability of the exchange rate is due to a fixed-rate regime or simply due to lack of shocks in the foreign exchange market. In the empirical analysis, however, the 13 "inconclusive regimes" are subsumed into fixed regimes as both exhibit stable exchange rates in practice.

[11] In the empirical analysis we will use the larger data set with 203 country-year observations. If we use the smaller data set with only 149 observations, however, the

	$\sigma(e)$		$\sigma(\Delta e)$		$\sigma(r)$	
	Mean	Median	Mean	Median	Mean	Median
Fixed*	1.92	0.97	2.37	0.99	10.62	9.86
Intermediate	4.84	2.89	5.98	3.46	10.02	6.10
Flexible	17.64	8.14	28.28	13.78	6.29	4.66

* Not including "inconclusive regimes."

Table 1: Volatility Measures Across De Facto Exchange Rate Regimes (in per cent)

the empirical analysis presented below, we use this classification as the dependent variable to investigate the determination of the choice of the de facto exchange rate regimes.[12]

3 Determinants of De Facto Exchange Rate Regimes

In this section we discuss the potential determinants of de facto exchange rate regimes and their qualitative influences on these regime choices. We also explain briefly the empirical proxies for the potential determinants. Detailed information on the definition and data source of each variable can be found in the Appendix.

3.1 Official Exchange Rate Regimes

De facto exchange rate policies can be influenced by the choices of official exchange rate regimes. From a theoretical perspective, if countries choose their official exchange rate regimes based on careful evaluations of costs and benefits, they will in general make exchange rate policies consistent with the declared formal exchange arrangements, unless deviations from the official regimes are well justified by other considerations. Moreover, changing official regimes incurs costs, including loss of repu-

results hardly change. This is because for the 54 observations where data on reserves volatility is not available, there are missing values on one or another variable used in the estimation, so they are not included in the regression analysis anyway.

[12]We also construct an index of exchange rate flexibility, which is the ratio of the volatility of the exchange rate ($\sigma(e)$) to the volatility of international reserves ($\sigma(r)$). The estimation results with this index as the dependent variable are generally consistent with those of the probit model where de facto regimes classified by the cluster analysis are used as the dependent variable.

tation if a formal currency peg is abandoned, or constraints on policy autonomy if a floating regime is replaced by a more rigid one. As a result, countries have a tendency to run de facto exchange rate policies within the framework of the official regimes. This suggests that, at least to some extent, the choice of the official exchange rate regime will guide that of the de facto regime.[13] From an empirical perspective, the choice of the official exchange rate regime can be viewed as a proxy for the economic fundamentals, which may influence the choice of de facto regimes, but not included in the empirical model. For these reasons we include the choice of official exchange rate regimes as a determinant of de facto regimes.

The classification of official exchange rate regimes is based on the new eight-regime IMF nomenclature, where currency unions, currency boards, and conventional fixed pegs are labeled as fixed regimes, horizontal bands, crawling pegs, and crawling bands as intermediate regimes, and managed floating without pre-announced exchange rate paths as well as independent floating and flexible regimes.[14] This leads to a trichotomous classification of the official exchange rate regimes, which takes a value of 0, 1, or 2 for fixed, intermediate, or flexible regimes respectively. Note that for each country in each year the official regime is the end-year observation, while the de facto regime is identified based on the behavior of the exchange rate and international reserves during that year. To attenuate the endogeneity of the official regime choice to the evolution of the exchange rate and international reserves and, as a result, to the de facto regime choice, we use the official regime prevailing at the end of the previous year as one that constrains the de facto regime choices in the current year, or use instrumental variables to project the current-year official regime choice.

3.2 Inflation Performance and Exchange Rate Pass-through

Inflation performance is expected to play a role in the determination of de facto exchange rate policies. On the one hand, high inflation coupled with fixed exchange rates leads to a real appreciation of the home currency and possibly a misalignment of the real exchange rate, which may raise the desirability of flexible exchange rates to facilitate adjustments of the exchange rate. On the other hand, high inflation makes an exchange rate anchor more attractive, since stabilizing the exchange rate

---

[13] In von Hagen and Zhou (2002b) we show that there is positive correlation between the choices of official and de facto exchange rate regimes.

[14] See von Hagen and Zhou (2002a) for the details of this classification.

can help pin down the whole price system and contributes to disinflation. Of these two contradicting effects, which one is more important in reality is an empirical question. We expect, however, that the latter effect should dominate in the contest, and that high inflation rates should raise the likelihood of a more stable exchange rate. The former effect may be less important in practice, since it can easily create a vicious inflation–depreciation spiral, especially when the pass-through effect from depreciation to inflation is strong. This reduces sharply the desirability of a flexible exchange rate regime, not only for its negative impact on price stabilization, but also for its inability to correct real misalignments. Therefore, the stronger is the pass-through effect, the less desirable a flexible exchange rate will be, and the more likely a de facto peg will be adopted.

We use annual growth rates of consumer prices as a measure of inflation performance (INFLATION). To dampen the influence of hyperinflationary episodes without deleting them as outliers, we follow Ghosh *et al.* (1997) to transform the original inflation rates (π) into a new data series (π^*) according to the formula $\pi^* = \pi/(1-\pi)$. To measure the extent of the pass-through effect, we follow Hausmann *et al.* (2000) to compute the correlation coefficient between monthly inflation rates and one-quarter lagged monthly depreciation rates, which is used as the proxy for the intensity of the pass-through effect (PASSTHRU). The one-quarter lag is intended to give the currency depreciation some time to work its effect out.[15]

3.3 Quality and Strength of Financial Institutions

The quality and strength of financial institutions is another potential determinant of de facto exchange rate policies. In order to defend a fixed or tightly managed exchange rate, it may be necessary to raise interest quickly and to high levels, leading to deterioration of banks' portfolios. The negative impact on banks' balance sheets will be particularly profound if many banks have heavy burdens of non-performing loans. This suggests that, in the presence of a weak banking sector, flexible exchange rate regimes may be more appropriate. If financial institutions are healthy and strong, they are able to endure the harshness of interest-rate hikes typically associated with fixed exchange rates, so a stable exchange rate is a more likely result.

---

[15] We also adjust the lag length to zero or one month in the construction of the pass-through variable. When they are used in empirical analysis, results concerning other variables are similar to those reported in the paper. The pass-through variables themselves become less significant but do not change their signs.

This prediction should be qualified if there is a substantial currency mismatch in banks' portfolios, especially when assets are denominated in the home currency but liabilities are "dollarized." If this is the case, then a depreciation of the home currency increases the home-currency value of foreign-currency denominated liabilities but does not change the value of assets, which is equivalent to the deterioration of banks' balance sheets. Since depreciations of the home currency are more often than not appreciations under a flexible regime in transition economies, a stable exchange rate is more beneficial than a flexible one in the presence of liability "dollarization."

For the empirical analysis we use two variables as proxies for the quality and strength of financial institutions.[16] One is the share of non-performing loans in total loans (NPL), which is inversely related to the strength of banks: the higher this share is, the weaker the banks are. The other is a measure of the quality of financial institutions (FINQUAL), which is the average of the index of banking sector reform and the index of reform of non-banking financial institutions. Both indices are compiled by the European Bank for Reconstruction and Development (EBRD) on a 1–4 scale, with 1 denoting little progress in financial reform and 4 full convergence of financial laws and regulations with Western standards.[17] The higher the FINQUAL index is, the better quality the financial institutions are expected to have.

3.4 Other Macroeconomic Factors

De facto exchange rate policies can also be influenced by other macroeconomic factors, such as fiscal discipline, monetary expansion, and current account positions. As pointed out by the theoretical literature on currency crises, fiscal discipline is critical for the sustainability of a fixed exchange rate.[18] Large fiscal deficits, especially when monetized, are likely to cause a loss of foreign exchange reserves and to lead to an attack on the home currencies, which is evidenced by many dramatic collapses of fixed-rate regimes (e.g., Argentina 2002). One of the lessons from these crises is that, if countries can not observe fiscal discipline, exchange rate flexibility is necessary as a preemptive measure against potential currency crises.

A related factor is the speed of monetary expansion. If fast mon-

---

[16] We do not consider currency mismatch or liability dollarization in the estimations due to lack of data.

[17] EBRD, Transition Report 1999.

[18] Krugman (1979).

etary expansion is a result of the monetization of large fiscal deficits, then exchange rate stability is difficult to maintain. A more viable exchange rate regime is a more flexible one. Monetary expansion can also be a result of financial deepening. Since a deeper financial market provides more chances to hedge exchange rate risks, a flexible exchange rate regime can be adopted, which frees the central bank from the daily management of the exchange rate and, as a result, allows more monetary autonomy.

Another factor that may influence de facto exchange rate flexibility is current account positions. In case of large current account deficits, exchange rates need to be adjusted to regain external competitiveness. The depreciation of the home currency can also dampen the excessive demand on foreign goods and services, leading to the improvement of the balance-of-payments position. However, the awareness of the possibility of a depreciation–inflation circle may delay the prescribed exchange rate adjustment. Moreover, while exchange rate flexibility is needed to facilitate these adjustments, they may take the form of infrequent but substantial devaluations of home currencies. To make things more complicated, if the J-curve effect exists, then the current account position may further deteriorate when the exchange rate is stable after a major adjustment. Given these contradicting forces in play, it is difficult to predict the nature of the influence of external positions on de facto exchange rate policies.

For the empirical analysis, fiscal discipline is proxied by the general government budget balance normalized by Gross Domestic Products (GDP). The variable is labeled FISCAL, which is negative (positive) for budget deficits (surpluses). Monetary expansion is proxied by the annual growth rate of broad money (M2GROW). Similar to the adjustment of the inflation data, we apply the same transformation (i.e., $x^* = x/(1-x)$) to avoid the influence of some episodes of extremely fast monetary expansion. Current account position is measured by the current account deficits ($-$) or surpluses ($+$) normalized by GDP (CURRACCT).

4 Empirical Analysis

4.1 The Model

We will consider three alternatives for the choice of de facto exchange rate regimes: fixed, intermediate, and flexible regimes. Since these three options are naturally ordered with rising degree of regime flexibility, an ordered probit model will be applied in the empirical analysis. Denoting the observed discrete choices of de facto exchange rate regimes by Q, we label fixed regimes by $Q = 0$, intermediate ones by $Q = 1$, and flexible ones by $Q = 2$. As a common practice in the analysis of discrete choices, we assume that the value of Q depends on the distribution of a continuous latent index Q^*, which can be interpreted in our case as reflecting the desired degree of flexibility of the de facto exchange rate regime. To be specific,

$$Q = 0 \text{ for fixed regimes if } Q^* \leq 0 \quad (1a)$$

$$Q = 1 \text{ for intermediate regimes if } 0 < Q^* \leq c \quad (1b)$$

$$Q = 2 \text{ for flexible regimes if } Q^* > c \quad (1c)$$

Here c ($c > 0$) is the threshold differentiating between intermediate and flexible regimes, while the lower threshold between fixed and intermediate regimes is normalized to zero.[19] This structure indicates that if the higher degree of regime flexibility is desired, the more flexible regime will in general be selected.

The latent index Q^* is assumed to be linear in the regime determinants discussed in the previous section, including official exchange rate regime choices and other explanatory variables. Let the country and time subscripts be denoted by i and t respectively. We have two versions of the model:

$$Q(i,t)^* = Y(i,t-1)\,\gamma + Z(i,t)'\,\beta + u(i,t) \quad (2)$$

$$Q(i,t)^* = 1\{Y(i,t-1) = 0\}\,\gamma_0 + 1\{Y(i,t-1) = 2\}\,\gamma_2 + Z(i,t)'\,\beta + u(i,t) \quad (3)$$

Here $Y(i,t)$ is a discrete-valued indicator for the choice of official exchange rate regimes by country i at the end of period t, which takes a value of 0, 1, 2, for fixed, intermediate, and flexible regimes, respectively. All the other determinants are summarized in the vector Z. The indicator function 1{A} has the property that it returns a value of 1 if the event "A" is true, and 0 otherwise. For ease of estimation, the error term $u(i,t)$ is assumed to be independently and identically distributed normal, which leads to a probit model.[20]

[19] This is a harmless normalization as long as a constant is included in the determination of Q^*.

[20] We do not assume autocorrelations among the error terms, since the autocorrelation in de facto regime choices can be captured by their dependence on lagged official regime choices, which are correlated with de facto regime choices contemporaneously (von Hagen and Zhou, 2002b).

In equation (2) we control for the existing official framework for exchange rate policies and allow the observed official regime flexibility to assert a monotonic influence on the determination of actual exchange rate policies in the current period. In equation (3), different official regimes are allowed to have different impacts on de facto regime choices, so that the influence of official regime flexibility may not be monotonic on the flexibility of de facto regimes. A common point, however, is that de facto exchange rate policies in the current period are constrained by the existing official exchange rate regimes.

An alternative modeling strategy is to relate the choice of de facto exchange rate regimes to the desired official regimes in the same period, i.e.,

$$Q(i,t)^* = \hat{Y}(i,t)\gamma + Z(i,t)'\beta + u(i,t) \tag{4}$$

$$Q(i,t)^* = 1\left\{\hat{Y}(i,t-1) = 0\right\}\gamma_0 + 1\left\{\hat{Y}(i,t-1) = 2\right\}\gamma_2 + Z(i,t)'\beta + u(i,t) \tag{5}$$

Here $Y(i,t)^*$ is a latent index for the desired degree of flexibility of the official exchange rate regime, while $Y(i,t)^*$ is its predicted value based on an auxiliary ordered probit model for the choice of official exchange rate regimes:

$$Y(i,t)^* = Y(i,t-1)\alpha + X(i,t)'\theta + v(i,t) \tag{6}$$

The mapping from $Y(i,t)^*$ to $Y(i,t)$ is similar to that of (1a)–(1c), except for a different upper threshold.[21] The predicted choice of official exchange rate regimes is denoted by $Y(i,t)$. The regime determinants summarized in $X(i,t)$ are the economic fundamentals selected based on our early study (von Hagen and Zhou, 2002a), and include trade openness, geographical and commodity concentration of trade, level of economic development, size of the economy, financial development, reserve sufficiency, and a CIS dummy.

Equations (4) and (5) incorporate the idea that it is the intention or desire to float, say, officially that influences the choice of de facto exchange rate regimes, and that the influence of the intended degree of flexibility can be linear (equation (4)) or non-linear (equation (5)). The dependence of de facto regime choices on the existing official framework as modeled by equations (2) and (3) is now, indirectly, reflected by the autoregressive process of the choice of official exchange rate regimes (equation (6)).

---

[21] The lower threshold is again normalized to zero.

4.2 Estimation Results

We estimate the models based on a sample of 25 transition economies over the period 1990–1999. Due to many missing values in one or another variable the effective sample size is about 130 country-year observations, roughly 5 annual observations for each country. Among the 25 countries under investigation, 12 countries are members of the Commonwealth of Independent States (CIS) and the rest are Central and Eastern European Countries (CEECs). The CIS countries are generally slower in their reform paces and more inclined to adopt flexible official exchange rate regimes than the transition economies in Central and Eastern Europe (von Hagen and Zhou, 2002a). In order to control for the unobserved group-specific features we include a dummy variable for the CIS countries (CISDUMMY). Except for CISDUMMY and the choice of official exchange rate regimes, all the variables are instrumentalized by their own one-year lagged values to attenuate potential endogeneity problems.

Table 2 reports the coefficient estimates of the ordered probit model for the determination of de facto exchange rate regimes. The dependent variable is the trichotomous classification of de facto exchange rate regimes. Given the rule of mapping ((1a)–(1c)), an increase of the variable with a positive coefficient raises the desired degree of regime flexibility (Q^*) and therefore the probability of more flexible defacto exchange rate regimes. Table 3 reports the marginal effects of the explanatory variables on the probability of each regime alternative. The marginal effects are evaluated at the sample mean of each variable, except for the dummy variables, whose marginal effects are derived as the changes in the probabilities when the dummy switches from zero to unity. Because the marginal effects on various regimes must sum up to zero, we only report the marginal effects on the probabilities of fixed or flexible regimes.

We first look at the role of official exchange rate regimes in the determination of de facto regimes. The results of equations (2) and (4) in Table 2 suggest that flexible official regimes tend to make flexible de facto regimes more likely (note the positive coefficients for $Y(i,t-1)$ and $\hat{Y}(i,t)$), but this effect is statistically insignificant, no matter whether the official-regime flexibility is measured by the observed regime choice or by the intended degree of flexibility. The positive influence of official-regime flexibility is also economically weak: when the existing official regime changes from fixed to intermediate or from intermediate to flexible, it reduces on average the probability for a fixed de facto regime by 3 per cent, raises that for intermediate regimes by 2 per cent, and that for flexible ones by 1 per cent. The influence is even weaker from the

Variables	Eqn (2)	Eqn (3)	Eqn (4)	Eqn (5)
$Y(i, t-1)$	0.09			
	(0.16)			
$1\{Y(i, t-1) = 0\}$		−0.87**		
		(0.42)		
$1\{Y(i, t-1) = 2\}$		−0.54		
		(0.34)		
$Y(i, t)^*$			0.01	
			(0.06)	
$1\{Y(i, t) = 0\}$				−1.14**
				(0.53)
$1\{Y(i, t) = 2\}$				−0.15
				(0.32)
INFLATION	−2.28**	−1.98**	−2.13**	−1.86*
	(0.96)	(0.97)	(0.96)	(0.99)
PASSTHRU	−1.79**	−1.86**	−1.93**	−1.91**
	(0.89)	(0.91)	(0.91)	(0.94)
NPL	1.74**	1.85**	1.92**	1.64**
	(0.78)	(0.78)	(0.79)	(0.79)
FINQUAL	−0.83**	−1.01**	−0.80**	−1.02**
	(0.29)	(0.30)	(0.30)	(0.32)
FISCAL	−3.27	−3.17	−3.80	−2.43
	(3.01)	(3.00)	(3.63)	(3.44)
M2GROW	2.33*	2.03	1.63	1.13
	(1.24)	(1.25)	(1.26)	(1.32)
CURRACCT	8.40 **	8.05 **	8.52 **	7.29 **
	(2.98)	(3.03)	(3.18)	(3.27)
CISDUMMY	0.34	0.25	0.40	0.13
	(0.36)	(0.36)	(0.38)	(0.37)
CONSTANT	1.05	2.08**	1.15	2.11**
	(0.85)	(0.96)	(0.88)	(1.00)
THRESHOLD	0.90**	0.92**	0.95**	0.98**
	(0.16)	(0.16)	(0.16)	(0.17)
Observations	133	133	129	129
Log-likelihood	−93.88	−91.76	−90.26	−87.31
Prediction (%)	68.4	70.7	68.2	67.4

Note: Standard errors are in parentheses.
Significance levels of 5% and 10% are denoted by **
and * respectively.

Table 2: Ordered Probit Model for the Choice of De Facto Exchange Rate Regimes

intended official-regime flexibility (Table 3).

One possible explanation of this weak correlation is that the relationship between the flexibility of de facto regimes and that of official regimes is not monotonic, so a single flexibility measure may not be able to capture this effect. This conjecture is supported by the results of equations (3) and (5) in Table 2, where dummies for fixed or flexible regimes are included, with intermediate regimes as the benchmark. Relative to the impact of intermediate official regimes, the existence of an officially fixed regime ($\mathbf{1}\{Y(i,t-1)=0\}$), or the intention to adopt such a regime ($\mathbf{1}\{\hat{Y}(i,t)=0\}$), significantly reduces the likelihood for flexible de facto regimes: it raises the probability for a de facto fixed regime by 26 per cent to 29 per cent (Table 3). Interestingly, the existence of ($\mathbf{1}\{Y(i,t-1)=2\}$) or the intention for ($\mathbf{1}\{\hat{Y}(i,t)=2\}$) a flexible official regime also reduces the likelihood for a flexible de facto regime, though the difference from the influence of intermediate official regimes is slight and insignificant. In other words, intermediate official regimes are associated with the most flexible de facto ones, flexible official regimes with somewhat less flexible de facto ones, and fixed official regimes with the least flexible de facto ones. The high correlation between formal pegs and de facto pegs is consistent with the view that deviating from a formal peg involves reputation costs and is less likely.

The negative and significant coefficients for INFLATION across all equations suggest that high inflation rates unambiguously reduce the chances for de facto flexible exchange rate regimes, reflecting the increasing attractiveness of a stable exchange rate anchor in such an environment. The marginal effects show that a 1 percentage-point increase in INFLATION[22] raises the probability for a de facto fixed regime by 0.6–0.8 per cent and reduces that for a flexible regime by 0.2–0.3 per cent. The concern for a vicious depreciation–inflation circle is certainly an important reason for choosing a de facto fixed regime. This is confirmed by the negative and significant coefficients for PASSTHRU, which imply that with strong pass-through effects exchange-rate flexibility will be less asked for, since a depreciation of the home currency can easily fuel into high inflation, nullifying the effect of an exchange-rate adjustment on aggregate demand. It can be shown that the probability for choosing a de facto fixed regime will be roughly 64 per cent higher in a country with perfect exchange-rate pass-through (PASSTHRU=1) than in one with no pass-through effect at all (PASSTHRU=0).

The two variables reflecting the strength and quality of financial in-

---

[22] Note that INFLATION is the transformed inflation rate. A one percentage-point increase in this variable corresponds to a two percentage-point increase in the original inflation rate around the sample mean.

	Eqn (2)		Eqn (3)	
Variables	Fix	Flex	Fix	Flex
$Y(i,t-1)^a$	−0.03	0.01		
$1\{Y(i,t-1)=0\}^b$			0.26	−0.09
$1\{Y(i,t-1)=2\}^b$			0.19	−0.08
$Y(i,t)^*$				
$1\{Y(i,t)=0\}^b$				
$1\{Y(i,t)=2\}^b$				
INFLATION	0.80	−0.34	0.68	−0.27
PASSTHRU	0.63	−0.26	0.64	−0.26
NPL	−0.61	0.26	−0.64	0.26
FINQUAL	0.29	−0.12	0.35	−0.14
FISCAL	1.14	−0.48	1.09	−0.44
M2GROW	−0.81	0.34	−0.70	0.28
CURRACCT	−2.93	1.23	−2.78	1.11
CISDUMMYb	−0.12	0.05	−0.09	0.04

	Eqn (4)		Eqn (5)	
Variables	Fix	Flex	Fix	Flex
$Y(i,t-1)^a$				
$1\{Y(i,t-1)=0\}^b$				
$1\{Y(i,t-1)=2\}^b$				
$Y(i,t)^*$	−0.00	0.00		
$1\{Y(i,t)=0\}^b$			0.29	−0.08
$1\{Y(i,t)=2\}^b$			0.05	−0.02
INFLATION	0.73	−0.28	0.61	−0.21
PASSTHRU	0.66	−0.25	0.63	−0.21
NPL	−0.66	0.25	−0.54	0.18
FINQUAL	0.28	−0.10	0.34	−0.11
FISCAL	1.31	−0.50	0.80	−0.27
M2GROW	−0.56	0.21	−0.37	0.13
CURRACCT	−2.93	1.11	−2.40	0.81
CISDUMMYb	−0.14	0.06	−0.04	0.02

Note: Marginal effects are measured at sample mean. Marginal effects on the probability of intermediate regimes are the negative of the sum of the two terms reported in the table.

[a] Average change of the probabilities when $Y(i,t-1)$ switches from 0 to 1 and from 1 to 2.

[b] Change of the probabilities when the dummy switches from 0 to 1.

Table 3: Marginal Effects on Choice Probabilities

stitutions are all significant with expected signs. Countries with weak financial institutions plagued with bad loans (high NPL) are likely to adopt flexible de facto exchange rate regimes, while countries whose financial institutions are close to the Western standard (high FINQUAL) are likely to choose de facto fixed regimes. These results indicate that the ability of the financial institutions to endure exchange rate fluctuations plays a central role in this regard. Table 3 shows that a 1 percentage-point increase of NPL raises the probability for flexible de facto regimes by roughly 0.2 per cent, while the same amount of increase of FINQUAL raises the probability of a fixed regime by about 0.3 per cent.

Among the remaining variables, fiscal balances have an expected influence on regime choices, i.e., fiscal deficits (negative FISCAL) make flexible de facto exchange rate regimes more likely. But this effect is insignificant. The marginal increase in the probability of flexible regime is 0.3–0.5 per cent if the fiscal deficit increases by 1 percentage-point. Faster monetary expansion also raises the probability of flexible de facto regimes, at a ratio of 0.1–0.3 per cent for each percentage-point increase in M2GROW. This effect, though consistent with our expectation, is again insignificant except in equation (2). In contrast, current account balances play a significant role in the choice of de facto exchange rate regimes across all equations. Its positive coefficients show that current account deficits (negative CURRACCT) make de facto flexible regimes less likely: a 1 percentage-point increase of current account deficits (normalized by GDP) reduces the probability of flexible regimes by 0.8–1.2 per cent, but raises that of fixed regimes by 2.4–2.9 per cent. One explanation for this result is that countries ease controls on their exchange rates only at times when their external account is in a good position, so that allowing more flexibility in the exchange rate policy does not lead to immediate currency depreciations. Another explanation is that countries tend to finance current account deficits by utilizing international reserves, which also stabilizes exchange rates at the same time. Since episodes with stable exchange rates and volatile international reserves are classified as representing a de facto fixed regime, an association between current account deficits and de facto fixed regimes is a natural result.

Finally, the insignificant coefficients for the CIS dummy suggests that, as far as the choices of de facto exchange rate regimes are concerned, the CIS countries are not very much different from the CEECs, although the positive signs suggest that the former are more likely to adopt flexible regimes than the latter, which is similar to the choices of official exchange rate regimes. The overall performance of the models are satisfactory: in all specifications we can correctly predict at least two-thirds of de facto regime choices in transition economies.

5 Conclusions

In this paper we provide an empirical analysis of the de facto exchange rate regimes in transition economies in the 1990s. We apply the cluster analysis to the data on the ex-post movements of exchange rates and international reserves in these countries, and classify de facto exchange rate regimes according to the behavior of these variables. In contrast to the commonly used binary regime classification, we construct a trichotomous choice structure, with fixed, intermediate, and flexible de facto regimes as alternatives. The rising flexibility of these regime alternatives make them suitable for an ordered-choice model, which we use in our empirical analysis.

Our estimation results suggest that the choice of official exchange rate regimes constrains to some extent the choice of de facto exchange rate regimes. The choice of a fixed official regime has particularly strong influences on the choice of de facto regime, and a de facto fixed regime is more likely if an official fixed regime is adopted or viewed as desirable. Among other determinants of de facto regimes, high inflation rates, strong exchange-rate pass-through, better financial institutions, and large current account deficits make a de facto fixed exchange rate regime a more likely choice. On the contrary, a heavy burden of non-performing loans, large fiscal deficits, and fast monetary expansion all raise the chance for a more flexible de facto exchange rate regime. We also find that the CIS countries, although still favoring more flexible regimes, are not statistically different from the CEECs when choosing their de facto exchange rate regimes.

Appendix: Definitions of Variables and Data Sources

CISDUMMY: Dummy for the member countries of the Commonwealth of Independent States, including Armenia, Arzebaijan, Belarus, Georgia, Kazakhstan, Kyrgyz Republic, Moldova, Russia, Tajikistan, Turkmenistan, Ukraine, and Uzbekistan.

CURRACCT: Current account surplus (+) or deficit (−) as a ratio of GDP. Data source is IMF, International Financial Statistics (various issues).

FINQUAL: Index of quality of financial institutions, measured by the average of the EBRD indices for banking reform and for non-banking financial institutions reform. Data source is EBRD, Transition Report (2000).

FISCAL: General government budget balance, normalized by GDP. A positive (negative) entry denotes a surplus (deficit). Data source is IMF, International Financial Statistics (various issues), and EBRD, Transition Report (1999).

INFLATION: Change in the consumer prices, annual average, transformed using the formula $x^* = x/(1+x)$. Data source is IMF, International Financial Statistics (various issues).

M2GROW: Annual growth rate of broad money, transformed using the formula $x^* = x/(1+x)$. Data source is IMF, International Financial Statistics (various issues).

NPL: Ratio of non-performing loans in total loans. Data are from EBRD, Transition Report (2000) and IMF, Country Report (various issues).

PASSTHRU: Pass-through effects from exchange rate depreciation to inflation, measured by the correlation coefficient between one-quarter lagged monthly depreciation rates and current monthly inflation rates. Data source is IMF, International Financial Statistics (various issues).

BIBLIOGRAPHY

[1] Bénassy-Quéré, A., and B. Coeuré, 2002, "The Survival of Intermediate Exchange Rate Regimes," CEPII Working Paper 2002-07.

[2] Bubula, A., and Ý. Ötker-Robe, 2002, "The Evolution of Exchange Rate Regimes Since 1990: Evidence from De Facto Policies," IMF Working Paper No. 02/155.

[3] Calvo, A. G., and C. M. Reinhart, 2000, "Fear of Floating," mimeo, University of Maryland.

[4] Edwards, S., 1996, "The Determinants of the Choice Between Fixed and Flexible Exchange-rate Regimes," NBER Working Paper No. 5756.

[5] European Bank for Reconstruction and Development, 1999 and 2000, Transition Report (London: EBRD).

[6] Ghosh, A. R., A.-M. Gulde, J. Ostry, and H. Wolf, 1997, "Does the Nominal Exchange Rate Matter?," NBER Working Paper 5874.

[7] Hausmann, R., U. Panizza, and E. Stein, 2000, "Why Do Countries Float the Way They Float?," Inter-American Development Bank Working Paper No. 418.

[8] Heller, H. R., 1978, "Determinants of Exchange Rate Practices," Journal of Money, Credit and Banking, Vol. 10 (August): 308–321.

[9] Holden, P., M. Holden, and E. C. Suss, 1979, "The Determinants of Exchange Rate Flexibility: An Empirical Investigation," The Review of Economics and Statistics, Vol. LXI, No. 3 (August): 327–333.

[10] Juhn, G., and P. Mauro, 2002, "Long-Run Determinants of Exchange Rate Regimes: A Simple Sensitivity Analysis," IMF Working Paper No. 02/104.

[11] Krugman, P., 1979, "A Model of Balance of Payments Crises," Journal of Money, Credit and Banking, vol. 11 (August): 311–325.

[12] Levy-Yeyati, E., and F. Sturzenegger, 2000, "Classifying Exchange Rate Regimes: Deeds vs. Words," mimeo, Universidad Torcuato Di Tella, Buenos Aires.

[13] Melvin, M., 1985, "The Choice of an Exchange Rate System and Macroeconomic Stability," Journal of Money, Credit and Banking, Vol. 17, No. 4 (November, Part 1): 467–478.

[14] Poirson, H., 2001, "How Do Countries Choose Their Exchange Rate Regime?," IMF Working Paper 01/46.

[15] Savvides, A., 1990, "Real Exchange Rate Variability and the Choice of Exchange Rate Regime by Developing Countries," Journal of International Money and Finance, vol. 9: 440–454.

[16] Von Hagen, J., and J. Zhou, 2002a, "The Choice of Exchange Rate Regimes: An Empirical Analysis for Transition Economies," ZEI Working Paper B02-03, University of Bonn.

[17] Von Hagen, J., and J. Zhou, 2002b, "Official and De Facto Exchange Rate Regimes in Transition Countries," ZEI Working Paper B02-13, University of Bonn.

7 News-Magazine Monetarism

Edward Nelson[1]

1 INTRODUCTION

Alan Walters (1987, p. 427) observed of Milton Friedman, 'In effectiveness, breadth and scope, his only rival among the economists of the 20th century is Keynes.' Similarly, Alan Greenspan (1997) has remarked, 'His views have had as much, if not more, impact on the way we think about monetary policy... as those of any person in the last half of the twentieth century.' John Taylor (2001, p. 101) comments that Greenspan's words 'are no exaggeration. Many would say they do not go far enough.'[2]

As the above quotations suggest, Friedman's influence on academic work on monetary policy in the last several decades has been pervasive. Alan Walters, writing in 1965, noted, 'The last decade has... seen a revival of interest in money... Many of these studies have been produced or stimulated by Professor Milton Friedman... ' (1965, p. 2). Robert Clower, writing in September 1970, observed, 'Contemporary discussion of monetary policy centres upon the work of Milton Friedman... ' (1971, p. 25). That remained true seven years later, when Lewis (1977, p. 1) opened his Ph.D. dissertation with the words, 'Much, if not most, of the present controversy about the appropriate role for monetary policy centres around the views of Milton Friedman.' Meltzer (1969, pp. 25, 29)

---

[1]Milton Friedman, Mervyn King, David Laidler, Mervyn Lewis, Allan Meltzer, Athanasios Orphanides, Nicholas Oulton, Anna Schwartz, Chris Sims, Lars Svensson, Alan Walters, and Ken West provided valuable comments on earlier drafts of this paper. The usual disclaimers apply. I also thank participants at the May 2002 European Monetary Forum Conference on Money in honour of Alan Walters. The views expressed in this paper are my own and should not be interpreted as those of the Federal Reserve Bank of St. Louis or the Federal Reserve System.

[2]Beside Walters's (1987) entry on Friedman for the *New Palgrave Dictionary*, see Brunner and Meltzer (1993) and Hafer and Wheelock (2001) for discussion of Friedman's contributions in the context of other monetarist studies.

offered this perspective: 'I notice that people take various positions. One is that Milton Friedman is completely wrong; another is that Friedman is almost completely wrong. A third is that there is a grain of truth to what Friedman says... If we develop our analysis and concentrate on improving our understanding of money... rather than on the issue of whether Milton Friedman is wholly right or wholly wrong, we will have more progress.' By the 1980s, some resolution had taken place, with Friedman and Schwartz (1982, p. 70) observing that '[t]he climate of professional opinion has changed greatly' since the 1950s, and that the framework that they had advocated was now 'more nearly in the mainstream'.

Friedman's work continues to feature prominently in discussions of current policy issues by central bankers. For example, the archive on the European Central Bank's (ECB's) web page indicates[3] that the President, Vice-President, and Chief Economist of the ECB have all given speeches that include publications of Friedman's in their bibliography, with a variety of articles from 1951 to 1992 cited. The reach of Friedman's influence on monetary policy discussions ranges from the acceptance by policy-makers of the absence of a long-run inflation/unemployment trade-off,[4] to their use of specific phrases due to Friedman. For example, Otmar Issing, Chief Economist and Member of the Executive Board of the ECB, refers (2001, p. 291) to 'the validity of Friedman's famous dictum that monetary policy lags are long and variable', while Laurence Meyer, member of the Board of Governors of the Federal Reserve System from 1996 to 2002, observes that, 'Few economists would disagree that inflation is, as Milton Friedman taught us long ago, always and everywhere a monetary phenomenon' (Meyer, 2001, p. 5).[5] Perhaps the ultimate testament to Friedman's influence is that the word 'Friedmanite' (adjective and noun) appears in the *Oxford English Dictionary*.[6]

---

[3]As of April 2002.

[4]For further discussion of Friedman's views on the trade-off, see Section 5 below.

[5]These speeches also illustrate the limitations of any attempt to quantify the extent of Friedman's influence on monetary economics and monetary policy: both Issing and Meyer explicitly mention and quote Friedman, but do not include any Friedman paper in their bibliography—such as sources for Friedman's 'long and variable lag' expression (e.g. Friedman, 1961, p. 464) and his 'always and everywhere a monetary phenomenon' statement (e.g. Friedman, 1963, p. 17). On many monetary issues, Friedman's contribution has become so well-known that explicit reference to his work has become almost superfluous.

[6]The dictionary entry (1989, p. 192) also gives the variant 'Friedmanian', an adjective that seems to have originated earlier (Pesek and Saving, 1963, p. 353), and that has appeared in Friedman's work as well as that of Robert Lucas, Paul Samuelson, and Lars Svensson (see Friedman, 1970, p. 325; Lucas, 1972, p. 121;

It would, however, trivialise Friedman's contribution—and be no compliment to a person whom the *Economist* magazine once described as 'able to argue the hind leg off a horse' (1970, p. 37)—to claim that his views have been so integrated into the mainstream that they are now uncontroversial. On the contrary, debate continues on the extent to which the current monetary policy practice of inflation targeting can be regarded as an evolution from, or a sharp departure from, Friedman's policy proposals (e.g. Gavin, 1996; Barro, 1998; Leeson, 2000; Meyer, 2001). Similarly, opinion differs on the question of whether models used in today's macroeconomic analysis include the features emphasised by Friedman, or whether these models, instead, constitute a rejection of Friedman's views (e.g. Goodfriend and King, 1997; Woodford, 1999; Alvarez, Lucas, and Weber 2001; Nelson, 2002; Svensson, 2002). Moreover, as discussed in Section 4 below, it has been claimed that the findings of the recent vector autoregression (VAR) literature reject Friedman's interpretation of the post-war data (Sims, 1998).

In this paper, I examine some monetary policy issues discussed in the recent literature—doing so in light of commentary on those issues contained in some of Friedman's work. The specific aspect of Friedman's work on monetary policy that I draw upon is his series of columns in *Newsweek* magazine from 1966 to 1984. The analysis and commentary in these columns clarify Friedman's positions on a number of issues, including the behaviour of velocity (discussed in Section 3) and the role of monetary policy shocks in business cycle fluctuations (Section 4).

Friedman's *Newsweek* columns have themselves been a source of controversy. Walters (1987, p. 426) contends that in Friedman's *Newsweek* columns, 'high professional standards of integrity were maintained'. Nevertheless, other prominent scholars have criticised the *Newsweek* columns, on the grounds that they take more extreme positions on monetary policy than are present in Friedman's scientific work. Tobin (1970, p. 301) claimed that '[i]n his less guarded and more popular expositions' of his views on monetary policy, such as in his *Newsweek* columns, Friedman came 'close to asserting that [changes in money] are the unique cause' of nominal income variations. In 1983, Robert Solow gave a similar characterisation of Friedman's *Newsweek* columns (see Section 3 below). More recently, Paul Krugman has appeared to endorse these criticisms by expressing the opinion that Friedman 'has often been wrong, and... is sometimes willing to cut corners to win an argument' (Krugman, 1994, p. 92).

Samuelson, 1973, p. 169; Persson, Persson, and Svensson, 1987, p. 1423). Still further variants have appeared: Kane (1967, p. 432), Bhagwati (1977, p. 225), and Goldfeld (1982, p. 362) use the word 'Friedmanesque'.

One aspect of Friedman's *Newsweek* columns, namely their position on the macroeconomic effects of bond-financed tax changes, has been examined in detail previously (Gordon, 1974). Gordon (1976, p. 55) states that, while he once believed that there was 'an inconsistency between "academic journal monetarism" and "news-magazine monetarism"', a close examination indicates that the analysis of the effects of a tax increase in Friedman's *Newsweek* columns is not different in substance from that in his scientific work.[7] This leaves open the possibility that Friedman's discussions of monetary policy in his *Newsweek* columns were indeed—as alleged by Solow and Tobin—inconsistent with, and more extreme than, his scientific work. On the basis of an examination of the *Newsweek* columns, I argue below that these criticisms are unwarranted—i.e., that the positions on monetary policy and the quantity theory of money presented in Friedman's *Newsweek* columns are fully consistent with the positions he presented on those subjects in his scientific writings.

I restrict myself to the *positive* analysis in Friedman's columns—his discussion of the consequences of, and forces driving, actual US monetary policy actions—and so place normative aspects, such as Friedman's advocacy of a constant money growth rule, beyond the scope of this paper.[8] This positive analysis, alongside Friedman's scientific work, establishes that his views on monetary policy as carried out in practice in the post-war United States, were both more eclectic and more realistic than many of his critics have acknowledged. This casts doubt, as I show, on the claims that the findings of the structural VAR literature dramatically undermine Friedman's empirical positions.

2 The Columns

The source material for this paper is the close to 300 columns that Milton Friedman contributed to *Newsweek* approximately every three weeks, beginning with the September 26, 1966 edition and finishing with the January 16, 1984 edition; see Friedman and Friedman (1998, pp. 356–

[7] Beside those mentioned in the text, journal articles and books that have referred to the analysis in Friedman's *Newsweek* columns include Laidler (1982, p. 299), Evans (1984, p. 205), Bruno and Sachs (1985, p. 195), Ball and Mankiw (1995, pp. 1161–1162), B. Friedman (1988, p. 61) and Barnett (1997, p. 1171).

[8] Some columns where Friedman made policy recommendations nevertheless prove useful for obtaining information about his positive economics, e.g. concerning behaviour of monetary velocity, and the use of output gaps in analysis of the state of the economy (see Sections 3 and 5 below).

364). All but one of the columns published to August 1972 were reprinted in Friedman (1972); 31 of the additional 38 columns published to October 1974 were reprinted in Friedman (1975); and 60 of the additional 137 columns to October 1982 were reprinted in Friedman (1983). In addition to relying on the reprinted material, I obtained copies of all the non-reprinted columns from the original *Newsweek* editions.[9] In total, I judged 189 of Friedman's columns to cover monetary or macroeconomic policy issues, and these were the ones used for the analysis below.

3 Behaviour of Velocity

In an interview given in 1983, Robert M. Solow stated,

> As far as Friedman's arguments are concerned, I always thought that he sang two tunes. In the economic[s] profession, he was absolutely reasonable. I could find no distinction between his modern quantity theory of money and eclectic Keynesian economics. But in writing for *Newsweek*, he argued a hard monetarism, as against the soft monetarism of the "modern quantity theory". In hard monetarism, velocity is constant and *nothing* but the money supply matters for nominal GNP. I thought that was just factually wrong [Quoted in Klamer, 1984, p. 145]

Was the analysis in Friedman's *Newsweek* columns based on a constant-velocity set-up where '*nothing* but the money supply matters for nominal GNP'?[10]

From his earliest columns, Friedman stressed a long and variable time lag between monetary policy changes and the economy (e.g. January 9, 1967).[11] This alone implies an acceptance that velocity is not constant. But the *Newsweek* columns also accepted many other sources of velocity movements. As in Friedman (1956), the columns acknowledged that interest rates affected the cost of holding money balances, and so, the amount of nominal income consistent with a given quantity of money (e.g. January 23, 1967; May 12, 1975). In line with the framework in

[9] I used the US editions, as, from 1976 onward, non-US editions of *Newsweek* frequently replaced Friedman's columns with local material.

[10] Krugman (2002) similarly characterises Friedman's position as an 'insistence that changes in the money supply explain all of the economy's ups and downs'.

[11] Dates given in parentheses refer to the edition of *Newsweek* that contains the relevant column.

Friedman (1956) that made the rate of return on physical assets a separate argument in the money demand function, the columns gave declining inflation as a reason why some money growth would be absorbed into cash balances and not reflected in higher spending (October 16, 1972). Friedman also cited 'the desire of people to hold somewhat more money relative to their income as they become richer' (June 3, 1968) as grounds for why the long-term money growth rate would exceed the growth in real income under stable prices—consistent with the somewhat higher-than-unity real income elasticity of long-run money demand estimated by Friedman (1959) and Friedman and Schwartz (e.g., 1982) on US data. Another argument of Friedman and Schwartz (1963, 1982), namely that there was a negative relationship between money demand and economic confidence (and so a negative relationship between velocity and uncertainty), is reflected in the columns. Among the events Friedman cited in the columns as triggering uncertainty, and therefore falls in nominal income growth relative to monetary growth, were President Nixon's 1971 introduction of price controls (February 7, 1972), the Vietnam War (October 16, 1972), and the volatile behaviour of interest rates and the economy during the early 1980s recessions (July 25, 1983).

In addition to these money-demand-based factors, the columns accepted that other events could create divergences of nominal income growth from monetary growth, one example given being the 1970 General Motors strike (January 10, 1972).

Clearly, the economic analysis in Friedman's *Newsweek* columns was not based on a constant-velocity assumption. Rather, by stressing the long and variable lags in the money-income relationship, and by permitting variables that affect the cost of holding money to produce discrepancies between money supply growth and nominal income growth, the columns are consistent with Friedman's scientific writings on the subject.

4 Monetary Policy Shocks and Federal Reserve Policy

Christopher Sims (1998) argued that:

> There is a view, which Milton Friedman used to restate regularly some years ago, that erratic variation in monetary policy is the primary source of business cycle fluctuations, with each post-war US business cycle largely explainable via the pattern of monetary policy variations preceding it. Friedman used to defend this view via statistical analysis that took the time path of a monetary aggregate as a sufficient statistic

> for the time path of monetary policy. The recent VAR literature decisively undercuts this way [of] looking at history... [Its] conclusion [is] that the contribution of policy shocks to business cycle variation is modest...' [Sims, 1998, p. 934]

Leeper, Sims, and Zha (1996, p. 2) elaborate on the vector autoregression (VAR) findings that they believe contradict Friedman's statements:[12]

> Another robust conclusion, common across these [structural VAR] models, is that a large fraction of the variation in monetary policy instruments can be attributed to the systematic reaction of policy authorities to the state of the economy.

By way of contrast, Michael Woodford (1998, p. 393) writes:

> The VAR evidence... implies that the *unsystematic* component of monetary policy has not been a very important source of disturbances to the economy. That finding might be disquieting to some monetarists, though I actually suspect that it would be cheerfully accepted by Friedman and Schwartz.

And Bennett McCallum (1998, p. 307) has remarked,

> Friedman, Brunner and Meltzer have never contended that typical central bank behaviour does *in fact* feature exogenous money growth rates. On the contrary, these writers have frequently been critical of actual central banks precisely because of their responses (in terms of money growth rates) to cyclical conditions.

Similarly, Kenneth West (1993, p. 162) observes that the hypothesis 'that the money supply... is set in total disregard to the state of the economy' is 'not a view that Friedman or anyone else has advocated, as far as I know'.

The dispute implicit in the above quotations can be clarified by considering what is the appropriate parameterisation, in describing post-war US data, of the following reaction function for quarterly growth in the nominal money stock (Δm_t):

$$\Delta m_t = b_0 + b(L)\, e_{mt} + c(L)\boldsymbol{x}_t' \qquad (1)$$

[12] See also Sims (1980, p. 2; 1996, p. 117).

where b_0 is a constant, $\{e_{mt}\}$ is a sequence of exogenous policy shocks, x_t' is a vector of non-policy shocks, and $b(L)$ and $c(L)$ are (possibly infinite-order) polynomials in the lag operator L (so e.g. $b(L)\, e_{mt}$ is a distributed lag of the e_{mt} series). Equation (1) can be regarded as the money supply function implied by a monetary policy that permits money growth to expand or contract in response to movements in, for example, output, the exchange rate, or inflation. For since these endogenous variables can be written (using the Wold representation) as a function of the history of all the shocks hitting the economy, monetary policy can be regarded as allowing Δm_t to be a function of those shocks (see Christiano, Eichenbaum, and Evans, 1998).[13] Similarly, a version of equation (1) holds if the monetary authorities follow an interest rate rule; in that case, the shock vector x_t includes money demand shocks (see Poole, 1970).

At issue is whether, in his discussion of US monetary policy as it operated in practice in the post-war period,[14] Friedman's arguments implied that setting all elements of the coefficient matrix $c(L)$ to zero in the policy reaction function (1) was a good approximation. Sims's characterisation is that Friedman argued that policy shocks dominated the behaviour of Δm, and that these shocks contributed substantially to observed output variability. In that case, policy responses to non-policy shocks were not empirically important, so all entries of $c(L)$ could, indeed, be set to zero. On the other hand, the claim by West and others that Friedman accepted that monetary policy in practice reacted to the state of the economy, and so to non-monetary shocks, would imply that

---

[13] As a concrete example, suppose the policy rule implies a money supply reaction function of the form $\Delta m_t = d un_t + e_{mt}$, where $d > 0$ and un_t is the unemployment rate. Suppose further that in equilibrium, the policy rule and structure of the economy imply that the solution for unemployment in terms of underlying shocks is $un_t = c_1 e_{mt-1} + c_2 v_t + c_3 v_{t-1}$, where v_t is a real shock (assumed to be white noise). Then the equilibrium money relation is $\Delta m_t = d\,[c_1 e_{mt-1} + c_2 v_t + c_3 v_{t-1}] + e_{mt}$, which can be cast in the form of equation (1) by setting $b_0 = 0$, $b(L) = 1 + dc_1 L$, and $x_t = v_t$, and giving $c(L)$ a single row consisting of $dc_2 + dc_3 L$. Note that if either the policy shocks or non-policy shocks are serially correlated, it is assumed that they have been re-expressed, by substitution, in terms of underlying, white-noise innovations, with e_{mt} in equation (1) corresponding to the policy innovations and the x_t to the non-policy innovations.

[14] I stress that the Sims, Leeper–Sims–Zha, and Woodford discussions quoted above all refer to the post-war US data. For that reason, Woodford's characterisation of Friedman and Schwartz is not necessarily inconsistent with Cagan's (1978, p. 88) statement that Friedman and Schwartz (1963) found 'that money had been the most important source of disturbance to the economy over that [1867–1960] period'. In addition, Hetzel (2001) argues that the key inter-war monetary policy mistakes discussed by Friedman and Schwartz (1963) would not fall into the category of monetary policy shocks.

there is no presumption that $c(L)$ has only zero entries; nor that the policy shocks dominate the Δm_t series. In that case, Friedman's position on the importance of monetary policy would be disconnected from any claim about the empirical importance of monetary shocks—either for money growth variation, or for the behaviour of other variables, such as nominal income or physical output. Indeed, as discussed shortly, the Woodford argument quoted above rests on there being such a disconnection.

In a sense, the divergent positions of Sims and West given above can be regarded as different interpretations of Friedman's position on the exogeneity of money. But in discussing Friedman's position on exogeneity, it is important to distinguish two issues. Friedman and Schwartz certainly did regard it as 'appropriate to regard the money stock as exogenous (i.e., determined by the monetary authorities)' (Friedman and Schwartz, 1991, p. 42). That is, for particular paths for variables directly controllable by the central bank, such as open market operations or reserve requirement ratios, there was an implied path for money growth; and alterations in the paths of the control variables would change this money growth path in a predictable direction. That position of Friedman's is not the one principally under dispute by the recent VAR literature,[15] much of which implicitly takes a similar view by positing a money supply reaction function like equation (1) (e.g. Christiano, Eichenbaum, and Evans, 1998). Rather, the disputed question is a *second* exogeneity issue, namely whether Friedman's characterisation of actual Fed policy admitted non-zero responses to non-policy shocks in rule (1) above.[16]

Friedman's *Newsweek* columns provide a running commentary on Federal Reserve policy from the mid-1960s to the early 1980s, so they constitute a valuable basis for discriminating between Sims's and West's characterisations of Friedman's position on actual monetary policy. Here

---

[15] To be sure, some of the VAR literature, including Leeper, Sims, and Zha (1996), has focussed more on the details of the reserves market than Friedman typically did, and has included reserves-based measures of monetary policy in the analysis, rather than a single broader aggregate such as M1 or M2. But the Sims and Leeper-Sims-Zha papers quoted above do not claim that their crucial difference with Friedman is that money should be defined more narrowly; rather they argue that *all* monetary and reserve aggregates in practice respond to non-policy shocks, and that this contradicts Friedman's position.

[16] Alan Walters' position on the exogeneity of money in the United Kingdom is also clarified by making this distinction. It can reconcile his statement that 'the aggregate quantity of money is determined by the monetary authorities' (Walters, 1970, p. 42) with his observation that 'it is a fair caricature to suppose that the [UK] authorities fix the interest rate and supply the market with the quantity of money needed to sustain that rate... [T]here was in fact no control over the reserve base...' (Walters, 1970, pp. 43, 62).

are the most pertinent excerpts on the subject from the *Newsweek* columns:

'Throughout the post-war period... the Fed has tended to delay action and then, when it had to act, to go too far.' (October 30, 1967).

'Recent monetary growth partly reflects the Fed's reaction to the stock market crisis in May and to a Federal debt issue... .' (July 6, 1970).

'The early stages of the [1960s] inflation produced a sharp overreaction by the Fed that caused a credit crunch in 1966 and a mini-recession in 1967. Overreaction to that mini-recession set it off on the accelerating inflation of 1967 to 1969. Fine-tuning with a sledgehammer!' (July 26, 1971).

'... any attempt to use monetary policy for fine-tuning is likely simply to introduce additional instability. And this is indeed what has happened.' (February 7, 1972).

'The Fed currently attempts to control the money supply indirectly, by controlling a particular interest rate (the Federal funds rate).' (December 8, 1975).

'[Of the] pressures impinging on the [Federal Reserve] System... the most important are the pressures to create money in order to pay off exploding federal spending and in order to promote the goal of "full employment".' (October 3, 1977).

'... pressures from Congress and the Administration to finance rising government spending and to keep interest rates low are a major reason for high monetary growth... .' (April 24, 1978).

'In mid-1982, alarmed at the severity of the recession and at the threat of an international debt crisis, [the Fed] stepped hard on the accelerator.' (January 16, 1984).

As the above quotations indicate, the columns recognised that the Federal Reserve reacted to economic developments, including movements in the stock market, the international economy, inflation, output, and federal deficits. They are also explicit in recognising the Fed's use of an interest rate instrument.[17] They clearly do not imply a monetary

[17] As Goodhart (1989, p. 331) observes, when discussing 'the level of short-term interest rates, [Friedman] had no doubts that these were normally determined by the authorities, and could be changed by them'. In his analysis of the UK situation, Alan Walters also recognised that policy-makers had an interest rate reaction function, observing that '[t]he government increases Bank rate when prices start or are likely to start rising too rapidly' (Walters, 1970, p. 46). In comments on an earlier version of this paper, Allan Meltzer has remarked, 'We all understood that central banks controlled interest rates not money. But looking at interest rates cannot tell me whether money is easier or tighter unless I observe how the stock of money changes relative to the demand for money.'

policy reaction function in which only policy shocks matter for monetary growth.

What does this imply for Friedman's stress on the importance of monetary policy? There is no doubt that, both in his scientific work and elsewhere, Friedman argued, as he put it in his October 30, 1967 column, that '[i]nstead of offsetting other forces making for economic instability, the Fed has itself been a major source of instability', and that he described US monetary policy as 'erratic', as Sims notes.[18] Sims's characterisation of Friedman's view is that monetary policy generated output volatility in the post-war US by injecting an extra source of disturbance, namely the policy shocks e_{mt} in equation (1). In the same vein, Yoshikawa (1993, p. 121) claims that Friedman is among the 'monetarists... [who] consider unanticipated changes in the money supply exogenously caused by central banks to be the major shock driving economic fluctuations'.[19]

But monetary policy does not have to generate policy shocks in order to be a contributor to total output volatility. A systematic monetary policy rule, that feeds back on the state of the economy and contributes no extra type of shock, is capable of magnifying cyclical variability. In terms of equation (1), such policies correspond to zero values for the $b(L)$ coefficients combined with non-zero, but inappropriate, choices for the feedback coefficients that appear in the $c(L)$ matrix. Such a policy would not introduce policy shocks, but would instead, exacerbate cyclical fluctuations by propagating the effects of non-policy shocks.

The evidence from the *Newsweek* columns suggests that Friedman did recognise that there was considerable response of monetary policy to the state of the economy. That Friedman nevertheless blamed the Fed for creating instability is in keeping with the point in Friedman's scientific work that stabilisation policy can be destabilising (e.g. Friedman, 1953).[20] Bad feedback rules, not an emphasis on the importance

---

[18] For example, in his July 5, 1971 column, Friedman asked, 'Why must the Federal Reserve swing so erratically from side to side?'

[19] Similarly, Canova and De Nicoló (2002, p. 1132) claim: 'Friedman and Schwartz (1960) [*sic*]... argued that rates of change in money were good approximations to monetary policy disturbances.'

[20] LeRoy (1995, p. 238) argues that 'Friedman opposed discretionary policy on substantive grounds: policy-makers can be expected neither to diagnose the problem accurately enough nor to implement a policy response quickly enough to affect the macroeconomic environment in the right direction.' This opposition in principle applies to versions of rule (1) with no policy shock terms. For explicit denials by monetarists that they emphasise only policy shocks, see Friedman and Schwartz (1982, p. 552) and Brunner (1983, p. 50).

of monetary policy shocks, are central to this critique.[21] In keeping with this, Congdon (1982, p. 15) observes that 'Friedman has... only contended that [monetary] targets prevent [the effects of] non-monetary disturbances... from being exaggerated'.

To avoid misunderstanding, the present author does not disagree with the finding of the structural VAR literature, such as Leeper, Sims, and Zha (1996), that monetary policy shocks account for a relatively small fraction of the post-war variation in both monetary policy instruments and in output. Rather, my point is that such findings are not a contradiction of Friedman's position. The above quotations from Friedman reinforce West's contention that Friedman accepted the existence of systematic monetary policy responses to the state of the economy.[22] And the relative unimportance of monetary policy shocks certainly does not imply that systematic monetary policy cannot matter very much for cyclical fluctuations, nor that ill-chosen systematic monetary policy rules are not destabilising. As Woodford (1998, p. 393) observes, 'The VAR evidence... in no way implies that the nature of *systematic* monetary policy does not greatly matter for the effects (upon both inflation and output) of *other* kinds of disturbances.' Christiano, Eichenbaum, and Evans (1999, fn. 4) concur that the VAR literature 'is silent' regarding 'the impact of the systematic component of monetary policy on aggregate output and the price level.' Walsh (1998, p. 33) gives an example: 'If policy is completely characterised as a feedback rule on the economy, so that there are no exogenous policy shocks, then the VAR methodology would conclude that monetary policy doesn't matter... [I]t does not follow that policy is unimportant; the response of the economy to non-policy shocks may depend importantly on the way monetary policy endogenously adjusts.' Indeed, as Brunner and Meltzer (1993, p. 24) argue, 'choice of monetary regime can increase stability... by eliminating

[21] The closest to a contradiction of this position that I know of in Friedman's writings is his criticism of the real business cycle (RBC) literature on the grounds that its emphasis on 'technological change as the chief source of disturbances... has exaggerated their importance relative to monetary disturbances' (Friedman, 1993, p. 173). The RBC literature, however, attributes literally *no* output variability to monetary shocks. So RBC work can be criticised for understating the importance of monetary shocks, even if these shocks in practice account for only a modest portion of cyclical variability.

[22] Indeed, Friedman and Schwartz pointed to the fact that US history had featured several different monetary policy feedback rules (different arrangements for the provision of money to the economy), yet considerable consistency in the money/nominal income relation, as evidence of the importance of money for economic behaviour. On this, see e.g. Friedman (1961, p. 450), Friedman and Schwartz (1970, p. 139), Brunner (1986, p. 45), Hammond (1996, p. 97), and Batini and Nelson (2001).

(or reducing) the induced monetary responses that augment real shocks.'

It is also worth noting that, unlike the present VAR literature, two of Friedman's most prominent contemporary critics—James Tobin in the US and Nicholas Kaldor in the UK—did not interpret Friedman's analysis of the data as resting on the proposition of negligible response of monetary policy to the state of the economy. For example, Tobin (1976, p. 95) observed that 'central banks, according to Friedman's own criticism of them, supplied money to accommodate the economy's demands.' And Kaldor (1985, p. 13) noted that '[i]t was nowhere stated in the writings of Friedman... that the quantity theory of money *only* holds...[when] the monetary authorities are sufficiently "competent" to regulate the money supply.'

All in all, I find that there is considerable support in the *Newsweek* columns for Woodford's conjecture that the VAR findings 'would be cheerfully accepted by Friedman and Schwartz'.

5 Comparisons with Paul Samuelson's *Newsweek* Columns[23]

For much of Friedman's period as a *Newsweek* columnist, Paul Samuelson also had a *Newsweek* column.[24] Though Samuelson's column often dealt with macroeconomic policy, he rarely covered precisely the same subject matter as Friedman's contemporaneous column, so a systematic comparison of forecasts made in each column is difficult. However, on two key macroeconomic issues, there is a major contrast in the positions advanced by each columnist.

5.1 The Inflation/Unemployment Trade-off

In his academic work, Paul Samuelson was jointly responsible for the proposition that there was a permanent trade-off between unemployment and inflation in the US (Samuelson and Solow, 1960). He continued this theme in his *Newsweek* columns in the late 1960s. In his July 14, 1969,

---

[23]The exercise reported in this section was independently suggested by Milton Friedman, Athanasios Orphanides, and Anna Schwartz in their comments on an earlier version of this paper.

[24]Approximately 250 columns by Samuelson were published in the editions from September 19, 1966 to May 11, 1981. All but seven of the columns to April 1973 were reprinted in Samuelson (1973); an additional hundred columns to 1981 were reprinted in Samuelson (1983). I examined these reprints and also obtained copies of all the non-reprinted columns from the original *Newsweek* editions.

column, Samuelson stated that the inflation experienced by the US since 1965 had confirmed his 1960 belief in a Phillips curve. In his October 26, 1970 column, Samuelson again affirmed, 'The trade-off between full employment and price stability does constitute a cruel dilemma for any Administration... .'

Friedman, of course, argued in his scientific work that there was no long-run trade-off: real benefits of inflationary policies would wear off once the new inflation rate was embedded in inflationary expectations (Friedman, 1958, 1966). Macroeconomic stimulus that pushed inflation to a higher rate could not lower unemployment permanently below its natural rate—or, to put the point more positively, full employment and growth at potential were not incompatible with price stability. Friedman expressed these themes in an early *Newsweek* column entitled 'Inflationary Recession' (October 17, 1966). There he noted that in recent years, 'rising prices stimulated economic activity because they were rising faster than people had anticipated... The only way to make an expansion of this kind last is... still more rapid inflation'. Instead, he recommended a monetary and fiscal program consistent policy would 'prepare the basis for a subsequent non-inflationary expansion'.

The views advanced by Friedman in the 1960s that the long-run Phillips curve was vertical, and that inflation and unemployment could rise together as the short-run trade-off wore off, have proved more durable than Samuelson's 1960s view that there existed a permanent trade-off. Indeed, in his March 21, 1973 column, Samuelson conceded, 'Years ago we'd have called you neurotic if you worried about inflation and recession at the same time. Now... [w]e've learned about "stagflation"... .'

5.2 Productive Potential and the Output Gap

Orphanides (2000a, 2000b) argues that a major source of monetary policy errors in the US in the 1960s and 1970s was inaccurate information on the degree of slack in the economy. A key problem was that '[a]s is now evident, real-time estimates of potential output severely overstated the economy's capacity' (Orphanides, 2000a, p. 16). Orphanides notes that Friedman was consistently cautious about relying on output gap estimates, but contends that policy-makers and other influential outside economists took the official output gap series seriously. As a result, policy-makers permitted what now appear easy monetary policy settings—a serious mistake in light of the double-digit inflation that resulted. Taylor (2000), by contrast, argues that 'potential GDP and its growth rate became politicised as early as the late 1960s; serious economic analysts... paid no attention' to the official figures. Paul Samuelson's views on the output gap over this period are of interest because they suggest whether some 'serious' economists did accept the validity of the official gap estimates.

Samuelson supported the use of the output gap in monetary policy and, in the late 1960s, endorsed the official quantitative estimates of the gap. In his July 14, 1969 column, Samuelson praised the Kennedy Administration's economists for introducing the output gap concept into policy, and declared that their estimate of 'growth of [US] real potential [GDP] at 4-plus per cent a year' had been vindicated.

In his August 2, 1971 column, Samuelson reaffirmed that the US had a 'more than 4 per cent' potential output growth rate, and that 'to get [unemployment] down to... the full-employment level, we need real growth rates of 5 and 6 per cent from now to November 1972'. He emphasised that this was based on a conservative (i.e. high) estimate of the full-employment rate of unemployment. His estimate of the required real growth needed to restore full employment implies an output gap of about −2.25 per cent in mid-1971. Yet this estimate, which Samuelson considered if anything biased toward zero, compares to a present (2002) Congressional Budget Office estimate of the 1971 Q2 output gap of only −0.4 per cent.[25] Thus even a lower-bound estimate by Samuelson of the gap appears in retrospect to have overestimated the amount of slack in the economy in 1971 by nearly 2 per cent. Later, in his February 18, 1974, column, Samuelson described 5.5 to 6 per cent unemployment as not 'remotely near' full employment.

Errors in real-time estimates of the output gap became larger in the mid-1970s due to failure to incorporate the effects of the slowdown in productivity growth from 1973 (Orphanides, 2000a). Taylor (2000) argues that while this slowdown was not incorporated into published output gap estimates until 1977, and then only partially, it was recognised by practitioners and observers much earlier, so that the official series—which gave a double-digit negative gap in 1975—was not taken seriously.

The evidence suggests, however, that Samuelson, while not as erroneous in his views on the output gap as the official estimates, did seriously overstate the degree of excess capacity in the economy in the mid-1970s. For example, in his January 12, 1976, column, Samuelson

[25] My figure for Samuelson's estimate is based on assuming that he set potential growth to 4 per cent a year, and believed that 5.5 per cent average growth was needed in the six quarters from 1971 Q3 to 1972 Q4 inclusive to deliver a zero output gap in 1972 Q4. Other interpretations of Samuelson's statement give a larger estimate of the output gap in 1971 Q2. For example, if I take Samuelson's statement that 'more than 4 per cent' potential GDP growth rate is to mean 4.25 per cent, and his estimate of '5 to 6 per cent' required growth to mean 6 per cent, then the implied estimate of the output gap is about −2.6 per cent.

wrote, 'What we need is a couple of years of 6 to 7 per cent real growth followed in the final years of the 1970s by a growth rate of about 5 per cent.'[26] In addition, in his 1975 and 1976 columns Samuelson was still giving the US potential output growth rate as 4 per cent, failing to acknowledge a post-1973 slowdown (May 6, 1975; July 28, 1975; October 18, 1976).[27] Together, these statements suggest Samuelson's 1976 estimate of the output gap in the US as of late 1975 was −7 per cent, not as pessimistic as the official output gap estimate at the time,[28] but much more so than the current CBO estimate of a 1975 Q4 output gap of −3.6 per cent. Moreover, as is clear from the quotations, Samuelson advocated targets for real GDP expansion based on his estimate of the gap.

By contrast, output gap measurement issues and the productivity slowdown had little effect on the analysis in Friedman's columns. This was not because of superior judgement on his part regarding the behaviour of productive potential; Friedman's columns provide no evidence of greater insight than other observers about the extent and timing of the 1973 productivity slowdown. But both Friedman's inflation forecasts and his policy recommendations were largely insulated from output gap measurement error. Because Friedman eschewed recommendations of countercyclical monetary policy, he did not advance, as Samuelson did, target paths for real GDP growth based on the estimated distance of the economy from full employment. And his inflation forecasts were informed mainly by the behaviour of prior monetary growth. This approach was vulnerable to lasting changes in velocity growth—for example, the break in the trend of M1 velocity in the early 1980s. But one advantage of Friedman's inflation projections was that they were relatively insensitive to errors in measuring the output gap. A slowdown in potential GDP

---

[26] Similarly, in his May 6, 1975 column, Samuelson wrote that '[a] prudent target for annual real GNP growth... would be at least 6 per cent for some time'.

[27] Samuelson's columns of August 19, 1974 and January 1, 1979 instead presented a range for potential GDP growth of '3 to 4 per cent', which still seems high by post-1973 standards. Earlier, in a May 21, 1973 column, Samuelson gave a range of '4 to 5 per cent' for annual growth in potential.

[28] Estimates of the output gap in real time had the series at around −12 per cent at the end of 1975 (Orphanides, 2000a, Figure 11). Prominent economists other than Samuelson also overestimated the output gap in the 1970s. For example, Tobin (1975) proposed a programme of 10 per cent GDP growth in 1976 and 7 per cent in 1977, contended that this programme was consistent with falling inflation, and stated that the growth of potential was (still) 4 per cent per year. This implies an output gap in late 1975 of −9 per cent, which, like Samuelson's and the real-time official series, suggested considerably more slack than today's estimates of the output gap in 1975. Tobin's denial of a change in the behaviour of potential output in the 1970s was noted by Brunner (1983, p. 50).

growth does raise the inflation rate associated with a maintained money growth rate, and so will induce a bias in inflation forecasts based on money growth. But this error does not grow over time, whereas forecasts of inflation using the output gap have cumulating errors when a productivity slowdown is not recognised.

Friedman's and Samuelson's different approaches were reflected in the January 10, 1977 edition of *Newsweek*, a rare occasion where both economists contributed columns to the same issue. Each column provided recommendations for economic policy to the new administration. Samuelson endorsed 'the 6 per cent real rate of growth [for 1977] agreed upon a reasonable target by President-elect Carter and Fed chairman Arthur Burns', and recommended an ongoing programme of monetary expansion to bring the unemployment rate 'to below 6 per cent' by 1979.[29] Friedman argued for 'a gradual reduction in the rate of monetary growth to a level consistent with zero inflation... That is the policy I favoured a year ago, six months ago, and shall favour six months from now.'

If the evidence from Samuelson's columns is any indication, two main points emerge regarding outside observers' estimates of the output gap during the 1970s. First, Taylor (2000) appears correct that some key commentators did not believe that the output gap was as negative in the mid-1970s as the official statistics suggested. Secondly, there is nevertheless support for Orphanides' contention that outside observers in the 1970s did have estimates of the output gap based on potential GDP growth assumptions that were no longer valid, and that 'none of these estimates was anywhere as pessimistic as the present perspective would suggest would have been appropriate' (2000a, p. 24). Samuelson's columns also support Orphanides' claim that economists made policy recommendations based on these severely exaggerated estimates of the output gap. Friedman's *Newsweek* discussions, like his other work, are notable for not making these kinds of policy prescriptions.

6 Conclusions

In this paper, I looked at Milton Friedman's *Newsweek* columns on monetary policy. This examination provided support for Walters's (1987)

[29] Unemployment did fall to consistently below 6 per cent in the first half of 1979, by which time monetary policy had shifted to tightening in response to the behaviour of inflation, which, by the CPI annual inflation measure, had risen from around 5 per cent in late 1976 to over 11 per cent by mid-1979. See Orphanides (2000a, 2000b) for discussion of monetary policy developments in the 1970s.

position that the columns were consistent with Friedman's academic writings. I established that the columns did not claim that the money supply was the only variable relevant for nominal income fluctuations; the columns instead took an eclectic view on the issue consistent with the modern quantity theory familiar from Friedman's scientific work. The columns also shed light on Friedman's position that post-war monetary policy (up to the early 1980s) primarily contributed to, rather than dampened, variations in physical output. Some have interpreted this position as implying that the Fed added to overall cyclical variability by contributing exogenous policy shocks; others have interpreted it as implying that the Fed magnified the effects of non-policy shocks through an inappropriate monetary policy reaction function. The *Newsweek* columns, like many of Friedman's scientific writings, are consistent with the second view, and so indicate that recent VAR evidence on the relative unimportance of monetary policy shocks does not undercut Friedman's position. And, like Friedman's other work, the columns were sceptical about the trade-offs and growth opportunities faced by the US economy—a scepticism not shared by many of Friedman's contemporaries, but now part of consensus macroeconomic opinion.

BIBLIOGRAPHY

[1] Alvarez, Fernando, Robert E. Lucas, Jr, and Warren E. Weber (2001). 'Interest Rates and Inflation', American Economic Review (Papers and Proceedings), 91, 219–225.

[2] Ball, Laurence, and N. Gregory Mankiw (1995). 'Relative Price Changes as Aggregate Supply Shocks', Quarterly Journal of Economics, 109, 161–193.

[3] Barnett, William A. (1997). 'Which Road Leads to Stable Money Demand?', Economic Journal, 107, 1171–1185.

[4] Barro, Robert J. (1998). 'Milton Friedman: Being Right Is the Best Revenge', Business Week, July 13, 13.

[5] Batini, Nicoletta, and Edward Nelson (2001). 'The Lag from Monetary Policy Actions to Inflation: Friedman Revisited', International Finance, 4, 381–400.

[6] Bhagwati, Jagdish N. (1977). 'Harry G. Johnson', Journal of International Economics, 7, 221–229.

[7] Brunner, Karl (1983). 'Has Monetarism Failed?', Cato Journal, 3, 23–62.

[8] Brunner, Karl (1986). 'Fiscal Policy in Macro Theory: A Survey and Evaluation'. In R.W. Hafer (ed.), The Monetary Versus Fiscal Policy Debate: Lessons from Two Decades, Rowman and Allanheld. 33–116.

[9] Brunner, Karl, and Allan H. Meltzer (1993). Money and the Economy: Issues in Monetary Analysis, Cambridge University Press.

[10] Bruno, Michael, and Jeffrey Sachs (1985). Economics of Worldwide Stagflation, Harvard University Press.

[11] Cagan, Phillip (1978). 'Monetarism in Historical Perspective'. In T. Mayer *et al.*, The Structure of Monetarism, W.W. Norton. 85–93.

[12] Canova, Fabio, and Gianni De Nicoló (2002). 'Monetary Disturbances Matter for Business Fluctuations in the G-7', Journal of Monetary Economics, 49, 1131–1159.

[13] Christiano, Lawrence J., Martin Eichenbaum, and Charles L. Evans (1998). 'Modeling Money'. NBER Working Paper No. 6371.

[14] Christiano, Lawrence J., Martin Eichenbaum, and Charles L. Evans (1999). 'Monetary Policy Shocks: What Have We Learned and to What End?'. In J.B. Taylor and M. Woodford (eds.), Handbook of Macroeconomics, Vol 1A, North Holland. 65–148.

[15] Clower, Robert W. (1971). 'Theoretical Foundations of Monetary Policy'. In G. Clayton, J.C. Gilbert, and R. Sedgwick (eds.), Monetary Theory and Monetary Policy in the 1970s, Oxford University Press. 15–28.

[16] Congdon, Tim (1982). Monetary Control in Britain, Macmillan.

[17] The Economist (1970). 'Review: The Optimum Quantity of Money and Other Essays', January 3, 37.

[18] Evans, Paul (1984). 'The Effects on Output of Money-Growth and Interest-Rate Volatility in the United States', Journal of Political Economy, 92, 204–222.

[19] Friedman, Benjamin M. (1988). 'Lessons on Monetary Policy from the 1980s', Journal of Economic Perspectives, 2, 51–72.

[20] Friedman, Milton (1953). 'The Effects of a Full-Employment Policy on Economic Stability: A Formal Analysis'. In M. Friedman, Essays in Positive Economics, University of Chicago Press. 117–132.

[21] Friedman, Milton (1956). 'The Quantity Theory of Money—A Restatement'. In M. Friedman (ed.), Studies in the Quantity Theory of Money, University of Chicago Press. 3–21.

[22] Friedman, Milton (1958). 'The Supply of Money and Changes in Prices and Output'. In The Relationship of Prices to Economic Stability and Growth. Joint Economic Committee, 85th Congress, 2nd session. 241-256. Reprinted in M. Friedman, The Optimum Quantity of Money and Other Essays, Aldine, 1969. 171–187.

[23] Friedman, Milton (1959). 'The Demand for Money: Some Theoretical and Empirical Results', Journal of Political Economy, 67, 327–351.

[24] Friedman, Milton (1961). 'The Lag in Effect of Monetary Policy', Journal of Political Economy, 69, 447–466.

[25] Friedman, Milton (1963). Inflation: Causes and Consequences, Asia Publishing House.

[26] Friedman, Milton (1966). 'Comments'. In G.P. Shultz and R.Z. Aliber (eds.), Guidelines: Informal Controls and the Market Place, University of Chicago Press. 55–61.

[27] Friedman, Milton (1970). '"Money and Income: Post Hoc Ergo Propter Hoc?": Comment', Quarterly Journal of Economics, 84, 318–327.

[28] Friedman, Milton (1972). An Economist's Protest, Thomas Horton.

[29] Friedman, Milton (1975). There's No Such Thing as a Free Lunch, Open Court.

[30] Friedman, Milton (1983). Bright Promises, Dismal Performance: An Economist's Protest, Harcourt Brace Jovanovich.

[31] Friedman, Milton (1993). 'The "Plucking Model" of Business Fluctuations Revisited', Economic Inquiry, 31, 171–177.

[32] Friedman, Milton, and Rose Friedman (1998). Two Lucky People: Memoirs, University of Chicago Press.

[33] Friedman, Milton, and Anna J. Schwartz (1963). A Monetary History of the United States, 1867–1960, Princeton University Press.

[34] Friedman, Milton, and Anna J. Schwartz (1970). Monetary Statistics of the United States, Columbia University Press.

[35] Friedman, Milton, and Anna J. Schwartz (1982). Monetary Trends in the United States and the United Kingdom: Their Relation to Income, Prices, and Interest Rates, 1867–1975, University of Chicago Press.

[36] Friedman, Milton, and Anna J. Schwartz (1991). 'Alternative Approaches to Analyzing Economic Data', American Economic Review, 81, 39–49.

[37] Gavin, William T. (1996). 'The FOMC in 1995: A Step Closer to Inflation Targeting?', Federal Reserve Bank of St Louis Review, 78, 29–47.

[38] Goldfeld, Stephen M. (1982). 'Rules, Discretion, and Policy', American Economic Review (Papers and Proceedings), 72, 361–366.

[39] Goodfriend, Marvin, and Robert G. King (1997). 'The New Neoclassical Synthesis and the Role of Monetary Policy', NBER Macroeconomics Annual, 12, 231–283.

[40] Goodhart, Charles A.E. (1989). 'The Conduct of Monetary Policy', Economic Journal, 99, 293–346.

[41] Gordon, Robert J. (ed.) (1974). Milton Friedman's Monetary Framework: A Debate with His Critics, University of Chicago Press.

[42] Gordon, Robert J. (1976). 'Comments on Franco Modigliani and Albert Ando'. In Jerome L. Stein (ed.), Monetarism, North Holland. 52–66.

[43] Greenspan, Alan (1997). 'Remarks at the 15th Anniversary Conference of the Center for Economic Policy Research at Stanford University', September 5.

[44] Hafer, R.W., and David C. Wheelock (2001). 'The Rise and Fall of a Policy Rule: Monetarism at the St. Louis Fed, 1968–1986', Federal Reserve Bank of St. Louis Review, 83, 1–24.

[45] Hammond, J. Daniel (1996). Theory and Measurement: Causality Issues in Milton Friedman's Monetary Economics, Cambridge University Press.

[46] Hetzel, Robert L. (2001). 'Identification: The Taylor Rule', Manuscript, Federal Reserve Bank of Richmond.

[47] Issing, Otmar (2001). 'The Monetary Transmission Process: Concluding Remarks'. In Deutsche Bundesbank (ed.), The Monetary Transmission Process: Recent Developments and Lessons for Europe. Palgrave. 283–293.

[48] Kaldor, Nicholas (1985). 'How Monetarism Failed', Challenge, 28, 4–13.

[49] Kane, Edward J. (1967). 'Topics in Money: Discussion', American Economic Review (Papers and Proceedings), 57, 432–433.

[50] Klamer, Arjo (1984). The New Classical Macroeconomics: Conversations with the New Classical Economists and Their Opponents, Wheatsheaf Books.

[51] Krugman, Paul (1994). Peddling Prosperity: Economic Sense and Nonsense in the Age of Diminished Expectations, W.W. Norton.

[52] Krugman, Paul (2002). 'Missing James Tobin', New York Times, March 12.

[53] Laidler, David (1982). 'Friedman and Schwartz on Monetary Trends: A Review Article', Journal of International Money and Finance, 1, 293–305.

[54] Leeper, Eric M., Christopher A. Sims, and Tao Zha (1996). 'What Does Monetary Policy Do?', Brookings Papers on Economic Activity, 27, 1–63.

[55] Leeson, Robert (2000). 'Inflation, Disinflation, and the Natural Rate of Unemployment: A Dynamic Framework for Policy Analysis'. In D.W.R. Gruen (ed.), The Australian Economy in the 1990s, Reserve Bank of Australia. 124–175.

[56] LeRoy, Stephen F. (1995). 'On Policy Regimes'. In K.D. Hoover (ed.), Macroeconometrics: Developments, Tensions, and Prospects, Kluwer. 235–251.

[57] Lewis, Mervyn K. (1977). Time Lags and the Effectiveness of Monetary Policy in Australia. Ph.D. Thesis, University of Adelaide, September.

[58] Lucas, Robert E., Jr. (1972). 'Expectations and the Neutrality of Money', Journal of Economic Theory, 4, 103–124.

[59] McCallum, Bennett T. (1998). 'Comment: Mayer's Version of the Monetarist vs. Keynesian Debate'. In R.E. Backhouse, D.M. Hausman, U. Maki, and A. Salanti (eds.), Macroeconomics and Methodology, Macmillan. 303–310.

[60] Meltzer, Allan H. (1969). 'The Role of Money in National Economic Policy: Panel Discussion'. In Controlling Monetary Aggregates. Proceedings of the Monetary Conference held on Nantucket Island, June 8–10, 1969, Federal Reserve Bank of Boston. 25–29.

[61] Meyer, Laurence H. (2001). 'Inflation Targets and Inflation Targeting', Federal Reserve Bank of St Louis Review, 83, 1–13.

[62] Nelson, Edward (2002). 'The Future of Monetary Aggregates in Monetary Policy Analysis'. Manuscript, Bank of England.

[63] Orphanides, Athanasios (2000a). 'The Quest for Prosperity without Inflation'. ECB Working Paper No. 15.

[64] Orphanides, Athanasios (2000b). 'Activist Stabilisation Policy and Inflation: The Taylor Rule in the 1970s'. FEDS paper 2000-13, Federal Reserve Board.

[65] The Oxford English Dictionary: Second Edition, Volume VI (1989), Clarendon Press.

[66] Persson, Mats, Torsten Persson, and Lars E.O. Svensson (1987). 'Time Consistency of Fiscal and Monetary Policy', Econometrica, 55, 1419–1431.

[67] Pesek, Boris P., and Thomas R. Saving (1963). 'Monetary Policy, Taxes, and the Rate of Interest', Journal of Political Economy, 71, 347–362.

[68] Poole, William (1970). 'Optimal Choice of Monetary Policy Instruments in a Simple Stochastic Macro Model', Quarterly Journal of Economics, 84, 197–216.

[69] Samuelson, Paul A. (1973). The Samuelson Sampler' W. W. Norton.

[70] Samuelson, Paul A. (1983). Economics from the Heart: A Samuelson Sampler, Harcourt Brace Jovanovich.

[71] Samuelson, Paul A., and Robert M. Solow (1960). 'Analytical Aspects of Anti-Inflation Policy', American Economic Review, 50, 177–194.

[72] Sims, Christopher A. (1980). 'Macroeconomics and Reality', Econometrica, 48, 1–48.

[73] Sims, Christopher A. (1996). 'Macroeconomics and Methodology', Journal of Economic Perspectives, 10, 105–120.

[74] Sims, Christopher A. (1998). 'Comment on Glenn Rudebusch's "Do Measures of Monetary Policy in a VAR Make Sense?"', International Economic Review, 39, 933–941.

[75] Svensson, Lars E.O. (2002). Lecture Notes: Macroeconomic Theory, Monetary Theory and Policy. Manuscript, Princeton University.

[76] Taylor, John B. (2000). 'Comments on Athanasios Orphanides' "The Quest for Prosperity without Inflation"'. Manuscript, Stanford University.

[77] Taylor, John B. (2001). 'An Interview with Milton Friedman', Macroeconomic Dynamics, 5, 101–131.

[78] Tobin, James (1970). 'Money and Income: Post Hoc Ergo Propter Hoc?', Quarterly Journal of Economics, 84, 301–317.

[79] Tobin, James (1975). 'Monetary Policy, Inflation, and Unemployment'. In A.T. Sommers (ed.), Answers to Inflation and Recession: Economic Policies for a Modern Society, Conference Board. 2–19. Reprinted in J. Tobin, Essays in Economics: Theory and Policy, The Papers of James Tobin, Volume 3, MIT Press, 1982. 14–31.

[80] Tobin, James (1976). 'The Nobel Milton', The Economist, 23 October. 94–95.

[81] Walsh, Carl E. (1998). Monetary Theory and Policy, MIT Press.

[82] Walters, Alan A. (1965). 'The Revival of the Quantity Theory of Money', Malayan Economic Review, 10, 1-6. Reprinted in K. Matthews (ed.), The Economics and Politics of Money: The Selected Essays of Alan Walters, Edward Elgar, 1998. 3–8.

[83] Walters, Alan A. (1970). 'The Radcliffe Report — Ten Years After: A Survey of Empirical Evidence'. In D.R. Croome and H.G. Johnson (eds.), Money in Britain, 1959–1969, Oxford University Press. 39–68. Reprinted in K. Matthews (ed.), The Economics and Politics of Money: The Selected Essays of Alan Walters, Edward Elgar, 1998. 91–120.

[84] Walters, Alan A. (1987). 'Milton Friedman'. In J. Eatwell, M. Milgate, and P. Newman (eds.), The New Palgrave: A Dictionary of Economic Theory and Doctrine, Macmillan. 422–427.

[85] West, Kenneth D. (1993). 'An Aggregate Demand–Aggregate Supply Analysis of Japanese Monetary Policy, 1973–1990'. In K.J. Singleton (ed.), Japanese Monetary Policy, University of Chicago Press. 161–188.

[86] Woodford, Michael (1998). 'Comment on John Cochrane, "A Frictionless View of US Inflation"', NBER Macroeconomics Annual, 13, 390–418.

[87] Woodford, Michael (1999). 'Revolution and Evolution in Twentieth-Century Macroeconomics'. Manuscript, Princeton University.

[88] Yoshikawa, Horoshi (1993). 'Monetary Policy and the Real Economy in Japan'. In K.J. Singleton (ed.), Japanese Monetary Policy, University of Chicago Press. 121–159.

8 Alan Walters and the Demand for Money: An Empirical Retrospective

Kent Matthews[1], Ivan Paya, and David A. Peel[2]

1 INTRODUCTION

Empirical studies of the demand for money have been one of the most researched areas of monetary economics. It is sometimes easy to forget that barely two-score years ago, empirical studies of the demand for money were in their infancy. The first of the empirical studies on the role of money in the UK came out of Birmingham University in the 1960s, led by Alan Walters. Walters' work on the demand for money and the monetary multiplier was a turning point for British monetarism. The dominant view was Keynesian. Government intervention and discretionary policy was the accepted norm. Monetarism was for cranks. Argument alone would not have won against the economic establishment. It was important that empirical evidence support the monetarist camp. But empirical study of the monetary economy was not just dismissed by the economics establishment, it was positively discouraged.[3] Spurred on by the work of Friedman and others[4] and the debate that followed,

[1]**Corresponding author.** E-mail address: matthewsk@cardiff.ac.uk. Tel.: +44 (0)2920-875855.

[2]The author gratefully acknowledges financial support by ESRC grant *L/138/25/1004*.

[3]In Walters (1989) he reveals that he applied to the Bank of England for a modest grant to construct a historical data series on money. His request was refused on the grounds that the quantity of money was irrelevant and that there was little interest in such statistics.

[4]Friedman and Meiselman (1963), Friedman and Schwartz (1963).

Walters and his colleagues produced empirical studies of the monetary multipliers and the long-run demand for money. The principal purpose of their efforts was to demonstrate the existence of a long-run demand for money.

The purpose of this paper is to replicate the earliest study of the demand for money undertaken for the UK. The study by Kavanagh and Walters (1966) confirmed the existence of a long-run demand for money in the UK in the period 1877–1961. However, it argued that the long-run results were of limited use in policy except as a guide to long-term trends. For policy purposes, the short-run results were more important, and thus the study attempted to estimate the short-run parameters using first-differences and sub-samples in estimation. However, as Walters readily accepted, the Kavanagh and Walters (1966) paper can be criticised for ignoring dynamic adjustment and for the inappropriate modelling of the short-run parameters.[5] This paper replicates Walters' estimates of the long-run demand for money using the modern econometric method of cointegration. The short-run demand for money and dynamic adjustment is approached through the now conventional methodology of a dynamic equilibrium-correction. The paper firstly examines the veracity of Walters' original findings, in the light of modern econometric technology. Secondly, using the appropriate methodology, we attempt to confirm his findings for the short-run demand for money. Finally, in keeping with a number of recent studies on the UK demand for money, we attempt to identify a nonlinear dynamic adjustment.

The paper is organised in the following way. The next section examines the data and reports the results of the replication of the Kavanagh and Walters (1966) paper. The third section reports the results from cointegration and dynamic adjustment. The fourth section reviews the non-linear dynamic adjustment specification. The final section concludes with an analysis of Walters' original findings.

2 THE KAVANAGH AND WALTERS RESULTS

Our aim was to replicate the Kavanagh and Walters results using the original data series used in their study. We were unable to obtain the exact data used by Kavanagh and Walters,[6] but we used the monetary series produced by Sheppard (1971) who was part of the original Birmingham team that led the monetarist counter-revolution in the UK

---

[5] Walters (1973) p. 15.

[6] Reported in Walters and Kavanagh (1964).

(missing values were taken from Capie and Webber, 1985). The measures of money were M1 (currency plus bank deposits), M2 (M1+savings bank deposits), and M3 (M2+deposits of other non-bank financial institutions 1926–61). The data for the M1 series closely corresponded with the Bank of England £M3 data that was subsequently collected from 1963. The nominal GNP series, the GNP deflator and interest rates are taken from Capie and Webber (1985).[7] Following Kavanagh and Walters, all variables are measured in logarithmic form. The sample periods cover two world wars that could arguably affect the time series properties.[8] Four dummies are then included to correct for possible structural breaks, D1, D2, D3, and D4. In particular, D1 covers the first world war (1914-1918), D2 the interwar period (1919-1938), D3 the second world war (1939–1945), and D4 covers the post-war era (1946–1966).[9]

As a preliminary exercise, we investigate the unit root properties of the time series under consideration. The order of integration has a clear implication for the OLS estimations carried out in their original paper. If the series appear to be I(1) the OLS statistics would be 'acceptable' only in the case of cointegration between the I(1) series. All three monetary aggregates, real balances, the GNP series and interest rates are I(1) in levels according to the augmented Dickey–Fuller (ADF) and Phillips–Perron tests, and I(0) processes in first differences.[10]

Tables 1–4 below compare our results with Kavanagh and Walters (K–W).

The results are strikingly similar to Kavanagh and Walters' original findings although some differences emerge with the inclusion of addi-

---

[7] Nominal GNP corresponds to Table III(12) column I. GNP deflator is Table III(12) column III. Table III(10) column VIII is the yield on consols that will be used as the long-term interest rates. Table III(10) column V is the prime bank bill rate that will be used as the short-term interest rate.

[8] This possibility is also taken into consideration by Walters (1966, p.272):

> For the annual data the period 1877–1962 has 'natural breaks' with the two World Wars. Monetarily these wars and their immediate aftermath produced the most dramatic changes.

[9] The dummies used here are the same as the ones employed in Sarno *et al.* (2002) in a similar study of the US money demand.

[10] The number of lags in the unit root tests was chosen such that no remaining residual autocorrelation was present in the unit root test regressions. Apart from the number of observations used in the unit root test, almost a hundred, in a study about the low frequency characteristics of time series processes, Shiller and Perron (1985) discussed the relevance of the length of the sample span in terms of years, and that is more important than the number of observations *per se*. Although the results are not displayed for space consideration, they are avaible from the authors upon request.

Dependent variable	Independent variables					R^2	DW
$M1_t$	$1.149y_t$	$-0.306r_t$			K–W	0.98	0.114
	(0.021)	(0.086)					
$M1_t$	$1.129y_t$	$-0.364r_t$			MPP	0.98	0.148
	(0.042)	(0.174)					
$M1_t$	$1.191y_t$	$-0.280r_t$	$-0.081p_t$		K–W	0.98	0.115
	(0.080)	(0.099)	(0.149)				
$M1_t$	$0.998y_t$	$-0.427r_t$	$0.231p_t$		MPP	0.98	0.144
	(0.105)	(0.185)	(0.195)				
$M1_t$	$1.203y_t$	$-0.303r_t$	$-0.782p_t$	$0.708p_{t-1}$	K–W	0.98	0.134
	(0.076)	(0.095)	(0.284)	(0.248)			
$M1_t$	$1.041y_t$	$-0.414r_t$	$-0.414p_t$	$0.591p_{t-1}$	MPP	0.98	0.141
	(0.106)	(0.189)	(0.423)	(0.307)			
$M1_t$	$0.621y_t$	$0.011y_{t-1}$	$0.542y_{t-2}$	$-0.333r_t$	K–W	0.99	0.093
	(0.275)	(0.485)	(0.277)	(0.079)			
$M1_t$	$0.640y_t$	$-0.048y_{t-1}$	$0.563y_{t-2}$	$-0.400r_t$	MPP	0.98	0.113
	(0.220)	(0.352)	(0.251)	(0.152)			
$M2_t$	$1.272y_t$	$-0.461r_t$	$-0.112p_t$		K–W	0.99	0.152
	(0.072)	(0.090)	(0.135)				
$M2_t$	$1.091y_t$	$-0.600r_t$	$0.190p_t$		MPP	0.99	0.187
	(0.092)	(0.180)	(0.175)				

Notes: Numbers in parentheses are standard errors. The standard errors in the replicated estimates are Newey–West corrected for autocorrelation and heteroskedasticity. DW denotes the estimated Durbin–Watson statistic.

Table 1: Money Demand 1880–1961

tional lags in the independent variables. In particular, we find marginally stronger interest elasticities both in the levels and first differenced form. There are also some differences between the impact and dynamic effects of GNP. However, the long-run patterns of the demand for money show strong similarities. While in some cases these differences are significant, there is sufficient correspondence in the main results to warrant confidence that we are using approximately the same data set and further econometric investigation will reveal the short-run dynamic adjustment.

Dependent variable	Independent variables					R^2	DW
$M1_t$	$0.964y_t$	$-0.499r_t$			K–W	0.97	0.240
	(0.030)	(0.089)					
$M1_t$	$0.945y_t$	$-0.598r_t$			MPP	0.98	0.341
	(0.033)	(0.123)					
$M1_t$	$0.107y_t$	$-0.754r_t$	$1.331p_t$		K–W	0.98	0.630
	(0.197)	(0.092)	(0.303)				
$M1_t$	$0.094y_t$	$-0.777r_t$	$1.319p_t$		MPP	0.99	0.799
	(0.145)	(0.079)	(0.226)				
$M1_t$	$0.159y_t$	$-0.836r_t$	$0.480p_t$	$0.822p_{t-1}$	K–W	0.98	0.671
	(0.188)	(0.095)	(0.491)	(0.385)			
$M1_t$	$0.090y_t$	$-0.776r_t$	$1.348p_t$	$-0.025p_{t-1}$	MPP	0.99	0.800
	(0.147)	(0.086)	(0.372)	(0.296)			
$M1_t$	$0.455y_t$	$-0.433y_{t-1}$	$1.008y_{t-2}$	$-0.616r_t$	K–W	0.98	0.380
	(0.383)	(0.685)	(0.394)	(0.078)			
$M1_t$	$0.277y_t$	$0.099y_{t-1}$	$0.628y_{t-2}$	$-0.704r_t$	MPP	0.98	0.456
	(0.128)	(0.267)	(0.207)	(0.081)			
$M3_t$	$0.188y_t$	$-0.905r_t$	$1.353p_t$		K–W	0.98	0.666
	(0.226)	(0.106)	(0.348)				
$M3_t$	$0.349y_t$	$-0.876r_t$	$1.080p_t$		MPP	0.99	0.862
	(0.195)	(0.065)	(0.296)				

Notes: Numbers in parentheses are standard errors. The standard errors in the replicated estimates are Newey–West corrected for autocorrelation and heteroskedasticity. DW denotes the estimated Durbin–Watson statistic.

Table 2: Money Demand 1926–1960

3 New Econometric Results

The basic money demand equation relates nominal money to nominal income and long-term interest rates. Our second step is to identify a stable long-term relationship between these three variables over the period 1870–1966. We assume long-run income homogeneity, thus the coefficient on nominal income in the cointegrating equation was constrained to equal unity.[11] Thus, the cointegration test will include the

[11]This assumption is made on the grounds that cointegration tests with money, GNP and consol yield gives a cointegrating vector where the hypothesis of unit coefficient for the GNP cannot be rejected at any conventional significant level. This

Dependent variable	Independent variables (NB all variables are in differenced form)					R^2	DW
$M1_t$	$0.655y_t$	$-0.223r_t$			K–W	0.49	0.816
	(0.074)	(0.068)					
$M1_t$	$0.562y_t$	$-0.228r_t$			MPP	0.41	1.291
	(0.081)	(0.068)					
$M1_t$	$0.164y_t$	$-0.257r_t$	$0.566p_t$		K–W	0.58	1.007
	(0.137)	(0.062)	(0.138)				
$M1_t$	$0.110y_t$	$-0.343r_t$	$0.643p_t$		MPP	0.56	1.723
	(0.118)	(0.077)	(0.127)				
$M1_t$	$0.140y_t$	$-0.260r_t$	$0.426p_t$	$0.277p_{t-1}$	K–W	0.65	0.940
	(0.125)	(0.057)	(0.130)	(0.067)			
$M1_t$	$0.163y_t$	$-0.319r_t$	$0.477p_t$	$0.173p_{t-1}$	MPP	0.58	1.652
	(0.109)	(0.087)	(0.131)	(0.057)			
$M1_t$	$0.480y_t$	$0.220y_{t-1}$	$0.172y_{t-2}$	$-0.240r_t$	K–W	0.62	0.737
	(0.075)	(0.081)	(0.068)	(0.059)			
$M1_t$	$0.427y_t$	$0.193y_{t-1}$	$0.194y_{t-2}$	$-0.261r_t$	MPP	0.54	1.494
	(0.074)	(0.095)	(0.087)	(0.080)			
$M2_t$	$0.619y_t$	$-0.259r_t$			K–W	0.46	0.787
	(0.073)	(0.067)					
$M2_t$	$0.536y_t$	$-0.251r_t$			MPP	0.41	1.128
	(0.076)	(0.066)					

Notes: Numbers in parentheses are standard errors. The standard errors in the replicated estimates are Newey–West corrected for autocorrelation and heteroskedasticity. DW denotes the estimated Durbin–Watson statistic.

Table 3: Money Demand (first differences) 1881–1961

ratio of nominal money over nominal income (the Cambridge k) and the yield on consols. The analysis was undertaken for the three different monetary aggregates defined above (M1, M2, M3). To formally test for cointegration, we apply the Johansen (1988, 1995) maximum likelihood procedure in a VAR formed by the three variables.[12] The VAR lag length

result is in line with Kavanagh and Walters (1966) results: 'money is neither a luxury nor a necessity'.

[12]As Sarno (1999) points out in a study about the money demand in Italy with a similar set up, Monte Carlo results provided by Balke and Fomby (1997) suggest that the long-run linear equilibrium estimated using the Johansen cointegration procedure does not provide misleading results in terms of loss of power when the true adjustment

Dependent variable	Independent variables NB all variables are in differenced form					R^2	DW
$M1_t$	$0.378y_t$ (0.144)	$-0.247r_t$ (0.086)			K–W	0.23	0.588
$M1_t$	$0.436y_t$ (0.123)	$-0.349r_t$ (0.076)			MPP	0.35	1.388
$M1_t$	$-0.031y_t$ (0.233)	$-0.247r_t$ (0.081)	$0.555p_t$ (0.256)		K–W	0.31	0.770
$M1_t$	$0.042y_t$ (0.171)	$-0.424r_t$ (0.074)	$0.795p_t$ (0.274)		MPP	0.47	1.838
$M1_t$	$-0.291y_t$ (0.239)	$-0.263r_t$ (0.075)	$0.475p_t$ (0.239)	$0.491p_{t-1}$ (0.197)	K–W	0.41	0.874
$M1_t$	$0.067y_t$ (0.177)	$-0.417r_t$ (0.075)	$0.629p_t$ (0.249)	$0.230p_{t-1}$ (0.183)	MPP	0.47	1.863
$M1_t$	$0.188y_t$ (0.174)	$0.107y_{t-1}$ (0.197)	$0.304y_{t-2}$ (0.166)	$-0.279r_t$ (0.081)	K–W	0.33	0.781
$M1_t$	$0.350y_t$ (0.146)	$0.053y_{t-1}$ (0.178)	$0.319y_{t-2}$ (0.193)	$-0.401r_t$ (0.073)	MPP	0.43	1.817
$M3_t$	$0.344y_t$ (0.157)	$-0.259r_t$ (0.093)			K–W	0.19	0.441
$M3_t$	$0.342y_t$ (0.105)	$-0.304r_t$ (0.066)			MPP	0.34	1.146

Notes: Numbers in parentheses are standard errors. The standard errors in the replicated estimates are Newey–West corrected for autocorrelation and heteroskedasticity. DW denotes the estimated Durbin–Watson statistic.

Table 4: Money Demand (first differences) 1926–1961

was chosen using the Akaike information criterion and an F-test for the significance of the removed lags starting from a VAR structure of five lags and parsimoniously removing the insignificant ones. Both criteria yielded a lag of two in the three cases for the three different monetary aggregates. The Johansen test statistics suggested in all cases a unique cointegrating vector between k_i $(i = 1, 2, 3)$ and the log of the consol yield rate, r.[13] All coefficients were significant at the one per cent level

towards equilibrium is nonlinear.

[13] In the case of the k_3 cointegration test, the interest of the deposit account was also initially included, expecting to enter the long-run relationship with a positive sign. However in the Johansen cointegrating vector the coefficient of the interest on

of significance. The estimated long-run relationships were:

$$\begin{aligned} k_1 &= 0.319 - 0.729r \\ k_2 &= 0.649 - 0.814r \\ k_3 &= 0.593 - 0.696r \end{aligned}$$

Testing for the exogeneity of the rate of interest we found that the Granger (1969) noncausality tests could not reject the null that lagged values of k_i had explanatory power over the rate of interest. But a weak exogeneity test in the sense of Engle et al. (1983), produced different results, that showed an effect on the long-term interest rate through the error-correction term.

We proceed to estimate the corresponding equilibrium-correction model (ECM):

$$\Delta k_i = \beta_{i0} + \sum \beta_{i1j} \Delta k_{it-j} + \sum \beta_{i2j} \Delta r_{t-j} + \delta u_{t-1}$$

where u_{t-1} are the lagged estimated cointegrating residuals.[14] Table 5 presents the results of the estimated linear ECM. The linear ECM results are similar across different monetary aggregates. The estimated coefficients are statistically significant with plausible magnitudes and signs. The adjustment towards the long-run equilibrium (u_{t-1}) is negative and significant in all cases with a high coefficient of around 0.3 suggesting a relatively fast speed of adjustment.[15] The diagnostic tests show satisfactory results in terms of autocorrelation. However, the normality test is rejected in all cases, and conditional heteroskedasticity tests are also rejected strongly for k_3. The RESET test provides evidence of misspecification especially in the case of k_1. This evidence suggests that possible nonlinearity may be present in the residuals of the linear ECMs for money velocity. Our next step is to formally test for nonlinearity and nonlinear model specification.

---

the deposit account was not significant at the ten per cent significance level.

[14]The cointegrating residuals used in this equation, u_{t-1}, are clean of structural breaks. That is, these are the residuals of a regression based on the cointegrating residuals regressed on the dummies for the inter-war, world war II and post-war periods.

[15]Sarno *et al.* (2002) report much slower equilibrium correction coefficient (0.075) for a similar time period (1869–1997) for the US in the case of demand for real balances. Terasvirta and Eliasson (2001) also find a slower adjusment (0.069) towards the esimated long-run demand for real balances in the UK for the period 1878–1993.

$$\Delta k_1 = \underset{(0.004)}{-0.0004} + \underset{(0.112)}{0.276}\Delta k_{1,t-1} + \underset{(0.123)}{0.275}\Delta k_{1,t-2} - \underset{(0.077)}{0.375}\Delta_2 r_t \underset{(0.074)}{-0.201}\Delta_2 r_{t-1} - \underset{(0.015)}{0.241}u_{t-1}$$

R^2_{adj}	σ	DW	LB	$ARCH$	JB	$RESET$
0.30	0.0426	1.88	0.861	0.082	0.000	0.067

$$\Delta k_2 = \underset{(0.004)}{-0.0001} + \underset{(0.133)}{0.262}\Delta k_{2,t-1} + \underset{(0.121)}{0.252}\Delta k_{2,t-2} - \underset{(0.073)}{0.392}\Delta_2 r_t \underset{(0.079)}{-0.203}\Delta_2 r_{t-1} - \underset{(0.065)}{0.295}u_{t-1}$$

R^2_{adj}	σ	DW	LB	$ARCH$	JB	$RESET$
0.40	0.0413	2.02	0.710	0.091	0.003	0.141

$$\Delta k_3 = \underset{(0.004)}{0.0008} + \underset{(0.152)}{0.223}\Delta k_{3,t-1} + \underset{(0.117)}{0.195}\Delta k_{1,t-2} - \underset{(0.060)}{0.338}\Delta_2 r_t \underset{(0.079)}{-0.185}\Delta_2 r_{t-1} - \underset{(0.051)}{0.285}u_{t-1}$$

R^2_{adj}	σ	DW	LB	$ARCH$	JB	$RESET$
0.39	0.0404	2.08	0.503	0.001	0.057	0.121

The figures in parentheses are the estimated standard errors. σ is the standard error of the OLS regression. DW is the Durbin–Watson statistic. LB is the Ljung–Box test for residual autocorrelation up to order three. $ARCH$ is the statistic for autoregressive conditional heteroskedasticity up to order three. JB is the Jarque–Bera test of normality. $RESET$ is the Ramsey (1969) test of the null hypothesis that the coefficient on the powers of fitted value are all zero, where the alternative model considered involves a third-order polynomial. The figures under the latter four statistics are the corresponding p-values.

Table 5: Estimated Parsimonious Linear ECM for Δk_i

4 NONLINEARITY

Evidence of nonlinearity in money demand equilibrium correction mechanisms is now relatively common place. Hendry and Ericsson (1991) calculate an ECM model for the demand for money in the UK for the period 1878–1970. Following Escribano (1985), they included the square and cube terms of the lagged error correction term in their equations. The significance of those terms predicted a different speed of adjustment towards the long-run equilibrium depending on the magnitude of the disequilibrium. In an updated study Ericsson *et al.* (1998) find virtually no change with respect to the original model in terms of the coefficients in the dynamic model. However, Terasvirta and Eliasson (2001) reconsider the Ericsson *et al.* (1998) nonlinear error-correction in the demand for broad money and refine it by estimating a smooth transition regression (STR) model. Their estimated STR models evidenced nonlinearity in the dynamics of the demand for real balances towards the long-run equilibrium. They also found that the adjustment process would depend on the size of the deviation from the long-run equilibrium as well as on changes in real income.

Similar analyses have been applied to studies of the dynamic properties of the demand for money in other countries. Notably, Sarno *et al.* (2003) estimate a nonlinear equilibrium correction model for the change in US real money balances of the form of an exponential STR using annual data from 1869 to 1997.[16] They find a significant nonlinear adjustment on real money balances that depend on the size of the lagged long-run equilibrium error. The nonlinear empirical money demand equation appears to be stable over time and implies a notable reduction on the residual variance compared to the linear adjustment. Sarno (1999) studies the demand for narrow money in Italy using annual data from 1861 to 1991 using a similar set up. He finds that the ESTAR model of the error term in the ECM of demand for real money is superior to the linear ECM in terms of a set of diagnostic tests. Previously, Muscatelli and Spinelli (1996) had also found a significant cube term for the error-correction term in a model similar to the one proposed by Hendry and Ericsson (1991) in the money demand for Italy. Lutkepohl *et al.* (1995) and Wolters *et al.* (1998) examined the linearity properties of the demand for money in Germany using quarterly post-war data. While the former study finds evidence of nonlinearity in the M1 equation, the latter study is unable to find any misspecification in the linear ECM for the demand of broad money, M3.

---

[16] See also Michael *et al.* (1999) for a discussion on the US post-war period.

The smooth transition regression (STR) model is discussed at length in Granger and Terasvirta (1993) and Terasvirta (1998) and an extensive survey of recent developments is presented in Van Dijk, Terasvirta and Franses (2000). The model can be written as,

$$y_t = \pi_{1,0} + \pi_1^{'} x_t + (\pi_{2,0} + \pi_2^{'} x_t) F_1(s_t; \gamma_1, c_1) + u_t \tag{1}$$

where u_t is a white noise process, x_t is a vector of lagged endogenous and exogenous variables and the transition function $F(.) \in [0,1]$ is assumed to be either a logistic function,

$$F_1(s_t; \gamma_1, c_1) = (1 + \exp\{-\gamma_1(s_t - c_1)/\sigma_{s_t}\})^{-1}, \quad \gamma_1 > 0 \tag{2}$$

or an exponential function

$$F_1(s_t; \gamma_1, c_1) = (1 - \exp\{-\gamma_1(s_t - c_1)^2/\sigma_{s_t}^2\}) \tag{3}$$

where s_t is the transition variable, σ_{s_t} is the standard deviation of s_t, γ_1 is a slope (transition) parameter and c_1 is a location parameter. The restriction $\gamma_1 > 0$ is an identifying restriction and the value of γ_1 measures the speed of transition between two underlying regimes. These regimes are represented for $F_1 = 0$ or $F_1 = 1$. Model (1) with (2) is called LSTR (logistic STR) and (1) with (3) is called ESTR (exponential STR). The transition variable could be a weakly stationary process. In the transition variable, s_{t-d}, d is called the delay parameter, and y_t in model (1) is called either LSTAR or ESTAR given its autoregressive character. Notice that the LSTAR model allows different dynamics to be present for low and high values of s_{t-d}, thus it offers advantages when modelling processes that generate asymmetric cycles. But function (3) is symmetric about c_1 so local dynamics are the same for low and high values of s_{t-d} but differ when "mid-range" values of s_{t-d} are involved.

Terasvirta (1998) proposes a modelling cycle consisting of the following stages:

a) Specification of a linear model.

Given our particular application we will specify linear ECM for money velocity.

b) Testing for linearity.

We conducted a linearity test of the null hypothesis of linearity $H_{L,0}$: $\gamma = 0$ by estimating the following auxiliary regression by OLS:

$$v_t = \beta_0 + \beta_1^{'} x_t + \beta_2^{'} x_t s_{t-d} + \beta_3^{'} x_t s_{t-d}^2 + \beta_4^{'} x_t s_{t-d}^3 + w_t \tag{4}$$

where v_t denotes the residuals from the linear ECM of Δk_i as a function of the vector x_t that includes all significant explanatory variables including the lagged estimated cointegrating residuals. The linearity test has null hypothesis $H_{L,0} : \beta_2^{'} = \beta_3^{'} = \beta_4^{'} = 0$, where 0 is a null vector, and the original hypothesis can be tested by applying LM type tests. The appropriate transition variable lag in the STR model can be determined without specifying the form of the transition function. We can compute the F-statistic for $H_{L,0}$ for various values of d (and the s_t variable is the lagged cointegrating residuals) and select the one for which the p-value of the test is smallest.

c) Selecting the transition function.

The choice between ESTR and LSTR models can be based on the following sequence of null hypotheses:

$$H_{03} : \beta_4 = 0 \tag{5}$$

$$H_{02} : \beta_3 = 0 \mid \beta_4 = 0 \tag{6}$$

$$H_{01} : \beta_2 = 0 \mid \beta_3 = \beta_4 = 0 \tag{7}$$

If the p-value for the F-test of H_{02} provides the strongest rejection of linearity, that is, a smaller p-value than that for H_{01}, H_{03} we select the ESTR model. Otherwise, we choose the LSTR model.

The results of the linearity tests for the three money velocities are displayed in Table 6 Panel A. The tests report the p-values corresponding to equation (4) estimates for three different lags ($d = 1, 2, 3$) of the transition variable, s_{t-d}. In the case of k_1, the strongest rejection of linearity appears at lag 2, although linearity is also rejected for lags 1 and 3. The nonlinear model selection tests for k_1 have the smallest p-value in the F_{02} statistic suggesting an exponential STAR (ESTAR) model. As the results are qualitatively similar for the three different lags of the transition variable and taking into account that the data is annual, we estimate a nonlinear ECM model using s_{t-1} as the transition variable as a plausible dynamic framework. The nonlinearity tests for broader money aggregates do not present such a clear cut result. For velocity k_2 and k_3 we can only reject the linearity hypothesis at lags 3 and 2 respectively. The model selection tests displayed in Panel C and D indicate an ESTAR model for k_2 and k_3.

The ESTAR model of the form described in equation (3) is estimated using nonlinear least squares.[17] The fact that the γ_1 coefficient was very high suggested a very high speed of transition between regimes. This high coefficient may be indicative of a threshold-autoregressive model (TAR) instead of a smooth transition autoregressive model (STAR).[18]

[17] Klimko and Nelson (1978) prove that the nonlinear least squares estimates of (4) are asymptotically normal.

[18] The linearity tests carried on before have also power against a threshold au-

Case	$d = 1$	$d = 2$	$d = 3$
Panel A: Lag transition variable (s_{t-d})			
k_1	0.0323	0.024	0.055
k_2	0.547	0.295	0.018
k_3	0.256	0.093	0.416
Panel B: Selecting transition function for k_1			
F_{03}	0.489	0.052	0.317
F_{02}	0.049	0.019	0.003
F_{01}	0.052	0.670	0.930
Panel C: Selecting transition function for k_2			
F_{03}			0.217
F_{02}			0.000
F_{01}			0.994
Panel D: Selecting transition function for k_3			
F_{03}		0.179	
F_{02}		0.095	
F_{01}		0.370	

Table 6: Linearity Test: F_L

We then next consider the threshold autoregression[19] (TAR) model. Specifically

$$\Delta k = \alpha_0 + \sum \alpha_{1j} \Delta k_{t-j} + \sum \alpha_{2j} \Delta r_{t-j} + \gamma u_{t-1} \text{ if } z_{t-d} \leq c$$

$$\Delta k = \beta_0 + \sum \beta_{1j} \Delta k_{t-j} + \sum \beta_{2j} \Delta r_{t-j} + \delta u_{t-1} \text{ if } z_{t-d} > c \quad (8)$$

The integer d is called the delay lag and typically it is unknown so it must be estimated. As we will shortly explain, the least-squares principle allows d to be estimated along with the other parameters. Parameter c is the "threshold" that distinguishes two regimes, i) transition variable z_{t-d} is below c (lower regime), ii) transition variable z_{t-d} is above c (upper regime). Then, parameter vectors $\boldsymbol{\alpha} = (a_0, a_1, a_2, \gamma)'$ and $\boldsymbol{b} = (b_0, b_1, b_2, \delta)'$ determine the total money velocity response to changes in last period's cointegrating disequilibrium.

toregressive type of nonlinearity, that is, a STR model but with very high speed of adjustment and just few observations in the transition interval.

[19] The idea of approximating a general nonlinear autoregressive structure by a threshold autoregression with a small number of regimes is due to Tong (1983, 1990).

If the threshold value, c, were known, then to test for threshold behaviour all one needs is to test the hypothesis $H_0 : \boldsymbol{\alpha} = \boldsymbol{b}$. Unfortunately, the threshold value is typically unknown and, under the null hypothesis, parameter c is not identified.[20] The second difficult statistical issue associated with TAR models is the sampling distribution of the threshold estimate. Our model specification and inference will closely follow Hansen (1997) who a) provides a bootstrap procedure to test H_0, b) develops an approximation to the sampling distribution of the threshold estimator free of nuisance parameters and c) develops a statistical technique that allows confidence interval construction for c. In particular, we write TAR model (8) compactly as,

$$\Delta k_i = x_t(c)^{'}\theta + u_t \tag{9}$$

where

$$x_t(c) = \left(x_t^{'}\mathbf{1}\left\{z_{t-d} \leq c\right\} x_t^{'}\mathbf{1}\left\{z_{t-d} > c\right\}\right)^{'}$$

with

$$x_t = (1, \Delta k_{it-j}, \Delta r_{t-j}, u_{t-1})^{'}, \mathbf{1}\{.\}$$

the indicator function and $\theta = (\boldsymbol{\alpha}^{'}, \boldsymbol{b}^{'})^{'}$. For a given value of c the least squares (LS) estimate of θ is

$$\hat{\theta}(c) = \left(\sum x_t(c)x_t(c)^{'}\right)^{-1}\left(\sum x_t(c)\Delta y_t^k\right) \tag{10}$$

with LS residuals $\hat{\xi}(c)_t$ and LS residual variance $\sigma_T^2(c) = (1/T)\sum_{t=1}^{T}\hat{u}^2(c)_t$. Then the LS estimate of c is the value,

$$\hat{c} = \arg\min_{c \in C} \sigma_T^2(c) \tag{11}$$

where C is an interval (usually trimmed) that covers the sample range of the transition variable. Problem (11) can be solved by a direct search over C. The LS estimate of θ is then, $\hat{\theta} = \hat{\theta}(\hat{c})$. Furthermore, the LS principle allows us to estimate the, typically, unknown value of d by extending problem (11) to a search across the discrete space $[1, \bar{d}]$.

The hypothesis $H_0 : \boldsymbol{\alpha} = \boldsymbol{b}$ is tested as follows: Let $\{e_t\}_{t=1}^{T}$ be an *i.i.d.* sequence of $N(0,1)$ draws. Regress e_t on x_t to obtain the residual variance $\hat{\sigma}_T^2$ and on $x_t(c)$ to obtain $\hat{\sigma}_T^2(c)$ and compute $F(c) = T\left(\frac{\hat{\sigma}_T^2 - \hat{\sigma}_T^2(c)}{\hat{\sigma}_T^2(c)}\right)$. Then compute $F = \sup_{c \in C} F(c)$. Repeat the procedure

[20]Nothing can be learned about c from the data when the null hypothesis is true.

n times (we set $n = 1000$) and the asymptotic p-value of the test is given by the percentage of samples for which F exceeds the observed F_T.

Finally, Hansen (1997) provides critical values and a method to construct asymptotically valid confidence intervals. Estimate the model using the actual data for a set of values of c in the range C and in each case calculate the likelihood ratio statistic $LR(c)$ for that value of c against the value of the likelihood obtained by unrestricted LS, that is, $LR(c) = T\left(\frac{\hat{\sigma}_T^2(c)-\hat{\sigma}_T^2(\hat{c})}{\hat{\sigma}_T^2(\hat{c})}\right)$. Notice that for $c = \hat{c}$ we get $LR(c) = 0$. Then plot $LR(c)$ against c and draw a flat line that corresponds to the β-level critical value $c^*(\beta)$ given in Hansen (1997, table 1, p.5). For $\beta = 5\%$ we have $c^*(\beta) = 7.35$. The confidence interval LR^c is given by $LR^c = \{c : LR(c) \leq c^*(\beta)\}$.

We set z_{t-d} to be the absolute value of the cointegrating residuals u_{t-1}.[21] So, evidence of a threshold value would be indicative of a symmetric band around zero where money velocity has different dynamics depending on the size of the last period disequilibrium in money holdings. The search interval was set to be $C = [\underline{c}, \bar{c}] = [\min\{z_{t-d}\} + 0.05, \max\{z_{t-d}\} - 0.05]$. Notice that in order to "gain" observations, we arbitrarily add or subtract 0.05 to construct the boundaries $\underline{c}, \bar{c}$ and then we divided C into 200 discrete points.

if $|u_{t-1}| < 0.028$:

$$\underset{}{\Delta k_1 =} \underset{(0.014)}{0.009} + \underset{(0.215)}{0.885}\Delta k_{1,t-2} - \underset{(0.058)}{0.403}\Delta_2 \text{yield}_{t-1}$$

if $|u_{t-1}| > 0.028$:

$$\Delta k_1 = \underset{(0.0051)}{-0.0011} + \underset{(0.127)}{0.469}\Delta k_{1,t-1} - \underset{(0.073)}{0.387}\Delta_2 r_t - \underset{(0.065)}{0.281} u_{t-1}$$

R^2_{adj}	σ	DW	LB	$ARCH$	JB	$RESET$	σ_{NL}/σ_L
0.48	0.037	2.03	0.960	0.834	0.082	0.377	0.863

Table 7: Estimated TAR ECM for k_1

The estimated TAR model is reported in Table 7 for the case of k_1 where the nonlinearity was found to be significant with respect to the cointegrating residuals at one lag. The estimated threshold value, $\widehat{c}$, for the absolute value of u_{t-1} is 0.028 with a p-value of the F-statistic of 0.000. The F-test strongly rejects the null of equal parameters above

[21] In this case, u_{t-1} is the same variable used in the linear ECMs. That is, clean of determistic trends or dummy variables.

and below the threshold. This result implies that changes in velocity do not adjust towards the long-run equilibrium relationship between velocity and interest rates when the disequilibrium is small. This is consistent with the type of S-S framework in the money demand developed in Miller and Orr (1966) where economic agents allow their money holdings to follow a random walk within a fixed band but have a rapid adjustment process outside the bands. This result implies a different adjustment process of k_1 towards its equilibrium value depending on whether the previous period misalignments lie below or above $\widehat{c}$. In particular, if the misalignment, u_{t-1}, was lower than 0.028, money velocity would not adjust to its equilibrium level, i.e., the coefficient of u_{t-1} in the equation of Δk_1 is insignificant. However, k_1 adjusts to its equilibrium value when u_{t-1} is above 0.028. In this case, the adjustment process, 0.28, is faster than in the simple linear case, 0.24. The nonlinear model is also superior in terms of adjusted R^2. The nonlinear residuals diagnostic tests are all satisfactory in terms of autocorrelation, conditional heteroskedasticity and normality. Moreover, Table 7 also reports a RESET type test. We regress the residuals of each model on the squared and cube fitted values and we report the p-value of the F-statistic. The results were qualitatively similar with the ones obtained with only squared fitted values or with fourth powers included. The residuals appear to be free of any additional nonlinearity. The last column of the diagnostic analysis shows the ratio σ_{NL}/σ_L (standard error of the nonlinear regression over the standard error of the linear one) that provides a measure of in-sample fit comparison for the alternative models. Given that it is less than one it implies better fit and typically if the σ_{NL}/σ_L ratio is below 0.90 this indicates that nonlinearity explains more than just exceptional observations in the sample. The nonlinear model appears to outperform the linear one as the ratio of standard errors is 0.86.

Figure 1 plots the actual and the fitted values of the linear and nonlinear models for Δk_1. The nonlinear fit is closer to the actual figure than the linear fit along the sample period. These results shed light on the adjustment process of narrow money velocity between 1880 and 1966. The adjustment towards the equilibrium velocity depended on the size of the disequilibrium above a specified threshold. Above that point agents were adjusting their balances at a much faster rate than if the disequilibrium was below the threshold.

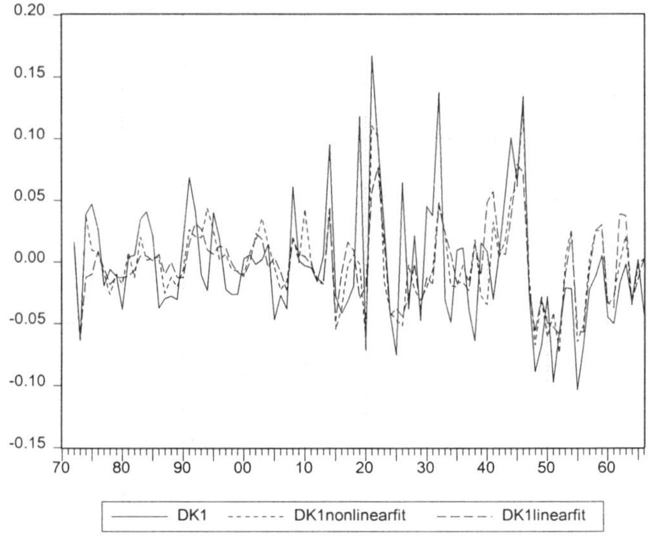

Figure 1: Fitted and Actual Values of Δk_1

5 Concluding Remarks

In their concluding remarks, Kavanagh and Walters argue that their results provide a framework for the discussion of monetary policy. Their main results were that the income elasticity of demand for money was found to be unity in the long-run but less than unity in the short-run. The implied interest elasticity of demand for money was in the region -0.8 to -0.2. Different specifications of the dependent variable produced changes to the numerical values of the parameters. Alternative measures of money produced qualitatively the same results and if anything using the broader measures produced an increase in the interest elasticity.

Our results confirm the finding that the long-run income elasticity is unity on all three measures and unlike Kavanagh and Walters we found that this restriction also held in the short-run. The interest elasticity is negative in both the short-run and the long-run and lies in the bounds found by Kavanagh and Walters.

The linear dynamic specification confirms the findings of K-W and so it can be argued that little is gained from the application of sophisticated econometric techniques to the original data. Indeed it was clear that Walters was well aware of the problems of estimation with trended variables and made some effort to deal with this by re-estimating the functions in first-differences. He was also aware that the dynamic specification was primitive which said little if anything about the adjustment to equilibrium. Our results confirm that a stable demand for money existed in this period. We have estimated a short-run demand for money and in contrast to many other findings, we found that the speed of adjustment was relatively swift (30 per cent in the first year).

The value-added of this exercise is that we are able to identify a richer disequilibrium adjustment process for the demand for M1 (which in reality looks much like the Bank of England former M3 measure). The finding that the speed of adjustment responds to the magnitude of the disequilibrium is novel but is being increasingly confirmed by recent research. The result that the demand for money has a symmetric zone has also been confirmed by Terasvirta and Eliasson (2001) for UK broad money.

In his critique of the Radcliffe Report, Walters (1970) recognised that unanticipated monetary shocks would produce longer lag responses than if anticipated. In this, Walters was himself anticipating the main conclusions of the rational expectations revolution which was reflected in his 1971 paper on Consistent Expectations (Walters, 1971). However, he did not (to our knowledge) recognise the potential for nonlinear disequilibrium adjustment in the demand for money. While our results confirm Walters' findings on the long-run demand for money, the finding of a significant nonlinear disequilibrium adjustment is something we think would have met with his approval.

BIBLIOGRAPHY

[1] Balke, N.S. and T.B. Fomby (1997) "Threshold Cointegration," *International Economic Review*, 38, pp. 627–645

[2] Capie, F. and A. Webber (1985) *A Monetary History of the United Kingdom 1870–1982,* Vol. 1, London: George Allen & Unwin.

[3] Engle, R.F., Hendry, D.F. and J. Richard (1983) "Exogeneity," *Econometrica,* 51, pp. 277–304.

[4] Ericsson, N.R., Hendry, D.F. and K.M. Prestwich (1998) "The demand for broad money in the United Kingdom, 1878–1993," *Scandinavian Journal of Economics,* 100, pp. 289–324.

[5] Escribano, A. (1985) "Nonlinear error correction: The case of money demand in the UK (1878–1970)," *Mimeo, University of California at San Diego*, La Jolla, California.

[6] Friedman, M. and D. Meiselman (1963) "The Relative Stability of Monetary Velocity and the Investment Multiplier in the United States, 1897–1958. In *Commission on Money and Credit, Stabilization Policies*, Englewood Cliffs, New Jersey: Prentice-Hall.

[7] Friedman, M. and A.J. Schwartz (1963) "Money and Business Cycles," *Review of Economics and Statistics*, 45, part 2, supp, February.

[8] Granger, C.W.J. (1969) "Investigating causal relations by econometric models and cross-spectral methods," *Econometrica,* 37, pp. 424–438.

[9] Granger, C.W.J and T. Terasvirta, (1993) *Modelling Nonlinear Economic Relationships*, Oxford: Oxford University Press.

[10] Hansen, B.E. (1997) "Inference in TAR Models," *Studies in Nonlinear Dynamics and Econometrics,* 2, pp. 1–14.

[11] Hendry, D.F. and N.R. Ericsson (1991) "An econometric analysis of UK money demand in Monetary trends in the United States and the United Kingdom by Milton Friedman and Anna J. Schwartz," *American Economic Review,* 81, pp. 8–38.

[12] Johansen, S. (1988) "Statistical analysis of cointegrating vectors," *Journal of Economic Dynamics and Control,* 12, pp. 231–254.

[13] Johansen, S. (1995) *Likelihood-based Inference in Co-integrated VAR Models*, Oxford: Oxford University Press.

[14] Kavanagh, N.J. and A.A. Walters (1966) "Demand for money in the UK, 1877–1961 some preliminary findings," *Bulletin of the Oxford Institute of Economics and Statistics,* 28, pp. 93–116.

[15] Klimko, L.A. and P.I. Nelson (1978) "On conditional least squares estimation for stochastic processes," *Annals of Statistics, 6*, pp. 629–642.

[16] Lutkepohl, H., Terasvirta, T. and J. Wolters (1995) "Investigating stability and linearity of a German M1 money demand function," *Stockholm School of Economics, Working Paper Series in Economics and Finance* No. 64.

[17] Michael, P., Nobay, A.R. and D.A. Peel (1999) "Nonlinear Adjustment Towards Long-Run Money Demand," in *Nonlinear Time Series Analysis of Economic and Financial Data* (ed.) P. Rothman, Dordrecht: Kluwer Academic Publishers.

[18] Miller, M. and D. Orr (1966) "A model of the demand for money by firms," *Quarterly Journal of Economics,* 80, pp. 68–72.

[19] Muscatelli, V.A. and F. Spinelli (1996) "Modeling monetary trends in Italy using historical data: The demand for broad money 1861–1990," *Economic Inquiry,* 34, pp. 579–596.

[20] Ramsey, J.B. (1969) "Tests for specification errors in classical linear least-squares regression analysis," *Journal of Royal Statistical Society, Series B*, 31, pp. 350–371.

[21] Sarno, L. (1999) "Adjustment costs and nonlinear dynamics in the demand for money: Italy, 1861–1991," *International Journal of Finance and Economics.* 4, pp. 155–177.

[22] Sarno, L., Taylor, M.P. and D.A. Peel (2003) "Nonlinear equilibrium correction in US real money balances, 1869–1997," *Journal of Money, Credit and Banking,* 35, October.

[23] Sheppard, D.K. (1971) *The growth and role of UK Financial Institutions, 1880–1962*, London: Methuen & Co.

[24] Shiller, R.J. and P. Perron (1985) "Testing the random walk hypothesis: Power versus frequency of observation," *Economics Letters,* 18, pp. 381–386.

[25] Smith, G.W. (1986) "A dynamic Baumol–Tobin model of money demand," *Review of Economic Studies,* 53, pp. 465–469.

[26] Terasvirta, T. (1998) "Modelling Economic Relationships with Smooth Transition Regressions," in A. Ullah and D.E.A. Giles (editors), *Handbook of Applied Economic Statistics*, New York: Marcel Dekker, pp. 507–552

[27] Terasvirta, T. and A. Eliasson (2001) "Non-linear error correction and the UK demand for broad money, 1878–1993," *Journal of Applied Econometrics,* 16, pp. 277–288.

[28] Tong, H (1983) *Threshold Models in Non-linear Time Series Analysis*: Lecture Notes in Statistics 21, Berlin: Springer-Verlag.

[29] Tong, H (1990) *Non-Linear Time Series: A Dynamical System Approach.* New York: Oxford University Press.

[30] Van Dijk, D. Terasvirta, T., and P.H. Franses (2000) "Smooth Transition Autoregressive Models — A survey of recent developments," *SSE/EFI Working paper series in Economics and Finance,* No. 380.

[31] Walters A.A. (1966) "Monetary multipliers in the UK 1880–1962," *Oxford Economic Papers,* 18, pp. 270–283.

[32] Walters, A.A. (1970) "The Radcliffe Report — Ten Years After: A Survey of Empirical Evidence," in *Money in Britain* 1959–1969 (eds.) D.R. Croome and H.G. Johnson, Oxford: Oxford University Press, pp. 39–68.

[33] Walters A.A. (1971) "Consistent Expectations, Distributed Lags and the Quantity Theory," *Economic Journal*, 81, pp. 273–281

[34] Walters A.A. (1973) (ed.) *Money and Banking*, Penguin Modern Economics Readings.

[35] Walters A.A. (1989) "A Life Philosophy," *American Economist,* Fall, pp. 18–24.

[36] Walters, A.A. and N.J. Kavanagh (1964) "Demand for money in the UK," *University of Birmingham Discussion Paper No. 48.*

[37] Wolters, J., Terasvirta, T. and H. Lutkepohl (1998) "Modeling the demand for M3 in the unified Germany," *Review of Economics and Statistics,* 80, pp. 399–409.

9 The Interaction of Monetary and Fiscal Policy: Solvency and Stabilisation Issues

Jagjit S. Chadha and Charles Nolan[1]

1 Introduction

The interaction between monetary and fiscal policy remains a topic of intense interest to macroeconomists. The underlying concerns here are that should the inherent and mutual constraint upon such policies not be respected and/or the correct mix between the two arms of stabilisation policy not obtain then the extent of inefficient economic fluctuations may be exacerbated (Woodford, 2001). This chapter tries to contribute to our understanding of both these key questions. First, we examine some issues surrounding the tension between these two arms of policy by teasing out some implications of the present value budget constraint for the setting of the interest rate. Second, we analyse the optimal mix in stabilisation for monetary and fiscal policy in a micro-founded general equilibrium model.

These debates promulgated a number of key contributions to economics, touching on the theory of optimal policy (Mundell, 1971) and on the development of the need for systematic rules over policy discretion (Lucas, 1996). For example, the early debate between Monetarists and Keynesians was to some extent dominated by the question of which arm of macroeconomic policy was most effective at stabilising the economy,

[1]Corresponding author. We thank Matthew Canzoneri, Sugata Gosh, Dale Henderson, Andrew Hughes Hallett, Campbell Leith, Simon Wren-Lewis, Bennett McCallum, Patrick Minford, David Peel, Mark Salmon, Gabriel Talmain, Mike Wickens, conference participants at Cardiff University and York University for useful comments. All remaining errors are due to the authors.

given the budget constraint faced by the government.[2]

More recently, the celebrated contribution of Sargent and Wallace (1981), and the (still more recent) fiscal theory of the price-level develop concerns that monetary policy makers may not ultimately be able to control inflation for reasons largely grounded in the conduct of fiscal policy. And finally, with monetary and fiscal policy now in many countries conducted by separate agencies, there are concerns that these arms of policy may be uncoordinated resulting in suboptimal macroeconomic outcomes.

In this chapter we shall revisit aspects of this debate that have resurfaced following the rational expectations revolution of the 1970s.[3] In particular, in Section 2 we shall set out some of the solvency concerns raised by Sargent and Wallace (1981) and others, and then look briefly at some of the ensuing debate. Much of this literature has characterised monetary policy as control over the money supply in an environment of flexible prices. More recently, however, theoretical discussion has tended to model monetary policy as a rule for the interest rate. So in Section 3 we shall recast the solvency debate in terms of interest rate bounds. We show that fiscal plans necessarily place restrictions on the available set of interest rate choices that may be available to monetary policy makers.

The sorts of restrictions on the interest rate that we generate will be useful, at least conceptually, in Section 4. In that section we set up a dynamic stochastic general equilibrium model that permits monetary and fiscal policy to influence aggregate demand, whilst fiscal policy over the long run is being conducted in a 'sustainable' manner, reflecting the concerns highlighted in Sections 3 and 4. Section 5 discusses the design of optimal policy for our model and sets out our key results on optimal weights in the policy reaction functions for monetary and fiscal policy. Section 6 offers some conclusions.

2 The Solvency Debate

In this section, then, we review some of the issues raised by Sargent and Wallace (1981) and some subsequent analysts. The framework we adopt for this discussion will be that of a representative agent. Each period each identical agent in the economy receives an endowment. The

---

[2]See, for example, Blinder and Solow (1973), Barro (1974), Stein (1976) and McCallum (1981).

[3]This chapter draws heavily on some results reported in Chadha and Nolan (2002a,b).

allocation problem faced by an agent, and all the others just like it, is to consume, save and accumulate money balances through time in order to maximise utility. Holdings of money are considered to ease transactions costs encountered in the act of obtaining real consumption units, as in Sidrauski (1965) and Brock (1975). The discounted present value of utility of this agent is given by

$$V_t = \sum_{t=0}^{\infty} \beta^t U\left(C_t, \frac{M_t}{P_t}\right) \tag{1}$$

where $U(\cdot)$ denotes a utility function increasing in both arguments, separable in both arguments and strictly concave. $\beta \in (0,1)$ is the discount factor which equals $(1+\delta)^{-1}$, where $\delta > 0$ is the subjective rate of time preference. The representative agent maximises (1) each period subject to the following sequence of flow budget constraints;

$$P_t C_t + M_t + \frac{B_t}{1+i_t} \leq M_{t-1} + B_{t-1} + P_t Y_t - P_t T_t \quad \forall t \geq 0, \tag{2}$$

M_{-1} and B_{-1} given. P_t is the price-level in period t, M_t and B_t are, respectively, nominal money balances and one period (discount) nominal government debt held at the end of period t. Y_t is the endowment in period t and T_t denotes lump sum taxes. The optimal choices that the agent makes with respect to consumption, saving and the amount of base currency to hold can be found by maximising a Lagrangian function for this problem with respect to $\{C_t\}_{t=0}^{\infty}$, $\{B_t\}_{t=0}^{\infty}$ and $\{M_t/P_t\}_{t=0}^{\infty}$. This function may be written as:

$$L = \sum_{t=0}^{\infty} \beta^t \left\{ U\left(C_t, \frac{M_t}{P_t}\right) + \lambda_t \begin{pmatrix} M_{t-1} + B_{t-1} + P_t Y_t - P_t T_t - \\ P_t C_t - M_t - \frac{B_t}{1+i_t} \end{pmatrix} \right\}.$$

We find that the optimal plan for consumption is then determined by

$$\beta \frac{u'(C_{t+1})}{u'(C_t)} \frac{P_t}{P_{t+1}} = \frac{1}{1+i_t} \quad \forall t \geq 0. \tag{3}$$

The optimal amount of money balances is implied by

$$\frac{v'(M_t/P_t)}{u'(C_t)} = \frac{i_t}{1+i_t} \quad \forall t \geq 0. \tag{4}$$

To these first-order necessary conditions we add (2) with equality at each date and

$$\lim_{T \to \infty} \left\{ \prod_{j=0}^{T-1} (1 + i_{t+j}) \right\}^{-1} W_{t+T} \to 0, \tag{5}$$

where $W_t \equiv M_{t-1} + B_{t-1}$. This is called the no-Ponzi finance condition and helps ensure that the agent's consumption set is well defined. In doing so it can also be shown to play an additional role of ruling out equilibria in which, for a given money stock, the price level tends to zero.

We assume that a government exists and spends an amount each period. Let G_t denote real government expenditure in period t. Since there is only one type of good in this economy, this expenditure, which yields no direct utility to agents in the economy, is necessarily on final goods. In equilibrium, when planned expenditure equals supply, it follows that the economy–wide resource constraint is given by,

$$C_t + G_t = Y_t \quad \forall t \geq 0. \tag{6}$$

Equations (6) and (2) in turn imply that the government's budget constraint is

$$\frac{B_t}{(1+i_t)} = B_{t-1} + P_t(G_t - T_t) - (M_t - M_{t-1}) \quad \forall t \geq 0. \tag{7}$$

Since the representative agent's optimal consumption programme is constrained by lifetime resources it follows that the sequence of equations (7) will be consistent with the representative agent's consumption programme if and only if a requirement analogous to (5) is imposed on the government's net issue of debt,

$$\lim_{T\to\infty} \left\{ \prod_{j=0}^{T-1} (1 + i_{t+j}) \right\}^{-1} W_{t+T} \to 0. \tag{8}$$

In turn, then, it follows that (7) and (8) together imply that,

$$B_{t-1} + M_{t-1} = \sum_{j=0}^{\infty} \left\{ \begin{array}{c} \prod_{s=j}^{j-1} \left(\frac{1}{1+i_{t+s}}\right) \times \\ \left[P_{t+j}\left(T_{t+j} - G_{t+j}\right) + \frac{i_{t+j}}{1+i_{t+j}} M_{t+j}\right] \end{array} \right\}. \tag{9}$$

This equation is labelled the public sector's present value budget constraint (PVBC). The traditional interpretation of it is that it requires the government, given outstanding liabilities, $B_{t-1} + M_{t-1}$, to plan to raise sufficient net surpluses (primary surpluses plus seigniorage), in a present discounted sense, to meet these obligations.

It will be convenient to consider the implications of the present value constraint in real terms. To that end, note that $P_{t+1}/P_t \equiv (1 + \pi_{t+1})$, and also that, for any variable X_t, deflated by the previous period's price-level we may write $X_{t+1}/P_t = (X_{t+1}/P_{t+1})(1 + \pi_{t+1})$. Let $m \equiv M/P$, and $b \equiv B/P$. Let us further assume that the real interest rate, r, is constant. It can be shown that the PVBC may, in real terms, be written as:

$$b_{t-1} + m_{t-1} = \sum_{j=0}^{\infty} \left(\frac{1}{1+r} \right)^j \left[\frac{r + (1+r)\pi_{t+j+1}}{1+r} \right] m_{t+j} + \sum_{j=0}^{\infty} \left(\frac{1}{1+r} \right)^j [T_{t+j} - G_{t+j}] . \quad (10)$$

Some of the issues raised by Sargent and Wallace may now be observed from the standpoint of the PVBC. Let K denote the present value of outstanding liabilities and primary deficits. That is,

$$\sum_{j=0}^{\infty} \left(\frac{1}{1+r} \right)^j \left[\frac{r + (1+r)\pi_{t+j+1}}{1+r} \right] m_{t+j} = K. \quad (11)$$

We assume that the arm of government responsible for seigniorage revenue takes the right hand side of (11) as given. Consider, now, the consequences of a temporary decline in seigniorage revenue raised in period t, but compensated for with a one-off rise in period $t+T$. It follows that,

$$\frac{dm_{t+T}}{dm_t} = -\frac{[r + (1+r)\pi_{t+1}]\,(1+r)^T}{[r + (1+r)\pi_{t+T+1}]} . \quad (12)$$

We can see that a fall in the amount of seigniorage 'today' implies a larger increase in seigniorage in T-periods time, which implies a powerful constraint operating on future policy. The concerns highlighted by Sargent and Wallace are normally taken to imply that monetary and fiscal policy ought to be conducted by separate agencies and underpins much of the case for introduction of independent central banks. Eichengreen and Wyplosz (1998) provide an interesting discussion of some of these issues with respect to the European Central Bank and the conduct of fiscal policy in the Eurozone area, with particular reference to the Stability and Growth Pact.

2.1 Persistent Deficits and the Constraints on Monetary Policy

One of the implications of the Sargent and Wallace worries is that an accumulating debt may ultimately lead to inflation: at some point agents in the economy may refuse to hold new government debt issue and sell their existing holdings of such debt. At that point, as suggested by (12), recourse to an inflationary monetary policy may be the only option left to fiscal authorities. The simple model developed above incorporates just this kind of limit which in fact is a necessary requirement for equilibrium. The transversality condition, equation (8), demonstrates that government cannot have unbounded resort to debt issue, or monetary issue.

Fiscal deficits in the US and the UK became large and persistent following the collapse of the Bretton Woods system. In the UK this behaviour quickly undermined credibility and led to IMF support in 1976 and an incoming government in 1979 committed to establishing financial credibility: subsequently much of the persistence in deficits disappeared. In the US, however, large deficits persisted from the second half of the 1970s through to the first half of the 1990s. This caused some economists to question whether or not the US economy was actually violating its PVBC. Hamilton and Flavin (1986) initiated a whole empirical literature that tested whether the PVBC was violated. In retrospect, it may be difficult to know what to make of such studies as it is difficult to analyse 'off-equilibrium' behaviour. Indeed Bohn (1995) makes just this point in a critique of the empirical literature that followed the Hamilton and Flavin (1986) contribution. In any event, the concerns raised by Sargent and Wallace (1981) seemed very relevant at that time and continued to exercise the minds of policy makers.

Perhaps a more fruitful line of enquiry was to enquire just how tolerant monetary policy could be of persistent deficits. Might a run of deficits or even a *permanent* sequence of deficits be inflationary? This was the subject of McCallum (1984). McCallum enquired whether or not monetary policy might retain control of the price-level in the face of just such a sequence of permanent deficits. We will define a monetarist equilibrium to be one in which the price-level does not grow, and then investigate whether a given sequence of deficits is consistent with such an equilibrium. We shall assess the feasibility of this joint sequence of monetary and fiscal policies by assessing their compatibility with the transversality condition. Our monetarist equilibrium is given by: $m_t(1+\pi_{t+1}) - m_{t-1} = 0, \ \forall\, t$. In this case the per-period budget constraint (in real terms) may be written as,

$$\frac{b_t}{1+r_t} = b_{t-1} + (g_t - \tau_t). \tag{13}$$

If we iterate on this expression, assuming a constant real interest rate, we find at some arbitrary date in the future, T, that

$$\frac{b_{t+T}}{(1+r)^{T+1}} = b_{t-1} + d\sum_{j=0}^{T}\left(\frac{1}{1+r}\right)^{j}, \tag{14}$$

where we have used the following notation, $(g_t - \tau_t) \equiv d$, $\forall t$.[4] The final term on the right hand side may be written as $d\left[\frac{1-\left(\frac{1}{1+r}\right)^T}{1-\left(\frac{1}{1+r}\right)}\right]$. Clearly, this expression does not converge to zero through time since as $T \to \infty$ we see that

$$\frac{b_{t+T}}{(1+r)^{T+1}} = b_{t-1} + \frac{1+r}{r}d. \tag{15}$$

However, since the PVBC must hold, a zero inflation equilibrium is not feasible under rule (13): permanent deficits in this sense are inconsistent with the monetarist equilibrium. In contrast to (13), now consider a process for debt of the following sort:

$$b_t = b_{t-1} + d_t^*(1+r), \tag{16}$$

where d^* denotes the deficit inclusive of interest payments, $d_t^* \equiv (g_t + \frac{rb_{t-1}}{1+r} - \tau_t)$. Furthermore, let us assume that the fiscal authority attempts to fix the deficit to its value at time t for all $t+j$, for $j \geq 0$. This rule implies that at time T the outstanding level of debt will be given by,

$$\frac{b_{t+T}}{(1+r)^{T+1}} = \frac{b_{t-1}}{(1+r)^{T+1}} + \frac{(T+1)d^*}{(1+r)^T}. \tag{17}$$

Note that the first term on the right hand side of this expression clearly converges to zero for $T \to \infty$. The second term on the right is likely to rise initially before falling. Intuitively, whilst the numerator is rising linearly through time, the denominator is rising exponentially through time. As $T \to \infty$, it follows then that $\frac{b_{t+T}}{(1+r)^{T+1}} \to 0$, as required. The intuition is that by including interest payments in the definition of the deficit, the government repays a sufficient amount of debt each period and hence meets the PVBC.[5] Loosely speaking, agents in the model can always be sure of being able to transform their holdings of government debt into real consumption. So permanent deficits — inclusive of interest payments — is a feasible policy for the fiscal authority in the presence of a zero inflation monetary policy.

On this definition for the deficit, then, the message seems reasonably optimistic: a long-lasting sequence of deficits may not necessarily

---

[4] An intermediate step is missing. Iterating on the period budget constraint yields $b_{t+T} = (1+r)^{T+1}b_{t-1} + (1+r)d\sum_{j=0}^{T}(1+r)^j$. To put this in a form amenable to comparison with the transversality condition divide through by $(1+r)^{T+1}$. This yields equation (14) in the text.

[5] The ever-rising interest receipts on the outstanding debt enables agents to pay the ever-rising taxes. See below.

compromise monetary policy. And to some extent, providing credibility is not compromised, that may be the story to tell about post-Bretton Woods US fiscal policy. Of course, in one sense this observation merely begs the question as to what exactly makes the government resort to taxes when inflation will do just as well.

However, even on this definition of the deficit, there are some unappealing implications for the evolution of taxes. In particular, the sequence of taxes required to support such a permanent deficit is itself unbounded. It can be shown that the sequence of taxes necessary for $d_t^* = d^*$ for all t is given by,

$$\{\tau_{t+j}\}_{j=0}^{\infty} = \left\{ g_{t+j} + \frac{rb_{t-1}}{1+r} + (1 - jr)\, d^* \right\}_{j=0}^{\infty}.$$

We see therefore that debt must be growing through time.[6] However, the rate of growth is declining by construction, as the economy is running a constant-valued deficit each period. As a result, taxes are rising through time in an unbounded manner such that the interest payments on the current level of debt are met. Consequently, as may be seen in Figure 1, the growth in taxes is also falling through time, reflecting the decline in the growth of interest service required on outstanding debt.

McCallum's contribution raises a number of important issues. However, from our perspective the interesting point is the interplay between the sustainability of debt and the interest payments required to 'back' the taxes. In the next section we explore in further depth the interplay between interest rates and fiscal solvency. This will be useful in designing sustainable fiscal policies for our model in section 4.

3 Fiscal Policies, Budget Constraints and Interest Rate Bounds

Recently macroeconomic and monetary models have incorporated the nominal interest rate as the instrument of monetary policy. In this section, and as a prelude to our discussion of the joint conduct of monetary and fiscal policy in a full macro-model, we consider the interaction of

[6] This formula can also be used in turn to yield a formula for the deficit inclusive of interest:

$$\frac{r}{1+r}\left[\sum_{j=0}^{\infty}\left\{\left(\sum_{s=0}^{j-1} b_{t+s} - b_{t+s-1}\right) + (1 - jr)\, d\right\}\right].$$

We adopt the convention, $\sum_s \equiv 0$, for $j = 0$.

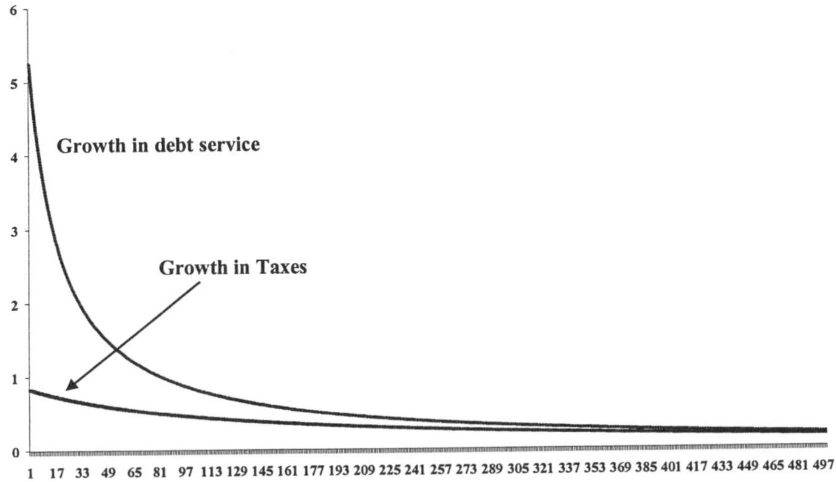

Figure 1: Debt Service and Tax Implications of Long-Lasting Deficits

monetary and fiscal policy from the perspective of the interaction of sequences of interest rates and deficits. We continue to work within a deterministic framework. The following analysis does not incorporate the behaviour of the private sector, as the main points can be made without doing so.

Let financial wealth continue to take one of two forms: money, which earns no interest, and one-period discount nominal bonds. We may think of a fiscal authority setting fiscal variables (taxes and debt, given expenditure), and a monetary authority determining the path for the interest rate. The seigniorage sequence determined as a result of the interest rate sequence is assumed to be determined endogenously (via a money demand equation). As before, the one-period public sector flow budget constraint is given by:

$$\frac{B_t}{(1+i_t)} = B_{t-1} + P_t(G_t - T_t) - (M_t - M_{t-1}). \tag{18}$$

B_{t-1} is the nominal quantity of debt issued last period, and maturing this period, i_t is the nominal interest rate between period t and $t+1$, P_t is the aggregate price level, $(G_t - T_t)$ is the real primary deficit in period t, and $(M_t - M_{t-1})$ is seigniorage raised in period t. A central assumption is that the monetary–fiscal sequences avoid Ponzi schemes,[7] such that,

$$\lim_{T\to\infty} B_{t+T}\left(\prod_{j=0}^{T}(1+i_{t+j})\right)^{-1} = 0. \tag{19}$$

What we found in Section 2 was that a condition similar to (19) is necessary to ensure that the PVBC is satisfied. This condition ensures that for a given level of outstanding liabilities at the start of any time period the ensuing intertemporal sequence of net surpluses plus seigniorage is sufficient to meet those liabilities.

We shall analyse fiscal rules (or regimes) of the following form:

$$T_t = \lambda_t G_t - \frac{(M_t - M_{t-1})}{P_t} + \gamma\frac{B_{t-1}}{P_t}, \tag{20}$$

where T_t denotes tax revenue generated in period t. Fiscal policy is characterised by the sequence $\{(\lambda_{t+s}, \gamma_{t+s})\}_{s=0}^{T}$. In other words, we may think of fiscal policy as determining the amount of debt retired, and the size of the primary deficit (i.e., γ and $(1-\lambda_{t+s})G_{t+s}$). We assume that $\gamma \in (0,1)$ is fixed for all time. This is a useful assumption that makes it more easy to characterise the kind of restrictions on the interest rate and γ that we are seeking. Finally, again for simplicity, we assume that seigniorage revenue is rebated lump sum to the private sector. The particular fiscal rules that we analyse will then be indexed simply by restrictions on the sequence $\{\lambda_{t+s}\}_{s=0}^{T}$.

Equation (19) represents a general statement of the restrictions we require on monetary and fiscal policy to ensure that the PVBC is satisfied. However, we can rewrite this statement in a manner more applicable to the class of fiscal rules under consideration. First, since $\gamma > 0$, the fiscal authority, looking forward from any time t, will always do enough to repay the outstanding debt in existence at the start of time t, that is

$$\lim_{T\to\infty}(1-\gamma)^{T+1}B_{t-1} = 0.$$

Consequently, for monetary and fiscal policy to be consistent with fiscal solvency there must be a sufficient amount of (discounted) net surpluses

[7] As we noted before, the no-Ponzi game restriction is consistent with optimal private sector behaviour. O'Connell and Zeldes (1988) demonstrate that no rational individual will hold the liabilities of a government that attempts to run a Ponzi game. That is because the welfare of any individual holding such government debt for any period will be strictly lower than under an alternate feasible consumption programme.

looking forward from date t. Therefore

$$\lim_{T\to\infty} B_{t+T}\left(\prod_{j=0}^{T}(1+i_{t+j})\right)^{-1}=0$$

if and only if

$$\sum_{s=0}^{T}\left[\left\{\prod_{j=0}^{s-1}(1+i_{t+j})\right\}^{-1}(1-\gamma)^{T-s}(1-\lambda_{t+s})P_{t+s}G_{t+s}\right]\to 0, \qquad (21)$$

as $T\to\infty$. It is straightforward to show that a balanced budget regime results in fiscal policy placing no restrictions on the feasible sequence of interest rates. To see this note that in this case fiscal policy is simply the sequence $\{(\lambda,\gamma)\}_{s=0}^{T}$ with $\lambda=1$ and $0<\gamma<1$, $\forall s$.

However, it is perhaps more interesting to go to the opposite extreme of a permanent deficit, the case where $\lambda\in(0,1),\forall t$. Assume that there is a lower bound on taxes determined by the debt repayment parameter γ. The fiscal rule is now:

$$T_t=\lambda G_t-\frac{(M_t-M_{t-1})}{P_t}+\gamma\frac{B_{t-1}}{P_t}. \qquad (22)$$

Substituting (22) into (18) yields

$$\frac{B_t}{(1+i_t)}=(1-\gamma)B_{t-1}+(1-\lambda)P_tG_t. \qquad (23)$$

The public sector is now running a deficit in every period. This policy is sustainable if and only if the following expression goes to zero in the limit:

$$B_{t+T}\left(\prod_{j=0}^{T}(1+i_{t+j})\right)^{-1}=(1-\gamma)^{T+1}B_{t-1}+$$
$$(1-\lambda)\sum_{s=0}^{T}\left[\left\{\prod_{j=0}^{s-1}(1+i_{t+j})\right\}^{-1}(1-\gamma)^{T-s}P_{t+s}G_{t+s}\right]. \qquad (24)$$

Clearly the first term on the right hand side goes to zero in the limit. So, for the posited fiscal regime to be feasible, we require the second term on the right hand side to converge to zero. We shall analyse this term by considering some interesting special cases. For instance, consider the case where the sequence of nominal government expenditures is fixed:

$$(1-\lambda)P_{t+s}G_{t+s}=(1-\lambda)\overline{PG} \qquad \forall s. \qquad (25)$$

Now substitute (25) into (24) to see that the second expression on the right hand side of (25) may be written as

$$(1-\lambda)\overline{PG}\sum_{s=0}^{T}\left[\left\{\prod_{j=0}^{s-1}(1+i_{t+j})\right\}^{-1}(1-\gamma)^{T-s}\right]. \qquad (26)$$

This expression brings out clearly the potential tension between monetary and fiscal policy. Given the rate of retirement of outstanding debt (γ), it is left to monetary policy to ensure convergence of this expression to zero. On the other hand, if the monetary authority had a stronger commitment technology we would regard (26) as determining a bound on γ. An interesting example of the implications for monetary policy is where interest rates are set at the level given in equation (27)

$$i_{t+s} = \left\{(1-\gamma)^{-2} - 1\right\} \qquad \forall s \geq 0. \qquad (27)$$

If monetary policy follows this path then expression (26) can be written as

$$(1-\gamma)^{T}\sum_{s=t}^{T}\left[(1-\gamma)^{s-t}(1-\lambda)\overline{PG}\right] \qquad (28)$$

where the expression in square braces converges to

$$\frac{1-\lambda}{\gamma}\overline{PG}. \qquad (29)$$

Consequently, as $T \to \infty$ expression (28) tends to zero. Although it is clear that (27) is not unique, in the spirit of McCallum (1984) we find that (27) is a sufficient condition for permanent deficits to be a feasible fiscal policy. But, and more importantly, we find that permanent fiscal deficits effectively place an upper bound on the sequence of interest rates and so do not imply complete 'separability' in the feasible set of monetary and fiscal choices. We illustrate this result in Figure 2, which shows that the upper bound constraint on the interest rate sequence, $\{i_{t+s}\}_{s\geq 0}$, seems somewhat less likely to bite as the rate of debt retirement increases. We cannot necessarily infer from this deterministic analysis the correct stochastic policy, but if we suspect that the equilibrium, or steady-state, interest rate was around 5 per cent then any rate of debt repayment less than 2.5 per cent per annum would ensure that 5 per cent lies above the upper bound. The result here is intuitive insofar as the bound increasingly constrains the interest rate sequence as the fiscal authority's chosen rate of debt retirement becomes smaller.

The assumption of completely fixed prices is not crucial to these arguments. What is critical, as we now make explicit, is that, for a

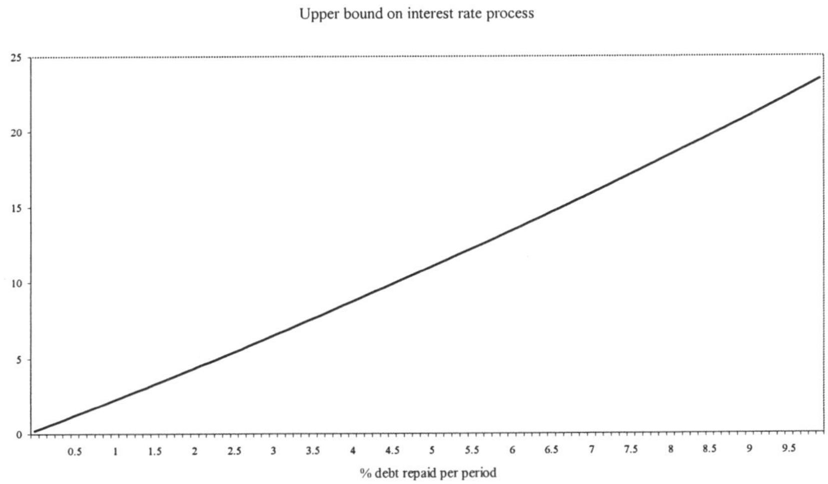

Figure 2: Upper Bound on Interest Rates Resulting from Debt Repayment Schedules

given value of γ, the monetary authority needs *sufficient* control over the real short-term interest rate. We continue to assume that government expenditure is constant. Rewriting the solvency condition in real terms yields

$$(1-\lambda)\overline{G}\sum_{s=0}^{T}\left[\left\{\prod_{j=0}^{s-1}\frac{(1+\pi_{t+1+j})}{(1+i_{t+j})}\right\}(1-\gamma)^{T-s}\right]. \tag{30}$$

As in the previous example, the expression in square braces must tend to zero in the limit if the requirements of fiscal solvency are to be met. Expression (30) can usefully be rewritten as

$$(1-\lambda)(1-\gamma)^{T}\overline{G}\sum_{s=0}^{T}\left[\left\{\prod_{j=0}^{s-1}\frac{(1+\pi_{t+1+j})}{(1+i_{t+j})}\right\}\left(\frac{1}{1-\gamma}\right)^{s}\right]. \tag{31}$$

A sufficient condition for this expression to reach zero in the limit is simply that the term in square braces is convergent, as opposed to having a zero limiting value.[8] It can then be shown that this will be the case

[8]See Rudin (1976), Theorem 3.3(c), page 49.

when the following requirement is (eventually) met infinitely often:[9]

$$i_s - \pi_{s+1} < \gamma \qquad \forall s \geq T. \tag{32}$$

This expression has a very obvious interpretation that is clearly analogous to McCallum's arguments: it requires that the fiscal authority must eventually repay a sufficient portion of the debt each period.[10] The alternative interpretation of course is that the debt retirement schedule places an upper bound on the feasible real interest rate sequence.

There are intermediate cases, which are analysed further in Chadha and Nolan (2002e).[11] However, the key point for current purposes is that debt retirement (γ) and the interest rate are linked by the requirement of fiscal solvency. In the simulations in section 4 we shall require γ to be sufficiently high such that fiscal policy ensures the public sector PVBC is met. As a consequence, monetary policy will be unconcerned with such issues.

3.1 Do Fiscal Solvency Concerns Impede the Conduct of Monetary Policy? Some Evidence

The bounds on interest rates that we have derived can loosely be interpreted as having to hold 'eventually' or in the steady-state. But what about the conduct of monetary policy in practice: is there evidence that monetary policy is systematically being hampered by fiscal concerns? Table 1 provides some evidence on this point for some advanced economies.

The data in Table 1 are seigniorage receipts as a percentage of GNP. We see that seigniorage revenue does not appear to be *systematically* deployed in the G7 as a major source of revenue for the public sector, despite the public sector typically allocating between 30 and 55 per cent of GNP expenditure in developed economies (see Offer 2002). Naturally, major bursts of inflation can do wonders for the debt service burden (see the discussion in King, 1995) but these have hardly been systematic in

[9] We are essentially drawing on d'Alembert's ratio test. This says that for a convergent series: $\limsup_{n \to \infty} |a_{n+1}/a_n| < 1$. In the text, however, we are unwinding the unstable roots forward to ensure convergence.

[10] Actually this expression is an approximation, since we ignore the cross term: $[(p_{t+1}/p_t) - 1] \times \gamma$.

[11] For example, consider a deficit $D_t = \rho D_{t-1}$, where $\rho > 1$ and where $D_t \equiv (1 - \lambda)P_t G_t$. Then one can show that a condition analogous to (32) occurs:

$$(1 - \rho) + i_s - \pi_{s+1} < \gamma \qquad \forall s \geq T.$$

Year	Ca	Fr	Ge	It	Ja	UK	US	G-7*
1950s	0.3	1.5	1.1	1.9	0.7	0.5	0.2	0.7
1960s	0.4	1.1	0.6	1.6	1.2	0.4	0.3	0.7
1970s	0.7	0.7	1.0	3.2	1.3	0.8	0.5	1.0
1980s	0.1	0.4	0.3	1.8	0.7	0.1	0.4	0.5
1990-94	0.2	−0.2	0.6	1.2	0.3	0.2	0.4	0.4
Average	0.5	0.7	0.7	1.9	0.8	0.4	0.4	0.7

Reported in King (1995). Data from Grilli *et al.* (1991) and Hudson and Nolan (1996). Seigniorage receipts are given as a percentage of GNP.

Table 1: Seigniorage Receipts as a Percentage of GNP

these economies. However, when we come to model monetary and fiscal policy in the next section, as it will be the systematic components of these policies that we are interested in, we shall model fiscal policy as being Ricardian.

4 A Model for Business Cycle Analysis Under Fiscal–Monetary Interactions

If much concern hitherto in the academic literature has centred around the issue of fiscal solvency, in policy circles that concern may be partially giving way to a concern that fiscal policy may not be being adequately coordinated with monetary policy at the business cycle frequencies. In other words, there is concern that the systematic component of fiscal policy may be being constrained such that output may be more volatile than it otherwise would be. As a consequence, monetary policy may be more activist as a result.

In this section, then, we construct a simple model in which both monetary and fiscal policy have influence over aggregate demand, and we ask how a policy maker might go about designing the systematic components of monetary and fiscal policy. The model is constructed around a finite horizon model, following Yaari (1965) and Blanchard (1985). We extend this framework in a number of important directions. First following Cardia (1991) Chadha *et al.* (2001) and Chadha and Nolan (2002b) we translate the model into discrete time. We incorporate an imperfectly competitive production technology, to motivate the existence of sticky prices. Like the latter authors, we model price stickiness in the manner of Calvo (1983), in what has become something of a benchmark for sticky-price models (see Woodford, 1997). Our exposition of the model will be relatively brief as it is set out in detail elsewhere.[12] The utility function for the representative agent, j, is given by

$$V_0 = E_0 \sum_{t=0}^{\infty} \left\{ \left(\frac{1}{1+\delta} \right)^t \left(\frac{1}{1+\lambda} \right)^t U \left(C_t^j, \frac{M_t^j}{P_t}, L_t^J \right) \right\}. \quad (33)$$

Here δ is the subjective discount rate and λ the probability of death. We assume that this is constant. This set-up is consistent with the expected remaining lifetime of the agent being equal to λ^{-1}, a constant. Because of this the model is sometimes dubbed the 'perpetual youth' model. We make the usual assumptions on the shape of the utility function. Expected utility is maximised subject to a sequence of per period budget constraints,

$$P_t C_t^j + M_t^j + \frac{B_t^j}{(1+i_t)} \leq (1+\lambda) M_{t-1}^j + (1+\lambda) B_{t-1}^j + P_t Y_t^j - T_t^j, \quad (34)$$

where

$$P_t C_t^j = \int_0^1 \int_0^1 p_t(k,z) c_t^j(k,z) dz dk$$

and

$$P_t Y_t^j = \int_0^1 \int_0^1 p_t(j,z) y_t(j,z) dz$$

and where (34) holds for all $t \geq 0$, and in each state of nature. Here $c_t^j(k,z)$ denotes the representative agent's consumption of good (k,z) where z indexes agents in the economy. Similarly, $y_t(j,z)$ indicates the amount of z output produced by the agent. This formulation follows Woodford (1997) and assumes that each agent is a monopoly supplier of all goods that it supplies, while each agent also consumes a basket of all goods. In this way, we partial out any wealth effects that might otherwise have occurred due to price rigidity, retaining the ability to work in a symmetric representative agent set-up.[13] $P_t C_t^j$ denotes total nominal consumption, M_t^j holdings of the money stock, B_t^j is the nominal bond

[12] See Chadha and Nolan (2002d,e).

[13] By not modelling factor markets and the corporate sector explicitly, we can develop the key aggregate equations with a minimum of fuss. However, in doing so we gloss over some important aggregation issues, see Chadha and Nolan (2002e) and an appendix to that paper, available on request.

portfolio $P_t Y_t^j$ is income and T_t^j lump sum government transfers. The accumulation of wealth is given by

$$W_t^j = (1+\lambda) M_{t-1}^j + (1+\lambda) B_{t-1}^j, \tag{35}$$

where we assume, following Blanchard (1985), that perfect capital markets return all financial wealth to the population as windfall dividends in the event of death. Combining (34) and (35), we get that

$$W_t^j = \left(\frac{1}{1+i_t}\right)\left(\frac{1}{1+\lambda}\right) E_t W_{t+1}^j + P_t C_t^j - P_t Y_t^j + \frac{i_t}{1+i_t} M_t^j. \tag{36}$$

This implies if $\lim_{T\to\infty}\left(\frac{1}{1+\lambda}\right)^T E_0 \prod_{j=0}^{T-1}(1+i_{t+j})^{-1} W_{t+T}^j \to 0$, that

$$W_t^j = -E_t \sum_{s=t}^{\infty}\prod_{j=t}^{s-1}\left\{ \begin{array}{c} \left(\frac{1}{1+i_{t+j}}\right)\left(\frac{1}{1+\lambda}\right)^{s-t} \times \\ \left[P_s(C_s^j - Y_s^j) + T_s^j + \frac{i_s}{1+i_s} M_s^j\right] \end{array} \right\}. \tag{37}$$

Equation (37) may be interpreted in the usual manner, that 'borrowing' is limited by lifetime resources and is analogous to (5) above. However, we note that both (36) and (37) reflect now the probability faced by the agent of not being alive in any subsequent period. The simple way we have incorporated this effect means that the probability of death serves merely to act to increase the effective rate of discount. Consumption is defined over the Dixit–Stiglitz aggregator function,

$$C_t^j \equiv \left[\int_0^1\int_0^1 c_t^j(k,z)^{\frac{\theta-1}{\theta}} dz dk\right]^{\frac{\theta}{\theta-1}}, \tag{38}$$

with the aggregate price-level defined accordingly as:

$$P_t \equiv \left[\int_0^1\int_0^1 p_t(j,z)^{1-\theta} dz dj\right]^{\frac{1}{1-\theta}}. \tag{39}$$

4.1 The Demand Side

The first-order conditions of the representative agent from any cohort are familiar. At each date and in each state we have that an interior optimum will be characterised by

$$(1+\delta)^{-1} E_t U'(C_{t+1}^j)/P_{t+1}(1+i_t) = U'(C_t^j)/P_t, \tag{40}$$

and

$$U'_M(C^j_t, M^j_t/P_t, L^j_t)/U'_c(C^j_t, M^j_t/P_t, L^j_t) = i_t/(1+i_t). \tag{41}$$

Despite the probability of death we see no tilting of consumption towards the present, and no reduction in the demand for money, as one might have supposed. In fact, given our assumptions on the operation of the capital/equity markets and the money market this makes perfect sense. Any windfall gain from agents dying and leaving unconsumed real resources (either in the form of 'unspent' bonds or money) are simply passed on to those agents left alive. However, those agents, in turn, face an excess interest premium (in order to ensure a zero profit equilibrium).

4.2 The Supply Side

Agents are assumed to meet demand at the posted price, whether or not prices have been changed in the current period or not. We follow Calvo (1983), then, and many subsequent analysts and assume that when a price is set in period t it will remain at that nominal level with probability α $(0 \leq \alpha < 1)$. More generally, an agent that re-prices some part of his or her output this period faces the probability α^k of having to charge the same price in k-periods time. We consider the re-pricing by an agent j of one good, z. We demonstrate that the optimal price is a function of aggregate economy wide variables only. As a consequence we can easily aggregate across all goods in our economy. It will be convenient now to introduce a specific functional form for our utility functional and we shall assume the following $U\left(C^j_t, \frac{M^j_t}{P_t}, L^j_t\right) \equiv \log C + \log(M/P) - \int_0^1 \varpi[y_t(j,z)]dz$. This will also be the functional form assumed in our simulation results reported in Section 5. $\int_0^1 \varpi[y_t(j,z)]dz$ denotes the marginal disutility of supplying labour across all z goods. For any individual good, then, it follows that the optimal level of $p(z)$, say, p^*_t will be that which maximises the following function

$$\Phi = E_0 \sum_{k=0}^{\infty} (\alpha\beta')^k \left\{ \mu_{t+k} p(z) \left(\frac{p(z)}{P_{t+k}}\right)^{-\theta} Y_{t+k} - \varpi\left[\left(\frac{p(z)}{P_{t+k}}\right)^{-\theta} Y_{t+k}\right]\right\}. \tag{42}$$

So calculating $\frac{\partial \Phi}{\partial p(z)}$ it follows that

$$E_0 \sum_{k=0}^{\infty} \left\{ (\alpha\beta')^k \mu_{t+k} \left(\frac{p(z)}{P_{t+k}}\right)^{-\theta} Y_{t+k} p(z) \frac{1-\theta}{\theta} \right\} =$$

$$- E_0 \sum_{k=0}^{\infty} \left\{ (\alpha\beta')^k \mu_{t+k} \left(\frac{p(z)}{P_{t+k}}\right)^{-\theta} Y_{t+k} \varpi' \left[\frac{\left(\frac{p(z)}{P_{t+k}}\right)^{-\theta} Y_{t+k}}{\mu_{t+k}} \right] \right\},$$

and hence finally that

$$p_t^* = \frac{\theta}{\theta - 1} \frac{E_0 \sum\limits_{k=0}^{\infty} \left\{ (\alpha\beta')^k \mu_{t+k} \left(\frac{p(z)}{P_{t+k}}\right)^{-\theta} Y_{t+k} \varpi' [\cdot] \right\}}{E_0 \sum\limits_{k=0}^{\infty} \left\{ (\alpha\beta')^k \mu_{t+k} \left(\frac{p(z)}{P_{t+k}}\right)^{-\theta} Y_{t+k} \right\}}. \tag{43}$$

Here μ_{t+k} is a measure of aggregate marginal utility, and $\beta = \beta^{'}(1+\lambda)^{-1}$. Expression (43) indicates that the optimal price is a function of expected future demand and cost conditions. It follows that the evolution of the aggregate price-level is given by,[14]

$$P_t = \left[(1-\alpha)p_t^{*1-\theta} + \alpha P_{t-1}^{1-\theta}\right]^{1/(1-\theta)}. \tag{44}$$

4.3 Aggregation

Our aggregator function is a discrete time analogue of Blanchard (1985). Chadha and Nolan (2002e) is a detailed description of our discretisation of the Blanchard (1985) model.

First we note that the size of the cohort born each period is given by

$$\left(\frac{\lambda}{1+\lambda}\right)\left(\frac{1}{1+\lambda}\right)^t.$$

As a result of this, the size of the cohort decreases monotonically with time, and the sum of all currently alive cohorts is equal to unity. That is

$$\frac{\lambda}{1+\lambda} \sum_{j=-\infty}^{t} \left(\frac{1}{1+\lambda}\right)^{(t-j)} = 1. \tag{45}$$

This makes aggregating the model, for the most part, straightforward. In Chadha and Nolan (2002e) we provide more details on these calculations. In particular, for any variable x_t^a (where a indicates an aggregate

[14] A strict interpretation of our set-up implies then that a proportion of each cohort will never get to price some of its output. This is an artifact of combining a yeoman-farmer with a probability of death set-up. If we modelled the corporate sector separately, as in Chadha and Nolan (2002e), this anomaly disappears. Consequently, we ignore it in what follows. Alternatively, one may think of the newly born agents inheriting the price tags of the currently expiring agents.

magnitude) it follows that,

$$x_t^a = \frac{\lambda}{1+\lambda} \sum_{s=-\infty}^{t} \left(\frac{1}{1+\lambda}\right)^{t-s} x_{s,t}$$

where $x_{s,t}$ denotes variable x pertaining to cohort s at time t. The derivation of aggregate consumption dynamics is slightly more involved and we go through that derivation in detail in an appendix. We show that aggregate consumption dynamics are given by the following expression,

$$E_t P_{t+1} C_{t+1} = (1 + i_t)\beta P_t C_t - \lambda\phi E_t W_{t+1}. \tag{46}$$

In the infinite horizon case (where $\lambda = 0$) this expression is simply $E_t P_{t+1} C_{t+1} = (1 + i_t)\beta P_t C_t$, the familiar consumption Euler equation. This equation describes how aggregate consumption evolves through time — and importantly we see that temporal variations in bonds plays no part in determining contemporaneous consumption. In other words, in the absence of distortionary taxation, liquidity constraints, or other financial frictions, deviations from rational expectations and in the presence, as we make clear below, of a Ricardian fiscal policy (and other ingredients of Ricardian equivalence, see Barro, 1974), we see that it makes no odds to the economy whether taxes are raised now or in the future. Agents will consume out of their present value of net wealth, and since lower taxes now resulting in higher taxes in the future does not alter the present value of net wealth, there will be no leverage for fiscal policy to operate in this model via that channel. However, in the case of finite horizons, $\lambda \neq 0$ variations in the temporal allocation of taxes are not 'neutral'. Net wealth is affected by the time profile of taxes. In our simple set-up, that is essentially because the probability of a currently alive cohort facing a given tax bill has fallen and hence the consumption set has expanded.[15]

4.4 Monetary and Fiscal Policy

We shall think of policy makers as setting the per period interest rate and taxes in order to stabilise both output and inflation. That is we are envisaging policy rules of the following sort:

$$i_t = \phi(i)\left[\tilde{Y}_t, \pi_t, E_t\pi_{t+1}, i_{t-1}\right], \tag{47}$$

[15] See Buiter (1988) for an important discussion of non-Ricardian equivalence due to the interplay between birth, death and productivity growth.

and

$$T_t = \phi(T)[G_t, B_{t-1}], \tag{48}$$

where i_t is the short nominal interest rate set in period t, $\tilde{Y}_t$ is the output gap, π_t is the inflation rate in period t, and T_t is per period lump sum taxes. While the monetary rule is fairly standard the rule for the tax needs some explanation. We shall assume that the process for government expenditure is exogenous, and that the fiscal authority sets taxes in response to the level of contemporaneous government expenditure. Following our earlier discussion, we shall also assume that taxes are a function of the level of outstanding debt. The parameter γ in (50) below indicates the proportion of debt that is retired each period, as in Section 3. We shall assume that seigniorage is remitted lump-sum to the private sector.

4.5 The Government Budget

As we saw in Section 3 γ is a key parameter. Here we give another example in this vein for an example of a fiscal rule that we actually use in our simulations below. Recall that the period public sector budget constraint, reproduced here for convenience, may be written as,

$$\frac{B_t}{(1+i_t)} = B_{t-1} + P_t(G_t - T_t) - (M_t - M_{t-1}). \tag{49}$$

The rule for taxes mentioned above is given by

$$T_t = \chi_t G_t - \frac{(M_t - M_{t-1})}{P_t} + \gamma \frac{B_{t-1}}{P_t}. \tag{50}$$

Together these two equations imply that real debt will evolve in the following manner,

$$\frac{b_t}{1+r_t} = (1-\gamma)b_{t-1} + (1-\chi_t)G_t. \tag{51}$$

So we call $(1-\chi_t)G_t$ the per period deficit which we denote D_t. Following the same steps as in Section 3, we see that at $t = T$

$$E_t \frac{b_{t+T}}{\prod_{j=0}^{T}(1+r_{t+j})} = (1-\gamma)^{T+1} b_{t-1} + E_t \sum_{s=0}^{T} \prod_{j=0}^{s-1} \left(\frac{1}{1+r_{t+j}}\right) (1-\gamma)^{T-s} D_{t+s}. \tag{52}$$

To ensure fiscal solvency is obtained via the fiscal authority's choice over the sequence $\{T\}_{t=0}^{\infty}$, we shall assume that the coefficient γ is sufficiently large. In particular that will ensure that policy is Ricardian and that the PVBC is satisfied for any feasible path for the relevant variables.

4.5.1 Why does fiscal policy matter in this model?

In our discussion of consumption dynamics we indicated one way in which fiscal policy has leverage over the economy. In this section we demonstrate this point explicitly. Recall that fiscal policy matters for the level of aggregate demand in this model because it affects the discounted present value of human wealth. Define human wealth, H_t, as equal to the difference between present-value income (let Y_t denote income in period t) and present-value lump-sum taxes (where T_t denotes such taxes in period t). That is,

$$H_t = \sum_{j=0}^{\infty} \left\{ \left(\frac{1}{1+r}\right)^j \left(\frac{1}{1+\lambda}\right)^j Y_{t+j} \right\} - \sum_{j=0}^{\infty} \left\{ \left(\frac{1}{1+r}\right)^j \left(\frac{1}{1+\lambda}\right)^j T_{t+j} \right\}. \quad (53)$$

For simplicity we assume here that the real interest rate is constant, although it will be apparent that nothing crucial hinges on this assumption. Now consider a change in the temporal profile of taxes such that the present discounted value of government surpluses remains unchanged. That is, consider a variation in taxes at time t offset by a one-time change at $t + j$,

$$T_t(1+\triangle) + \left(\frac{1}{1+r}\right)^j (1+\triangle)T_{t+j} = 0.$$

That is,

$$\triangle T_{t+j} = -(1+r)^j \triangle T_t, \quad (54)$$

such that

$$B_{t-1} = \sum_{j=0}^{\infty} \left\{ \left(\frac{1}{1+r}\right)^{t+j} T_{t+j} \right\} - \sum_{j=0}^{\infty} \left\{ \left(\frac{1}{1+r}\right)^{t+j} G_{t+j} \right\}. \quad (55)$$

In the simple representative agent model such an amendment to fiscal policy would leave all real variables unaltered since it would leave the present value of human wealth unchanged, $\triangle H = 0$. Here, however, it is straightforward to show that this will not be the case. First note that the change in human wealth will be given by

$$\triangle H_t = T_t(1+\triangle) + \left\{ \left(\frac{1}{1+r}\right)^j \left(\frac{1}{1+\lambda}\right)^j \right\} (1+\triangle)T_{t+j}. \quad (56)$$

It follows that for $\lambda \neq 0$

$$\triangle H_t = \triangle T_t \left\{ 1 - \left(\frac{1}{1+\lambda} \right)^j \right\} \neq 0. \tag{57}$$

Clearly, if the representative agent here faces a zero (anticipated) probability of death, then the change in present-value human wealth is identically zero, $\triangle H_t = 0$, and the time profile of consumption remains the same despite the temporal reallocation of taxes. So a government that cuts taxes today but leaves fiscal solvency intact can nevertheless influence the level of private sector demand. And the longer the fiscal authority waits to tighten fiscal policy to offset today's relaxation, the larger will be the impact on aggregate demand.

However there are additional effects from fiscal policy. To see this note that in our model aggregate demand is simply given by

$$Y_t^d = C_t + G_t. \tag{58}$$

The *aggregate* consumption function at time t is given by

$$C_t = \frac{1+\lambda-\beta}{1+\lambda} \times \left[b_{t-1} + E_t \sum_{s=t}^{\infty} \prod_{j=t}^{s-1} \left\{ \left(\frac{1}{1+r_{t+j}} \right) \left(\frac{1}{1+\lambda} \right)^{s-t} (Y_s - T_s) \right\} \right], \tag{59}$$

where we are ignoring the effect of money balances. We see that the path of taxes impacts negatively on consumption as it reduces net wealth. Following Blanchard (1985) we construct an index of fiscal stance, IFS_t, which characterises the net effect of fiscal variables on aggregate demand:

$$IFS_t = G_t - \frac{1+\lambda-\beta}{1+\lambda} \left[E_t \sum_{s=t}^{\infty} \prod_{j=t}^{s-1} \left\{ \left(\frac{1}{1+r_{t+j}} \right) \left(\frac{1}{1+\lambda} \right)^{s-t} G_s \right\} \right]$$
$$+ \frac{1+\lambda-\beta}{1+\lambda} \left[\begin{array}{c} b_{t-1} + \\ E_t \sum_{s=t}^{\infty} \prod_{j=t}^{s-1} \left\{ \left(\frac{1}{1+r_{t+j}} \right) \left(\frac{1}{1+\lambda} \right)^{s-t} (G_s - T_s) \right\} \end{array} \right]. \tag{60}$$

The first line is the effect of government expenditure on aggregate demand when it is financed out of contemporaneous taxation, whilst the second line is the effect of financing via debt issue. To see this more clearly, recall that the government's present-value budget is

$$b_{t-1} = -E_t \sum_{s=t}^{\infty} \prod_{j=t}^{s-1} \left\{ \left(\frac{1}{1+r_{t+j}} \right) (G_s - T_s) \right\}, \tag{61}$$

where we have again partialled out the seigniorage term. Hence the index may now be written as,

$$IFS_t = G_t - \frac{1+\lambda-\beta}{1+\lambda}\left[E_t \sum_{s=t}^{\infty}\prod_{j=t}^{s-1}\left\{\left(\frac{1}{1+r_{t+j}}\right)\left(\frac{1}{1+\lambda}\right)^{s-t} G_s\right\}\right]$$
$$+\frac{1+\lambda-\beta}{1+\lambda}\left[E_t \sum_{s=t}^{\infty}\prod_{j=t}^{s-1}\left\{\frac{\left(\frac{1}{1+r_{t+j}}\right)}{\left[1-\left(\frac{1}{1+\lambda}\right)^{s-t}\right]}(G_s - T_s)\right\}\right]. \quad (62)$$

Here, if $\lambda = 0$ we see that the second line is identically zero, and there is no net wealth effect. If, however, $b_{t-1} > 0$, then outstanding bonds will tend to boost aggregate demand. The correspondence between the second line in this expression and equation (57) is clear.

5 Optimal Simple Rules for Fiscal and Monetary Policy

In our set-up the policy maker needs to decide on monetary policy *and* fiscal policy. Rather than simply impose a monetary rule that conforms to the Taylor principle we therefore optimise over the parameter space that spans both the monetary and fiscal policy rules, for a given functional form for both rules. We shall see in what ways the addition of fiscal policy affects the optimal simple monetary rule — which in principle need not now conform to the Taylor principle.[16] To be more specific, we shall assume that monetary and fiscal policy are set jointly optimal, under the assumption of perfect credibility and assuming that the policy maker has a quadratic criterion function in annualised output, inflation and interest rates. In effect, then, there is here a single policy maker which determines monetary and fiscal policy jointly, subject to the requirement that fiscal

[16] We extend the King and Watson (1997) code to perform what is, in effect, a grid search over the policy parameters such that the policy maker's loss function is minimised. Alternative code has been written by Richard Dennis (2001) to solve for optimal simple rules under rational expectations. This latter algorithm, however, requires something close to what we call the B matrix in (63) below to be non-singular. For larger models that is often inconvenient since then some manual system reduction is required. Our code requires neither A nor B to be singular. The King and Watson (1997) reduction algorithm deals with singular A matrices whilst our method of calculating the model's asymptotic variance-coviariance matrix does not require the inversion of B at any step along the way. Dennis' (2001) code however can also be used to solve for the case when precommitment is not feasible.

policy must at all times ensure that policy is Ricardian, in the sense of Woodford (2000).[17]

5.1 Solving the Model and Optimal Simple Rules

We use our model developed in the previous section to solve for equilibrium processes for the evolution of aggregate wealth, consumption, money holdings, inflation, the short-term nominal interest rate, the level of taxation, the level of government interest-bearing debt and aggregate output. To do this we used the following equations (converted into aggregate form as required): (35), (41), (43), (44), (46), (47), (48) together with an equation describing the aggregate economy-wide resource constraint. The feedback coefficients in the policy rules, equations (47) and (48), are left unspecified and we solve for these adopting a quadratic criterion for the policy maker. In practice that means we need to calculate, for a given stochastic structure for the economy's driving processes, the asymptotic variance-covariance matrix for the economy's endogenous variables. We first linearise the model around its non-stochastic steady state. Then we make an initial guess about the optimal policy parameters (given the other parametric assumptions we have made) and verify that the model admits a unique stable rational expectations equilibrium under this parameter constellation. In the event that such an equilibrium exists we are able to calculate the loss function of the policy maker. We then redo this calculation for an alternative selection of policy rule parameter values, and compare losses, and continue in this way until a minimum for the loss function is located. The linearised model can be represented in the following way with all variables in percentage deviation from the steady state:

$$AE_t y_{t+1} = By_t + Cx_t \qquad \forall t \geq 0, \tag{63}$$

where y_t is a vector of endogenous variables comprising both predetermined and non-predetermined variables including policy rules for the nominal interest rate and taxes, x_t is a vector of exogenous variables, and A, B and C are matrices of fixed, time-invariant, coefficients. E_t is the expectations operator conditional on information available at time t. King and Watson (1997) demonstrate that if a solution to (63) exists

[17] There have been a few recent studies which have solved for optimal simple rules. These are Williams (1999), Erceg, Henderson and Levin (2000). These studies both focussed on Taylor-type rules. Batini, Harrison and Millard (2001) subject an open economy DSGE model to a battery of optimised rules, including Taylor rules, nominal income targteing rules, exchange rate rules and inflation targeting rules. None of the above papers have focussed on the fiscal policy issues.

and is unique then we may write that solution in state-space form as follows,

$$\begin{aligned} y_t &= \Pi s_t \\ s_t &= M s_{t-1} + G e_t, \end{aligned} \tag{64}$$

where the s_t matrix includes the state variables of the model (predetermined variables along with exogenous state variables), and e_t is a vector of shocks to the state variables. The y_t matrix has also been augmented to include the model's exogenous state variables. To proceed, iterate on the second set of equations. Since there are a sufficient number of stable roots, we have that

$$s_t = G \sum_{j=0}^{\infty} M^j e_{t-j}. \tag{65}$$

Using this in the first set of equations in (64), defining $\Phi \equiv \Pi G$, and noting that the stochastic shocks to the economy are covariance stationary, it follows that we may write,

$$y_t y_t' \equiv \Sigma = \sum_{j=0}^{\infty} \Phi M^j \Omega M^{j\prime} \Phi', \tag{66}$$

where a prime denotes a transpose and $\Omega \equiv e_t e_t'$. Let Σ_x denote the asymptotic variance of the annualised value of x. Then, using the relevant entries from the Σ matrix for given policy rules we can evaluate the policy maker's loss function which we assume is given by

$$L = \alpha_1 \Sigma_\pi + \alpha_2 \Sigma_y + \alpha_3 \Sigma_i. \tag{67}$$

Following Chadha and Nolan (2002d) we set $\alpha_1 = \alpha_2 = 1$, and $\alpha_3 = 0.25$. In what follows we generate sequences of systems (63) under alternative guesses on the optimal parameters in our policy rules which we then evaluate using (67). Our aim, of course, is to find parameter values which minimise (67), given the functional form of the rules under consideration. In an appendix we set out the parameter values that we adopt for our calibration exercises as well as our assumptions on the forcing processes.

5.2 Simulations

Recall that our aim is to identify the jointly optimal rules for monetary and fiscal policy given our assumed criterion for the policy maker. Our benchmark simple rules are of the following form for monetary policy;

$$R_t = \alpha_1(\pi_t - \pi^*) + \alpha_2(E_t \pi_{t+1} - \pi^*) + \alpha_3(y_t - y_t^*) + \alpha_4 R_{t-1},$$

Interest rate rule		Fiscal rule	
$\pi_t - \pi^*$	1.1513	$\pi_t - \pi^*$	0
$y_t - y_t^*$	0.0631	$y_t - y_t^*$	1.7522
R_{t-1}	0.2511	D_{t-1}	0.5712

Table 2: The Simple Taylor Rule

and

$$D_t = \beta_1(\pi_t - \pi^*) + \beta_2(E_t\pi_{t+1} - \pi^*) + \beta_3(y_t - y_t^*) + \beta_4 D_{t-1},$$

for fiscal policy. In all of the simulations we have constrained $\beta_1 = \beta_2 = 0$. From the literature on Taylor rules (see, for example, Woodford, 1999) it is often argued that a weight of greater than unity on inflation and a weight close to zero on output has desirable stabilising properties (see also Christiano and Gust, 1999). In fact, in most studies these parameters are simply imposed and the behaviour of the model analysed under these imposed rules. Our first simulation sets $\alpha_2 = 0$. Our results are given in Table 2.

The numbers in this table correspond to the values of the optimised coefficients associated with the arguments (indicated to the left) in the reaction functions. As regards the monetary policy rule, there is much that looks familiar. First, the feedback from inflation, at just over 1.5 (i.e., 0.06 ÷ (1 – 0.25)) conforms to the Taylor principle, with Taylor himself arguing for a number in the region of 1.5. The weight on output, on the other hand, is somewhat lower than Taylor suggested, but is in keeping with the more recent work of Christiano and Gust (1999) and Woodford (2000). The fiscal rule suggests that the response of the fiscal surplus:GDP ratio should be in the region of 0.75 contemporaneously and somewhat larger than this in the long run. Taylor, on the other hand, argues for a value of around 0.5.[18]

One way to interpret this result is to argue that in a model where both monetary and fiscal policy act to stabilise economic fluctuations, the Taylor principle for interest rates — that rates should move at least equi-proportionally with inflation — needs to be respected alongside an active counter-cyclical fiscal policy. In other words the optimality of the Taylor principle seems, in some degree, to be predicated on similar optimality on fiscal policy.

[18] The simulations actually involve the (log linearised) surplus. Straightforward algebra recovers the implied response of the D/Y ratio.

5.3 Model Responses and Matching Data

We study the impulse responses of output, interest rates, the fiscal balance and inflation to 1 per cent shocks from each of the forcing variables given the optimised coefficients reported in Table 2. From the plots of these responses, a picture emerges of monetary and fiscal policy working as complementary sequences of choices.[19]

The economy's response to a symmetric persistent productivity shock is as follows. Naturally, output responds positively and with a high degree of persistence to a productivity shock. Inflation mirrors the response by falling below baseline for 7 quarters, as falling marginal costs put downward pressure on firms' prices. The optimal policy response sees the nominal interest rate fall below base, while the fiscal surplus rises. Nominal interest rates are cut in order to stabilise falling inflation and lump-sum taxation tempers aggregate demand.

The response of the economy to innovations in the economy's interest rate rule involves output remaining below its steady-state level for some 10 quarters, although it is within 0.1 per cent of base after only 3 quarters. Output falls because a monetary policy shock increases real rates. Fiscal policy responds to this monetary tightening by running a (persistent) deficit. The maximal response is in the first period where the deficit increases by 1.0 per cent, which is some 0.4 per cent greater than the fall in output. Inflation responds quickly to the monetary shock, falling by just under 0.5 per cent in the first period and returns more than half way to base by period 2.

Fiscal policy shocks impact on output, nominal interest rates and inflation as follows. The fiscal impact on output operates via government expenditure and bonds. The increase in output and inflation caused by the impact on aggregate demand leads to a persistent but small rise in nominal interest rates. The effects of government expenditure are analysed in Baxter and King (1993). Briefly, a rise in government expenditure on final goods results in a rise in labour supply which boosts aggregate output (despite pushing down on aggregate consumption). It turns out that the transmission channel of fiscal policy identified by Baxter and King (1993) is also dominant in the current set-up. In other words the wealth effect of outstanding government bonds is of second-order importance. Chadha and Nolan (2002e) demonstrate this point in more detail.

A dichotomy can be drawn between the response of inflation and

[19] For a full set of impulse responses the reader is referred to Chadha and Nolan (2002d).

output to monetary as opposed to fiscal shocks, as monetary shocks, see Figures 3–6, induce large initial responses that tail away relatively quickly whereupon fiscal shocks induce smaller but significantly more persistent responses. This dichotomy provides a clue as to why Table 2 suggests that monetary policy concentrates on inflation and fiscal policy on output. In the forward-looking Phillips curve, inflation jumps and therefore can be well stabilised by an initially strong impetus from monetary policy. Output, on the other hand, inherits considerable persistence from the exogenous equilibrium process for the determination of potential and appears to best be stabilised by a policy with similar characteristics.

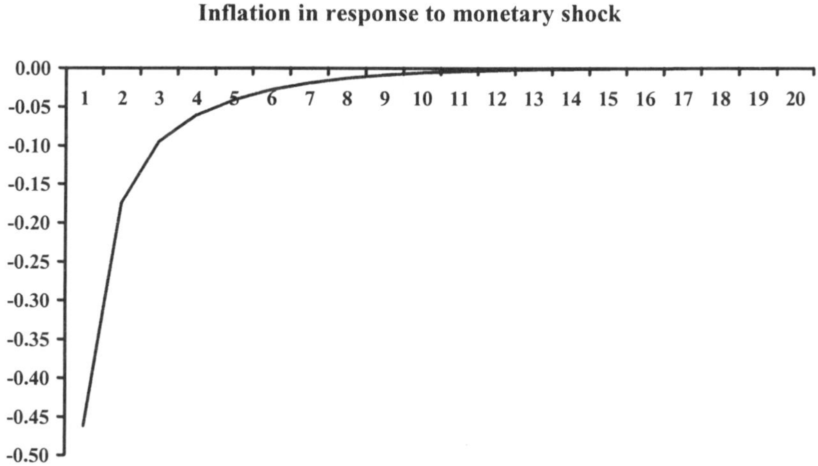

Figure 3: Monetary Transmission Mechanism: Inflation

In Chadha and Nolan (2002e) we calibrated these simple optimised rules to the US and UK data. Here we just look at the UK data and optimised rules (Figures 7 and 8). This exercise is intended to see if these rules — particularly for the deficit — look plausible. The monetary policy rule does a reasonably good job of tracking the data. Similarly, the fiscal rule follows the general movement in the actual data. However, towards the start of the sample the optimised fiscal rule appears to imply large swings in the deficit. This reflects relatively large swings in the output gap in the UK and the effects of the strong feedback from the output gap in our optimised rule. (These same features are also evident

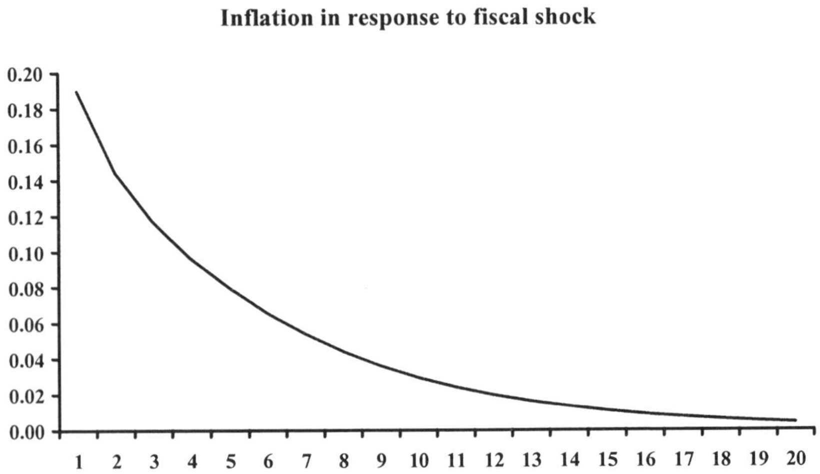

Figure 4: Fiscal Transmission Mechanism: Inflation

in our simulations on US data.) Our assumption that all government expenditure is on final goods and that it is financed ultimately only out of lump sum tax means that it is relatively costless for the fiscal authority to design a systematic component for fiscal policy that implies potentially wide swings in net expenditure. Nevertheless, given that our model has such a simple structure, the ability of the model to capture some of the movement in actual data provides us with comfort that our results provide some insight.

5.3.1 Monetary–fiscal interactions

We now turn to three further experiments. First, there has been much recent interest in the welfare and stabilisation properties of inflation (forecast) targeting regimes. This interest has, of course, been the result of a number of countries adopting such a nominal regime, and with a degree of success that has often appeared elusive under alternative nominal frameworks.[20] Some analysts have argued that feedback from expected inflation may have desirable stabilisation properties (see, for example, Taylor, 1999). We therefore augmented our simple Taylor rule

[20] See Canzoneri, Nolan and Yates (1997) for a discussion of why this may be the case when credibility is an issue.

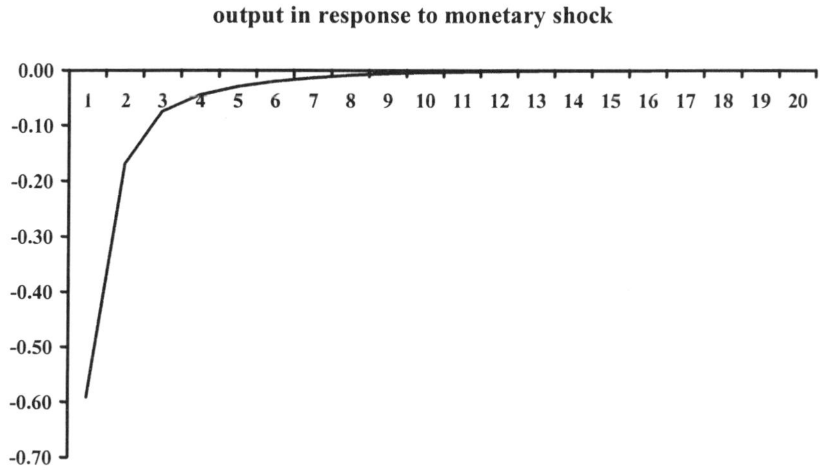

Figure 5: Monetary Transmission Mechanism: Output

to include the possibility of some feedback from expected inflation. The results are given in Table 3. Again the monetary policy rule has familiar properties, with a response of the interest rate to inflation of just under 1.3 ($(\alpha_1 + \alpha_2) \div (1 - \alpha_4)$), and to output of around 0.06. To a first-order approximation, then, the inclusion of inflation expectations substitutes for the lagged interest rate in Table 2. By and large the fiscal rule is unaltered, which is unsurprising given that the monetary policies reported in Tables 2 and 3 are very similar.

	Interest rate rule		Fiscal rule
$\pi_t - \pi^*$	1.0981	$\pi_t - \pi^*$	0
$E_t\pi_{t+1} - \pi^*$	0.2927	$E_t\pi_{t+1} - \pi^*$	0
$y_t - y_t^*$	0.0548	$y_t - y_t^*$	1.8151
R_{t-1}	0.0958	D_{t-1}	0.5271

Table 3: Inflation Expectations Augmented Taylor Rule

Next, we assess a suggestion of Robert Mundell (1971) that monetary policy should focus on inflation control, and fiscal policy on real objectives. We take this regime to be one where $\alpha_2 = \alpha_3 = 0$, and as before $\beta_1 = \beta_2 = 0$. As pointed out in the Section 5.3, it seems that the impact of the respective arms of stabilisation policy should concentrate

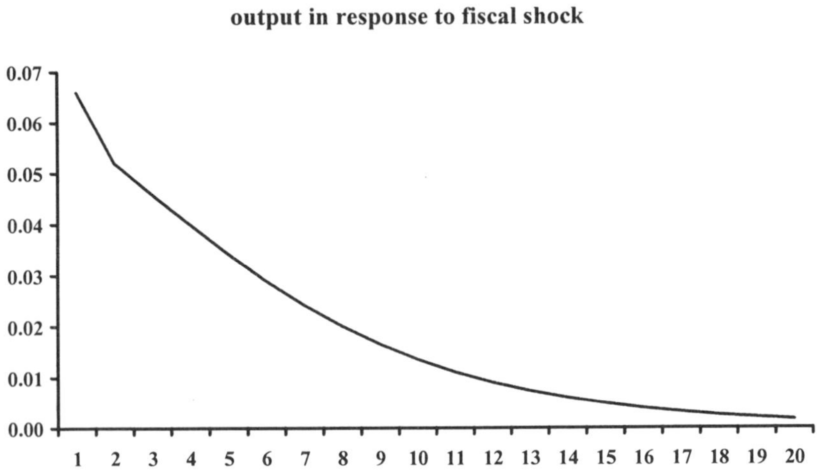

Figure 6: Fiscal Transmission Mechanism: Output

on where they have most efficacy, as suggested by Mundell.

	Interest rate rule		Fiscal rule
$\pi_t - \pi^*$	1.07	$\pi_t - \pi^*$	-
$y_t - y_t^*$	-	$y_t - y_t^*$	1.11
R_{t-1}	0.19	D_{t-1}	0.65

Table 4: Mundell Assignment Rule

Table 4 shows that the weights in the optimal rules derived in Tables 2 and 3 are not particularly far from that which would be implied by the implementation of Mundell's (1971) suggestion. Again, the monetary feedback on inflation at 1.3 seems reasonable, while the fiscal feedback remains similar to before. It is interesting to note that both rules seem a little less vigorous than before.

Our final illustration in Table 5 shows the implications for optimal monetary and fiscal policy from an 'active' fiscal policy, in the sense of Chadha and Nolan (2002d). That is where the weight on output in the fiscal rule is constrained to be greater than the long-run consumption multiplier i.e. $(1 - c/y)^{-1}$. The table shows that active fiscal policy in this case engenders similarly active monetary policy in order to reach the optimum. This means that aggressive fiscal policy will be complemented

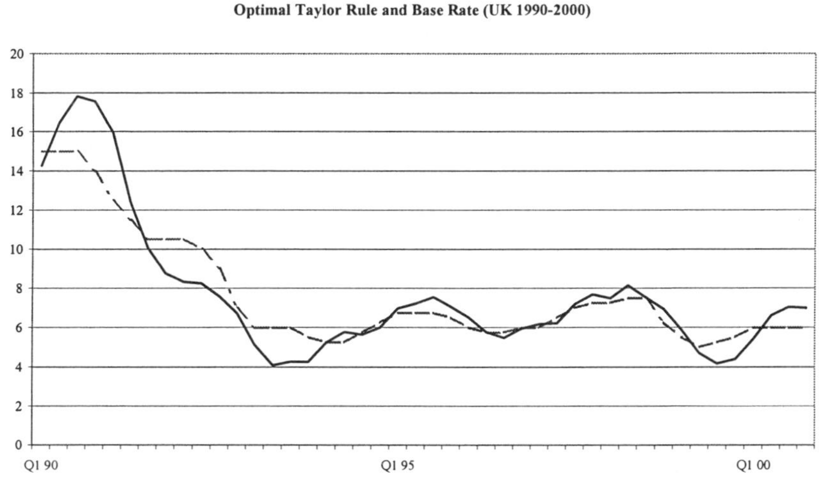

Figure 7: Optimal Taylor Rule and Base Rate (UK 1990–2000)

	Interest rate rule		Fiscal Rule
$\pi_t - \pi^*$	2.1404	$\pi_t - \pi^*$	0
$y_t - y_t^*$	0.3257	$y_t - y_t^*$	3.6755
R_{t-1}	0.5	D_{t-1}	0.5

Table 5: The Simple Taylor Rule under Active Fiscal Policy

by a similar monetary policy, driving the long-run reaction of interest rates to inflation to 4.28 in order to stabilise the economy optimally: aggression breeds aggression. In Chadha and Nolan (2002e) a number of further experiments are conducted. However the same basic intuition is present, in that when one rule is constrained to deviate from its optimised form, the other rule ends up acting to try to compensate.

The three simulations in this section indicate a number of issues worth pursuing further. The Mundellian assignment strategy is near the optimum of our constrained optimal rules. Inflation targeting, or at least our version of it, does not appear to make much difference to the behaviour of our model economy as the feedback from anticipated inflation substitutes for the lack of a feedback from the lagged interest rate. Finally, aggressive behaviour in one rule generates a complementary response from the other: in our final example an aggressive fiscal policy optimally engendered an aggressive monetary policy.

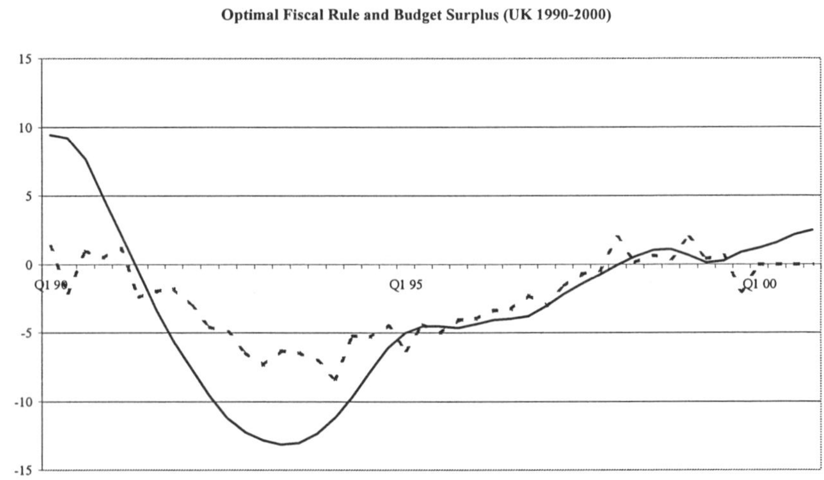

Figure 8: Optimal Fiscal Rule and Budget Surplus (UK 1990–2000)

6 Conclusions

In this paper we have reviewed two dimensions of the interaction of monetary and fiscal policy, which have been of prominent concern to policy makers. How should fiscal policy operate so that monetary policy is constrained to a minimal extent? And how should we design optimal simple rules for both monetary and fiscal policy. We have stressed that the clearest link in the two arms of stabilisation policy is that of the interest rates. The interest rate regulates demand in the economy but as it also sets the cost of any given fiscal plans, we therefore have to formulate acceptable plans that respect this inherent tension.

Fiscal solvency remains an important concern in the design of macroeconomic policy. The Growth and Stability Pact in Europe is one example of an attempt to deal with this concern. And although fiscal constraints are clearly necessary for monetary flexibility it seems unlikely, in light of our analysis, that a once-and-for-all limit of 3 per cent on the fiscal deficit can be considered anything other than arbitrary. We need more work to calibrate the optimal fiscal plans for economies that are members of a monetary union.

Our results in Sections 4 and 5 present an initial attempt to analyse that second issue by assuming the adoption of jointly optimal plans. There are a number of important directions in which that analysis may be taken. Obvious extensions include the incorporation of distortionary taxation and of 'useful' government expenditure.[21]

Appendix: Parameterisation of Model

Table 6 outlines the baseline parameter values that we adopt for the calibration of the model. More discussion of these and the driving processes that we adopt can be found in Chadha and Nolan (2002e).

Symbol	Value	Description
λ	0.00357	Expected life remaining: 70 years
r	0.0125	Real interest rate
β	0.95	Subjective discount factor
δ	0.053	Subjective discount rate
γ	0.06	Rate of debt retirement
$\frac{c}{y}$	0.6	Steady-state consumption–output ratio
$\frac{m}{w}$	0.1	Steady-state money–wealth ratio
κ	0.5	Phillips curve slope
$\frac{w}{c}$	0.7	Steady-state wealth–consumption ratio

Table 6: Calibration Parameters for Quarterly Model

The model is calibrated at a quarterly frequency using more or less standard parameter values. We assume that λ is determined as a result of the representative agent expecting to live to 70. The discount factor, β, is set at 0.95. Numerical investigations led us to set the debt retirement rate, γ, to 0.06. The consumption:income ratio, c/y, is equal to 0.6, while the steady-state money:wealth ratio, m/w, was chosen to be 0.1. Roughly speaking the average size of the UK debt-to-GDP ratio over the post-war period has been some 40 per cent. Together with our assumption for c/y, implies that the steady-state wealth:income ratio for this simple model economy is 0.7.

Let a_t, f_t, and h_t denote the log detrended processes for productivity, fiscal and monetary innovations, respectively. We then assume they can be described adequately for our purposes as follows,

$$\begin{bmatrix} a_t \\ f_t \\ h_t \end{bmatrix} = \begin{bmatrix} \rho_a & 0 & 0 \\ 0 & \rho_f & 0 \\ 0 & 0 & \rho_q \end{bmatrix} \begin{bmatrix} a_{t-1} \\ f_{t-1} \\ h_{t-1} \end{bmatrix} + \begin{bmatrix} x_t \\ g_t \\ q_t \end{bmatrix},$$

[21] Also as Finn (1998) notes, the distinction between government expenditure on final goods and government employment is likely to be important.

where x_t, g_t, and q_t are the shocks respectively to productivity, fiscal and monetary innovations. We adopted an agnostic strategy for setting the covariation structure of the forcing variables. First we estimated Solow residuals, Taylor rules and fiscal rule equations on US and UK data and found little difference in the standard errors of the respective equations. Similarly Cardia (1991) found that the standard deviation of shocks to the monetary and fiscal processes were of similar magnitude in the US data, whilst in the German data the standard deviations of fiscal and productivity shocks were of a similar size. In practice, then, we decided simply to set $\sigma_a = \sigma_f = \sigma_q = 0.01$. In terms of the persistence parameters we chose the following: $\rho_a = 0.9$, $\rho_f = 0.9$, and $\rho_q = 0$. In Chadha and Nolan (2002e) we discuss these stochastic settings further and show the full set of impulse response functions. We found that our results were fairly insensitive to alternative plausible assumptions vis à vis persistence and volatility of underlying shocks.

Bibliography

[1] Aiyagari, S.R., L.J. Christiano and M. Eichenbaum (1992), "The Output, Employment, and Interest Rate Effects of Government Consumption", *Journal of Monetary Economics* (30)1, pp. 73–86.

[2] Barro, R.J. (1974), "Are Government Bonds Net Wealth?", *Journal of Political Economy*, 82(6), pp 1095–1117.

[3] Barro, R.J. (1979), "On the Determination of the Public Debt", *Journal of Political Economy*, 87(5:1), pp 940–71.

[4] Barro, R. J. (1981), "Output Effects of Government Purchases", *The Journal of Political Economy*, 89(6: December), pp. 1086–1121.

[5] Batini, N., R. Harrison and S.P. Millard (2001), "Monetary Policy Rules for an Open Economy", Bank of England Working Paper No. 149.

[6] Baxter, M. and R.G. King (1991), "Productive externalities and business cycles," Discussion Paper / Institute for Empirical Macroeconomics 53, Federal Reserve Bank of Minneapolis.

[7] Blanchard, O.J. (1985), "Debts, Deficits and Finite Horizons" *Journal of Political Economy, 93,* pp. 223–247.

[8] Blinder, A.S. and R.M. Solow (1973), "Does Fiscal Policy Matter", *Journal of Public Economics*, Jan/Feb, 2, pp. 319–337.

[9] Bohn, H. (1998a), "The Behaviour of U.S. Public Debt and Deficits", *Quarterly Journal of Economics*, 113(3), pp. 949–963

[10] Bohn, H. (1998b), "Comment on John Cochrane, 'A frictionless view of US inflation"', NBER Macroeconomics Annual, edited by Ben S. Bernanke and Julio J. Rotemberg, MIT Press, Cambridge, Massachusetts, pp. 323–384

[11] Bohn, H. (1995), "The Sustainability of Government Deficits in a Stochastic Economy", *Journal of Money, Credit and Banking*, 27(1:February), pp. 257–271.

[12] Brock, W.A. (1975), "A Simple Perfect Foresight Monetary Model" *Journal of Monetary Economics*, 1, pp. 133–150.

[13] Buiter, W. H., (1988), "Death, Birth, Productivity Growth and Debt Neutrality", *The Economic Journal*, 98(391:June), pp. 279–293.

[14] Buiter, W.H. (1998), "The Young Person's Guide to Neutrality, Price Level Indeterminacy, Interest Rate Pegs and Fiscal Theories of the Price Level", NBER Working Paper, no 6396, Cambridge, Massachusetts.

[15] Buiter, Willem (1999), "The Fallacy of the Fiscal Theory of the Price-Level", Mimeo.

[16] Calvo, G.A. (1983), "Staggered Prices in a Utility Maximising Framework", *Journal of Monetary Economics,* 12(3:September), pp. 983–998.

[17] Calvo, G.A. (1985), "Macroeconomic Implications of the Government Budget Constraint: Some Basic Considerations", *Journal of Monetary Economics*, 15, pp. 95-112.

[18] Canzoneri, M.B., R.E. Cumby and B.T. Diba (2001), "Is The Price Level Determined by the Needs of Fiscal Solvency?", *American Economic Review*, 91(5), December 2001, 1221–1238

[19] Canzoneri, M.B., C. Nolan and A. Yates, (1997), "Mechanisms for Achieving Monetary Stability: Inflation Targeting versus the ERM", *Journal of Money, Credit and Banking*, 29(1), pp. 46–60.

[20] Cardia, E. (1991), "The Dynamics of a Small Open Economy in Response to Monetary, Fiscal and Productivity Shocks", *Journal of Monetary Economics*, 28(3), pp. 411–434.

[21] Chadha, J.S., N. Janssen and C. Nolan (2001), "Productivity and Preferences in a Small Open Economy", *The Manchester School*, 69(1:September), pp. 57–80.

[22] Chadha, J.S. and C. Nolan (2002a), "Price Level versus Inflation Targeting in a New Keynesian General Equilibrium Macro-Model", *The Manchester School, 70(4),* Special Issue, pp. 570–595.

[23] Chadha, J.S. and C. Nolan (2002b), "Supply Shocks and the Natural Rate of Interest: An Exploration" in *The Theory and Practice of Monetary Transmission in Diverse Economies*" edited by P.J. Sinclair *et al.*, Cambridge University Press, Cambridge.

[24] Chadha, J.S. and C. Nolan (2002c), "Output, Inflation and the New Keynesian Phillips Curve", DAE Working Paper No. 0204.

[25] Chadha, J.S. and C. Nolan (2002d), "The Interaction of Monetary and Fiscal Policy: Forthcoming in Dynamic Macroeconomic Analysis: — Theory and Policy in General Equilibrium, Cambridge University Press, edited by S. Altug, J.S. Chadha and C. Nolan.

[26] Chadha, J.S. and C. Nolan (2002e), "Optimal Simple Rules for the Conduct of Monetary and Fiscal Policy". Working paper, available at http://www.dur.ac.uk/charles.nolan/index.html

[27] Chari, V.V. and P. Kehoe (1999), "Optimal Fiscal and Monetary Policy", Handbook of Macroeconomics, J. Taylor and M. Woodford, (eds.), North Holland: Amsterdam

[28] Christiano, L.J., and T.J. Fitzgerald (2000), "Understanding the Fiscal Theory of the Price Level", *Federal Reserve Bank of Cleveland Economic Review*, 36(2), pp. 1–37

[29] Christiano, L. J and C. J. Gust (1999), "Taylor Rules in a Limited Participation Model", NBER Working Paper No. w7017, March.

[30] Cochrane, J. (1998), "A frictionless view of US inflation", NBER Macroeconomics Annual, edited by Ben S. Bernanke and Julio J. Rotemberg, MIT Press, Cambridge, Massachusetts, pp. 323–384

[31] Cochrane, J. (2001a), "Long term debt and optimal policy in the fiscal theory of the price level", *Econometrica,* 69(1:January), pp. 69-116.

[32] Cochrane, J. (2001b), "Money as Stock", Revised June 2001 (Original August 1999), Mimeo, Chicago.

[33] Dennis, R. (2001), "Solving for Simple Rules in Rational Expectations Models", Working Paper, Federal Reserve Bank of San Francisco Number 00-14.

[34] Eichengreen, B. and C. Wyplosz (1998), "Stability Pact: More than a Minor Nuisance?", *Economic Policy*, April, pp. 67-113.

[35] Erceg, C., D. Henderson and A. Levin (2000), "Optimal monetary policy with staggered wage and price contracts", *Journal of Monetary Economics*, 46, pp. 281–313.

[36] Fatas, A. and I. Mihov (1999), "Government Size and Automatic Stabilizers: International and International Evidence", CEPR Working Paper No. 2259.

[37] Finn, M.G. (1998), "Cyclical Effects of Government's Employment and Goods Purchases", *International Economic Review*, 39(3), pp. 635–657.

[38] Friedman, M. and A.J. Schwartz (1963), A Monetary History of the United States, 1867–1960 Princeton University Press.

[39] Grilli, V., D. Masciandaro, and G. Tabellini (1991), "Political and Monetary Institutions and Public Financial Policies in the Industrial Countries", *Economic Policy,* 13, pp. 341–92.

[40] Hamilton, J.D. and M.A. Flavin (1986), "On the Limitations of Government Borrowing: A Framework for Empirical Testing", *American Economic Review*, 76(4), pp. 808–819

[41] Hansen, L.P. and Sargent, T.J.(1998), *Recursive Linear Models of Dynamic Economies*, Chicago: University of Chicago Press.

[42] Hudson, S. and C. Nolan (1996), "Seigniorage Revenues in the G7", Bank of England *mimeo.*

[43] Janssen, N., C. Nolan and R.S. Thomas (1999), "Money, Debt and Prices in the UK 1705–1996", Working Paper, Forthcoming in *Economica.*

[44] King, M.A. (1995), Comment on "Monetary Policy Implications of Greater Fiscal Discipline", by J.B. Taylor, Paper presented at Federal Reserve Bank of Kansas City Jackson Hole Symposium, Wyoming, August 31–September 2, 1995.

[45] King, R.G. and M.W. Watson, (1997), Testing Long-Run Neutrality. *Economic Quarterly*, Federal Reserve Bank of Richmond, 83/3 summer, pp. 69–101.

[46] Kocherlakota, N. and C. Phelan (1999), "Explaining the Fiscal Theory of the Price Level", *Federal Reserve Bank of Minneapolis Quarterly Review*, 23(4), pp. 14–23

[47] Leeper, E (1991), "Equilibria Under 'Active' and 'Passive' Monetary Policies", *Journal of Monetary Economics*, 27(1), pp. 129–47.

[48] Lucas, R.E., Jr (1996), "Nobel Lecture: Monetary Neutrality", *Journal of Political Economy*, 104(4), pp. 661–682.

[49] McCallum, B.T. (1981), "Monetarist Principles and the Money Stock Growth Rule", *The American Economic Review*, 71(2), Papers and Proceedings of the Ninety-Third Annual Meeting of the American Economic Association. (May), pp. 134–138.

[50] McCallum, B.T. (1984), "Are Bond-Financed Deficits Inflationary? A Ricardian Analysis", *Journal of Political Economy*, 91(1), pp. 123–135.

[51] McCallum, B.T. (2001), "Indeterminacy, Bubbles and the Fiscal Theory of Price-Level Determination", *Journal of Monetary Economics*, 47(1:February), pp. 19–30.

[52] Mundell, R.A. (1971), "The Dollar and the Policy Mix: 1971", *Essays in International Finance No 85*, International Finance Section, Princeton University.

[53] Obstfeld, M. and K. Rogoff (1983), "Speculative Hyperinflations in Maximizing Models: Can We Rule Them Out?", *Journal of Monetary Economics*, 91(4), pp. 675–687.

[54] O'Connell, S.A. and S.P. Zeldes (1988), "Rational Ponzi Games", *International Economic Review*, 29. pp. 431–450.

[55] Offer, A (2002), "Why has the Public Sector Grown So Large in Market Societies? The Political Economy of Prudence in the UK, c1870–2000:", Inaugural Lecture for the Chichele Chair in Economic History at the University of Oxford, November 2001.

[56] Rudin, W. (1976), *Principles of Mathematical Analysis*, Third Edition, McGraw-Hill International Edition.

[57] Sargent, T.J. (1987), *Dynamic Macroeconomic Theory,* Harvard University Press.

[58] Sargent, T.J. and Neil Wallace (1975), "'Rational Expectations', the Optimal Monetary Instrument, and the Optimal Money Supply Rule", *Journal of Political Economy*, 83(2), pp. 241–254.

[59] Sargent, T.J. and N. Wallace (1981), "Some Unpleasant Monetarist Arithmetic", *Federal Reserve Bank of Minneapolis Quarterly Review*, 5(3), pp. 1–17

[60] Sidrauski, M (1965) "Rational Choice and Patterns of Growth in a Monetary Economy", *American Economic Review*, 57(2:May), pp. 534–544.

[61] Sims, C. (1994), "A Simple Model for the Study of the Price Level and the Interaction of Monetary and Fiscal Policy", *Economic Theory*, 4(2), pp. 381–399

[62] Sims, C. (1999), "The Precarious Fiscal Foundations of EMU", *De Economist*, 147(4), pp. 415–436

[63] Stein, J.L. (ed) (1976), *Monetarism*, Amsterdam.

[64] Taylor, J.B. (1999), *Monetary Policy Rules*, Chicago: University of Chicago Press, NBER.

[65] Taylor, J.B. (1993), "Discretion versus Rules in Practice", *Carnegie-Rochester Conference Series on Public Policy*, 39, pp. 195–214.

[66] Williams, J.C. (1999), "Simple Rules for Monetary Policy", Board of Governors of the Federal Reserve System, Finance and Economics Discussion Paper, No. 1999-12, February, Washington.

[67] Woodford, M. (1995), "Price Level Determinacy without Control of a Monetary Aggregate", *Carnegie-Rochester Conference Series on Public Policy*, 43, pp. 1–46

[68] Woodford, M (1997), "Control of the Public Debt: A Requirement for Price Stability?", in *The Debt Burden and Monetary Policy*, eds: G.A. Calvo, and M.A. King, London: MacMillan.

[69] Woodford, M. (1998a), Public Debt and the Price Level, Princeton University, mimeo.

[70] Woodford, M. (1998b), "Comment on John Cochrane, 'A frictionless view of US inflation"', in *NBER Macroeconomics Annual*, edited by B.S. Bernanke and J.J. Rotemberg, MIT Press, Cambridge, Massachusetts, pp. 400–428

[71] Woodford, M. (2000), A Neo-Wicksellian Framework for the Analysis of Monetary Policy, Princeton University, mimeo.

[72] Woodford, M. (2001), "Fiscal Requirements for Price Stability", *Journal of Money, Credit and Banking*, 33(3:August) pp. 669–728.

[73] Yaari, M.E. (1965), "Uncertain Lifetime, Life Insurance, and the Theory of the Consumer", *Review of Economic Studies*, 32(April), pp. 137–150.

10 Monetary Policy under Banking Oligopoly

Michael Beenstock

1 Introduction

Much if not all of macroeconomic theory assumes that the banking sector is perfectly competitive, e.g. Brunner and Meltzer (1990) and Modigliani and Papademus (1990). Textbooks too in macroeconomics take for granted that the banking sector is perfectly competitive. However, there are empirical indications which suggest that the banking system may not be perfectly competitive, e.g. Klein (1971). These indications are very strong in Israel (Elkayam 1994, Ruthenberg, Geva and Samet 1988) where margins of intermediation have been much greater than perfect competition would support. Most probably the situation in Israel is not dissimilar to that in other economies in which the banking system is cartelized, or the market structure is oligopolistic. Indeed, it may even be the case that the model proposed below is relevant to economies such as the US and UK, if their banking systems are competitive, but not perfectly so.[1]

The industrial organization of banking has been exclusively limited to microeconomics (Freixas and Rochet, 1998).[2] Here I discuss its macroeconomic ramifications. In particular, I show that the assumption of perfect competition has major implications for the conduct of monetary policy. If perfect competition does not prevail, the quantities of money and credit are less than otherwise would be the case, which in turn has

[1] For example, Neuberger and Zimmerman (1990) argue that the retail deposit market in American banking is not perfectly competitive.

[2] Curiously, Freixas and Rochet have a chapter on the macroeconomic consequences of financial imperfections, but they do not discuss the macroeconomic implications of the IO aspects that are raised here.

the effect of repressing inflation. This means that if the banking system becomes more competitive, money and credit expand, and repressed inflation is released. I also show that as the banking system becomes more competitive the central bank's ability to control money supply is enhanced. This means that a given change in the central bank's interest rate has a greater effect on the supply of money and credit the greater the degree of competition that prevails in the banking sytem. I refer to this phenomenon as "monetary leverage", i.e. monetary leverage varies directly with the degree of competition.

The absence of perfect competition is more difficult to model than perfect competition itself. In the case of banking systems it is most probably inappropriate to assume that competition is imperfect (in the sense of Robinson and Chamberlin). The latter suggests the existence of a large number of banks, which happen to face downward sloping demand curves. This is not the case in banking sytems, where the number of banks tends to be small, and banking services tend to be highly substitutable. If perfect competition does not prevail it is most probably because the banking sytem is oligopolistic.

The theory of oligopoly is considerably more intricate than either or both of perfect and imperfect competition. Klein (1971) and Monti (1972) examined the case of monopoly banks. Freixas and Rochet (1998) extended this model to the case of Cournot competition, which, as shown below, is observationally equivalent to the Klein–Monti model. I take this theme a stage further by relaxing the standard Cournot assumptions, and by allowing for strategic interactions between banks. What results is a model of "Effective Oligopoly" that is not observationally equivalent to the Klein–Monti model, because it contains a crucial new parameter, which I refer to as the "culture of competition". This model implies that even if the number of banks does not change, margins of intermediation may alter as a result of changes in the culture of competition.

The paper is organized as follows. I begin by discussing how the absence of perfect competition might be detected and measured. I use data for Israel's banking system to illustrate these ideas. The data show that during the 1990s the banking system has become steadily and even dramatically more competitive. Next, I present a benchline model in which the banking system is perfectly competitive. This is followed by a theoretical investigation of oligopolistic competition in the market for bank credit, and the results are compared with the perfectly competitive benchmark. Finally, an econometric model of the Israeli economy is simulated to illustrate the empirical effect of greater competition in the banking sector.

2 Detecting the Absence of Competition

In what follows, N denotes the number of banks and S_n denotes market share of bank n. Herfindahl's index of concentration, $H = \sum_{n=1}^{N} S_n^2$, is frequently used to measure absence of competition; i.e. competition varies inversely with $H \in 0, 1$. Since $\sum_{n=1}^{N} S_n^2 = N\text{var}(S) + \frac{1}{N}$, H increases when the variance of S increases, and it decreases with N because $\text{var}(S) < N^{-2}$. This means that H varies inversely with the number of competitors. A problem is that H abstracts from contestability, since potential competitors are excluded from N.

A Lerner index (M) is a more satisfactory measure of the absence of competition. It measures the degree of market power by comparing the marginal revenue from intermediation with its marginal cost. $M = 0$ when marginal cost equals marginal revenue. In what follows interest rates are denoted by i, and a bank's balance sheet may be simplified to $R + L = D + BR$, where R denotes reserves, L denotes loans, D denotes deposits and BR denotes borrowed reserves. It may be shown that $M = i_L - i_D + \rho(i_R - i_L) + \frac{BR}{D}(i_L - i_{BR})$, where ρ denotes the reserve ratio. When $\rho = 0$, and banks do not borrow from the central bank, M is equal to the spread between the rate of interest that banks charge on loans and the rate they offer on deposits. M varies directly with spread between lending and deposit rates, inversely with the reserve ratio (because $i_R < i_L$), and it varies directly with the spread between bank lending rates and the cost of borrowing from the central bank. In the presence of inflation (π) the real Lerner index is $\frac{M}{1+\pi}$.

Table 1 shows that in the late 1980s the real margin of intermediation exceeded 10 per cent. However, by 1993 these extraordinary margins had been greatly reduced. Subsequently, the margin gradually declined towards levels that currently prevail in the US and the UK. These data suggest that a major transformation occurred in the Israeli banking sector. Having been highly uncompetitive, the banking system became increasingly competitive. To some extent, the Herfindahl index echoes these developments. However, since the mid 1990s the market for shekel credit became more concentrated, and the absolute fall in H understates the major changes that took place.

It should be noted that the number of banks did not change over the period. Two large banks have dominated the banking sector over the entire period. Foreign banks have been reluctant to operate in Israel for fear of upsetting Arab governments, especially in the Arabian Gulf. However, recently some foreign banks have opened branches in the wholesale sector. The large fall in the Lerner index in the early 1990s resulted from the liberalization policy, which permitted companies to

Year	Herfindahl Index	Lerner Index, % p.a.
1988	0.252	16.4
1989	0.251	12.1
1990	0.250	9.9
1991	0.247	10.3
1992	0.241	8.1
1993	0.230	5.0
1994	0.220	4.3
1995	0.215	5.6
1996	0.211	5.2
1997	0.215	4.1
1998	0.217	3.4
1999	0.218	3.6
2000	0.222	3.0
2001	0.239	2.6

Source: The Banking System in Israel 2001, Bank of Israel.

Table 1: Measurements of Lack of Competition in the Market for Shekel Bank Credit

raise capital abroad, and which substantially reduced the market power of the banks. The subsequent fall in the Lerner index reflects ongoing changes in the culture of competition in Israel. During the 1990s, trade became substantially freer, the power of the Histadrut trade union movement was reduced, and the ethos of free markets and competition became more pervasive. The fruits of this ethos continue to permeate to the banking sector, as well as other sectors of the economy.

3 Perfect Competition

We begin by discussing the case in which banks are perfectly competitive, and in which goods prices are perfectly flexible.

3.1 Identities

The balance sheet of the banking system is:

$$L + R = D_S + D_T + BR + NDL \tag{1}$$

Using (1) to determine D_S and using the definition of NBB to determine C, the quantity of money must be equal to:

$$M = NBB + L - D_T - NDL \tag{2}$$

$H = NBB + BR$	High powered (base) money
$NBB = C + NBR$	Non-borrowed base money
BR	Borrowed reserves
C	Notes and coins held by public
NBR	Non-borrowed reserves
$R = RR + ER = BR + NBR$	Bank reserves
RR	Required reserves
ER	Excess reserves
$NFR = NBR - RR = ER - BR$	Net free reserves
L	Bank lending
D_S	Demand deposits
D_T	Time deposits
NDL	Non-deposit liabilities
$M = D_s + C$	Money stock
$D = D_s + D_T$	Bank deposits
P	Price level
i_L	Rate of interest on bank credit
i_T	Rate of interest on time deposits
i_{BR}	Rate of interest on borrowed reserves
π	Inflation

Table 2: Glossary of Terms

An alternative way of defining the stock of money is the "money multiplier" approach. Since the borrowed base is endogenous if the central bank controls its lending rate (i_{BR}), we express the money supply identity in terms of the non-borrowed base, $M = \mu NBB$ where the multiplier $\mu = (C + D_S)/NBB$. The definitions in Table 2 imply that $NBB = C + RR + NFR$. Dividing numerator and denominator by D_S we conclude that:

$$\mu = \frac{1 + c}{c + (\rho * + f)(1 + \tau)} \tag{3}$$

where $c = C/D_S$, $\rho^* = RR/D$, $f = NFR/D$ and $\tau = D_T/D_S$. Equation (3) states that the multiplier varies inversely with τ , ρ^*, f and c. The public affects the multiplier by deciding upon c and τ , the banks by deciding on f (the net free reserves ratio) and the central bank by deciding upon ρ^*. There is, of course, no difference between equations (2) and μNBB, because they are identically equal. To see this, we note that $\rho^* + f = 1 - \frac{L}{D} + \frac{NDL}{D}$. This treatment assumes the so-called "Free Reserves Doctrine" (Meigs 1962) where banks are indifferent between excess reserves and borrowed reserves, i.e. only free reserves matter.

3.2 The Model

The model developed here refers to a closed economy whose financial assets comprise money, credit, time deposits, reserves, and bonds. To simplify matters, the bond market is left in the background by implicitly assuming that the rate of interest on bonds is exogenous. Alternatively, the bond market is segmented from the money market. The central bank is assumed to set the rate of interest on borrowed reserves, which implies that borrowed reserves are infinitely elastic in supply, and their quantity is demand determined. An alternative policy is to fix the quantity of borrowed reserves as part of a policy of Money Base Control, leaving their rate of interest to be set by market forces. However, since most central banks set interest rates rather than quantities, I assume the former.

The demand for real bank credit is hypothesized to depend upon a scale variable (α_0) and to vary inversely with the real rate of interest on bank credit:

$$\frac{L^D}{P} = \alpha_0 - \alpha_1 \left(i_L - \pi\right) \tag{4}$$

It may be shown that if banks engage in perfect competition, and seek to maximize real profits, the supply schedule for bank credit depends upon a scale variable (bank capital) and the difference between the nominal rate of interest on bank lending and the rate of interest on borrowed reserves, and the difference between the nominal rate of interest on bank lending and the rate of interest on time deposits, grossed-up by their reserve requirement:

$$\frac{L^S}{P} = \beta_0 + \beta_1 \left[i_L - i_{BR}\right] + \beta_2 \left[i_L - i_T \left(1 + \rho_T\right)\right] \tag{5}$$

i.e. banks wish to expand credit when it is more profitable to do so. Note that reserve requirements reduce the incentive to supply bank credit because they raise the cost of liabilities.

The demand for real money balances is assumed to depend upon scale variables (δ_0) and to vary inversely with the nominal rate of interest:

$$\frac{M^D}{P} = \delta_0 - \delta_1 i_T \tag{6}$$

The real demand for time deposits is assumed to vary directly with their real rate of interest:

$$\frac{D_T^D}{P} = \theta_0 + \theta_1 (i_T - \pi) \tag{7}$$

Liability management theory implies that their supply is:

$$\frac{D_T^S}{P} = \eta_0 + \eta_1 \left[i_{BR} - i_T(1 + \rho_T)\right] + \eta_2 \left[i_L - i_T(1 + \rho_T)\right] \tag{8}$$

which assumes that borrowed reserves and time deposits are imperfect substitutes in liability management. If borrowed reserves become more expensive relative to time deposits, banks substitute time deposits for borrowed reserves. If the rate of interest on bank credit increases, it becomes more profitable to incur liabilities, and the supply of time deposits expands.

3.3 Equilibrium

To simplify matters it is assumed that there is no inflation, i.e. $\pi = 0$, and we focus upon the determinants of the general price level P. Equilibrium in the market for bank credit (i.e. $L^S = L^D$) and in the market for time deposits (i.e. $D_T^D = D_T^S$) implies:

$$i_T = \lambda_0 + \lambda_1 i_{BR} \tag{9}$$

$$i_L = \psi_0 + \psi_1 i_{BR} \tag{10}$$

where

$$\lambda_0 = \frac{1}{\lambda_2}\left(\eta_0 - \theta_0 + \frac{\eta_1(\alpha_0 - \beta_0)}{\alpha_1 + \beta_1 + \beta_2}\right)$$

$$\lambda_1 = \frac{1}{\lambda_2}\left(\eta_1 + \frac{\eta_2\beta_1}{\alpha_1 + \beta_1 + \beta_2}\right)$$

$$\lambda_2 = \theta_1 + (\eta_1 + \eta_2)(1 + \rho_T) - \frac{\eta_2\beta_2(1 + \rho_T)}{\alpha_1 + \beta_1 + \beta_2} > 0$$

$$\psi_0 = \frac{\alpha_0 - \beta_0 + \beta_1\lambda_1(1 + \rho_T)}{\alpha_1 + \beta_1 + \beta_2}$$

$$\psi_1 = \frac{\beta_1 + \beta_2\lambda_1(1 + \rho_T)}{\alpha_1 + \beta_1 + \beta_2}$$

The rates of interest on time deposits and credit vary directly with the rate of interest set by the central bank. In the case of perfect asset substitution $\lambda_1 = \psi_1 = 1$. More generally these reduced form parameters will be less than unity.

Substituting equation (9) into (6) gives the relationship between the demand for money and the central bank's rate of interest:

$$M^D = P(\delta_0 - \delta_1\lambda_0 - \delta_1\lambda_1 i_{BR}) \tag{11}$$

i.e. the demand for money falls when the central bank raises its rate of interest. The extent of this varies directly with δ_1 and λ_1. Substituting equations (9) and (10) into (2), and assuming for simplicity that $NDL = 0$, provides the relationship between the supply of money and the central bank's rate of interest:

$$M^S = NBB + P(\gamma_0 - \gamma_1 i_{BR}) \tag{12}$$

where:

$$\begin{aligned}\gamma_0 &= \alpha_0 - \theta_0 - \alpha_1\psi_0 - \theta_1\lambda_0\\ \gamma_1 &= \alpha_1\psi_1 + \theta_1\lambda_1\end{aligned}$$

The supply of money also varies inversely with the central bank's rate of interest for two main reasons, which are apparent in equation (2). First, credit contracts when the central bank raises its rate of interest. Secondly, the public wishes to hold more time deposits because the rate of interest that they bear increases.

Finally, when the supply of money is equal to the demand for money the equilibrium price level is determined. Equations (11) and (12) imply:

$$P = \frac{NBB}{\delta_0 - \delta_1\lambda_0 - \gamma_0 + (\gamma_1 - \delta_1\lambda_1)i_{BR}} \tag{13}$$

Equation (13) states that the equilibrium price level is homogeneous to degree one in the non-borrowed base. Since the borrowed base is endogenous, the nominal anchor is not base money as a whole, which includes "inside" base money, but only its exogenous component, or the "outside" money base. Note that the evolution of NBB depends upon the fiscal deficit and purchases of foreign exchange by the central bank. Here, however, NBB has been assumed to be fixed. Equation (13) indicates that the price level varies inversely with autonomous money demand and directly with autonomous money supply. It will also vary inversely with the central bank's rate of interest if $\gamma_1 > \delta_1\lambda_1$, otherwise the effect of monetary policy would be perverse. Below it is argued that this condition is easily fulfilled empirically, because the demand for money is less interest sensitive than the demand for time deposits and the demand and supply of credit.

Figure 1 illustrates the equilibrium that has just been derived. Schedule D_0 plots the demand for money balances that is implied by equation (11). Its location depends upon the price level (P_0) and scale variables, $q = \delta_0 - \delta_1\lambda_1$, which in practice vary directly with the level of economic activity. Schedule S_0 plots the supply schedule for money that is implied by equation (12). Its location depends upon scale variables, such as the level of economic activity and wealth. Its location also depends upon the non-borrowed base. Note that whereas the demand schedule depends upon P, the supply schedule does not. Schedule S is assumed to be flatter than schedule D because $\gamma_1 > \delta_1\lambda_1$. The central bank's rate of interest is assumed to be i_0. The initial equilibrium is at A, in which case the price level is initially P_0. If the central bank raises its rate of interest to i_1 the new equilibrium will be at B, and the price level will fall to P_1. The reduction in P shifts schedule D_0 to D_1. An increase in outside base money (NBB) would shift S_0 to the right, which given i_0 would induce a proportionate increase in the price level. Finally, an increase in economic activity would raise the demand for money, hence schedule D would shift to the right. However, so would schedule S shift to the right because the demand for credit increases. If the supply of money is more affected than the demand for money, the price level would increase, given the central bank's rate of interest and the outside money base.

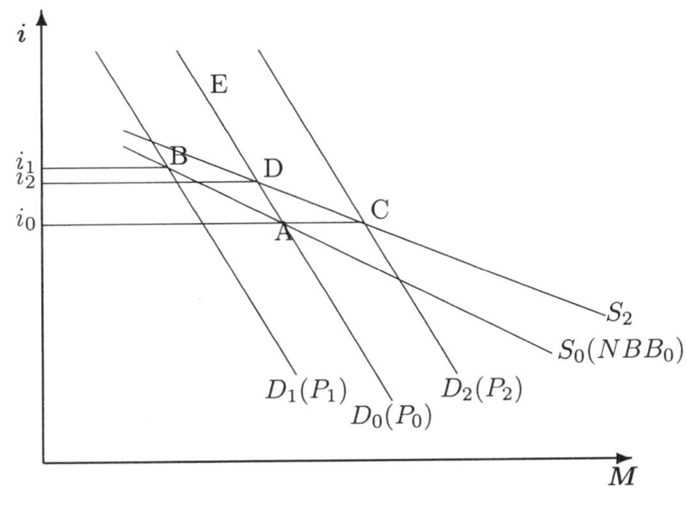

Figure 1: General Monetary Eqilibrium Under Banking Oligopoly

The story told here is incomplete because the long run rate of interest in the economy is determined by productivity and thrift, and not by the central bank, as suggested in Figure 1. However, because these factors are off the present agenda, the equilibrium characterized in Figure 1 relates to the medium run, rather than the very long run. Schedule S_2 is discussed in the next section.

4 Effective Oligopoly Theory

Thus far banks have been assumed to be perfectly competitive. Here we discuss modifications which take account of the possibly oligopolistic character of the banking system. To simplify matters we assume that there are no reserve requirements, that the marginal cost of bank liabilities is fixed at i_b, and that because bank credit is assumed to be perfectly substitutable between banks, banks cannot set independent rates of interest. It is also assumed that the market for time deposits is competitive or separable.[3] The real profit of bank n is defined as $z_n = \frac{L_n(i_L - i_b)}{P}$. We assume that each of the N oligopolistic banks sets L_n to maximize profits. For convenience, P is normalized to unity and there is price stability. The first order condition for profit maximization is:

$$\frac{\partial z_n}{\partial L_n} = i_L - i_b + L_n \frac{di_L}{dL_n} = 0 \tag{14}$$

where:

$$\frac{di_L}{dL_n} = \frac{\partial i_L}{\partial L_n} + \sum_{k \neq n}^{N} \frac{\partial i_L}{\partial L_k} \frac{\partial L_k}{\partial L_n}$$

We denote $\phi_n = \sum_{k \neq n}^{N} \frac{\partial L_k}{\partial L_n}$ to be bank n's expectation of the supply reaction of other banks to its own supply decisions.

4.1 Conjectural Variations

Multiplying the first order condition by N and using equation (4)[4] implies that the oligopolistically determined rate of interest is:

$$i_L = \theta \frac{\alpha_0}{\alpha_1} + (1 - \theta) i_b \tag{15}$$

where $\frac{\alpha_0}{\alpha_1} > i_b$, and where $1 - \theta = N/(1 + N + \phi)$ with $\phi_n = \phi$ for all banks. This last cognitive assumption implies that all banks have the same conjectural variation about their rival's supply reaction. As N tends to infinity θ tends to zero implying that price converges upon marginal cost, i.e., the market for bank credit becomes perfectly competitive. Moreover, as N tends to infinity ϕ will tend to zero, because each bank will believe that its decisions have no effect on the decisions of competing banks, as is appropriate when competition is perfect. When $N = 1$ the solution to equation (15) becomes the standard solution for a monopolist since $\phi = 0$ in which case $\theta = 0.5$.

---

[3] This assumption is merely made for simplicity and to separate the loan and deposit markets. However, Elkayam (1994) notes that the market for time deposits in Israel is competitive despite the fact that the market for bank credit is not competitive. In the absence of risk, the deposit and loan markets are separable (Dermine 1986). Beenstock *et al.* (2002) discuss the case of banks, which have monopsonistic power in deposit markets.

[4] I.e. $\sum_n L_n = L$ and $\frac{\partial i_L}{\partial L} = -\frac{1}{\alpha_1}$.

When $\phi = 0$, the solution to equation (15) is the Cournot solution obtained by Freixas and Rochet (1998); each bank assumes that its rival does not react. If each bank believes that its rival will cut supply when it expands its own supply, i.e. $\phi < 0$, this will lower θ below its Cournot solution, thereby lowering the equilibrium rate of interest on bank credit. In principle, ϕ may vary independently of the number of banks. Equation (15) states that the rate of interest on bank credit varies directly with ϕ. When $\phi = -1$, $\theta = 0$ in which event the rate of interest on bank credit is what it would be under perfect competition. We may therefore regard ϕ as a parameter which expresses the competitive culture; the smaller it is the more oligopoly mimics perfect competition, regardless of the number of banks.

Alternatively, we may think of $N^* = N/(1+\phi)$ as the effective number of banks, in the sense that N banks generate the same degree of Cournot competition as would N^* banks. If $-1 < \phi < 0$, $N^* > N$, i.e. there is more competition than Cournot would have expected to detect. For example, in Israel there may only be 4 main commercial banks, but they would generate the degree of Cournot competition of 8 banks if $\phi = -0.5$. If $\phi = -1$ the effective number of banks would be infinite, as in perfect competition. If $\phi > 0$ the effective number of banks would be less than the actual number.

Equation (15) also states, quite conventionally, that the rate of interest on bank credit varies directly with its demand (α_0), and inversely with the slope of the demand curve for credit (α_1). For example, a decision to enable companies to borrow abroad would reduce α_0, because companies cease to be the captive customers of the domestic banks, and increase α_1, because there is greater scope for substitution. Such a double-edged policy therefore reduces the market power of domestic banks. Finally, equation (15) states that the effect of interest rate policy upon the rate of interest on bank credit varies inversely with ϕ. Under perfect competition the effect is equal to unity because $\theta = 1$. Under monopoly the effect is only 0.5. Under oligopoly the effect lies in the interval of 0 and 1. The corollary of this is, that as the climate of competition improves, monetary aggregates can be expected to expand, and the money stock becomes more sensitive to interest rate policy, due to enhanced monetary leverage.

4.2 Best Response

The previous discussion has been cast in terms of conjectural variations. As is well known, this rather unsatisfactorily applies the static assumptions of a one-shot game to an ongoing situation, which is a repeated game. An appealing alternative to conjectural variations is "best response", where the reaction of one firm is optimal in the face of its rivals' behavior. It may be shown that the optimal policy of bank n is to supply credit according to the following rule:

$$\widetilde{L}_n = \frac{1}{2}(\alpha_0 - \widehat{L}_n - \alpha_1 i_b) \tag{16}$$

where $\widehat{L}_n$ denotes the credit supplied by the rivals of bank n. Equation (16) states that bank n supplies more credit when the overall demand (α_0) for credit is greater, it supplies less credit when the cost of liabilities increases, and it supplies less credit when its rivals expand their supply. In fact in this particular model, the best response of bank n is to set $\phi = -0.5$. If each bank understands that when it expands credit by a shekel its rivals' best combined response is to cut their credit supply by half a shekel, then $\phi = -0.5$ and the effective number of banks is twice the actual number. If, for example, $N = 2$ the effective number of banks is 4, and the total supply of credit may be shown to be:

$$L = \frac{1}{5}(2\alpha_0 - 6\alpha_1 i_b) \tag{17}$$

This model solves for ϕ in terms of the structural parameters; it is not an independent parameter. If demand is linear, as in equation (4), then $\phi = -0.5$. To induce a change in ϕ it would be necessary to assume that demand has become nonlinear. This means that best response theory is less capable of explaining changes in the competitive culture than the theory of conjectural variation, unless of course, demand just happened to become nonlinear in a way that induced a fall in ϕ.

5 Empirical Illustration

5.1 Macroeconomic Effects of ϕ

In terms of Figure 1 a spontaneous increase in the competitive culture following a reduction in ϕ has two theoretical effects. The first is to induce an expansion in the money supply schedule, which is brought about by the expansion of bank credit. The discussion in the previous section has shown that when ϕ decreases banks cut their margins of intermediation, credit becomes cheaper, which in turn brings about an expansion of bank credit, under the assumption that the supply of borrowed reserves is elastic, i.e. i_{BR} is fixed. The expansion of bank credit will be greater the more elastic is the demand for credit, i.e. the larger is α_1. The second effect is to make the money supply schedule flatter. This happens because monetary leverage is enhanced when ϕ decreases, i.e. a given change in the central bank's rate of interest has a greater effect on market rates of interest, and therefore a larger effect upon the supply of money. In short, schedule S_0 in Figure 1 shifts outwards, and becomes flatter, and the new supply schedule of money is S_2.

The demand for money is not affected by ϕ, hence the demand schedule for money continues to be D_0. If the central bank does not alter its rate of interest, the new equilibrium would be at B in Figure 1, and the equilibrium price level would be higher, inducing an outward shift in schedule D to D_2. If, instead, the central bank sterilizes this "repressed inflation", it would have to raise its interest rate to i_2, where schedule S_2 intersects schedule D_0. Note that this increase may not be so large, because the monetary leverage of the central bank is greater. In the absence of enhanced monetary leverage the central bank would have had to raise its rate of interest according to point E on schedule D_0.

5.2 The Econometric Model

Details of the econometric model for Israel that is used for the simulation may be found in Beenstock *et al.* (2002). The model incorporates aggregate supply and aggregate demand, and it has a monetary sector which is specified as discussed above. It incorporates equations for the supply and demand for time deposits, the demand for money, and the demand for credit. There is no equation for the supply of credit because the banking system is modelled according to the theory of oligopolistic competition as described above. The model is quarterly. In the theoretical model that has been discussed prices are flexible and all relationships are instantaneous. In the econometric model the price level is sticky and most relationships incorporate lag distributions. This means that the econometric model is inherently dynamic, in contrast to the theoretical model, which is static. However, the econometric model grinds out in the long run the static properties of the theoretical model.

The interest rate elasticities are as follows: currency −0.8, demand deposits −2.0, time deposits −9.0, i.e. the interest elasticity of demand for money is about −1.5, and the public demand for time deposits is very sensitive to interest rates. The interest elasticity of demand for bank credit is −1.8, which is quite large too. The supply of time deposits (8) varies directly with the central bank's rate of interest (elasticity 2.2), and the rate of interest on bank credit (elasticity 3.44), and it varies inversely with the rate of interest on time deposits. These elasticities imply that the money supply schedule in Figure 1 is much flatter than the money demand schedule, and that both schedules slope downwards.

When the central bank raises its rate of interest by 1 percentage point, the demand for money falls by about 1.5 per cent whereas the supply of money falls by about 9 per cent.

A noteworthy feature in the econometric model, which is absent in the theoretical model, is the direct effect of the competitive culture on the demand for credit. In the theoretical model a reduction in ϕ indirectly increases the demand for credit because it reduces the margin of intermediation. This indirect effect features in the econometric model. But the latter also embodies a direct effect; when banks become more competitive the demand for credit expands. It seems that more competitive banks are also more consumer friendly and less forbidding, and therefore attract more business. This direct effect implies that the rightward shift in schedule S in Figure 1 is larger than previously suggested.

Because the money markets are underdeveloped in Israel, open market operations are not used as an instrument of monetary policy. Instead, the key instrument is the cost of borrowing (or the return to depositing) from the central bank. The Bank of Israel sets its interest rate monthly. It announces about 10 days in advance the rate of interest that it intends to set for the following month. During this month the rate of interest does not alter, implying that the supply of borrowed reserves is infinitely elastic in the short run. If the Bank of Israel regrets the rate of interest that it has chosen, it must wait until the following month to alter it.[5] In the simulations described below, the rate of interest is assumed to be fixed. It is well known that nominal instability may be induced if the rate of interest is fixed for too long. The model suggests that nominal instability begins to develop after about 3 quarters.

5.3 Econometric Simulation for Israel

Table 3 reports the results of simulating a permanent decrease in θ of 1 percentage point (see 15), which constitutes a minor improvement in the climate of competition. Banks cut their margin of intermediation, which results in an immediate (quarter 1) fall in interest rates, despite the fact that the Bank of Israel is assumed to keep its rate of interest unchanged. At these lower rates of interest the demand for credit increases. Also, the demand for time deposits decreases by 0.35 per cent (not shown in Table 3) because they bear a lower rate of interest. The expansion in credit accompanied by the reduction in time deposits induces an expansion of the money stock equation (2) of 0.6 per cent in the first quarter.

---

[5] Very occasionally the rate of interest was changed during the month, such as in October 1998 during the Rouble Crisis.

Quarter	GDP	Price Level	Rate of Interest	Credit	Money Stock
1	0	0	-0.01	0.04	0.6
2	0	0.07	0.02	0.09	1.7
3	0	0.3	0.11	0.17	3.9
4	0	0.8	0.34	0.34	9.3
5	0.04	2.0	0.55	0.73	23.8
6	0.14	4.9	1.15	1.67	52.9

(percentage deviation from base-run)

Table 3: Simulating an Increase in Competition: ($\Delta\theta = -0.01$)

The price level begins to rise in quarter 2 as a result of the money expansion. Nominal interest rates begin to rise because of the Fisher effect. The real cost of borrowing from the central bank falls because the Bank of Israel does not alter its rate of interest. The borrowed base consequently expands and the money stock rises further, by 1.7 per cent after 2 quarters. This slide continues in subsequent quarters, and turns into a severe problem by quarter 3. Note that while inflation has increased by about 3 per cent a quarter by quarter 6, there is a slight output expansion due to the fall in real rates of interest.

The simulation illustrates two phenomena. First, even slight improvements in banking competition can induce substantial money supply expansions. Secondly, if the Bank of Israel does not change its rate of interest sufficiently quickly nominal stability (after 3 quarters) rapidly rears its head. However, the Bank of Israel can easily put matters right by raising its rate of interest in time, to offset the credit expansion induced by the increase in competition.

During the 1990s the banking system became increasingly competitive. Margins of intermediation were steadily and even dramatically reduced. The result was persistent money expansion, which prevented inflation from falling more rapidly than it did. It was no coincidence that once the margin of intermediation stabilized at a low level towards the end of the 1990s, the money supply stabilized and inflation finally fell to about 2 per cent per year, having averaged about 12 per cent during the decade as a whole. Had the banking system been competitive in 1990, or had the banking system continued to remain uncompetitive, inflation would most probably have fallen in the early part of the 1990s. The spread of competition delayed the conquest of inflation by about 7 years.

6 Conclusions

The spread of competition to the banking sector is desirable on microeconomic grounds, but it may destabilize the macroeconomy. In particular, the volume of credit increases, which, if the central bank does not respond appropriately, induces an expansion in the supply of money. This happened in Israel during the 1990s, and it happened in Britain during the early 1970s with the policy of Competition and Credit Control. This policy induced an expansion of bank credit, which destabilized the money supply, which in turn induced inflation. Banking competition is desirable, but it must be accompanied by tightness in monetary policy, to prevent adverse macroeconomic fall-out.

The model that has been proposed is no doubt relevant to economies with cartelized banking systems. In such economies central bankers need to keep a watchful eye on competitive developments in the banking system when they operate monetary policy. In this context Lerner indices are preferable to concentration indices for detecting changes in the climate of competition. They should also take account of the fact that their rate of interest has a greater monetary effect the more competitive is the banking system.

The model that has been proposed may even be relevant in countries such as the US and the UK, where the banking system is competitive, but imperfectly so. Since even minor changes in the degree of competition can have large monetary consequences, US and UK central bankers might find that seemingly inexplicable monetary aberrations are in fact caused by marginal changes in competition.

Bibliography

[1] Beenstock M., E. Azulay, A. Offenbacher and O. Sulla (2002) A macroeconometric model with oligopolistic banks: monetary control, inflation and growth in Israel. *Economic Modelling,* 20: 455–486.

[2] Brunner K. and A.H. Meltzer (1990) Money Supply, in Friedman B.M. and F.H. Hahn (eds) *Handbook of Monetary Economics*, Elsevier.

[3] Dermine J. (1986) Deposit rates, credit rates, and bank capital: the Monti–Klein model revisited. *Journal of Banking and Finance*, 10: 99–114.

[4] Elkayam D. (1994) The effect of monetary policy on the interest rate spread in the unindexed local currency segment, 1986–1990. *Bank of Israel Economic Review,* 68: 1–22.

[5] Freixas X. and J-C. Rochet (1998) *Microeconomics of Banking,* MIT Press, Cambridge.

[6] Klein M. (1971) A theory of the banking firm. *Journal of Money, Credit and Banking.* 3: 205–218.

[7] Meigs J. (1962) *Free Reserves and the Money Supply,* University of Chicago Press.

[8] Modigliani F. and L. Papademus (1990) The supply of money and the control of nominal income, in Friedman B.M. and F.H. Hahn (eds) *Handbook of Monetary Economics*, Elsevier.

[9] Monti M. (1972) Deposit, credit, and interest rate determination under alternative bank objectives, in Szego, G.P. and K. Shell (eds) *Mathematical Methods in Investment and Finance*, North-Holland, Amsterdam.

[10] Neuberger J. and G. Zimmerman (1990) Bank pricing of retail deposits accounts and "the California rate mystery". *Economic Review*, Federal Reserve Bank of San Francisco, Spring 1990(2): 3–16.

[11] Ruthenberg, D., D. Geva and Z. Samet (1988) An investigation of the interest rate spread in the non-indexed market for shekel credit in Israel's banking system. *Issues in Banking*, 7: 3–144 (Hebrew).

11 Money Targeting

Harris Dellas

1 Introduction

The last few years have witnessed a reorientation in the conduct of monetary policy away from monetary targeting and towards explicit inflation targeting. Two main factors seem to have contributed to this development. The first is the apparent instability of velocity that was caused by the increase in the level of variability of inflation in the seventies and which persisted into the eighties. As implied by Poole's, 1970 seminal analysis, the pace of financial innovation and the resulting instability in velocity creates a presumption in favor of controlling interest rates — rather than the money supply — as a means of smoothing fluctuations in aggregate economic activity and inflation.

The second factor is the almost unanimous acceptance of the so called new neoclassical model as the mainstream model for the analysis of monetary policy (Goodfriend and King, 1997; King and Wolman, 1999; Woodford, 2000). A key implication of this model is that inflation targeting,[1] conducted typically through a short term nominal interest rate instrument, represents the optimal monetary policy (Gali, 2000). While the properties of inflation targeting in more general specifications have not yet been thoroughly investigated, a widespread presumption seems to have emerged that some sort of direct inflation targeting is approximately optimal within this class of models. Because inflation stabilization brings about also output stabilization in this model, the new model has proved very popular among central bankers as it allows them to pursue output stabilization under the disguise of the pursuit of price stability.

[1] Perfect targeting in the absence of cost-push factors and imperfect targeting in their presence.

The objective of this paper is to evaluate this view by comparing the properties of a standard Taylor type of inflation targeting rule and strict monetary targeting within a model that is more general than those typically used in the literature. We use the standard NNS model but with money explicitly modeled, capital accumulation and three shocks (supply, fiscal and monetary) and, more importantly, we do not have the fiscal authority eliminate the imperfect competition distortion via subsidies. Two findings stand out.

First, as far as macroeconomic volatility is concerned, money targeting generates more stable inflation but less stable output than the Taylor rule inflation in the face of individual supply and fiscal shocks. A Taylor rule, on the other hand, performs better for macroeconomic stability in the face of money demand shocks. Hence, the NNS produces a pattern of macroeconomic volatility for aggregate demand shocks that is different from the standard IS-LM model. Moreover, when we combine all three shocks taking into account their relative contribution to macroeconomic instability, we find that monetary targeting leads to less stable output but more stable *inflation*.

Whether a Taylor rule contributes to lower inflation volatility in comparison to money targeting under supply shocks depends critically on whether the monetary authorities also have output stabilization objectives. Even a small emphasis on output stability can be associated with inflation instability. With zero weight on output stabilization, on the other hand, a Taylor rule is associated with lower inflation variability.

Third, the welfare rankings are not related to the output–inflation volatility rankings. Money targeting generates higher welfare, both for each individual shock and for all three shocks combined. One of the reasons that welfare is higher under M-targeting even for money demand shocks is that inflation targeting requires a much more volatile nominal interest rate in order to offset the effects of the various shocks. Volatility in the nominal interest rates destabilizes real balances and exerts a negative effect on utility.

The rest of the paper is organized as follows. Section 1 presents the model. Section 2 describes the choice of parameters and Section 3 the main findings concerning the volatility and welfare properties of the two targeting procedures.

2 The Model

The set up is standard. The economy is populated by a large number of identical infinitely-lived households and the economy consists of two sectors: one producing intermediate goods and the other final goods. The intermediate good is produced with capital and labor and the final good with intermediate goods. The final good is homogeneous and can be used for consumption (private and public) and investment purposes.

2.1 The Household

Household preferences are characterized by the lifetime utility function:[2]

$$E_t \sum_{\tau=0}^{\infty} \beta^{\tau} U\left(C_{t+\tau}, \frac{M_{t+\tau}}{P_{t+\tau}}, \ell_{t+\tau}, \zeta_{t+\tau}\right) \tag{1}$$

where $0 < \beta < 1$ is a constant discount factor, C denotes consumption, M/P real balances and ℓ leisure. The utility function, $U\left(C, \frac{M}{P}, \ell\right) : \mathbb{R}_+ \times \mathbb{R}_+ \times [0,1] \longrightarrow \mathbb{R}$ is increasing and concave in its arguments. Finally, ζ is a stochastic money demand shock that will be defined later.

The household is subject to the following time constraint

$$\ell_t + h_t = 1 \tag{2}$$

where h denotes hours worked. The total time endowment is normalized to unity.

In each and every period, the representative household faces a budget constraint of the form

$$B_t + M_t + P_t(C_t + I_t + T_t) \leq \\ R_{t-1}B_{t-1} + M_{t-1} + N_t + \Pi_t + P_t W_t h_t + P_t z_t K_t$$

where B_t are M_t are nominal bonds and money acquired during period t, P_t is the nominal price of the final good, R_t is the nominal interest rate, W_t and z_t are the real wage rate and real rental rate of capital. The household owns K_t units of physical capital, makes an additional investment of I_t, consumes C_t and supplies h_t units of labor. It pays lump sum taxes T_t, receives a transfer of money N_t from the government and finally claims the profits, Π_t, earned by the firms.

Capital accumulates according to the law of motion

$$K_{t+1} = I_t - \frac{\varphi}{2}\left(\frac{I_t}{K_t} - \delta\right)^2 K_t + (1-\delta)K_t \tag{3}$$

where $\delta \in [0,1]$ denotes the rate of depreciation. The second term captures the existence of capital adjustment costs.

---

[2] $E_t(.)$ denotes mathematical conditional expectations. Expectations are conditional on information available at the beginning of period t.

The first order conditions lead to the following money demand equation

$$\zeta_t \left(\frac{M_t}{P_t C_t}\right)^{\eta-1} = \frac{R_t - 1}{R_t} \tag{4}$$

2.2 Final Sector

The final good is produced by combining intermediate goods. This process is described by the following CES function

$$Y_t = \left(\int_0^1 X_t(i)^\theta \mathrm{d}i\right)^{\frac{1}{\theta}} \tag{5}$$

where $\theta \in (-\infty, 1)$. θ determines the elasticity of substitution between the various inputs. The producers in this sector are assumed to behave competitively and to determine their demand for each good, $X_t(i)$, $i \in (0,1)$ by maximizing the static profit equation

$$\max_{\{X_t(i)\}_{i\in(0,1)}} P_t Y_t - \int_0^1 P_t(i) X_t(i) \mathrm{d}i \tag{6}$$

subject to (5), where $P_t(i)$ denotes the price of intermediate good i. This yields demand functions of the form:

$$X_t(i) = \left(\frac{P_t(i)}{P_t}\right)^{\frac{1}{\theta-1}} Y_t \tag{7}$$

and the following general price index

$$P_t = \left(\int_0^1 P_t(i)^{\frac{\theta}{\theta-1}} \mathrm{d}i\right)^{\frac{\theta-1}{\theta}} \tag{8}$$

The final good may be used for consumption — private or public — and investment purposes.

2.3 Intermediate Goods Producers

Each firm i, $i \in (0,1)$, produces an intermediate good by means of capital and labor according to a constant returns-to-scale technology, represented by the production function

$$X_t(i) = A_t K_t(i)^\alpha h_t(i)^{1-\alpha} \text{ with } \alpha \in (0,1) \tag{9}$$

where $K_t(i)$ and $h_t(i)$ respectively denote the physical capital and the labor input used by firm i in the production process. A_t is an exogenous stationary stochastic technology shock, whose properties will be defined later. Assuming that each firm i operates under perfect competition in the input markets, the firm determines its production plan so as to minimize its total cost

$$\min_{\{K_t(i),h_t(i)\}} P_t W_t h_t(i) + P_t z_t K_t(i)$$

subject to (9). This yields the following expression for total costs:

$$P_t \mathcal{C}_{m,t} X_t(i)$$

where the real marginal cost, $\mathcal{C}_m$, is given by $\frac{W_t^{1-\alpha} z_t^{\alpha}}{\chi A_t}$ with $\chi = \alpha^{\alpha}(1-\alpha)^{1-\alpha}$

Intermediate goods producers are monopolistically competitive, and therefore set prices for the good they produce. We follow Calvo (1983) in assuming that firms set their prices for a stochastic number of periods. In each and every period, a firm either gets the chance to adjust its price (an event occurring with probability γ) or it does not. We assume that the price set by the firm incorporates a nominal growth component Ξ_t, that is the nominal price in period t is $P_t(i) = \Xi_t p_t(i)$ where $p_t(i)$ is the deflated fixed price. A firm i sets its price, $\widetilde{p}_t(i)$, in period t in order to maximize its discounted profit flow:

$$\max_{\widetilde{p}_t(i)} \widetilde{\Pi}_t(i) + E_t \sum_{\tau=1}^{\infty} \Phi_{t+\tau}(1-\gamma)^{\tau-1}\left(\gamma\widetilde{\Pi}_{t+\tau}(i) + (1-\gamma)\Pi_{t+\tau}(i)\right)$$

subject to the total demand it faces:

$$X_t(i) = \left(\frac{P_t(i)}{P_t}\right)^{\frac{1}{\theta-1}} Y_t$$

and where

$$\Pi_{t+\tau}(i) = (\Xi_{t+\tau}\widetilde{p}_t(i) - P_{t+\tau}\mathcal{C}_{m,t+\tau})X_{t+\tau}(i)$$

is the profit attained when the price is maintained, while

$$\widetilde{\Pi}_{t+\tau}(i) = (\widetilde{p}_{t+\tau}(i) - P_{t+\tau}\mathcal{C}_{m,t+\tau})X(i, s^{t+\tau})$$

is the profit attained when the price is reset. $\Phi_{t+\tau}$ is an appropriate discount factor related to the way the household values future as opposed to current consumption. This leads to the price setting equation

$$\widetilde{p}_t(i) = \frac{1}{\theta} \frac{E_t \sum_{\tau=0}^{\infty}(1-\gamma)^{\tau}\Phi_{t+\tau}\Xi_{t+\tau}^{\frac{1}{\theta-1}} P_{t+\tau}^{\frac{2-\theta}{1-\theta}} \mathcal{C}_{m,t+\tau} Y_{t+\tau}}{E_t \sum_{\tau=0}^{\infty}(1-\gamma)^{\tau}\Phi_{t+\tau}\Xi_{t+\tau}^{\frac{\theta}{\theta-1}} P_{t+\tau}^{\frac{1}{\theta-1}} Y_{t+\tau}} \tag{10}$$

Since the price setting is independent of any firm specific characteristic, all firms that reset their prices will choose the same price.

In each period, a fraction γ of contracts ends, so there are $\gamma(1-\gamma)$ contracts surviving from period $t-1$, and therefore $\gamma(1-\gamma)^j$ from period $t-j$. Hence, from (8), the aggregate intermediate price index is given by

$$P_t = \left(\sum_{i=0}^{\infty} \gamma(1-\gamma)^i \left(\Xi_{t-i}\widetilde{p}_{t-i}\right)^{\frac{\theta}{\theta-1}} \right)^{\frac{\theta-1}{\theta}} \tag{11}$$

2.3.1 The monetary authorities

We consider two types of policy rules. Under the first rule, the central bank simply targets the growth rate of the money supply

$$\mu_t = \overline{\mu} \tag{12}$$

The nominal interest rate then adjusts to clear the money market.

Under the second policy, the central bank uses a standard Taylor rule. In particular, monetary policy is conducted according to

$$\widehat{R}_t = \rho \widehat{R}_{t-1} + (1-\rho)k_y \widehat{y}_t + (1-\rho)k_\pi \widehat{\pi}_t \text{ with } \rho = 0.01, k_y = 0.5 \text{ and } k_\pi = 1.5 \tag{13}$$

where y is output and π_t is the rate of inflation. A $\widehat{}$ stands for log-deviations from the deterministic steady state. Under this rule, the money supply adjusts in order to clear the money market.

2.3.2 The government

The government finances government expenditure on the domestic final good using lump sum taxes. The stationary component of government expenditures is assumed to follow an exogenous stochastic process, whose properties will be defined later.

2.4 The Equilibrium

We now turn to the description of the equilibrium of the economy.

Definition 2.1 An equilibrium of this economy is a sequence of prices $\{\mathcal{P}_t\}_{t=0}^{\infty} = \{W_t, z_t, P_t, R_t, P_t(i), i \in (0,1)\}_{t=0}^{\infty}$ and a sequence of quantities $\{\mathcal{Q}_t\}_{t=0}^{\infty} = \{\{\mathcal{Q}_t^H\}_{t=0}^{\infty}, \{\mathcal{Q}_t^F\}_{t=0}^{\infty}\}$ with

$$\{\mathcal{Q}_t^H\}_{t=0}^{\infty} = \{C_t, I_t, B_t, K_{t+1}, h_t, M_t\}$$

$$\{\mathcal{Q}_t^H\}_{t=0}^{\infty} = \{Y_t, X_t(i), K_t(i), h_t(i); i \in (0,1)\}_{t=0}^{\infty}$$

such that:

(i) given a sequence of prices $\{\mathcal{P}_t\}_{t=0}^{\infty}$ and a sequence of shocks, $\{\mathcal{Q}_t^H\}_{t=0}^{\infty}$ is a solution to the representative household's problem;

(ii) given a sequence of prices $\{\mathcal{P}_t\}_{t=0}^{\infty}$ and a sequence of shocks, $\{\mathcal{Q}_t^F\}_{t=0}^{\infty}$ is a solution to the representative firms' problem;

(iii) given a sequence of quantities $\{\mathcal{Q}_t\}_{t=0}^{\infty}$ and a sequence of shocks, $\{\mathcal{P}_t\}_{t=0}^{\infty}$ clears the markets

$$Y_t = C_t + I_t + G_t \tag{14}$$

$$h_t = \int_0^1 h_t(i)\mathrm{d}i \tag{15}$$

$$K_t = \int_0^1 K_t(i)\mathrm{d}i \tag{16}$$

$$G_t = T_t \tag{17}$$

and the money market.

(iv) Prices satisfy (10) and (11).

3 Calibration

The model is parameterized in order to match closely the postwar US economy. The parameters are reported in Table 1. The nominal growth of the economy is set equal to 7.4 per cent per year. The depreciation rate, δ, is set at 0.025, implying an annual depreciation of about 10 per cent. θ is set such that markups in the economy are 20 per cent. α, the elasticity of the production function to physical capital is set such that the labor share in the economy is 0.6. $a_t = \log(A_t/A)$ is assumed to follow a stationary AR(1) process of the form

$$a_t = \rho_a a_{t-1} + \varepsilon_{a,t}$$

with $|\rho_a| < 1$ and $\varepsilon_{a,t} \sim \mathcal{N}(0, \sigma_a^2)$. We set $\sigma_a = 0.008$ and $\rho_a = 0.95$.

The instantaneous utility function takes the form

$$U\left(C_t, \frac{M_t}{P_t}, \ell_t\right) = \frac{1}{1-\sigma}\left[\left(\left(C_t^{\eta} + \zeta_t \frac{M_t}{P_t}^{\eta}\right)^{\frac{\nu}{\eta}} \ell_t^{1-\nu}\right)^{1-\sigma} - 1\right]$$

Technology		
Capital elasticity of intermediate output	α	0.2500
Capital adjustmenbt costs parameter	φ	10.0000
Depreciation rate	δ	0.0250
Parameter of markup	θ	0.8000
Probability of price resetting	q	0.2500
Preferences		
Discount factor	β	0.9880
Relative risk aversion	σ	1.5000
Parameter of CES in utility function	η	-1.5600
Weight of money in the utility function	ζ	0.0500
CES weight in utility function	ν	0.3405
Interest rate persistence in the Taylor rule	ρ	0.01
Output reaction coefficient in the Taylor rule	k_y	0.5
Inflation reaction coefficient in the Taylor rule	k_π	1.5
Shocks		
Persistence of technology shock	ρ_a	0.9500
Standard deviation of technology shock	σ_a	0.0080
Persistence of government spending shock	ρ_g	0.9700
Volatility of government spending shock	σ_g	0.0200
Persistence of money demand shock	ρ_ζ	0.9500
Volatility of money demand shock	σ_ζ	0.0160

Table 1: Calibration: Benchmark Case

where ζ is set such that we match the ratio of M1 money to consumption expenditures in the US data ($M1/PC = 1.2$). σ, the coefficient ruling risk aversion, is set equal to 1.5 in the benchmark case. But we also carry out the analysis for alternative values (namely 0.5 and 3.5) as a means of assessing its role in the performance of monetary policy rules. It has been pointed out in the literature (for instance, Gali, 2000) that variation in the value of this parameter makes a difference for the properties of alternative rules. η is borrowed from Chari *et al.*, (2000), who estimated it on postwar US data. ν is set such that the model generates a total fraction of time devoted to market activities of 31 per cent. β, the discount factor is set such that households discount the future at a 4 per cent annual rate.

γ, the probability of price resetting is set in the benchmark case at 0.25, implying that the average length of price contracts is 4 quarters. We are also reporting results with higher price flexibility, namely $\gamma = 0.9$ in order to study the role played by price flexibility.

We set $\varphi = 10$ which means that increasing the investment capital ratio from its steady state value by one percentage point requires that about 1 per cent of the new investment be used to pay for capital adjustment. This value of φ is sufficient to generate a positive relationship between supply shocks and output even under the least favorable configuration employed, namely $\sigma = 3.5$ and $\gamma = 0.25$. Note that much larger values have been used in the literature. For instance, Ireland, (1999), sets $\varphi = 40$, following the suggestion by King and Watson, (1996), that high adjustment costs are necessary in order to generate sensible response of output to *monetary* shocks.

The government spending shock is assumed to follow an AR(1) process

$$\log(g_t) = \rho_g \log(g_{t-1}) + (1 - \rho_g)\log(\overline{g}) + \varepsilon_{g,t}$$

with $|\rho_g| < 1$ and $\varepsilon_{g,t} \sim \mathcal{N}(0, \sigma_g^2)$. ρ_g is set to 0.97, while $\sigma_g = 0.02$.

The money demand shock also follows an AR(1) process

$$\log(\zeta_t) = \rho_\zeta \log(\zeta_{t-1}) + (1 - \rho_\zeta)\log(\overline{\zeta}) + \varepsilon_{\zeta,t}$$

with $|\rho_\zeta| < 1$ and $\varepsilon_{\zeta,t} \sim \mathcal{N}(0, \sigma_\zeta^2)$. ρ_ζ is set to 0.95, while $\sigma_\zeta = 0.016$ to match HP-filtered inflation volatility under a money growth rule.

The parameters of the Taylor rule are taken directly from Taylor's original estimation.

4 The Results

Tables 3–4 describe the properties of the two targeting rules for $\gamma = 0.25$. Table 2 reports the elasticities of the key variables with regard to the individual shocks. Table 3 reports welfare[3] as well as the variability of the three components of utility, namely, consumption, real balances and leisure. We have computed welfare both in levels and in steady state consumption equivalents. Table 4 gives the corresponding volatilities for output and inflation. Tables 9–10 correspond to Tables 3–4 when $\gamma = 0.9$.

	M-Targeting			Taylor rule		
	A	g	ζ	A	g	ζ
	$\sigma = 1.50$					
y	0.161	0.228	−0.206	0.931	0.116	−0.005
c	0.252	−0.024	−0.183	1.104	−0.100	−0.008
R	−0.006	0.001	0.011	−0.892	−0.091	0.003
μ	0.000	0.000	0.000	11.670	0.974	0.341

Table 2: Elasticities: $q = 0.25$

	M-Targeting				
shock	sd(c)	sd(m/p)	sd(lp)	Welfare	x
Supply	2.83	2.98	0.53	−58.190708	−0.0102
Fiscal	0.82	0.92	0.69	−58.188391	−0.0039
Money	0.42	0.96	0.26	−58.188008	−0.0029
All	2.98	3.26	0.90	−58.193207	−0.0169
	Taylor rule				
shock	sd(c)	sd(m/p)	sd(lp)	Welfare	x
Supply	3.24	35.22	0.17	−58.297100	−0.2976
Fiscal	0.96	7.97	0.60	−58.195993	−0.0245
Money	0.04	1.75	0.02	−58.188376	−0.0039
All	3.38	36.15	0.62	−58.307569	−0.3259
note: sd: standard deviation					

Table 3: Money and Taylor rule targeting: Welfare $q = 0.25$

The main pattern is that M-targeting produces higher welfare for all three shocks. This is true for all values of σ and γ considered here.

[3]Following Woodford, (2000), we compute welfare by taking a quadratic approximation around the deterministic steady state and then inputting the generated variance covariance matrix of c, m/p, l and ζ.

		M-Targeting		R-Taylor	
shock	σ	sd(y)	sd(π)	sd(y)	sd(π)
Supply	1.50	2.55	0.34	2.58	2.53
Fiscal		1.19	0.10	0.92	0.77
Money		0.44	0.15	0.02	0.02
All		2.85	0.38	2.74	2.64
note: sd: standard deviation					

Table 4: Inflation and output volatility: $q = 0.25$

	M-Targeting				
shock	sd(c)	sd(m/p)	sd(lp)	Welfare	x
Supply	2.83	2.98	0.53	−58.190708	−0.0102
Fiscal	0.82	0.92	0.69	−58.188391	−0.0039
Money	0.42	0.96	0.26	−58.188008	−0.0029
All	2.98	3.26	0.90	−58.193207	−0.0169
	Taylor rule				
shock	sd(c)	sd(m/p)	sd(lp)	Welfare	x
Supply	3.35	7.36	0.12	−58.192879	−0.0160
Fiscal	0.97	2.35	0.60	−58.188686	−0.0047
Money	0.04	1.99	0.02	−58.188473	−0.0041
All	3.48	7.98	0.61	−58.196138	−0.0249
note: sd: standard deviation					

Table 5: Money targeting and Taylor rule: Welfare: $q = 0.25, k_y = 0$

		M-Targeting		Taylor rule	
shock	σ	sd(y)	sd(π)	sd(y)	sd(π)
Supply	1.50	2.55	0.34	3.02	0.21
Fiscal		1.19	0.10	1.01	0.07
Money		0.44	0.15	0.03	0.00
All		2.85	0.38	3.19	0.22
note: sd: standard deviation					

Table 6: Inflation and output volatility: $q = 0.25, k_y = 0$

	M-Targeting				
shock	sd(c)	sd(m/p)	sd(lp)	Welfare	x
Supply	2.82	2.97	0.53	−56.744759	−0.0097
Fiscal	0.82	0.91	0.69	−56.742585	0.0038
Money	0.38	0.98	0.25	−56.741171	−0.0000
All	2.96	3.26	0.90	−56.746189	−0.0135
	Taylor rule				
shock	sd(c)	sd(m/p)	sd(lp)	Welfare	x
Supply	2.37	29.15	0.50	−56.744684	−0.0095
Fiscal	1.20	6.13	0.50	−56.742660	−0.0040
Money	0.00	2.00	0.00	−56.741163	−0.0000
All	2.65	29.85	0.71	−56.746181	−0.0135
note: sd: standard deviation					

Table 7: Money targeting and Taylor rule: Welfare $q = 0.25$, low ζ

		M-Targeting		Taylor rule	
shock	σ	sd(y)	sd(π)	sd(y)	sd(π)
Supply	1.50	2.55	0.34	2.05	2.08
Fiscal		1.20	0.10	0.76	0.64
Money		0.42	0.15	0.00	0.00
All		2.85	0.38	2.19	2.17
note: sd: standard deviation					

Table 8: Inflation and output volatility: $q = 0.25$, low ζ

	M-Targeting				
shock	sd(c)	sd(m/p)	sd(lp)	Welfare	x
Supply	3.26	3.41	0.14	−58.190894	−0.0107
Fiscal	0.95	1.05	0.61	−58.188425	−0.0040
Money	0.08	1.18	0.03	−58.188176	−0.0033
All	3.40	3.76	0.62	−58.193595	−0.0180
	Taylor rule				
shock	sd(c)	sd(m/p)	sd(lp)	Welfare	x
Supply	4.99	55.85	0.61	−58.458020	−0.7305
Fiscal	0.47	13.64	0.80	−58.207766	−0.0563
Money	0.06	1.57	0.02	−58.188305	−0.0037
All	5.01	57.52	1.00	−58.480191	−0.7900
note: sd: standard deviation					

Table 9: Money targeting and Taylor rule: Welfare $q = 0.90$

		M–Targeting		Taylor rule	
shock	σ	sd(y)	sd(π)	sd(y)	sd(π)
Supply	1.50	2.98	0.78	4.20	4.07
Fiscal		1.02	0.24	1.37	1.20
Money		0.06	0.36	0.04	0.03
All		3.15	0.89	4.42	4.24
note: sd: standard deviation					

Table 10: Inflation and output volatility: $q = 0.90$

In order to understand these results let us look at the response of the economy to a particular shock in the benchmark case ($\sigma = 1.5$ and $\gamma = 0.25$). Consider first a positive supply shock. On impact, it increases output (first row in Table 2). It also leads to lower inflation. Due to the fact that the inflation reaction coefficient is greater than the output reaction, the nominal interest rate must be lowered in order to push inflation back towards its targeted value. This implies that monetary policy is conducted in a procyclical fashion, something that amplifies consumption movements in comparison to the passive policy of monetary targeting. At the same time, policy activism is associated with greater nominal interest rate volatility, which increases real balance volatility and lowers welfare.

Let us now turn to a positive fiscal shock. As in the textbook case, it increases both output and the nominal interest rates while it crowds private consumption out (table 2). Under inflation targeting, in order to prevent inflation from rising, the monetary authorities must decrease the supply of money. This implies procyclical monetary policy with regard to *consumption* and hence increased consumption volatility (Table 4). Again, a Taylor rule is associated with greater real balance instability (Table 3).

Let us now consider a positive money demand shock. Again, as in the textbook case, under M-targeting such a shock would lower output and consumption and raise nominal interest rates. A Taylor rule targeting then requires countercyclical monetary policy and hence leads to more stable output and consumption. But this increased consumption stability comes at a cost. By insulating consumption from the effects of the money shock, it forces real balances to absorb a greater share of the shock than they would have otherwise done (see equation 4). This results in greater real balance volatility. Under our parameterization, the former effect dominates, making the Taylor rule produce higher welfare.

Tables 9–10 show that similar patterns obtain when prices display greater flexibility ($\gamma = 0.9$).

We now examine the robustness of our results with regard to changes in two parameters of the model: The elimination of the output stabilization objective (setting $k_y = 0$) and the reduction of the weight of real balances in the utility function (ζ). Tables 5–6 report the results in the former case and Tables 7–8 in the latter.

Two results stand out. First, when the central bank does not pursue any output stabilization, then it manages to achieve greater inflation stability under supply shock with the activistic rule. Nevertheless, welfare remains higher under the passive money rule. And second, the reduction of the weight of money in the utility function to a very low value has mixed effects on both welfare and volatilities depending on the type of shock.

5 Conclusions

The modern literature on monetary policy has been preoccupied with the properties of Taylor type rules. There exists a widespread presumption that such a rule, with the emphasis it places on inflation targeting, is approximately optimal, especially in the presence of velocity shocks. Our analysis indicates that this is not the case and that a simple, passive rule of monetary targeting delivers better results. We have used the standard New Neoclassical Synthesis model with commonly used parameter values to demonstrate that money targeting generates higher welfare than the standard Taylor rule. And that it also tends to produce a more stable inflation path when the monetary authorities engage in — even limited — output stabilization (alongside their inflation targeting).

Our results offer a new dimension to the old debate on activism vs passivity in the conduct of monetary policy. Even in the absence of the considerations emphasized by Friedman (variable lags in the relationship between money and economic activity, moral hazard problems involved in policymaking and so on) and even when monetary policy is conducted according to a rule rather than via discretion, we argue that activistic monetary policies may still produce worse outcomes than a perfectly passive rule.

Bibliography

[1] Calvo, Guillermo A.,1983, "Staggered Prices in a Utility-Maximizing Framework," Journal of Monetary Economics 12, 383–398. 64

[2] Chari, V., Patrick Kehoe and Ellen McGrattan, 2000, "Can Sticky Price Models Generate Volatile and Persistent Real Exchange Rate Changes?" NBER working paper, No 7869.

[3] Gali, Jordi, 2000, "New Perspectives on Monetary Policy, Inflation, and the Business Cycle," invited paper at the 2000 World Congress of the Econometric Society, Seattle, August 11–16, 2000.

[4] Goodfriend, M. and R. King, 1997, "The New Neoclassical Synthesis and the Role of Monetary Policy," in Bernanke, B. and Rotemberg, J. eds. NBER Macroeconomics Annual, MIT Press.

[5] Ireland, Peter, 1999, "Interest Rates, Inflation, and Federal Reserve Policy Since 1980," mimeo, Boston College.

[6] King, Robert G. and Mark W. Watson, 1996, "Money, Prices, Interest Rates and the Business Cycle," *Review of Economics and Statistics* 78: 35–53.

[7] King, R. and A. Wolman, 1999, "What Should the Monetary Authority Do When Prices are Sticky?" in Taylor, J. ed. Monetary Policy Rules, Chicago University Press.

[8] Poole, William, 1970, "Optimal Choice of Monetary Policy Instruments in a Simple Stochastic Macro Model," *Quarterly Journal of Economics* 84: 197–216.

[9] Woodford, M., 2000, *Interest and Prices*, ch. 6.

12 Credit Value-at-Risk Constraints, Credit Rationing and Monetary Policy

Jan Frederik Slijkerman, David J.C. Smant and Casper G. de Vries[1]

1 Introduction

Banking supervisors and the banking industry have been discussing the wider application of the Value-at-Risk approach to risk management and capital regulation. To tie capital requirements more closely to the underlying risk in bank loan portfolios, the new Basle 2 framework allows for two main approaches to evaluate credit risk inherent in individual loans. Banks may use a standardised approach to risk assessment, which involves evaluating corporate loans by employing the ratings on unsecured debt issues provided by external credit rating agencies. Under this approach, loans to corporations would be allocated among a number of risk categories, each carrying predetermined risk weights. Alternatively, banks with sufficiently developed risk assessment systems may use an internal-ratings-based method to estimate the credit risk of their portfolios.

The consequences of the introduction of simple and risk-weighted capital adequacy requirements have been studied intensively, both empirically (see Basle Committee on Banking Supervision (1999) for an overview) and theoretically (see Freixas and Rochet (1997) for an overview). In this paper we show that a credit risk model based Value-at-Risk (CVaR) constraint distorts the operation of credit markets. This occurs,

[1]We would like to thank Dale Henderson, David B. Smith, Jürgen von Hagen and the participants of the Cardiff European Monetary Forum in honour of Sir Allen Walters for their useful suggestions.

because, when the constraint is binding, it induces credit rationing by banks. From the literature we know that imperfect information on loan applicants can cause credit rationing, see Stiglitz and Weiss (1981) and Williamson (1986). However, the influence of bank regulation is absent from these models. Thakor (1996) models bank lending in the case of adverse selection and bank capital requirements. However, he does not model VaR regulation. To the best of our knowledge the effect that CVaR regulation induces credit rationing is novel to the literature.

Understanding the distortionary effects on the credit market of Value-at-Risk based regulation is important, but the bank loan market is also relevant for monetary policy. There exists a broad literature on the transmission channels of monetary policy (see Mishkin (1996) for an overview). Dissatisfaction with conventional views of how interest rates explain the effects of monetary policy has recently led to a revival of the credit channel of monetary policy.

The new credit channel approach to monetary policy consists of both a general credit channel and a lending channel. According to the general balance sheet channel theory, the effects of monetary policy on interest rates are amplified by endogenous changes in the external finance premium, which is the difference in cost between funds raised externally and funds generated internally (Bernanke and Gertler, 1995). The size of this premium reflects imperfections in the credit markets. On the other hand, the bank lending channel of monetary policy states that specifically bank credit is special for firms. The information problem in the supply of credit from banks to firms generates frictions which make it difficult for banks to increase the supply of credit when demand rises. We model this friction in bank loan supply explicitly. Stein (1998) shows that asymmetric information between depositors and banks generates frictions in the lending channel. We model another aspect of the lending channel by modelling asymmetric information between banks and firms which results in adverse selection.

The structure of the remainder of this paper is as follows. In Section 2 we present our basic model of the bank loan market. We model the supply of bank loans in case of adverse selection but in absence of regulation. In Section 3 we introduce the Value-at-Risk constraint of bank credit risk regulation and show that CVaR regulation induces credit rationing. Section 4 concludes our paper.

2 The Bank Loan Market

Our model is a one period loan market in the spirit of Mankiw (1986). We assume that each firm can invest in a project that has a size of one unit. All firms are identical except for their probability of success with the investment project. Each investment project has two possible gross returns. These are $(X/\theta - k)$ with probability θ and zero with probability $(1-\theta)$, where $k > 0$ represents fixed costs of the investment. The expected return for firms thus becomes $X - k\theta$, and the variance is $(X - k\theta)^2(1/\theta - 1)$. Note that the expected returns are an increasing function of risk, consistent with basic finance theory.

For expository reasons the risk parameter θ of individual firms is here assumed to be uniformly distributed on the interval $[0, 1]$, see e.g. Mankiw (1986). Firms know their own risk parameter θ, but do not know the actual outcome of their project. Suppliers of external finance, i.e. banks, only know the sample distribution of θ for all firms. Bank loans can be obtained at the (gross) interest rate R $(R \geq 1)$.

2.1 The Demand for Bank Loans

Apart from the fixed costs, the firm also has to repay the loan at the going gross rate R. Adding up, the firm per unit (loan) profit function P^F becomes

$$P^F = \frac{X}{\theta} - R - k.$$

The expected profit for the firm is

$$E\left[P^F\right] = \theta\left(\frac{X}{\theta} - R - k\right).$$

A risk neutral firm only invests if expected profit $E[P^F] \geq 0$. The participation constraint for firms is therefore satisfied when $\theta \leq \frac{X}{R+k}$. By the assumption that θ follows a uniform distribution on $[0, 1]$, all projects will be undertaken when $1 \leq \frac{X}{R+k}$, which implies $R \leq X - k$. Let the average probability of success be denoted as $\pi^d = E[\theta]$. If all firms invest, the average probability of success is

$$\pi^d = 1/2. \tag{1}$$

If $1 > \frac{X}{R+k}$, that is when $R > X - k$, not all firms invest, only firms with $\theta < 1$ are active. The conditional expected value of θ for all firms that want to invest is

$$\pi^d(R) = \frac{1}{2}\frac{X}{R+k}. \tag{2}$$

Note that at any given loan rate the firms that choose to invest and turn out to be successful are always able to repay the bank loan in full, since for these firms $R \leq \frac{X}{\theta} - k$.

2.2 The Supply of Bank Loans

We assume that risk neutral banks offer standard debt contracts with limited liability. Because a firm's individual (X, θ) is private information of the borrower, R cannot be conditioned on this information. The expected per unit profit function for the bank is

$$E[P^B] = \pi(R)R - I.$$

This profit function consists of two parts. The first part, πR, denotes the expected gross return of all loans to firms that are successful. The second part, I, defines the funding costs of the bank loans. In a perfectly competitive market, bank profits are zero. In equilibrium the required expected probability of repayment in the pool of borrowers would be

$$\pi^s = \frac{I}{R}. \tag{3}$$

2.3 Equilibrium

Figure 1 displays the market equilibrium in the $(R, \pi(R))$ plane using the shape of the iso-profit curves and the shape of the expected repayment curve. As mentioned before, all firms want to participate in the loan market if $\frac{X}{R+k} \geq 1$ and this results in $\pi^d = 1/2$. This fact is represented by a straight line segment in the $(R, \pi(R))$ plane until the cost of borrowing, R, becomes too high at $R = X - k$, and the firms with high θ decide no longer to invest. This is the point where the adverse selection kicks in. Higher bank loan rates, $R > I$, are associated with lower π^s. For $\pi^s = 1$ and perfect competition the bank charges the loan rate $R = I$.

For $R > X - k$, loan demand equals loan supply when $\pi^d(R) = \pi^s$, which is the case if

$$R = \frac{2Ik}{(X - 2I)}. \tag{4}$$

It can be shown that at the loan market equilibrium the supply curve for banks is steeper than the demand curve for firms.

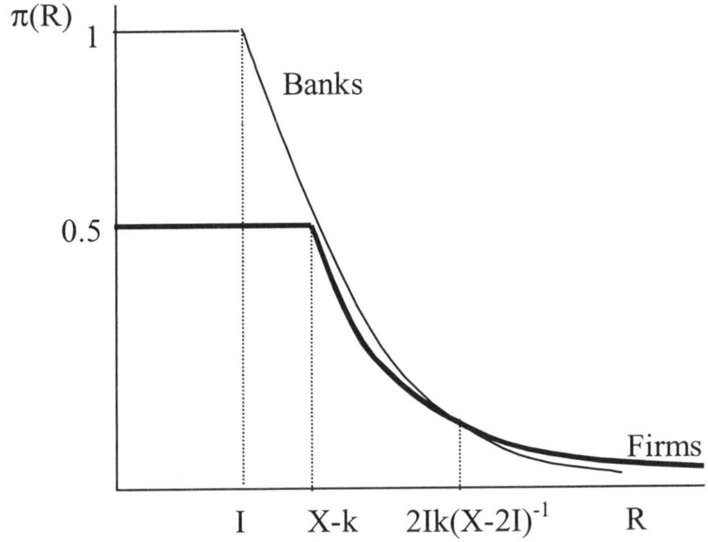

Figure 1: Bank Loan Market Equilibrium

3 Credit Risk Regulation

In this section we study the effect of a Value-at-Risk constraint on bank loans. We show that a credit risk model based Value-at-Risk constraint can distort the operation of credit markets by introducing credit rationing.

The motive for the minimum regulatory risk constraint for the bank loan portfolio is to counter adverse selection. It can be shown that in a perfect information setting the loan rate R, is lower than in the case of asymmetric information. A regulatory risk constraint which is equal to the equilibrium level of risk in the case of perfect information abates the adverse selection problem.

3.1 The Credit Risk Constraint

Now consider a banking supervisor and banking regulation under the new Basle accord. We assume that the supervisor has no better information than the bank. For this reason the supervisor imposes a risk limit using the average success rate of loans π in order to improve the quality of the loan portfolio. Note that the quality of the loan portfolio is strictly increasing in $\pi(R)$. Suppose therefore that credit risk regulation imposes a lower limit on the average probability of success on repayment $\pi(R)$, say $(1 - \pi(R)) < \delta$. We call δ the CVaR constraint on the loan book.

Figure 2 displays the credit risk constraint effective at the bank loan portfolio risk level π^v, where $\pi^v = 1 - \delta$. The iso-profit curve of the firms requires that the loan rate is no higher than R^A. From (4) one sees that when the risk restriction binds, $R^A < 2I_0k/(X - 2I_0)$. Here I_0 refers to the deposit rate which prevails in the unconstrained equilibrium $(2I_0k/(X-2I_0), (X-2I_0)/2k)$. At this lower interest rate R^A the quality (success rate) of the pool of loan contracts is higher, since more firms with relatively high quality projects apply for a loan, compared to the unconstrained equilibrium. So both the average quality as well as the number of loans demanded increases. At π^v and a given deposit rate I_0 banks require a loan rate of no less than R^B. In this situation loan demand and supply do not meet. What does it take for banks to be willing to offer (R^A, π^v)? This requires a shift in the bank iso-profit curve to the left. Note that the bank iso-profit curve implicitly defines the bank supply curve for loan (quality). From (3) it follows that the only shift parameter of this curve is the deposit rate I. By lowering I, the loan supply curve shifts to the left until it cuts the demand curve at (R^A, π^v). Assuming that the supply curve for deposits is an upward sloping function of the deposit rate, banks can reduce the deposit market rate by taking in fewer deposits. The implication of a lower deposit demand is a reduction in the supply of loans. Thus while at (R^A, π^v) the demand for loans increases vis à vis the free market solution, the supply is reduced. Loan market equilibrium can then be achieved only if banks ration the supply of loans at the given quality level π^v. Since the quality of the loan portfolio must at least be π^v, banks select the loan applicants randomly. Thus the equilibrium under a binding CVaR constraint requires random credit rationing.

It is interesting to note that regulation Q in the United States had similar consequences as the risk constraint δ. By limiting the loan rate R to a maximum, banks face an excess demand for loans. To achieve equilibrium the deposit rate should again be lowered. In this case the constraint is on the interest rate rather than on quality, but the effects are the same.

3.2 Effect on Money Supply

With a binding CVaR restriction imposed, the deposit rate I has to fall, lowering the volume of deposits as is explained in the previous paragraph. Introducing a binding CVaR constraint therefore reduces the money sup-

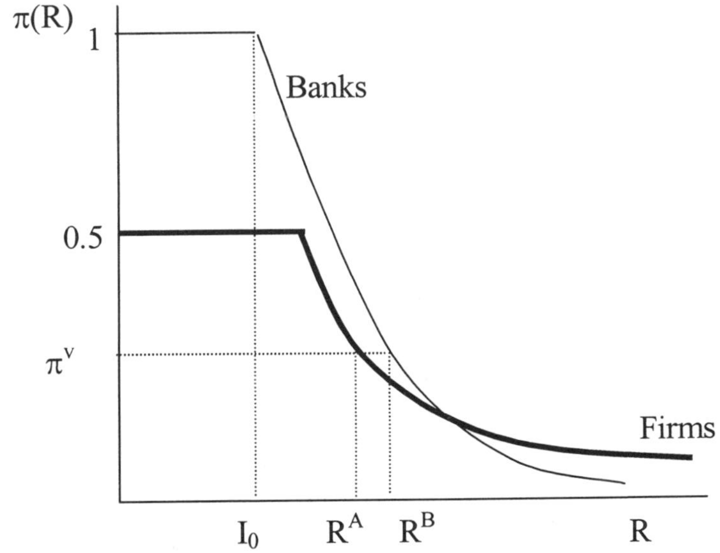

Figure 2: Bank Loan Market and Credit Risk Constraint

ply. In terms of the familiar IS/LM model this can be visualised by a shift of the LM-curve to the left. Evidence in Smith (2002) suggests that this may indeed have been the case. Shortly after the implementation of the Basle I 1988 agreement on bank capital ratios, the growth rate of the money supply was reduced considerably. Moreover, credit rationing also reduces investment, and hence the IS curve will also shift inwards.[2] Without a monetary policy response, the combined shifts of the LM and IS curves due to the regulatory shock could risk a significant reduction in economic activity.

4 Conclusion

Current proposals for a new Basle capital adequacy accord sponsor the idea that banks should be allowed to use internal credit risk models

[2] There is the positive dynamic effect of a quality improvement of the investments, something which cannot be analysed within the static IS/LM model. This issue warrants further investigation.

to compute the required capital adequacy on bank loans, in contrast to the existing but outdated BIS standards. We have shown that a credit risk model based Value-at-Risk constraint distorts the operation of credit markets by introducing credit rationing. The result is that in this rationing equilibrium the money supply experiences a negative shock if the risk constraint is binding.

BIBLIOGRAPHY

[1] Basle Committee on Banking Supervision, 1999, Capital requirements and bank behavior: The impact of the Basle Accord, Working Papers no.1, BIS, Basle

[2] Bernanke, B.S. and M. Gertler, 1995, Inside the black box: The credit channel of monetary policy transmission, Journal of Economic Perspectives, 9: 27–48

[3] Freixas, X. and J.C. Rochet, 1997, Microeconomics of Banking, MIT Press

[4] Mankiw, N.G., 1986, The allocation of credit and financial collapse, Quarterly Journal of Economics, 103: 101–130

[5] Mishkin, F.S., 1996, The channels of monetary transmission: Lessons for monetary policy, NBER working paper no. 5464

[6] Smith, D.B., 2002, Quarterly macroeconomic model of the UK and World Economies (Working Draft), 11th edition, Williams de Broë, London: 22–23

[7] Stein, J.C., 1998, An adverse-selection model of bank asset and liability management with implications for the transmission of monetary policy, RAND Journal of Economics, 29: 466–486

[8] Stiglitz, J. E. and A. Weiss., "Credit rationing in Markets with Imperfect Information", *American Economic Review*, 71 (3), June 1981, 393–410.

[9] Thakor, A.V., 1996, Capital requirements, monetary policy, and aggregate bank lending: Theory and empirical evidence, Journal of Finance, 51: 279–324

[10] Williamson, S.D., 1986, Costly monitoring, financial intermediation, and equilibrium credit rationing, Journal of Monetary Economics, 18: 159–179

13 Policy Games and the Optimal Design of Central Banks

Andrew Hughes Hallett and Diana N. Weymark

1 Introduction

Few studies of monetary delegation model the interaction between the government and the central bank as a game of strategy. Those that do allow for strategic policy formation, use non-cooperative simultaneous-move (Nash equilibrium) games to model the interaction between the fiscal and monetary authorities. In practice however, the institutional arrangements in many countries confer varying degrees of leadership on one of the policy authorities. In some cases, this is the result of statutory provisions or the institutional arrangements under which the central bank is required to operate. In other cases, it is simply a matter of convention or common practice built up over a number of years. But, in either event, a Nash equilibrium between the individual policy makers may not be the appropriate framework for analyzing the policies and performance of alternative central banking regimes.

Moreover, because most of the existing literature considers only the impact of monetary policy on inflation and output performance, it can offer no guidelines for choosing among regimes when there is some kind of leadership among the players; or when some of the institutional characteristics may be chosen by different players; or when fiscal policy with social equity (redistributional) objectives is being pursued by the government. In this article we analyze the implications of several alternative institutional configurations on economic performance.

No doubt there are many different institutional configurations that countries could employ in this context. For the purposes of this analysis we limit ourselves to just four representative alternatives that have practical counterparts in the real world. Our first case is represented by a two-stage game in which the government initially determines both the degree of independence and the conservatism of the central bank. Subsequently, in the second stage of the game, the government and the central bank move simultaneously in choosing fiscal and monetary policy. This constitutes our first case: it might be taken to represent the operation of the Federal Reserve System. We also include here a variant in which the central bank is free to choose a target inflation rate which is different from (less than) that preferred by the fiscal authorities. This is done to provide a second point of reference which will enable us to investigate the importance of target independence in the later stages of the paper.

Our second type of regime is one in which the government not only chooses the institutional design in the first stage of the game, but also exercises fiscal leadership in the second stage. This configuration might be taken as representative of the system under which the Bank of England now operates. In our third regime, we reverse the leadership roles and, in addition, grant the central bank target independence. In the first two regimes, by contrast, we assume that the inflation target pursued by the central bank coincides with that of the government. Our third case therefore captures some of the characteristics intended for the European Central Bank. But as the degree of target independence is incomplete and because the degree of conservatism is still set by the government, it is probably more representative of the strong monetary leadership found in Switzerland or Germany before the Euro. Finally, we consider the case of simultaneously set monetary and fiscal policies, but in a world in which the government(s) can only choose the central bank's degree of independence. The central bank determines its own degree of conservatism. Here again we allow for the possibility that the inflation targets of the two policy authorities may differ. This regime captures the salient features of current practice at the European Central Bank.

2 Economic Structure

The model used in Weymark (2001) provides a useful framework for the present analysis. For purposes of exposition, we suppress potential spillover effects between countries and focus on the following three equations to represent the economic structure of any country:

$$\pi_t = \pi_t^e + \alpha y_t + u_t \tag{1}$$

$$y_t = \beta(m_t - \pi_t) + \gamma g_t + \epsilon_t \tag{2}$$

$$g_t = m_t + s(b y_t - \tau_t) \tag{3}$$

where π_t is the inflation rate in period t, y_t is output growth in period t, and π_t^e represents the rate of inflation that rational agents expect will prevail in period t, conditional on the information available at the time expectations are formed. The variables m_t, g_t, and τ_t represent, respectively, the growth in the money supply, government expenditures, and tax revenues in period t. The variables u_t and ϵ_t are random disturbances which are assumed to be independently distributed with zero mean and constant variance. The coefficients α, β, γ, s, and b are all positive by assumption. The assumption that γ is positive may be considered controversial.[1] However, short-run impact multipliers derived from Taylor's (1993) multi-country estimation provide empirical support for this assumption.[2]

According to (1), inflation is increasing in the rate of inflation predicted by private agents and in output growth. Equation (2) indicates that both monetary and fiscal policies have an impact on the output gap. The microfoundations of the aggregate supply equation (1), originally derived by Lucas (1972, 1973), are well-known. McCallum (1989) shows that aggregate demand equations like (2) can be derived from a standard, multiperiod utility-maximization problem.

Equation (3) describes the government's budget constraint. In the interests of simplicity, we allow discretionary tax revenues to be used for redistributive purposes only. Thus, in each period, the government must finance its remaining expenditures by selling government bonds to the central bank or to private agents.[3] We assume that there are two types of agents, rich and poor, and that only the rich use their savings to buy government bonds. In (3), b is the proportion of pre-tax income (output) that goes to the rich and s is the proportion of after-tax income that the rich allocate to saving. The tax, τ_t, is used by the government to redistribute income from the rich to the poor.

Using (1) and (2) to solve for π_t^e, π_t and y_t yields the following

---

[1] Barro (1981) argues that government purchases have a contractionary impact on output. However, in contrast to those who argue that fiscal policy has little systematic or positive impact on economic performance, our model treats fiscal policy as important because (i) fiscal policy is used by governments to achieve redistributive objectives whose consequences need to be taken into account; and (ii) as Dixit and Lambertini (2001) point out, governments cannot precommit monetary policy with any credibility if fiscal policy is not also precommitted.

[2] For example, using Taylor's empirical results, Hughes Hallett and Weymark (2001) obtain short-run γ estimates of 0.57, 0.43, 0.60, and 0.58 for France , Germany, Italy, and the United Kingdom, respectively.

[3] Several variations which relax the restrictions on how fiscal policy may be financed are considered in Weymark (2001). Specifically, in one variation, bond financing is replaced by income taxes which can be used to finance both g_t and τ_t. In another variation, income taxes and newly-created general taxes are available to finance g_t and τ_t. However, the model's theoretical predictions are robust to these variations.

reduced forms:

$$\pi_t(g_t, m_t) = (1+\alpha\beta)^{-1}[\alpha\beta m_t + \alpha\gamma g_t + m_t^e + \frac{\gamma}{\beta} g_t^e + \alpha\epsilon_t + u_t] \quad (4)$$

$$y_t(g_t, m_t) = (1+\alpha\beta)^{-1}[\beta m_t + \gamma g_t - \beta m_t^e - \gamma g_t^e + \epsilon_t - \beta u_t] \quad (5)$$

Equations (5) and (3) then imply

$$\tau_t(g_t, m_t) = [s(1+\alpha\beta)]^{-1}[(1+\alpha\beta+sb\beta)m_t - (1+\alpha\beta - sb\gamma)g_t - sb\beta m_t^e - sb\gamma g_t^e + sb\epsilon_t - sb\beta u_t] \quad (6)$$

3 Government and Central Bank Objectives

In this paper, we allow for the possibility that the government and a fully independent central bank may differ in their objectives in some significant way. In particular, we assume that the government cares about inflation stabilization, output growth, and income redistribution, whereas the central bank, if left to itself, would be concerned only with the first two objectives. We also assume that the government has been elected by majority vote, so that the government's loss function reflects society's preferences over alternative economic objectives.

Formally, the government's loss function is given by

$$L_t^g = \frac{1}{2}(\pi_t - \hat{\pi})^2 - \lambda_1^g y_t + \frac{\lambda_2^g}{2}[(b-\theta)y_t - \tau_t]^2 \quad (7)$$

where $\hat{\pi}$ is the government's inflation target, λ_1^g is the relative weight that the government assigns to output growth, and λ_2^g is the relative weight assigned to income redistribution. The parameter θ represents the proportion of output that the government would, ideally, like to allocate to the rich. Galí and Monacelli (2002) have demonstrated that, under suitable assumptions, an objective function like (7) may be derived from the utility functions of individuals in a standard microfounded open economy model of the Obstfeld and Rogoff (1996) type. Demertzis *et al.* (2003) have likewise shown that such a function would emerge out of the electoral process involving those agents. Hence, fiscal policy in this model will always be anchored in the microfoundations of voters' preferences, and may be considered "precommitted" in that sense.

The first term on the right of (7) reflects the government's concern with inflation stabilization. Specifically, the government incurs losses when actual inflation deviates from the government's or society's inflation target. The second term is intended to capture what many believe is a political reality for governments — namely, that voters reward governments for increases in output growth and penalize them for reductions in the growth rate.[4] The third component in the government's loss function reflects the government's concern with income redistribution. The parameter θ represents the government's ideal degree of income inequality. For example, in an economy in which there are as many rich people as poor people, an egalitarian government would set $\theta = 0.5$. Ideally, in this case, the government would like to redistribute output in the amount of $(b \square 0.5)y_t$ from the rich to the poor.

We assume that the central bank has objectives which may differ from those of the government:

$$L_t^{cb} = \frac{1}{2}(\pi_t \square \bar{\pi})^2 \square (1 \square \delta)\lambda^{cb} y_t \square \delta\lambda_1^g y_t + \frac{\delta\lambda_2^g}{2}[(b \square \theta)y_t \square \tau_t]^2 \quad (8)$$

where $0 \leq \delta \leq 1$, and λ^{cb} is the weight that the central bank assigns to output growth. The parameter δ measures the degree to which the central bank is forced to take the government's objectives into account when formulating monetary policy. The closer δ is to 0, the greater is the independence of the central bank.

In (7) we have described $\bar{\pi}$ as the government's inflation target. The fact that the same inflation target appears in (8) reflects our assumption that the central bank has instrument independence but not target independence (we follow the definitions of Fischer, 1995, here). We relax that restriction below.

4 Four Policy Games

We characterize the strategic interaction between the government and the central bank as a two-stage non-cooperative game in which the structure of the model and the objective functions are common knowledge. Certain variations in institutional design are obtained by altering the assumptions about (i) which policy authority has control over the institutional parameters, δ and λ^{cb} in stage 1, and (ii) the timing of fiscal and monetary policy moves in stage 2. Our baseline is a game in which the government sets both δ and λ^{cb} in stage 1 and both policy authorities move simultaneously in stage 2. We then compare the outcomes

[4] In adopting a linear representation of the output objective, we follow Barro and Gordon (1983). In the monetary delegation literature, the output component in the government's loss function is more often represented as quadratic because the models employed typically preclude any stabilization role for monetary policy when the output term in the loss function is linear. In our model, the quadratic income redistribution term in the loss function allows monetary policy to play a direct role in output stabilization — the output variable being measured as deviations from full employment (capacity) output.

associated with our baseline case to three alternatives. In one, we retain the baseline assumption for stage 1, but alter stage 2 to give the fiscal authority leadership in policy formation. Our second variation retains the stage 1 baseline assumptions, but switches the role of Stackelberg leader to the central bank in stage 2.[5] Our third, and final, variant alters stage 1 by transferring control of λ^{cb} to the central bank, but retains the assumption of simultaneous policy moves in stage 2.

4.1 Simultaneous Moves — Government Chooses δ and λ^{cb}

In this section, we consider a situation in which the government chooses both of the institutional parameters, δ and λ^{cb} in the first stage of the game. In the second stage, the government and the monetary authority move simultaneously and set their policy instruments, given the δ and λ^{cb} values determined at the previous stage. Private agents understand the game and form rational expectations for future prices in the second stage. We consider two cases. In the first case, both government and central bank follow the same inflation target, $\hat{\pi}$, while in the second case the central bank's inflation target, $\hat{\pi}_i^{cb}$ may differ from that of the government.

4.1.1 Case 1

The simultaneous-move game with coincident inflation targets can be described as follows:

4.1.1.1 Stage 1

The government solves the problem

$$\min_{\delta,\, \lambda^{cb}} \mathrm{E}\, L^g\left(g_t, m_t, \delta,\, \lambda^{cb}\right) = \mathrm{E}\frac{1}{2}[\pi_t(g_t, m_t) - \hat{\pi}]^2 - \lambda_1^g[y_t(g_t, m_t)] + \frac{\lambda_2^g}{2}[(b-\theta)y_t(g_t, m_t) - \tau_t(g_t, m_t)]^2 \quad (9)$$

where $L^g(g_t, m_t, \delta,\, \lambda^{cb})$ is (7) evaluated at $(g_t, m_t, \delta,\, \lambda^{cb})$, and E is the expectations operator.

[5] In other words, the first three models test the degree of independence and the degree of conservatism as joint decisions by the two policy authorities — as emphasised by Rogoff (1985) or Alesina and Gatti (1995) — whereas the last variant treats them as separate decisions.

4.1.1.2 Stage 2

(i) Private agents form rational expectations about future prices before the shocks u_t and ϵ_t are realized.

(ii) The shocks u_t and ϵ_t are realized and observed by the government and by the central bank.

(iii) The government chooses g_t, taking m_t as given, to minimize

$$L^g(g_t, m_t, \bar{\delta}, \bar{\lambda}^{cb})$$

where $\bar{\delta}$ and $\bar{\lambda}^{cb}$ indicates that these variables were determined in stage 1.

(iv) The central bank chooses m_t, taking g_t as given, to minimize

$$L^{cb}\left(g_t, m_t, \bar{\delta}, \bar{\lambda}^{cb}\right) = \frac{(1-\bar{\delta})}{2}\left[\pi_t(g_t, m_t) - \hat{\pi}\right]^2 - (1-\bar{\delta})\bar{\lambda}^{cb}\left[y_t(g_t, m_t)\right] + \bar{\delta} L^g\left(g_t, m_t, \bar{\delta}, \bar{\lambda}^{cb}\right) \quad (10)$$

The timing of this game is illustrated in Figure 1.

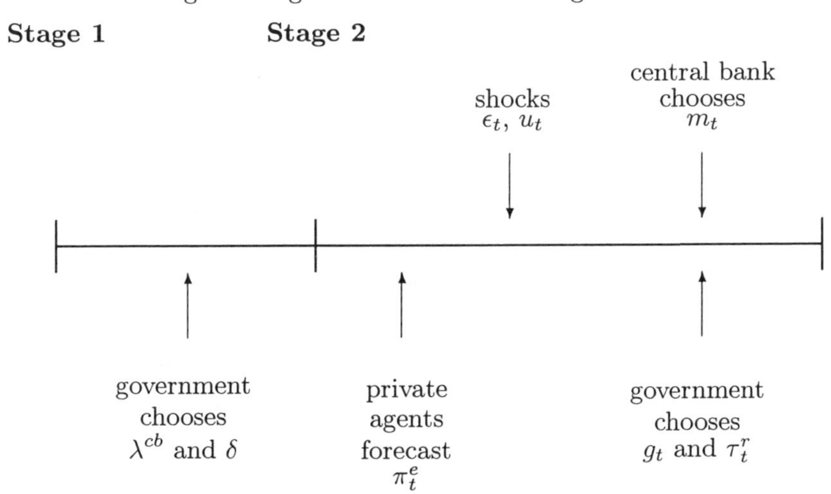

Figure 1: The Stages and Timing of the Simultaneous Move Game

This policy game can be solved by first solving the second stage of the game for the optimal money supply and government expenditure policies with δ and λ^{cb} fixed, and then solving stage 1 by substituting the stage 2 results into (9) and minimizing with respect to δ and λ^{cb}. The Nash equilibrium for stage 2 is

$$m_t(\delta, \lambda^{cb}) = \frac{\beta\hat{\pi}}{(\beta+\gamma)} + \frac{(1-\delta)\beta\left[\alpha\gamma^2 s^2 \;+\; \beta\phi\lambda_2^g\right]\lambda^{cb}}{\alpha\lambda_2^g[\beta\phi+\delta\gamma\Lambda](\beta+\gamma)} + \frac{\delta\beta(1+\alpha\beta)\lambda_1^g}{\alpha[\beta\phi+\delta\gamma\Lambda]}$$
$$- \frac{(1-\delta)\gamma^2\beta s^2\lambda_1^g}{(\beta+\gamma)\left[\beta\phi+\delta\gamma\Lambda\right]\lambda_2^g} - \frac{\epsilon_t}{(\beta+\gamma)} - \frac{(1-\beta\gamma+\gamma\theta-\gamma\theta s)u_t}{\alpha(\beta+\gamma)} \tag{11}$$

$$g_t(\delta, \lambda^{cb}) = \frac{\beta\hat{\pi}}{(\beta+\gamma)} + \frac{(1-\delta)\beta^2\left[\phi\lambda_2^g - \alpha\gamma s^2\right]\lambda^{cb}}{\alpha\lambda_2^g[\beta\phi+\delta\gamma\Lambda](\beta+\gamma)} + \frac{\delta\beta(1+\alpha\beta)\lambda_1^g}{\alpha[\beta\phi+\delta\gamma\Lambda]}$$
$$+ \frac{(1-\delta)\beta^2\gamma s^2\lambda_1^g}{(\beta+\gamma)[\beta\phi+\delta\gamma\Lambda]\lambda_2^g} - \frac{\epsilon_t}{(\beta+\gamma)} - \frac{(1+b\beta-\beta\theta+\beta\theta s)u_t}{\alpha(\beta+\gamma)} \tag{12}$$

where

$$\phi = 1 + \alpha\beta - \gamma\theta s \tag{13}$$
$$\Lambda = 1 + \alpha\beta + \beta\theta s \tag{14}$$

The sign of the composite parameter Λ has no bearing on the results that follow: it is positive anyway. The results are, however, sensitive to the sign of ϕ. The parameter ϕ is perhaps most easily interpreted by noting that from (5) and (6)

$$\frac{\partial[(b-\theta)y_t - \tau_t]}{\partial g_t} = \frac{\phi}{(1+\alpha\beta)} \tag{15}$$

The term $(b-\theta)y_t$ represents the transfer that the government would like to make to the poor. Equation (15) shows that the difference between the government's ideal transfer to the poor and actual transfer payment, τ_t^r, is positively (negatively) related to government expenditures when ϕ is positive (negative). The assumption that ϕ is positive therefore implies that increases in government expenditure make it more difficult for the government to achieve the optimal transfer. Because in this model, government expenditure is positively related to output growth, there is a conflict between government policies aimed at stimulating growth and those aimed at income redistribution when ϕ is positive. Although it is possible for ϕ to be negative, the implications of this are rather unappealing. In order for ϕ to be negative, the impact of government expenditure on output must be so large that the government can increase transfer payments without significantly reducing the funding available to finance its desired level of government expenditure. In this article, we restrict our analysis to the case in which ϕ is positive.

It is also assumed that the government and the central bank observe the white noise disturbances, u_t and ϵ_t, in the second stage before policies are chosen, but after private expectations have been formed. Although private agents cannot observe u_t and ϵ_t prior to forming expectations about future inflation rates, the characteristics of the institutions in place in the economy, represented by δ and λ^{cb}, are known to them with certainty. Under these conditions, it can be shown that (11) and (12) characterize a rational expectations equilibrium.

Taking the expectation of both sides of (11) and (12) to obtain m_t^e and g_t^e, respectively, and substituting the result, together with (11) and (12), into (4) and (5) yields the reduced-form solutions for π_t and y_t as functions of the institutional variables δ and λ^{cb}

$$\pi_t(\delta, \lambda^{cb}) = \hat{\pi} + \frac{(1-\delta)\beta\phi\lambda^{cb}}{\alpha[\beta\phi + \delta\gamma\Lambda]} + \frac{\delta[\beta\phi + \gamma\Lambda]\lambda_1^g}{\alpha[\beta\phi + \delta\gamma\Lambda]} \tag{16}$$

$$y_t(\delta, \lambda^{cb}) = \frac{-u_t}{\alpha} \tag{17}$$

From (6), the reduced-form solution for τ_t is given by

$$\tau_t(\delta, \lambda^{cb}) = \frac{(1-\delta)\beta\gamma s(\lambda^{cb} - \lambda_1^g)}{[\beta\phi + \delta\gamma\Lambda]\lambda_2^g} - \frac{(b-\theta)u_t}{\alpha} \tag{18}$$

Substituting (16)–(18) into (9), the government's stage 1 minimization problem can be expressed as

$$\min_{\delta, \lambda^{cb}} \; \mathrm{E}L^g(\delta, \lambda^{cb}) = \frac{1}{2}\left\{\frac{(1-\delta)\beta\phi\lambda_1^{cb}}{\alpha[\beta\phi \;+\; \delta\gamma\Lambda]} + \frac{\delta[\beta\theta + \Lambda\gamma]\lambda_1^g}{\alpha[\beta\phi + \delta\gamma\Lambda]}\right\}^2 + \frac{\lambda_2^g}{2}\left\{\frac{(1-\delta)\beta\gamma s(\lambda^{cb} - \lambda_1^g)}{[\beta\phi + \delta\gamma\Lambda]\lambda_2^g}\right\}^2 \tag{19}$$

Partial differentiation of (19) with respect to λ^{cb} and δ now yields the first-order conditions for choosing δ and λ^{cb}:

$$\frac{\partial \mathrm{E}L^g(\delta, \lambda^{cb})}{\partial \lambda^{cb}} = \frac{(1-\delta)^2(\beta\phi)^2\lambda^{cb} + \delta(1-\delta)\beta\phi[\beta\phi + \gamma\Lambda]\lambda_1^g}{\alpha^2[\beta\phi + \delta\gamma\Lambda]^2} + \frac{(1-\delta)^2(\beta\gamma s)^2(\lambda^{cb} - \lambda_1^g)}{\lambda_2^g[\beta\phi + \delta\gamma\Lambda]^2} = 0 \tag{20}$$

$$\frac{\partial \mathrm{E}L^g(\delta, \lambda^{cb})}{\partial \delta} = - \frac{\left\{(1-\delta)\beta\phi\lambda^{cb} + \delta[\beta\phi + \gamma\Lambda]\lambda_1^g\right\}\beta\phi[\beta\phi + \gamma\Lambda](\lambda^{cb} - \lambda_1^g)}{\alpha^2[\beta\phi + \delta\gamma\Lambda]^3}$$

$$-\left\{\frac{(1-\delta)(\beta\gamma s)^2[\beta\phi+\gamma\Lambda](\lambda^{cb}-\lambda_1^g)^2}{\lambda_2^g[\beta\phi+\delta\gamma\Lambda]^3}\right\}=0 \quad (21)$$

It is evident that $[\beta\phi+\delta\gamma\Lambda]=0$ is not a solution to the minimization problem. When $[\beta\phi+\delta\gamma\Lambda]\neq 0$, (20) and (21) yield, respectively, (22) and (23):

$$\lambda_2^g(1-\delta)\phi\left\{(1-\delta)\beta\phi\lambda^{cb}+\delta[\beta\phi+\gamma\Lambda]\lambda_1^g\right\} \\ +\alpha^2(1-\delta)^2\beta\gamma^2 s^2(\lambda^{cb}-\lambda_1^g)=0 \quad (22)$$

$$\lambda_2^g\phi\left\{(1-\delta)\beta\phi\lambda^{cb}+\delta[\beta\phi+\gamma\Lambda]\lambda_1^g\right\}(\lambda^{cb}-\lambda_1^g) \\ +\alpha^2(1-\delta)\beta\gamma^2 s^2(\lambda^{cb}-\lambda_1^g)^2=0 \quad (23)$$

There are two solutions that satisfy both of the first-order conditions given above. By inspection, it is apparent that (22) and (23) are both satisfied when $\delta=1$ and $\lambda^{cb}=\lambda_1^g$. This solution characterizes a central bank that is fully dependent. When $\delta\neq 1$ and $\lambda^{cb}\neq\lambda_1^g$, then (22) and (23) imply the following relationship between δ and λ^{cb}

$$\delta=\frac{\beta\phi^2\lambda^{cb}\lambda_2^g+(\alpha\gamma s)^2\beta(\lambda^{cb}-\lambda_1^g)}{\beta\phi^2\lambda^{cb}\lambda_2^g+(\alpha\gamma s)^2\beta(\lambda^{cb}-\lambda_1^g)-\phi[\beta\phi+\gamma\Lambda]\lambda_1^g\lambda_2^g} \quad (24)$$

or, equivalently,

$$\lambda^{cb}=\frac{(\alpha\gamma s)^2\lambda_1^g}{\phi^2\lambda_2^g+(\alpha\gamma s)^2}-\frac{\delta[\beta\phi+\gamma\Lambda]\phi\lambda_1^g\lambda_2^g}{(1-\delta)\beta[\phi^2\lambda_2^g+(\alpha\gamma s)^2]} \quad (25)$$

The solution that yields the minimum loss for the government, as measured by the government's loss function (7), can be identified by using (19) to compare the expected loss that would be suffered under the alternative institutional arrangements. Substituting $\delta=1$ and $\lambda^{cb}=\lambda_1^g$ into (19) results in

$$\mathrm{E}L^g=\frac{(\lambda_1^g)^2}{2\alpha^2} \quad (26)$$

Substituting (24) into the right-hand-side of (19) yields

$$\mathrm{E}L^g=\frac{(\lambda_1^g)^2}{2\alpha^2}\left\{\frac{(\alpha\gamma s)^2}{(\alpha\gamma s)^2+\phi^2\lambda_2^g}\right\} \quad (27)$$

The preference parameter λ_2^g is non-negative by assumption. For positive (non-negative) values of λ_2^g, the value of (26) exceeds (equals) that of (27) which establishes that (24) is the solution to the government's loss minimization problem.

4.1.2 Case 2

As a small but important variant on our reference case, we can also allow for the possibility that the central bank may adopt its own inflation target , $\hat{\pi}^{cb}$. This gives the central bank target independence. In what follows, we assume that the central bank's inflation target would be lower than that of the government (i.e., $\hat{\pi}^{cb} < \hat{\pi}$). As in case 1, institutional parameters, δ and λ^{cb} are chosen by the government.

It is comparatively easy to rework the previous case, but allowing the central bank to adopt its own inflation target, $\hat{\pi}^{cb} < \hat{\pi}$ in (8) or (10). The expressions that emerge are somewhat more complicated however. Repeating the same steps as in case 1 we get

$$\pi_t(\delta, \lambda^{cb}) = \frac{(1-\delta)\beta\phi\hat{\pi}^{cb} + \delta(\beta\phi + \gamma\Lambda)\hat{\pi}}{[\beta\phi + \delta\gamma\Lambda]} + \frac{(1-\delta)\beta\phi\lambda^{cb} + \delta[\beta\phi + \gamma\Lambda]\lambda_1^g}{\alpha[\beta\phi + \delta\gamma\Lambda]} \quad (28)$$

$$y_t(\delta, \lambda^{cb}) = \frac{-u_t}{\alpha} \quad (29)$$

$$\tau_t(\delta, \lambda^{cb}) = \frac{\alpha\beta\gamma s(1-\delta)(\hat{\pi}^{cb} - \hat{\pi})}{[\beta\phi + \delta\gamma\Lambda]\lambda_2^g} + \frac{(1-\delta)\beta\gamma s(\lambda^{cb} - \lambda_1^g)}{[\beta\phi + \delta\gamma\Lambda]\lambda_2^g} - \frac{(b-\theta)u_t}{\alpha} \quad (30)$$

The new institutional parameters are then given by

$$\delta = \frac{(\beta\phi)^2\lambda^{cb}\lambda_2^g - \Omega(\hat{\pi}, \hat{\pi}^{cb})}{(\beta\phi)^2\lambda^{cb}\lambda_2^g - \Omega(\hat{\pi}, \hat{\pi}^{cb}) - \beta\phi([\beta\phi + \gamma\Lambda]\lambda_1^g\lambda_2^g} \quad (31)$$

and

$$\lambda^{cb} = \alpha(\hat{\pi} - \hat{\pi}^{cb}) + \frac{(\alpha\gamma s)^2\lambda_1^g}{[\phi^2\lambda_2^g + (\alpha\gamma s)^2]} - \frac{\phi[\beta\phi + \gamma\Lambda]\lambda_1^g\lambda_2^g\delta}{\beta(1-\delta)[\phi^2\lambda_2^g + (\alpha\gamma s)^2]} \quad (32)$$

where $\Omega(\hat{\pi}, \hat{\pi}^{cb}) = \alpha(\beta\phi)^2(\hat{\pi} - \hat{\pi}^{cb})\lambda_2^g + (\alpha\beta\gamma s)^2[\lambda_1^g - \lambda^{cb} + \alpha(\hat{\pi} - \hat{\pi}^{cb})]$.

Substituting (28)–(32) back into (7) yields exactly the same welfare losses for the government (and society) as in case 1: i.e., we get (27) again.

The results obtained here may now be compared to case 1, where there is no target independence. Various conclusions follow. First, there is no advantage (or disadvantage) in granting target independence to the central bank as far as society and its elected government are concerned.[6] The reason is that, if the central bank were (expected) to choose a lower inflation target than the government ($\hat{\pi}^{cb} < \hat{\pi}$), the government would then choose its institutional parameters to compensate. It is easy to check that $\partial\delta/\partial(\hat{\pi} - \hat{\pi}^{cb}) > 0$ for any value of λ^{cb}; or that, because of the extra term in $(\hat{\pi} - \hat{\pi}^{cb})$, the value of λ^{cb} in case 2 always exceeds that in case 1 for any value of δ. Consequently, any attempt by the central bank to systematically exploit target independence by setting its own inflation target would cause an optimizing government to reduce the degree of independence conferred on the bank and/or the degree of conservatism of those appointed to manage monetary policy. In comparison to case 1, inflation is always lower in case 2 and income inequality greater; output stability is the same in both cases. Clearly, the different institutional arrangements can result in the same welfare outcome. This result shows that granting central banks target independence will not, on its own, be welfare improving. However, the degree of target independence granted the central bank is not a matter of indifference. First, because target independence can alter the mix of outcomes, changes in the degree of target independence may benefit certain groups in society over others. Second, a central bank that unexpectedly imposes its own inflation target will inevitably appear — from society's perspective — to be too independent or too conservative in its policies. Such criticisms have been a matter of great concern to the ECB.

4.2 Fiscal Policy Leadership — Government Chooses δ and λ^{cb}

In this variation, we maintain the same constitutional structure (i.e., stage 1 is unchanged), but allow the government to exercise leadership with its fiscal policy while the central bank may be (but does not have to be) fully independent in pursuit of its objectives. Thus, the government still chooses the institutional parameters δ and λ^{cb} in the first stage of the game. But the second stage is a Stackelberg game in which the government takes on a leadership role. That means the government and the monetary authority set their policy instruments, given values for δ and λ^{cb} determined at the previous stage, in the knowledge that the second stage would be a Stackelberg game with fiscal leadership. Formally, this policy game can be described as follows:

[6] That does not rule out the possibility that there may be some private advantage to the central bank.

4.2.1 Stage 1

The government solves the problem:

$$\min_{\delta,\,\lambda^{cb}} \; \mathrm{E}\,L^g(g_t, m_t, \delta,\, \lambda^{cb}) \;=\; \mathrm{E}\frac{1}{2}[\pi_t(g_t, m_t) - \hat{\pi}]^2 \;-\; \lambda_1^g[y_t(g_t, m_t)] \\ + \frac{\lambda_2^g}{2}[(b-\theta)y_t(g_t, m_t) - \tau_t(g_t, m_t)]^2 \quad (33)$$

where $L^g(g_t, m_t, \delta,\, \lambda^{cb})$ is (7) evaluated at $(g_t, m_t, \delta,\, \lambda^{cb})$, and E is the expectations operator.

4.2.2 Stage 2

(i) Private agents form rational expectations about future prices π_t^e before the shocks u_t and ϵ_t are realized.

(ii) The shocks u_t and ϵ_t are realized and observed by the government and by the central bank.

(iii) The government chooses g_t, before m_t is chosen by the central bank, to minimize $L^g(g_t, m_t, \bar{\delta},\, \bar{\lambda}^{cb})$, where $\bar{\delta}$ and $\bar{\lambda}^{cb}$ indicates that these variables were determined in stage 1.

(iv) The central bank chooses m_t, taking g_t as given, to minimize

$$L^{cb}(g_t, m_t, \bar{\delta},\, \bar{\lambda}^{cb}) = \\ \frac{(1-\bar{\delta})}{2}[\pi_t(g_t, m_t) - \hat{\pi}]^2 - (1-\bar{\delta})\bar{\lambda}^{cb}[y_t(g_t, m_t)] \\ + \; \bar{\delta}L^g(g_t, m_t, \bar{\delta},\, \bar{\lambda}^{cb}) \quad (34)$$

The timing of this game is illustrated in Figure 2.

This game can be solved by first solving the second stage of the problem for the optimal money supply and government expenditure policies with δ and λ^{cb} fixed, and then solving stage 1 by substituting the stage 2 results into (33) and minimizing with respect to δ and λ^{cb}. The equilibrium for the stage 2 leader–follower game is:

$$m_t(\delta, \lambda^{cb}) = \frac{\beta\hat{\pi}}{(\beta+\gamma)} + \frac{(1-\delta)\beta[\beta(\phi-\eta\Lambda)\lambda_2^g \;+\; \alpha\gamma(\beta\eta+\gamma)s^2]\lambda^{cb}}{\alpha(\beta+\gamma)[\beta(\phi-\eta\Lambda)+\delta\Lambda(\beta\eta+\gamma)]\lambda_2^g} \\ + \frac{\delta\beta[\beta\phi+\gamma\Lambda)\lambda_1^g}{\alpha(\beta+\gamma)[\beta(\phi-\eta\Lambda)+\delta\Lambda(\beta\eta+\gamma)]} - \frac{(1-\gamma\theta s)u_t}{\alpha(\beta+\gamma)}$$

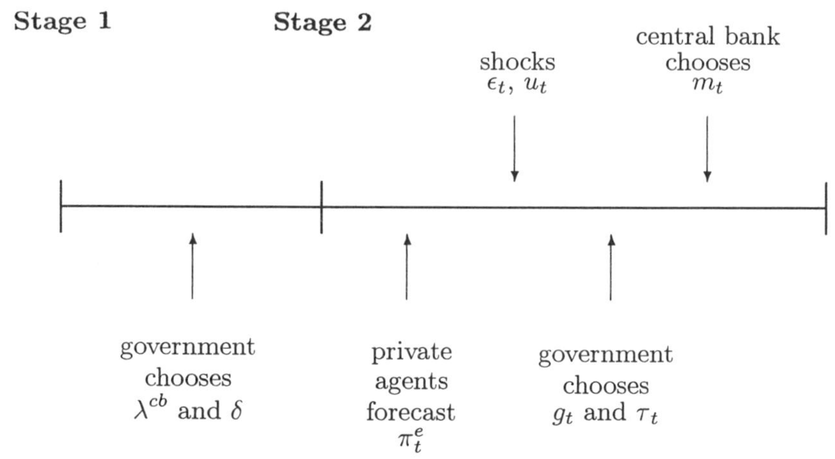

Figure 2: The Stages and Timing of the Government Leadership Game

$$-\frac{(1-\delta)\beta\gamma s^2(\beta\eta+\gamma)\lambda_1^g}{(\beta+\gamma)[\beta(\phi-\eta\Lambda)+\delta\Lambda(\beta\eta+\gamma)]\lambda_2^g}-\frac{\epsilon_t}{(\beta+\gamma)} \tag{35}$$

$$\begin{aligned} g_t(\delta,\lambda^{cb}) = {} & \frac{\beta\hat{\pi}}{(\beta+\gamma)}+\frac{(1-\delta)\beta^2[(\phi-\eta\Lambda)\lambda_2^g-\alpha s^2(\beta\eta+\gamma)]\lambda^{cb}}{\alpha(\beta+\gamma)[\beta(\phi-\eta\Lambda)+\delta\Lambda(\beta\eta+\gamma)]\lambda_2^g} \\ & +\frac{\delta\beta[\beta\phi+\gamma\Lambda)\lambda_1^g}{\alpha(\beta+\gamma)[\beta(\phi-\eta\Lambda)+\delta\Lambda(\beta\eta+\gamma)]}-\frac{(1+\beta\theta s)u_t}{\alpha(\beta+\gamma)} \\ & +\frac{(1-\delta)(\beta s)^2(\beta\eta+\gamma)\lambda_1^g}{(\beta+\gamma)[\beta(\phi-\eta\Lambda)+\delta\Lambda(\beta\eta+\gamma)]\lambda_2^g}-\frac{\epsilon_t}{(\beta+\gamma)} \end{aligned} \tag{36}$$

where

$$\eta=\frac{\partial m_t}{\partial g_t}=\frac{-\alpha^2\gamma\beta s^2+\delta\phi\Lambda\lambda_2^g}{(\alpha\beta s)^2+\delta\Lambda^2\lambda_2^g} \tag{37}$$

$$\phi=1+\alpha\beta-\gamma\theta s \tag{38}$$

$$\Lambda=1+\alpha\beta+\beta\theta s \tag{39}$$

Taking the mathematical expectation of both sides of (35) and (36) to obtain m_t^e and g_t^e, respectively, and substituting the result, together with (35) and (36), into (4) and (5) yields the reduced-form solutions for π_t and y_t as functions of the institutional variables δ and λ^{cb}

$$\pi_t(\delta,\lambda^{cb})=\hat{\pi}+\frac{(1-\delta)\beta(\phi-\eta\Lambda)\lambda^{cb}+\delta[\beta\phi+\gamma\Lambda]\lambda_1^g}{\alpha[\beta(\phi-\eta\Lambda)+\delta\Lambda(\beta\eta+\gamma)]} \tag{40}$$

$$y_t(\delta,\lambda^{cb})=\frac{-u_t}{\alpha} \tag{41}$$

From (6), the reduced-form solution for τ_t is given by

$$\tau_t(\delta, \lambda^{cb}) = \frac{(1-\delta)\beta s(\beta\eta+\gamma)(\lambda^{cb}-\lambda_1^g)}{[\beta(\phi-\eta\Lambda)+\delta\Lambda(\beta\eta+\gamma)]\lambda_2^g} - \frac{(b-\theta)u_t}{\alpha} \tag{42}$$

Substituting (40)–(42) into (33), the government's stage 1 minimization problem can now be expressed as

$$\min_{\delta,\lambda^{cb}} \; EL^g(\delta, \lambda^{cb}) = \frac{1}{2}\left\{\frac{(1-\delta)\beta(\phi-\eta\Lambda)\lambda^{cb}+\delta[\beta\phi+\gamma\Lambda]\lambda_1^g}{\alpha[\beta(\phi-\eta\Lambda)+\delta\Lambda(\beta\eta+\gamma)]}\right\}^2 + \frac{\lambda_2^g}{2}\left\{\frac{(1-\delta)\beta s(\beta\eta+\gamma)(\lambda^{cb}-\lambda_1^g)}{[\beta(\phi-\eta\Lambda)+\delta\Lambda(\beta\eta+\gamma)]\lambda_2^g}\right\}^2 \tag{43}$$

Partial differentiation of (43) with respect λ^{cb} and δ yields the first-order conditions

$$\frac{\partial \mathrm{E}L^g(\delta,\lambda^{cb})}{\partial\lambda^{cb}} = \frac{[(1-\delta)\beta(\phi-\eta\Lambda)\lambda^{cb}+\delta[\beta\phi+\gamma\Lambda]\lambda_1^g](1-\delta)\beta(\phi-\eta\Lambda)}{\alpha^2[\beta(\phi-\eta\Lambda)+\delta\Lambda(\beta\eta+\gamma)]^2} - \frac{(1-\delta)^2(\beta s)^2(\beta\eta+\gamma)^2(\lambda_1^g-\lambda^{cb})}{\lambda_2^g[\beta(\phi-\eta\Lambda)+\delta\Lambda(\beta\eta+\gamma)]^2} = 0 \tag{44}$$

$$\frac{\partial \mathrm{E}L^g(\delta,\lambda^{cb})}{\partial\delta} = \frac{(1-\delta)\beta(\phi-\eta\Lambda)\lambda^{cb}+\delta[\beta\phi+\gamma\Lambda]\lambda_1^g\beta[\beta\phi+\gamma\Lambda]\,(\lambda_1^g-\lambda^{cb})\left\{\delta(1-\delta)\Lambda\Omega+(\phi-\eta\Lambda)\right\}}{\alpha^2[\beta(\phi-\eta\Lambda)+\delta\Lambda(\beta\eta+\gamma)]^3} \frac{-(1-\delta)(\beta\eta+\gamma)(\beta s)^2[\beta\phi+\gamma\Lambda]\left\{(\beta\eta+\gamma)-(1-\delta)\beta\Omega\right\}(\lambda_1^g-\lambda^{cb})^2}{\lambda_2^g[\beta(\phi-\eta\Lambda)+\delta\Lambda(\beta\eta+\gamma)]^3} = 0 \tag{45}$$

where $\Omega = \partial\eta/\partial\delta$.

It is evident that $[\beta(\phi-\eta\Lambda)+\delta\Lambda(\beta\eta+\gamma)] = 0$ is not a solution to the minimization problem. But when $[\beta(\phi-\eta\Lambda)+\delta\Lambda(\beta\eta+\gamma)] \neq 0$, (44) and (45) yield (46) and (47), respectively:

$$(1-\delta)(\phi-\eta\Lambda)\lambda_2^g\left\{(1-\delta)\beta(\phi-\eta\Lambda)\lambda^{cb}+\delta[\beta\phi+\gamma\Lambda]\lambda_1^g\right\} - (1-\delta)^2(\beta\eta+\gamma)^2(\alpha s)^2\beta(\lambda_1^g-\lambda^{cb}) = 0 \tag{46}$$

$$\left\{(1-\delta)\beta(\phi-\eta\Lambda)\lambda^{cb}+\delta[\beta\phi+\gamma\Lambda]\lambda_1^g\right\}(\lambda_1^g-\lambda^{cb})$$
$$\{\delta(1-\delta)\Lambda\Omega+(\phi-\eta\Lambda)\}\,\lambda_2^g$$
$$-(1-\delta)(\beta\eta+\gamma)(\alpha s)^2\beta\{(\beta\eta+\gamma)-(1-\delta)\beta\Omega\}(\lambda_1^g-\lambda^{cb})^2=0 \quad (47)$$

There are two real-valued solutions that satisfy these two first-order conditions, and which fall within the permissible range for δ.[7] By inspection, it is apparent that (46) and (47) are both satisfied when $\delta = 1$ and $\lambda^{cb} = \lambda_1^g$. This solution characterizes a central bank that is fully dependent. The second solution is $\delta = \lambda^{cb} = 0$. In this case, the central bank is fully independent and concerned exclusively with the economy's inflation performance.

The solution that yields the minimum loss for the government, as measured by the government's loss function, can be identified by using (43) to compare the expected loss that would be suffered under the two alternative institutional arrangements. Substituting $\delta = 1$ and $\lambda^{cb} = \lambda_1^g$ into (43) results in

$$\mathrm{E}L^g = \frac{(\lambda_1^g)^2}{2\alpha^2} \quad (48)$$

Substituting $\delta = \lambda^{cb} = 0$ into the right-hand-side of (43) yields

$$\mathrm{E}L^g = 0 \quad (49)$$

It is evident that when institutional arrangements are such that the government is the Stackelberg leader in the second stage policy game, the optimal central bank design — from society's point of view — is one in which the central bank is required to use monetary policy to achieve the government's chosen inflation target, ignoring output growth and social equality objectives, and is granted full independence to do so.[8] In the following section we show that central bank leadership does not provide as good a result from society's point of view, *even if* the government is able to impose its own inflation target, and we explain why in Section 5.

---

[7] Because η is a function of δ, (47) is a quartic polynomial in δ. This polynomial has four distinct roots, of which only two are real-valued. We can discard the complex solutions as having no economic meaning. Details of the complete solution for these first-order conditions may be found in Appendix 1.

[8] Recall that $\hat{\pi} = \hat{\pi}^{cb}$ in this case. Since (49) shows an elected government would achieve $\mathrm{E}L^g = 0$, allowing $\hat{\pi}^{cb} < \hat{\pi}$ would not have generated any further improvements for society as a whole.

4.3 Monetary Policy Leadership — Government Chooses δ and λ^{cb}

In this section, we contrast the results of the last section, fiscal leadership, with the case where the central bank is granted leadership under the same constitutional arrangements. That is, when the government continues to choose the degree of monetary delegation (δ) and the general stance or conservatism of monetary policies (λ^{cb}). The words "is granted leadership" are significant because they indicate that there is a principal–agent relationship in which the government sets the parameters within which the central bank must operate. The government is therefore responsible for determining the degree of delegation and the institutional arrangements that the central bank must observe — the relationship between the German government and the Bundesbank before the advent of the Euro is an example of such an arrangement. This differs from the case in which the central bank "assumes leadership and ultimate responsibility" for monetary policy. In that case, the government chooses the degree of delegation which makes monetary leadership possible, but all other aspects of monetary policy design (including the degree of conservatism and inflation targets) are subject to choice by the central bank. An arrangement of this sort would imply a much greater degree of target (as well as instrument) independence and is a reasonably good description of the role of the ECB in the Eurozone. We consider the implications of monetary leadership of this type in Section 4.4 below.

Whichever form of central bank leadership we study, a leadership role inevitably involves a certain degree of target independence. We therefore allow the central bank to choose it own inflation targets as follows:

$$L_t^{cb} = \frac{1}{2}(\pi_t - \hat{\pi}^{cb})^2 - (1-\delta)\lambda^{cb} y_t - \delta\lambda_1^g y_t + \frac{\delta\lambda_2^g}{2}[(b-\theta)y_t - \tau_t]^2 \quad (50)$$

where the central bank's inflation target, $\hat{\pi}^{cb}$, may now differ from the government's inflation target value $\hat{\pi}$.

When the central bank has full target independence and is the Stackelberg leader, the reduced-form solutions for π_t, y_t, and τ_t are:

$$\pi_t = \frac{(\beta+\mu\gamma)\phi\hat{\pi}^{cb} + \delta\gamma(\Lambda - \mu\phi)\hat{\pi}}{(\beta+\mu\gamma)\phi + \delta\gamma(\Lambda-\mu\phi)} + \frac{(1-\delta)(\beta+\mu\gamma)\phi\lambda^{cb}}{\alpha[(\beta+\mu\gamma)\phi + \delta\gamma(\Lambda-\mu\phi)]} + \frac{\delta[\beta\phi + \gamma\Lambda]\lambda_1^g}{\alpha[(\beta+\mu\gamma)\phi + \delta\gamma(\Lambda-\mu\phi)]} \quad (51)$$

$$y_t = \frac{-u_t}{\alpha} \quad (52)$$

$$\tau_t = \frac{\alpha\gamma s(\beta+\mu\gamma)(\hat{\pi}-\hat{\pi}^{cb})}{[(\beta+\mu\gamma)\phi+\delta\gamma(\Lambda-\mu\phi)]\lambda_2^g} + \frac{(1-\delta)\gamma(\beta+\mu\gamma)s(\lambda_1^g-\lambda^{cb})}{[(\beta+\mu\gamma)\phi+\delta\gamma(\Lambda-\mu\phi)]\lambda_2^g} - \frac{(b-\theta)u_t}{\alpha} \quad (53)$$

where

$$\mu = \frac{\partial g_t}{\partial m_t} = \frac{-\alpha^2\beta\gamma s^2+\phi\Lambda\lambda_2^g}{(\alpha\gamma s)^2+\phi^2\lambda_2^g}$$

Substituting (51)–(53) into the government's loss function (7), and differentiating with respect to λ^{cb} and δ yields the necessary first-order conditions:

$$\frac{\partial \mathrm{E}L_t^g}{\partial\lambda^{cb}} = (1-\delta)\phi\lambda_2^g\left\{-\alpha\Gamma\phi(\hat{\pi}-\hat{\pi}^{cb})+\phi(1-\delta)\Gamma\lambda^{cb}+\delta[\beta\phi+\gamma\Lambda]\lambda_1^g\right\} - (\alpha\gamma s)^2\Gamma(1-\delta)\left[\alpha(\hat{\pi}-\hat{\pi}^{cb})+(1-\delta)(\lambda_1^g-\lambda^{cb})\right] = 0 \quad (54)$$

$$\frac{\partial \mathrm{E}L_t^g}{\partial\lambda^{cb}} = \phi\lambda_2^g\Gamma\Sigma\left\{\begin{array}{c}-\alpha(\beta+\mu\gamma)\phi(\hat{\pi}-\hat{\pi}^{cb})+\phi(1-\delta)\Gamma\lambda^{cb}\\ +\delta[\beta\phi+\gamma\Lambda]\lambda_1^g\end{array}\right\} - (\alpha\gamma s)^2\Gamma^2\Sigma\left[\alpha(\hat{\pi}-\hat{\pi}^{cb})+(1-\delta)(\lambda_1^g-\lambda^{cb})\right] = 0 \quad (55)$$

where

$$\Sigma = [\beta\phi+\gamma\Lambda](\lambda_1^g-\lambda^{cb})+\alpha\gamma(\hat{\pi}-\hat{\pi}^{cb})(\Lambda-\mu\phi)$$
$$\Gamma = (\beta+\mu\gamma)$$

There are two solutions that satisfy both of the first-order conditions given above. By inspection, it is apparent that (54) and (55) are both satisfied when $\delta = 1$ and $\Gamma = 0$. But when $0 \leq \delta < 1$ and $\Gamma \neq 0$, then (54) and (55) imply the following relationship between δ and λ^{cb}

$$\delta = \frac{(\beta+\mu\gamma)\left\{\begin{array}{c}\phi^2\lambda^{cb}\lambda_2^g+(\alpha\gamma s)^2(\lambda^{cb}-\lambda_1^g)-\alpha[\phi^2\lambda_2^g\\ +(\alpha\gamma s)^2](\hat{\pi}-\hat{\pi}^{cb})\end{array}\right\}}{(\beta+\mu\gamma)\left\{\phi^2\lambda^{cb}\lambda_2^g+(\alpha\gamma s)^2(\lambda^{cb}-\lambda_1^g)\right\}-\phi[\beta\phi+\gamma\Lambda]\lambda_1^g\lambda_2^g} \quad (56)$$

It is straightforward to show that the government's expected losses are minimized by combinations of δ and λ^{cb} that satisfy (56). Substituting (56) into the right-hand-side of (43) then yields

$$\mathrm{E}L^g = \frac{(\lambda_1^g)^2}{2\alpha^2}\left\{\frac{(\alpha\gamma s)^2}{(\alpha\gamma s)^2+\phi^2\lambda_2^g}\right\} \quad (57)$$

Comparing (57) with (27) shows that the government's (and society's) expected loss is greater under central bank leadership than under government leadership. In fact, the loss under central bank leadership is identical to the loss incurred by the government in a simultaneous move regime.

Furthermore, we can also see that target independence has no impact on economic outcomes or government losses as long as the government can alter the degree of central bank conservatism to compensate for the difference between its own inflation target and that of the central bank. To see this, note that when the central bank is fully independent (i.e., $\delta = 0$), the optimal degree of central bank conservatism (from 56) becomes

$$\lambda^{cb} = \frac{(\alpha\gamma s)^2 \lambda_1^g}{(\alpha\gamma s)^2 + \phi^2 \lambda_2^g} + \alpha(\hat{\pi} - \hat{\pi}^{cb}) \tag{58}$$

So, if the central bank was (expected) to choose to be target conservative compared to the government, the government would relax the constitutional arrangements in the direction of less weight conservatism. That is the reason why this regime gives the same outcomes and performance as the simultaneous moves game of Section 4.1. The government therefore only runs into difficulties if it does not have sufficient power to change those constitutional arrangements or operating procedures.

Since the delegation of monetary policy is a matter which governments decide for themselves, and which requires certain constitutional provisions that cannot be changed very frequently, it is reasonable to assume that the government would retain control of the choice of δ. But the degree of conservatism adopted in the policies of the central bank is more in the nature of an operating procedure which might more easily be changed as circumstances require. Hence the most likely development, if the government cannot adjust λ^{cb} according to (58), is that the government continues to choose the degree of monetary delegation (δ) while the central bank assumes target as well as instrument independence and chooses λ^{cb}, $\hat{\pi}^{cb}$, and then the monetary policy. The implications of institutional arrangements of this sort are examined next.

4.4 Simultaneous Moves — Central Bank Chooses λ^{cb}

If the central bank is potentially independent (i.e., δ is small) and able to choose its own inflation target ($\hat{\lambda}^{cb}$), then it is artificial to suppose that the government would be able to impose its preferred degree of conservatism (λ^{cb}) on the central bank's operations at the same time. In this section, we allow the central bank to choose λ^{cb} in order to define the stance of monetary policy.

However, because the central bank can now choose all of the characteristics of monetary policy for itself, it is reasonable to assume the bank and the government would choose their policies separately but at the same time in stage 2; and also their preferred institutional arrangements separately, but simultaneously in stage 1. The government's objective function is given, as before, by (7). However, since it does not have monetary leadership at stage 2, the central bank would try to minimize

$$L^{cb} = \frac{(1-\delta)}{2}(\pi_t - \hat{\pi}^{cb})^2 + \frac{\delta}{2}(\pi_t - \hat{\pi})^2 - (1-\delta)\lambda^{cb}y_t - \delta\lambda_1^g y_t + \frac{\delta\lambda_2^g}{2}[(b-\theta)y_t - \tau_t]^2 \quad (59)$$

which converges to the monetary leadership case, (50), as $\delta \rightarrow 0$. The Nash equilibrium policies at stage 2 are then:

$$\begin{aligned} m_t(\delta, \lambda^{cb}) = {} & \frac{\delta\beta\gamma\Lambda\hat{\pi}}{(\beta+\gamma)[\beta\theta+\delta\gamma\Lambda]} - \frac{\alpha\beta(\gamma s)^2(1-\delta)(\hat{\pi}-\hat{\pi}^{cb})}{(\beta+\gamma)[\beta\theta+\delta\gamma\Lambda]\lambda_2^g} \\ & + \frac{\beta^2\phi[\delta\hat{\pi}+(1-\delta)\hat{\pi}^{cb}]}{(\beta+\gamma)[\beta\theta+\delta\gamma\Lambda]} + \frac{(1-\delta)\beta[\alpha(\gamma s)^2+\beta\phi\lambda_2^g]\lambda^{cb}}{\alpha\lambda_2^g[\beta\phi+\delta\gamma\Lambda](\beta+\gamma)} \\ & + \frac{\delta\beta(1+\alpha\beta)\lambda_1^g}{\alpha[\beta\phi+\delta\gamma\Lambda]} - \frac{(1-\delta)\beta(\gamma s)^2\lambda_1^g}{(\beta+\gamma)[\beta\phi+\delta\gamma\Lambda]\lambda_2^g} \\ & - \frac{\epsilon_t}{(\beta+\gamma)} - \frac{(1-\gamma\theta s)u_t}{\alpha(\beta+\gamma)} \end{aligned} \quad (60)$$

$$\begin{aligned} g_t(\delta, \lambda^{cb}) = {} & \frac{\delta\beta\gamma\Lambda\hat{\pi}}{(\beta+\gamma)[\beta\theta+\delta\gamma\Lambda]} + \frac{\alpha\beta^2\gamma s^2(1-\delta)(\hat{\pi}-\hat{\pi}^{cb})}{(\beta+\gamma)[\beta\theta+\delta\gamma\Lambda]\lambda_2^g} \\ & + \frac{\beta^2\phi[\delta\hat{\pi}+(1-\delta)\hat{\pi}^{cb}]}{(\beta+\gamma)[\beta\theta+\delta\gamma\Lambda]} + \frac{(1-\delta)\beta^2[\phi\lambda_2^g-\alpha\gamma s^2]\lambda^{cb}}{\alpha\lambda_2^g[\beta\phi+\delta\gamma\Lambda](\beta+\gamma)} \\ & + \frac{\delta\beta(1+\alpha\beta)\lambda_1^g}{\alpha[\beta\phi+\delta\gamma\Lambda]} + \frac{(1-\delta)\beta^2\gamma s^2\lambda_1^g}{(\beta+\gamma)[\beta\phi+\delta\gamma\Lambda]\lambda_2^g} \\ & - \frac{\epsilon_t}{(\beta+\gamma)} - \frac{(1+\beta\theta s)u_t}{\alpha(\beta+\gamma)} \end{aligned} \quad (61)$$

Substituting (60) and (61), and their expectations, back into the model yields the following outcomes:

$$\pi_t = \frac{\delta\gamma\Lambda\hat{\pi}}{[\beta\phi+\delta\gamma\Lambda]} + \frac{\beta\phi[\delta\hat{\pi}+(1-\delta)\hat{\pi}^{cb}]}{[\beta\phi+\delta\gamma\Lambda]} + \frac{(1-\delta)\beta\phi\lambda^{cb}}{\alpha[\beta\phi+\delta\gamma\Lambda]} + \frac{\delta[\beta\phi+\gamma\Lambda]\lambda_1^g}{\alpha[\beta\phi+\delta\gamma\Lambda]} \quad (62)$$

$$y_t(\delta, \lambda^{cb}) = \frac{-u_t}{\alpha} \tag{63}$$

$$\tau_t(\delta, \lambda^{cb}) = -\frac{(1-\delta)\beta\gamma s(\hat{\pi} - \hat{\pi}^{cb})}{[\beta\phi + \delta\gamma\Lambda]\lambda_2^g} - \frac{(1-\delta)\beta\gamma s(\lambda_1^g - \lambda^{cb})}{[\beta\phi + \delta\gamma\Lambda]\lambda_2^g} - \frac{(b-\theta)u_t}{\alpha} \tag{64}$$

Moving back to stage 1, the first-order conditions for the central bank's choice of λ^{cb} yield

$$\bar{\lambda}^{cb} = \frac{\delta\left\{(1-\delta)\beta(\alpha\gamma s)^2 - [\beta\phi + \gamma\Lambda]\phi\lambda_2^g\right\}[\alpha(\hat{\pi} - \hat{\pi}^{cb}) + \lambda_1^g]}{(1-\delta)\beta[\phi^2\lambda_2^g + \delta(\alpha\gamma s)^2]} \tag{65}$$

if $\delta \neq 1$. But the government's first order conditions for the choice of δ imply that the government would have preferred, conditional on δ,

$$\lambda^{cb*} = \frac{\begin{array}{c}(1-\delta)\alpha[\beta\phi^2\lambda_2^g + \beta(\alpha\gamma s)^2](\hat{\pi} - \hat{\pi}^{cb}) + \\ \left\{-\delta\phi[\beta\phi + \gamma\Lambda]\lambda_2^g + (1-\delta)\beta(\alpha\gamma s)^2\right\}\lambda_1^g\end{array}}{(1-\delta)\beta[\phi^2\lambda_2^g + (\alpha\gamma s)^2]} \tag{66}$$

Two simple solutions are now obvious. If the government chooses $\delta = 0$, then $\bar{\lambda}^{cb} = 0$ follows. If, on the other hand, the government chooses $\delta = 1$, the central bank is indifferent about $\bar{\lambda}^{cb}$, so the government's preferred degree of conservatism $\lambda^{cb*} = \lambda_1^g + \alpha(\hat{\pi} - \hat{\pi}^{cb})$ would presumably prevail. In all other cases we need to solve (65) and (66) together to obtain δ. That yields four solutions when $\hat{\pi} \geq \hat{\pi}^{cb}$: $\delta = 1, \delta = 0$, $\delta > 1$, or $\delta < 0$. The latter two have no economic meaning, which implies that an optimizing government actually has only two solutions available:[9]

$$\begin{aligned} \delta &= 1 \quad \text{and} \quad \bar{\lambda}^{cb} = \lambda_1^g + \alpha(\hat{\pi} - \hat{\pi}^{cb}) \\ \delta &= 0 \quad \text{and} \quad \bar{\lambda}^{cb} = 0 \end{aligned} \tag{67}$$

Using these solutions, we can evaluate (7) to obtain

$$\mathrm{E}L_t^g = \frac{(\lambda_1^g)^2}{2\alpha^2} \quad \text{when} \quad \delta = 1$$

$$\text{and} \quad \mathrm{E}L_t^g = \frac{(\hat{\pi} - \hat{\pi}^{cb})^2}{2} + \frac{(\gamma s)^2[\alpha(\hat{\pi} - \hat{\pi}^{cb}) + \lambda_1^g]^2}{2\phi^2\lambda_2^g}$$

[9] $\delta > 1$ or $\delta < 0$ would violate convexity axioms on the central bank's objective function, and would imply that the bank was either keener on the government's goals than even the government itself, or wanted to maximize the deviations from its own inflation target. Neither situation is at all likely.

$$\text{when} \quad \delta = 0 \quad (68)$$

However, from (59), the central bank would achieve

$$\begin{aligned} \mathrm{E}L_t^{cb} &= \frac{[\alpha(\hat{\pi} - \hat{\pi}^{cb}) + \lambda_1^g]^2}{2\alpha} > 0 \quad \text{when} \quad \delta = 1 \\ \text{and} \quad \mathrm{E}L_t^{cb} &= 0 \quad \text{when} \quad \delta = 0 \end{aligned} \quad (69)$$

Hence, it is easy to see that the government would never choose $\delta = 1$ unless

$$(\hat{\pi} - \hat{\pi}^{cb}) > \left[\frac{\phi^2 \lambda_2^g - (\alpha\gamma s)^2}{\alpha^2[\phi^2 \lambda_2^g + (\alpha\gamma s)^2]} \right]^{1/2} \quad (70)$$

holds (a sufficient condition from (68)). That is, the government would not choose $\delta = 1$ unless the central bank threatened to be too ambitiously conservative with its inflation target; or if $\lambda_2^g \to 0$, in which case the government has no social or redistribution objectives. In all other cases, the government would rationally choose $\delta = 0$. And (69) implies that the bank would, in its own interest, never want to lower its inflation target so far that the government ends up wanting to choose $\delta = 1$. The upshot of this is that the central bank would have an incentive not to choose its inflation target $\hat{\pi}^{cb}$ too far below the government's target; but it would compensate for that by choosing a more conservative set of policies ($\bar{\lambda}^{cb} = 0$). The government for its part, would then always prefer a fully independent central bank. The outcomes of this regime would be more favorable to the central bank than in the other solutions. But they would be less favorable to the government than the fiscal leadership solution of Section 4.2 since $\mathrm{E}L_t^g$ is always positive in (68). However, they would probably be more favorable than the other two institutional designs.[10] Thus, since the government presumably retains the right to determine what form of policy delegation takes place, this particular institutional arrangement would not be chosen if fiscal leadership were possible. But if fiscal leadership is not acceptable, then it is probably worthwhile to allow the central bank to choose its own degree of conservatism — as the Federal Reserve System does — rather than have a fixed value imposed by statute as in the ECB's case.

---

[10] It is straightforward to show that when $(\hat{\pi} - \hat{\pi}^{cb})$ is small, allowing the central bank to choose λ^{cb} is more favorable for the government (and society as a whole) than the regimes considered in Sections 4.1 and 4.3, as long as $\phi^2 \lambda_2^g (s^2 + 1) \geq (\alpha\gamma s)^2$. That inequality is certain to hold unless λ_2^g is very small.

5 The Advantages of Fiscal Leadership

5.1 Central Bank Independence under Fiscal Leadership

Our results show that society's welfare, as measured by the inverse of (43), is maximized when there is fiscal leadership and the government appoints independent central bankers who are concerned only with the achievement of the mandated inflation target, and disregard the impact that their policies may have on output growth. However, our results also indicate that full central bank independence may be beneficial under more general conditions. When $\delta = 0$, $\beta\eta + \gamma = 0$ and (43) becomes

$$\mathrm{E}L^g = \frac{1}{2}\left\{\frac{\lambda^{cb}}{\alpha}\right\}^2 \tag{71}$$

for any value of λ^{cb} when $\delta = 0$. Clearly therefore, an independent central bank always produces better results as long as it is more conservative than the government ($\lambda^{cb} < \lambda_1^g$) — compare (48) — irrespective of the latter's commitment to growth (λ_1^g) or to social equality (λ_2^g).

Notice that, in deriving our results, we have assumed that the central bank has instrument independence but not target independence. Consequently, the fact that $\mathrm{E}L^g = 0$ can be achieved by setting $\delta = \lambda^{cb} = 0$ indicates that it is instrument independence which matters. Target independence is ultimately irrelevant when there is fiscal leadership: neither target independence nor central bank leadership would reduce society's expected losses to zero.

5.2 Leadership vs. Simultaneous Moves

A more interesting question is whether fiscal leadership with an independent central bank generally produces better outcomes, from society's perspective, than those obtained in the simultaneous move game. In the simultaneous move game, the solution to the government's stage 1 minimization problem was:

$$\delta = \frac{\beta\phi^2\lambda^{cb}\lambda_2^g + (\alpha\gamma)^2\beta(\lambda^{cb} - \lambda_1^g)}{\beta\phi^2\lambda^{cb}\lambda_2^g + (\alpha\gamma)^2\beta(\lambda^{cb} - \lambda_1^g) - \phi[\beta\phi + \gamma\Lambda]\lambda_1^g\lambda_2^g}$$

The optimal degree of conservatism for an independent central bank in this type of game can therefore be obtained by setting $\delta = 0$ to yield:

$$\lambda^{cb*} = \frac{(\alpha\gamma s)^2\lambda_1^g}{(\alpha\gamma s)^2 + \phi^2\lambda_2^g} \tag{72}$$

It is now straightforward to show that (71) is always less than (27) as long as

$$\lambda^{cb} < \left[\lambda_1^g \lambda^{cb*}\right]^{1/2} \tag{73}$$

It is also evident that $\lambda^{cb*} \leq \lambda_1^g$ for $\lambda_2^g \geq 0$. Consequently, fiscal leadership with any value of λ^{cb} such that $0 \leq \lambda^{cb} < \lambda^{cb*}$ will produce better outcomes, from society's point of view, than any simultaneous move game between the central bank and the government. This is an important observation because many inflation targeting regimes, such as those operated by the Bank of England, the Swedish Riksbank, and the Reserve Bank of New Zealand, operate with fiscal leadership; while several others, notably the European Central bank and the US Federal Reserve System, are better characterized as being engaged in a simultaneous move game with their governments.

5.3 Sources of the Leadership Advantage

Substituting $\delta = 0$ and $\lambda^{cb} = 0$ into (40)–(42) shows exactly where the advantages of fiscal leadership come from. We get

$$\pi_t = \hat{\pi}, \quad y_t = \frac{-u_t}{\alpha}, \quad \tau_t = \frac{-(b-\theta)u_t}{\alpha} \tag{74}$$

as the final outcomes. By contrast, from (16)–(18), the optimal outcomes for the associated simultaneous move policy game are

$$\pi_t^* = \hat{\pi} + \frac{\alpha(\gamma s)^2}{[(\alpha\gamma s)^2 + \phi^2\lambda_2^g]} \tag{75}$$

$$y_t^* = \frac{-u_t}{\alpha} \tag{76}$$

$$\tau_t^* = \frac{\gamma s(\lambda^{cb*} - \lambda_1^g)}{\phi\lambda_2^g} - \frac{(b-\theta)u_t}{\alpha} \tag{77}$$

Comparing the two sets of outcomes we see that fiscal leadership eliminates inflationary bias and therefore results in a lower rate of inflation for any given $\hat{\pi}$.[11] The optimal outcome under fiscal leadership is

[11] Notice that central bank independence alone implies a superior set of inflation outcomes. Setting $\delta = 0$ alone yields $\pi^* = \hat{\pi} + \lambda^{cb}/\alpha$ from (62), which is less than (75) if $\lambda^{cb}/\alpha < \alpha(\gamma s)^2/[(\alpha\gamma s)^2 + \phi^2\lambda_2^g]$. That inequality holds if $\lambda^{cb} < \lambda^{cb*}/\lambda_1^g$. Thus (73) is just a necessary, but not a sufficient condition for government leadership to produce lower inflation. But fiscal leadership can result in better welfare outcomes even if $\lambda^{cb*}/\lambda_1^g < \lambda^{cb} < [\lambda^{cb*}\lambda_1^g]^{1/2}$ because the social equality indicator is more satisfactory (even if inflation is not).

also characterized by higher taxes and therefore more income redistribution or social equality.[12] Moreover, these improvements in inflation control and income distribution can be achieved with no loss in expected growth.

One of the central issues addressed in the policy coordination literature is whether there are institutional arrangements that yield Pareto improvements over the non-cooperative outcome.[13] When such institutions can be identified, they are viewed as a coordination device. In our model, fiscal leadership in the second stage of the policy game results in better outcomes for both policy authorities and is therefore an example of a rule-based form of policy coordination.[14]

6 Conclusions

Our results show that different institutional arrangements for the central bank and the fiscal authorities matter. Furthermore, our analysis indicates that fiscal leadership, with an independent central bank directed whose sole objective is inflation control, provides the best outcomes for society as a whole and also for the financial interests represented by the central bank. The reason for this is that this regime produces the greatest coordination between monetary and fiscal policies, and the benefits of this coordination outweigh any potential threat to the inflation target that fiscal dominance might have been expected to pose.

If fiscal leadership is not acceptable, then an independent central bank choosing its own degree of conservatism is the next best regime — provided that the central bank's inflation target is not too far from the government's target, and that the government has some social or redistribution objectives. Monetary leadership or imposed degrees of conservatism are not desirable when economic performance is affected by both fiscal and monetary policies.

We also find that target independence is ultimately unimportant. Instrument independence is the crucial feature, even under reasonable variations in the central bank's preferred degree of conservatism or inflation

[12] Tax revenues are lower under the simultaneous move game because $\lambda^{cb*} < \lambda_1^g$. Redistribution is positively related to the amount of tax revenue because $(b-\theta)\mathrm{E}y_t^* = 0$, so that τ_t^* determines the amount of income redistribution actually achieved.

[13] See, for example, Currie, Holtham, and Hughes Hallett (1989); Currie (1990); and Currie and Levine (1991).

[14] See Currie (1990) for a discussion of the distinction between rule-based and discretionary, or *ad hoc*, forms of policy coordination.

target. The reason for this is that greater conservatism or lower inflation targets generate a reaction from governments using fiscal policies or other policy instruments. Governments will therefore compensate — which makes it important that our models should take into consideration the strategic elements of fiscal or other policies, alongside their analysis of a suitable monetary framework. Although this has been shown in an extremely stylized manner here, through the choice of policy independence and conservatism parameters, recent experience in Europe bears out the practical importance of considering the interaction of fiscal and monetary policies when designing monetary institutions. In particular, the trend towards lower inflation targets, increased conservatism, and greater central bank independence in Europe has led to a compensating expansion in fiscal positions — to the point where the Stability Pact appears to be threatened in many of the larger economies.

Appendix 1

Solutions to (46) and (47).

The first-order condition (47) can be written as a quartic polynomial in δ. As a consequence, there are four solutions that simultaneously satisfy (46) and (47). By inspection, it is apparent that one of these solutions is $\delta = 1$ and $\lambda^{cb} = \lambda_1^g$. When $\delta \neq 1$ and $\lambda^{cb} \neq \lambda_1^g$, the first-order conditions can be written

$$(\phi - \eta\Lambda)\lambda_2^g \left\{(1-\delta)\beta(\phi - \eta\Lambda)\lambda^{cb} + \delta[\beta\phi + \gamma\Lambda]\lambda_1^g\right\} - (1-\delta)(\beta\eta + \gamma)^2(\alpha s)^2\beta(\lambda_1^g - \lambda^{cb}) = 0 \quad \text{(A.1)}$$

$$\left[\delta(1-\delta)\Lambda\frac{\partial\eta}{\partial\delta} + (\phi - \eta\Lambda)\right] \left\{(1-\delta)\beta(\phi - \eta\Lambda)\lambda^{cb} + \delta[\beta\phi + \gamma\Lambda]\lambda_1^g\right\}\lambda_2^g - (1-\delta)(\beta\eta + \gamma)(\alpha s)^2\beta\left[(\beta\eta + \gamma) - (1-\delta)\beta\frac{\partial\eta}{\partial\delta}\right](\lambda_1^g - \lambda^{cb}) = 0 \quad \text{(A.2)}$$

But (??) can be expressed as

$$\text{(A.1)} + \delta(1-\delta)\Lambda\frac{\partial\eta}{\partial\delta}\left\{(1-\delta)\beta(\phi - \eta\Lambda)\lambda^{cb} + \delta[\beta\phi + \gamma\Lambda]\lambda_1^g\right\}\lambda_2^g + (1-\delta)^2(\beta\eta + \gamma)\frac{\partial\eta}{\partial\delta}(\alpha\beta s)^2(\lambda_1^g - \lambda^{cb}) = 0 \quad \text{(A.3)}$$

Consequently, when $\delta \neq 1$ and (A.1) is satisfied, (??) becomes

$$\delta\Lambda\left\{(1-\delta)\beta(\phi-\eta\Lambda)\lambda^{cb}+\delta[\beta\phi+\gamma\Lambda]\lambda_1^g\right\}\lambda_2^g \\ +(1-\delta)(\beta\eta+\gamma)(\alpha\beta s)^2(\lambda_1^g-\lambda^{cb})=0 \quad \text{(A.4)}$$

Replacing η with (37) yields

$$(\phi-\eta\Lambda)=\frac{\alpha^2\beta s^2[\beta\phi+\gamma\Lambda]}{(\alpha\beta s)^2+\delta\Lambda^2\lambda_2^g} \quad \text{and} \quad (\beta\eta+\gamma)=\frac{\delta\Lambda[\beta\phi+\gamma\Lambda]\lambda_2^g}{(\alpha\beta s)^2+\delta\Lambda^2\lambda_2^g} \quad \text{(A.5)}$$

It is evident that $(\beta\eta+\gamma)=0$ when $\delta=0$. Hence $\delta=\lambda^{cb}=0$ is one solution that satisfies (A.1) and (A.4).

The remaining potential solutions can be found by substituting (A.5) into (A.4) and solving for δ (under the assumption that $\delta \neq 0$ and $\delta \neq 1$, since we have already examined those solutions). We obtain:

$$\delta^2=\frac{-(\alpha\beta s)^2}{\Lambda^2\lambda_1^g\lambda_2^g} \quad \text{(A.6)}$$

Consequently, there are only two real-valued solutions that satisfy the first-order necessary conditions: (i) $\delta=1$ and $\lambda^{cb}=\lambda_1^g$, and (ii) $\delta=\lambda^{cb}=0$.

Bibliography

[1] Alesina, A. and R. Gatti (1995) "Independent Central Banks: Low Inflation at No Cost," *American Economic Review* **85**, 196–200.

[2] Barro, R.J. (1981) "Output Effects of Government Purchases," *Journal of Political Economy* **89**, 1086–1121.

[3] Barro, R.J. and D.B. Gordon (1983) "Rules, Discretion, and Reputation in a Model of Monetary Policy," *Journal of Monetary Economics* **12**, 101–121.

[4] Currie, D.A. (1990) "International Policy Coordination," in D.T. Llewellyn and C. Milner (eds.) *Current Issues in International Monetary Economics*, Macmillan, London, 125–148.

[5] Currie, D.A., G. Holtham, and A. Hughes Hallett, (1989) "The Theory and Practice of International Economic Policy Coordination: Does Coordination Pay?" in R. Bryant, D. Currie, J. Frenkel, P. Masson, and R. Portes (eds.) *Macroeconomic Policies in an Interdependent World*, International Monetary Fund, Washington DC.

[6] Currie, D.A. and P. Levine (1991) "The International Coordination of Monetary Policy – A Survey," in C.J. Green and D.T. Llewellyn (eds.) *Surveys in Monetary Economics*, Vol. 1, Oxford, Basil Blackwell.

[7] Demertzis, M., A. Hughes Hallett, and N. Viegi (2003) "An Independent Central Bank Faced with Elected Governments," *European Journal of Political Economy*, forthcoming.

[8] Dixit, A.K. and L. Lambertini (2001) "Fiscal Discretion destroys Monetary Commitment," Unpublished Manuscript, Department of Economics, Princeton University.

[9] Fischer, S. (1995) "Central Bank Independence Revisited," *American Economic Review* **85**, 201–206.

[10] Galí, J. and T. Monacelli (2002) "Monetary Policy and Exchange Rate Volatility in a Small Open Economy," Discussion Paper No. 3346, Center for Economic and Policy Research, London.

[11] Hughes Hallett, A. and D.N. Weymark (2001) "The Cost of Heterogeneity in a Monetary Union," Discussion Paper No. 3223, Center for Economic Policy Research, London; Working Paper No. 01-W28, Department of Economics, Vanderbilt University, <www.vanderbilt.edu/econ>.

[12] Lucas, R.E. (1973) "Some International Evidence on Output–Inflation Trade-Offs," *American Economic Review* **63**, 326–334.

[13] Lucas, R.E. (1972) "Expectations and the Neutrality of Money," *Journal of Economic Theory* **4**, 103–124.

[14] McCallum, B.T. (1989) *Monetary Economics: Theory and Policy,* Macmillan, New York.

[15] Obstfeld, M. and K. Rogoff (1996) *Foundations of International Macroeconomics*, Cambridge, MA: MIT Press.

[16] Rogoff, K. (1995), "The Optimal Commitment to an Intermediate Monetary Target," *Quarterly Journal of Economics,* **100**, 1056–1070

[17] Taylor, J.B. (1993) *Macroeconomic Policy in a World Economy: From Econometric Design to Practical Operation,* W.W. Norton and Company, New York.

[18] Weymark, D.N. (2001) “Inflation, Income Redistribution, and Optimal Central Bank Independence,” Working Paper No. 01-W02R, Department of Economics, Vanderbilt University. <www.vanderbilt.edu/econ>.

14 Policy Evaluation with a Forward-Looking Model

Rouben V. Atoian, Gregory E. Givens and Michael K. Salemi[1]

> Monetary policy rules are naturally amenable to modern econometric policy evaluation methods that were developed as part of the rational expectations revolution in macroeconomics in the early 1970's. When using these methods, researchers first build a structural model of the economy, consisting of mathematical equations with estimated numerical parameter values. They then test out different rules by simulating the model stochastically.... One monetary policy rule is better than another...if the simulation results show better economic performance. (Taylor, 1998).

Modern econometric policy evaluation entails two steps. In the first, the parameters of a structural model are either estimated or obtained through calibration. In the second, the performance of alternative policy rules is studied and conclusions about policy are reached. Fuhrer (1997) is a good example of the two part approach. He fits a small structural model to data for the US economy treating the coefficients of his policy rule as free parameters. He then derives an optimal policy frontier by varying the values of the policy-rule coefficients to minimize a weighted sum of the variance of output and the variance of inflation. He evaluates policy by comparing the variances of output and inflation achieved by the estimated rule with points on the policy frontier.

In this paper, we follow standard practice by setting out a small structural model, obtaining estimates of its parameters, and then evaluating

[1]Salemi is the corresponding author and may be reached via email at Michael_Salemi@unc.edu. The authors thank colleagues at UNC for valuable comments. Remaining errors are our own. Michael Salemi thanks participants at the European Monetary Forum Conference on Money in honor of Sir Alan Walters for their helpful comments on a related paper.

the performance of alternative policy rules while treating estimates of the structural parameters as fixed and known. We break with standard practice in an interesting way. Our maintained hypotheses include an auxiliary assumption that permits us to identify the covariance matrix of structural errors. On the assumption that structural covariances as well as structural parameters are known and fixed, we are able to compare the performance of backward- and forward-looking fixed coefficient rules. We are also able to compare the performance of fixed-coefficient rules to the performance of the optimal commitment policy and to the optimal policy under discretion. Our paper thus provides evidence on the practical importance to a central bank of obtaining a commitment mechanism and the loss in performance when the commitment mechanism takes the form of a simple and verifiable fixed-coefficient policy rule.

We evaluate the performance of a policy with a loss function with three inputs. The first input is a set of three weights that represent the relative importance to the central bank of stabilizing inflation, output, and interest rates. We compute optimal policies and corresponding loss values for different policy weights in order to determine whether conclusions about the relative performance of policies are sensitive to policy objectives. Policy weights range between zero and one and sum to one. The second input to the loss function is the covariance matrix of structural errors. For fixed-coefficient rules, we use the Klein algorithm to compute the covariance matrix of reduced form errors from the structural error covariance matrix, the structural parameters, and the coefficients of the policy rule. The reduced form error covariance matrix is then used to compute policy loss. The third input to the loss function is the state-transition coefficient matrix. For fixed-coefficient rules, we compute this matrix with the Klein algorithm. For optimal commitment and discretion, we derive the reduced form and compute policy loss with a version of Soderlind's (1999) algorithm.

Our policy analysis supports several interesting findings. First, the original Taylor rule, with *a priori* coefficient values, performs quite well when stabilizing inflation and stabilizing output are both important objectives. Its performance can, however, be very poor for other sets of weights. Second, for a wide variety of policy-objective weights, backward-looking rules perform as well as or better than rules that permit the central bank to adjust the rate of interest in response to current output and inflation. In fact, a backward-looking rule which permits the central bank to condition the rate of interest on the full state vector for the economy is the best performer for more than half of our policy objective weight configurations. Third, when the central bank makes output stabilization its chief objective, an optimized version of the Taylor rule where the interest rate depends on current values of output and inflation and the lagged interest rate is the best performer among the rules we consider.

We begin in Section 1 with an example that explains how the coefficients of a policy rule are computed when the structure is "backward-looking." The example highlights the challenges associated with computing optimal policies for " forward-looking" models. Section 1 also describes the algorithm we use to compute policy loss. In Section 2, we set out the forward-looking structural model that underlies our analysis and explain how we use the Klein algorithm to solve it and compute policy loss. In Section 3, we present the results of our policy evaluation for fixed-coefficient rules. In section 4, we explain how we compute loss for optimal commitment and discretionary policies and compare results for these policies with results for fixed-coefficient policies described in Section 3. Our concluding remarks are contained in Section 5.

1 Optimal Policy with a Backward-Looking Model

We begin with an example where monetary policy is like a game against nature in the sense that the parameters of the economy's state transition equation are independent of the policy chosen by the central bank. If the state transition equation is linear and the bank's objective function is quadratic, optimal policy is characterized by the matrix Ricatti equations. Given regularity conditions, backward iteration of the Ricatti equations shows that optimal policy is a fixed-coefficient rule. The example permits us to highlight the challenges that arise when, in contrast, the structural equations of the model are forward looking and optimal policies and state transition equations must be simultaneously determined.

The example is built around a three equation model for output, inflation, and the interest rate. The central bank wishes to stabilize the time paths of output and inflation by controlling the interest rate (r). Stabilizing output means keeping it close to its long run growth path. Stabilizing the inflation rate means keeping it constant. To keep the notation simple, y and p are defined as differences of output and inflation from target values so that the central bank wants to keep y and p as close to zero as possible.

The model is composed of three structural equations.

$$y_t = a_1 y_{t-1} + a_2 y_{t-2} - b\,(r_t - p_t) + u_t \tag{1}$$

$$p_t = \beta y_t + \alpha p_{t-1} + v_t \tag{2}$$

$$r_t = \theta_1 y_{t-1} + \theta_2 p_{t-1} + \theta_3 r_{t-1} + \theta_4 y_{t-2} + w_t \tag{3}$$

Equation (1) is a backward-looking IS schedule which implies that equilibrium output is inversely related to the real rate of interest which, for now, is defined as the interest rate minus the current inflation rate. Equation (2) is a backward-looking Phillips curve which implies that inflation tends to rise when output exceeds its steady state value. The lagged values of y in equation (1) and p in equation (2) capture the effects of partial adjustment mechanisms and govern the dynamic responses of output and inflation to shocks. Equation (3) explains how the central bank adjusts the nominal interest rate in response to changes in the economy. A monetary policy is a set of values for the parameters of the feedback equation. Structural shocks (u, v, and w) are assumed to have zero means and to be serially uncorrelated.

The model restricts monetary policy in two ways. First, the interest rate is a function only of past values of output and inflation which implies that the central bank can not respond contemporaneously to demand and supply shocks. Because the state of the economy is completely described by y_{t-1}, p_{t-1}, r_{t-1}, and y_{t-2}, adding additional lagged variables to the right hand side of (3) is superfluous. Second, the values of θ_1 through θ_4 are fixed, a sufficient but not a necessary condition for a time-consistent policy.

For equations (1)–(3), monetary policy is a game against nature because the parameters of the state transition equation for output and inflation are constant and independent of monetary policy. The reduced form y and p may be written as

$$Z_t = AZ_{t-1} + Cr_t + U_t \tag{4}$$

where $Z_t = (y_t, p_t, r_t, y_{t-1})'$, $U = (\eta_{1t}, \eta_{2t}, 0, 0)'$, $\eta_{1t} = d(u_t + bv_t)$, $\eta_{2t} = d(\beta u_t + v_t)$, $d = (1 - b\beta)^{-1}$ and where A and C are matrices given by:

$$A = \begin{bmatrix} da_1 & db\alpha & 0 & da_2 \\ d\beta\alpha_1 & d\alpha & 0 & dba_2 \\ 0 & 0 & 0 & 0 \\ 1 & 0 & 0 & 0 \end{bmatrix} \qquad C = \begin{bmatrix} -db \\ -db\beta \\ 1 \\ 0 \end{bmatrix}$$

We assume that the central bank chooses values for θ_1 through θ_4 that minimize the loss function

$$\Lambda = E_0 \sum_{t=0}^{\infty} \delta^t Z_t' W Z_t \tag{5}$$

where W is a (4×4) matrix of policy weights that determine the relative importance to the central bank of its stabilization objectives and where δ is the central bank's time rate of discount. We assume W is diagonal with $W_{1,1} = W_y$, $W_{2,2} = W_p$, $W_{3,3} = W_r$, $W_{4,4} = 0$ where W_y, W_p, and W_r are the weights assigned by the central bank to stabilizing output, inflation, and the interest rate. Since what matters is the relative size of weights, we normalize the sum of the weights to 1.0.

Because the state transition equation is linear and its objective function is quadratic, the central bank is a linear regulator and the solution to its problem is given by:

$$r_t = \Theta Z_{t-1} + w_t \tag{6}$$

where $\Theta = (\theta_1, \theta_2, \theta_3, \theta_4)$ is the (1×4) vector of reaction function coefficients.[2] The optimal value for Θ is the limit to the series Θ_T, Θ_{T-1}, Θ_{T-2}, computed with the matrix Ricatti equations:

$$\begin{aligned}
H_T &= \delta^T W \\
\Theta_T &= -\left(C' H_T C\right)^{-1} C' H_T A \\
H_{T-1} &= \delta^{T-1} W + A' H_T \left(A + C\Theta_T\right) \\
\Theta_{T-1} &= -\left(C' H_{T-1} C\right)^{-1} C' H_{T-1} A \\
&\vdots \\
H_{T-j} &= \delta^{T-j} W + A' H_{T-j-1} \left(A + C\Theta_{T-j-1}\right)
\end{aligned} \tag{7}$$

Certainty equivalence holds. The solution to the central bank problem is the same as the solution to the companion problem where random shocks are absent from the structural equations (Sargent, 1987). Inspection of the Ricatti equations confirms that the optimal reaction function coefficients do not depend on the covariance matrix of the model's error terms. McGratten (1990) reports that it is computationally efficient to compute the optimal θ by iterating the Ricatti equations to convergence.

For the forward-looking model presented in the following section, the optimal reaction function coefficients are not characterized by the Ricatti equations and must be computed by numerical minimization of loss. To see how this can be done, write the reduced form for y, p and r as a first-order vector autoregression:

$$X_t = G X_{t-1} + \Phi_t \tag{8}$$

where $X_t = (y_t, p_t, r_t, y_{t-1}, p_{t-1}, r_{t-1})'$, $\Phi_t = (\varphi_1, \varphi_2, \varphi_3, 0, 0, 0)'$, $\varphi_{1t} = d(u_t + bv_t - bw_t)$, $\varphi_{2t} = d(\beta u_t + v_t - b\beta w_t)$, $\varphi_{3t} = w_t$ and the (6×6)

[2] Strictly speaking there should not be an error present in the reaction function. Hansen and Sargent (1980) explain how to account for an error in a policy rule. An adaptation of the Hansen–Sargent argument to the current setting is given by Salemi (1995, p. 421).

matrix G is

$$G = \begin{bmatrix} G_{11} & G_{12} \\ 1 & 0 \end{bmatrix}$$

$$G_{11} = \begin{bmatrix} d(a_1 - b\theta_1) & db(\alpha - \theta_2) & -db\theta_3 \\ d\beta(a_1 - b\theta_1) & d(\alpha - b\beta\theta_2) & -db\beta\theta_3 \\ \theta_1 & \theta_2 & \theta_3 \end{bmatrix}$$

$$G_{12} = \begin{bmatrix} d(a_2 - b\theta_4) & 0 & 0 \\ d\beta(a_2 - b\theta_4) & 0 & 0 \\ \theta_4 & 0 & 0 \end{bmatrix}$$

Because they are linear combinations of the serially uncorrelated structural errors, the φ_{jt} are serially uncorrelated. The moving average representation for X_t is $(I - GL)^{-1}\Phi_t$ where L is the lag operator.

Next write Λ as a function of the forecast error variances of the model's variables.

$$\begin{aligned}
\Lambda &= E_0 \sum_{t=0}^{\infty} \delta^t X_t' \tilde{W} X_t \\
&= \sum_{t=0}^{\infty} \delta^t \text{ trace} \left[\tilde{W} E_0 (X_t X_t')\right] \\
&= \text{trace} \left[\tilde{W} \sum_{t=0}^{\infty} \delta^t E_0 (X_t X_t')\right] \\
&= \text{trace} \left[\tilde{W} \sum_{t=0}^{\infty} \delta^t \left(E_0 (X_t - E_0 X_t)(X_t - E_0 X_t)' + (E_0 X_t)(E_0 X_t)'\right)\right] \\
&= \text{trace} \left[\tilde{W} (M + N)\right] \qquad (9)
\end{aligned}$$

where $\tilde{W}$ is a (6×6) diagonal matrix with $(1,1)$, $(2,2)$, and $(3,3)$ elements equal to W_y, W_p, and W_r and with zeroes elsewhere. Λ involves two sums:

$$M = \sum_{t=0}^{\infty} \delta^t E_0 (X_t - E_0 X_t)(X_t - E_0 X_t)'$$

and

$$N = \sum_{t=0}^{\infty} \delta^t (E_0 X_t)(E_0 X_t)'$$

M is the discounted sum of forecast error variances of X computed at time zero when policy is set. N is the discounted sum of quadratic terms in expected departures of X from its target. Provided that the economy is on target at the time when policy is set, $N = 0$ and the objective of the central bank is to minimize the part of Λ that involves M. If the economy begins away from its target path, the central bank faces a tradeoff between returning the economy to its target path and minimizing the weighted sum of discounted error variances. Throughout this paper we assume $N = 0$.

The last step is derivation of a convenient expression for M. Let Ω be the (6×6) covariance matrix for Φ_t with $\Omega_{1,1}$, the (3×3) covariance matrix for the non-zero elements of Φ, in the upper left corner and zeroes elsewhere. Because Φ_t is serially uncorrelated, we have

$$E_0 (X_t - E_0 X_t)(X_t - E_0 X_t)' = \Omega + G\Omega G' + G^2\Omega (G^2)' + \ldots + G^{k-1}\Omega (G^{k-1})' \quad (10)$$

and

$$M = \Omega + \delta [\Omega + G\Omega G'] + \ldots + \delta^k \left[\Omega + G\Omega G' + \ldots + G^{k-1}\Omega (G^{k-1})'\right] + \ldots = (1-\delta)^{-1} \left[\Omega + \delta G\Omega G' + \delta^2 G^2 \Omega (G^2)' + \ldots\right] \quad (11)$$

The direct minimization strategy computes M by iterating the square-bracket term in (11) to convergence and computes loss as trace $(\tilde{W}M)$. Alternative techniques for computing M are discussed in Anderson *et al.* (1996).[3]

2 Optimal Policy with a Forward-Looking Model

In this section, we discuss computation of optimal policies for a forward-looking structural model in which agents have rational beliefs about future values of output and inflation.

$$y_t = \lambda E_t y_{t+1} + a_1 y_{t-1} + a_2 y_{t-2} - b(r_t - E_t p_{t+1}) + u_t \quad (12)$$

$$p_t = \beta y_t + \alpha_1 E_t p_{t+1} + \alpha_2 p_{t-1} + v_t \quad (13)$$

$$r_t = \theta_1 y_{t-1} + \theta_2 p_{t-1} + \theta_3 r_{t-1} + \theta_4 y_{t-2} + w_t \quad (14)$$

The IS schedule (12) may be obtained by combining a linearized Euler equation that characterizes a representative household's optimal choice

---

[3]The Matlab programs we used to compute optimal reaction function coefficients are available on request.

between consumption and saving and the market clearing condition for output. As explained by Clarida, Gali, and Gertler (1999), the presence of expected future output in the IS equation results from the desire of households to smooth consumption. When households expect higher consumption in the future, they want to consume more in the present which raises the current level of aggregate demand and, in equilibrium, introduces a positive association between the current and expected future levels of output. The presence of lagged output in the IS equation can be explained by habit persistence or adjustment costs. Woodford (1996) and Bernanke, Gertler, and Gilchrist (1998) provide the details. Svensson (2000) adapts the story to an open economy.

If α_2 is zero, equation (13) is a version of the new Phillips curve discussed by Gali and Gertler (1999), Clarida, Gali, and Gertler (1999), and Svensson (2000). The foundation for the new Phillips curve is a model in which monopolistically competitive firms adjust their prices on a staggered basis as in Calvo (1983). When it has the opportunity, an individual firm adjusts its price to maximize expected profits while taking account of the restriction it faces on future price adjustment and the expected future prices of its competitors. The staggered-price-setting story leads to an equation where the current rate of inflation is a function of the firm's current level of marginal cost and the expected future inflation rate. The new Phillips curve results when the output gap (y) is used as a proxy for marginal cost.

If α_2 is not zero, equation (13) is a version of the new hybrid Phillips curve developed by Gali and Gertler to explain inertia in the rate of inflation. The foundation is a model with two kinds of firms. The first kind is a Calvo firm. The second kind is a follower that sets its current price equal to the average of prices set by competitors in the previous period plus an adjustment for inflation. The existence of backward-looking firms is sufficient to introduce lagged inflation into the Phillips curve. Alternatively, Clarida, Gali, and Gertler (1999) account for lagged inflation in the Phillips curve by assuming serially correlated supply shocks.

As before, the model includes a fixed-coefficient reaction function (14) and the central bank chooses coefficient values to minimize expected loss. Equation (14) is essentially the same as (9) of Fuhrer and Moore (1995) and (4) of Fuhrer (1997).

Equations (12)–(14) introduce two layers of complexity to the control problem of the central bank. First, because agents' actions depend upon expected future output and inflation, there may be zero or many reduced form equations for y_t, p_t, and r_t. Second, because agents' beliefs are rational, changes in Θ cause changes in the parameters of the state transition equation. Thus, Θ and the state transition equation must be solved for simultaneously.

We address the issues of solution existence and multiplicity using the extension of Blanchard and Kahn (1980) proposed by Klein (2000). Equations (12)–(14) are written in Klein format as

$$\tilde{A}\begin{bmatrix} Z_t \\ E_t y_{t+1} \\ E_t p_{t+1} \end{bmatrix} = \tilde{B}\begin{bmatrix} Z_{t-1} \\ y_t \\ p_t \end{bmatrix} + \tilde{C} s_t \tag{15}$$

where $Z_t = (y_t, p_t, r_t, y_{t-1})'$, $S_t = (u_t, v_t, w_t)'$, and where $\tilde{A}$, $\tilde{B}$ and $\tilde{C}$ are given by:

$$\tilde{A} = \begin{bmatrix} 1 & 0 & 0 & 0 & 0 & 0 \\ 0 & 1 & 0 & 0 & 0 & 0 \\ 0 & 0 & 1 & 0 & 0 & 0 \\ 0 & 0 & 0 & 1 & 0 & 0 \\ 0 & 0 & -b & 0 & \lambda & b \\ 0 & 0 & 0 & 0 & 0 & \alpha_1 \end{bmatrix}$$

$$\tilde{B} = \begin{bmatrix} 0 & 0 & 0 & 0 & 1 & 0 \\ 0 & 0 & 0 & 0 & 0 & 1 \\ \theta_1 & \theta_2 & \theta_3 & \theta_4 & 0 & 0 \\ -a_1 & 0 & 0 & -a_2 & 1 & 0 \\ 0 & -\alpha_2 & 0 & 0 & -\beta & 1 \end{bmatrix}$$

$$\tilde{C} = \begin{bmatrix} 0 & 0 & 0 \\ 0 & 0 & 0 \\ 0 & 0 & 1 \\ 0 & 0 & 0 \\ -1 & 0 & 0 \\ 0 & -1 & 0 \end{bmatrix}$$

In the language of Klein, Z_{t-1} is the vector of backward-looking variables and y_t and p_t are the forward-looking variables. The Klein solution strategy computes a generalized "QZ" decomposition of $\tilde{A}$ and $\tilde{B}$. For any pair of conformable square matrices $\left(\tilde{A}, \tilde{B}\right)$, there exist orthonormal matrices Q and Z and upper triangular matrices S and T such that

$$\tilde{A} = Q'SZ' \qquad \tilde{B} = Q'TZ \qquad QQ' = ZZ' = I$$

The generalized eigenvalues of the system are the ratios T_{ii}/S_{ii} where T_{ii} and S_{ii} are the diagonal elements of T and S. Without loss of generality, the decomposition matrices can be transformed so that the generalized eigenvalues are arrayed in ascending modulus order (Klein, 2000, p. 1410).

Provided that the number of stable eigenvalues equals the number of backward-looking variables, Theorem 5.1 in Klein shows that the unique solution for the backward-looking variables is given by

$$Z_t = \left(Z_{11}S_{11}^{-1}T_{11}Z_{11}^{-1}\right) Z_{t-1} + LS_t \tag{16}$$

where Z_{11}, S_{11}, and T_{11} are the (4×4) upper left blocks of Z, S, and T and where L is a (4×3) matrix given by (5.23) in Klein. For our model, a unique solution will exist if there are four stable and two unstable eigenvalues.

Given our assumption that the Fed reacts neither to current values of output and inflation nor to current structural shocks, we can recover Σ, the covariance matrix of structural errors, from Ω, the covariance matrix of reduced form errors with the mapping $\Sigma = L^{-1}\Omega\left(L'\right)^{-1}$. We exploit this mapping in the policy experiments described in the following section.

With the forward-looking model, the central bank control problem is complicated by the fact that the parameters of the state transition equation depend on Θ. What the central bank may take as fixed is the structure of the economy and not its reduced form. An algorithm that the central bank could use to compute the coefficients of its policy rule has three steps. First, the algorithm chooses a starting value for Θ, uses (16) to compute the reduced form and the resulting G matrix, and then computes policy loss using (9) and (11). Second, it calculates partial derivatives of loss with respect to each element of Θ. For every change in Θ, G must be re-computed because private agents respond to policy changes by changing their beliefs and actions. Third, the algorithm updates Θ when doing so lowers policy loss provided that the Klein saddle path restriction is satisfied. The algorithm repeats steps two and three until it can no longer lower policy loss.

3 Monetary Policy Rules

A monetary policy rule specifies how a central bank will respond to changes in economic conditions. If the coefficients of the rule are chosen optimally, the rule is also an explicit commitment to a set of policy objectives. But why should a central bank adopt commitment in the form of a fixed coefficient rule?

The case for commitment builds on the realization that policy effectiveness depends not only on policy actions but also on public understanding of those actions and public expectations of future actions (Kydland and Prescott, 1977). Policy is more effective when its future course is predictable. Lacking a commitment mechanism, the central bank has an incentive to exploit stickiness in wages and prices to damp recessions. The public reacts with inflation expectations that incorporate future discretionary stimulus.

Commitment permits the central bank to distribute "policy medicine" over time. For example, suppose the central bank wishes to offset inflation that will result from a supply shock. Under commitment, it can raise interest rates moderately provided that it maintains higher rates for a period of time. Lacking commitment, a higher initial rate increase will be necessary because the public doubts that the central bank will sustain the rate increase.

Optimal commitment need not take the form of a fixed-coefficient reaction function. It is a state-contingent plan that gives the instrument setting as a function of the history of exogenous shocks. Optimal commitment is not practical for two reasons. First, it is not feasible to provide an advance listing of all relevant contingencies (Woodford, 2002). Second, it is difficult for the public to distinguish between discretion and a complicated contingency rule. Both problems are avoided when the central bank commits to a fixed-coefficient rule.

What form should a fixed-coefficient rule take? Most industrialized-economy central banks use a short-term interest rate as their control variable. An obvious example is the US Federal Reserve which sets a target level for the federal funds rate and controls the supply of bank reserves to keep the funds rate at the target. Because the Fed is able to closely control the federal funds rate, it makes sense to treat the funds rate itself as the policy instrument. In what follows, we limit attention to fixed coefficient rules that explain how the short-term interest rate should be adjusted in response to economic conditions.

The most famous examples of interest rate rules are those proposed by John Taylor which in our notation may be written as:

$$r_t = \theta_p p_t + \theta_y y_t + \theta_r r_{t-1} \tag{17}$$

The original Taylor rule (Taylor, 1993) assigns coefficient values that Taylor describes as providing both a sensible rule and an accurate description of Federal Reserve policy: $\theta_p = 1.5$, $\theta_y = 0.5$, and $\theta_r = 0$. The intuition for the large value of θ_p is that the central bank must raise the interest rate by more than any increase in inflation in order to raise the real rate of interest, cool the economy, and move inflation back toward its target. An interesting alternative to the original Taylor rule is a rule that sets θ_r to zero but chooses the values for θ_p and θ_r that minimize the loss function of the central bank. Taylor (1999) suggests another alternative that allows for interest rate smoothing so that θ_r is positive. McCallum (1997) and others argue that policymakers can react only to lagged and not to current values of output and inflation. In response, Taylor (1999) suggests an alternative where lagged values of output and inflation replace the current values in (17). In what follows, we will study the performance of all four forms of the Taylor rule.

The second type of rule we consider is the "full state" rule given by equation (14). There is one important difference between this rule and the lagged Taylor rule. Given our model, equation (14) permits the central bank to respond to all, rather than a subset, of the variables in the state vector. In theory, equation (14) would permit the central bank to better respond to business cycle momentum by conditioning the interest rate both on y_{t-1} and y_{t-2}. In practice, it is not clear whether conditioning policy on the full state vector will appreciably improve the performance of the rule. By comparing the performance of (14) and the Taylor rules, we can gather evidence on how important it is for the central bank to correctly specify the state vector.

Woodford (2002) attributes to Goodhart a simple rule where the central bank responds only to departures of the inflation rate from its target value. In terms of (17), the Goodhart rule amounts to setting $\theta_y = \theta_r = 0$ and choosing an optimal value for θ_p. Batini and Haldane (1998) recommend rules where the central bank reacts to expected future inflation. Clarida, Gali, and Gertler (1998) also suggest that forecast-based rules are optimal for a central bank with a quadratic objective function such as ours. We implement these recommendations with a version of (17), called the expected inflation rule, where $\theta_y = \theta_r = 0$, $E_t[p_{t+1}]$ replaces p_t, and where θ_p is chosen to minimize policy loss.

Slope Parameters						
λ	a_1	a_2	b	α_1	α_2	β
0.230	1.06	−0.305	0.030	0.600	0.401	.0006
Error Covariances ($\times 10^{-5}$)						
σ_{uu}	σ_{vv}	σ_{ww}	σ_{uv}	σ_{uw}	σ_{vw}	
1.53	1.38	1.78	−0.172	0.610	0.342	

Table 1: Structural Parameter Values Used to Compare Policy Rules

Our policy evaluation is based on estimates of the coefficients of (12)–(14) obtained by Salemi (2002) and reported in Table 1. Salemi fits (12)–(14) to quarterly data for the U.S. for 1983–2001 subject to the restriction that the coefficients of the policy rule minimize a quadratic loss function. We assume that correlation between the error (w_t) in the policy rule and the errors in the IS schedule (u_t) and the Phillips curve (v_t) are the result of contemporaneous responses of output and inflation to w_t rather than to the contemporaneous response of policy to structural shocks. It is then straightforward to back out an estimate of the structural error covariance matrix from Salemi's estimate of the reduced form error covariance matrix. Our estimate of the structural error covariance matrix is also reported in Table 1. We follow the literature by treating our estimates of structural parameters as fixed and known values. In future work, we intend to extend our analysis by treating the parameters as random variables.

Our results are summarized in Table 2 and in Figures 1–6. Table 2 reports the policy rule that achieved the lowest loss level for each set of policy-objective weights considered. The table takes the form of a triangular grid with W_p, the inflation weight, across the columns and W_y, the output weight, along the rows.[4] Nodes on the diagonal represent cases in which minimal weight was assigned to stabilizing the rate of interest. Nodes above the diagonal represent cases where higher weight was assigned to the objective of interest rate smoothing.

Legend
E: Expected Inflation Rule
F: Full-State Rule
T: Taylor Rule with Interest Rate Smoothing

Wy\Wp	0.05	0.10	0.15	0.20	0.25	0.30	0.35	0.40	0.45	0.50	0.55	0.60	0.65	0.70	0.75	0.80	0.85	0.90
0	E	E	E	E	E	E	E	E	E	E	E	E	E	E	E	E	E	E
0.05	E	E	E	E	E	E	E	E	E	E	E	E	E	E	E	F	F	
0.10	E	E	E	E	E	E	E	E	E	E	E	E	F	F	F	F		
0.15	E	E	E	E	E	E	E	E	F	F	F	F	F	F	F			
0.20	E	E	E	E	F	F	F	F	F	F	F	F	F	F				
0.25	F	F	F	F	F	F	F	F	F	F	F	F	F					
0.30	F	F	F	F	F	F	F	F	F	F	F	F						
0.35	F	F	F	F	F	F	F	F	F	F	F							
0.40	F	F	F	F	F	F	F	F	F	T								
0.45	F	F	F	F	F	F	F	F	T									
0.50	F	F	F	F	F	F	F	T	T									
0.55	F	F	F	F	F	F	T	T										
0.60	F	F	F	F	T	T	T											
0.65	F	F	T	T	T	T												
0.70	T	T	T	T	T													
0.75	T	T	T	T														
0.80	T	T	T															
0.85	T	T																
0.90	T																	

Table 2: The Minimum Loss Fixed Coefficient Rule

Our first finding is that the best policy rule is always one of three: the single-coefficient expected inflation rule (EI), the full state rule (FS), and

[4] In some cases when we allowed $W_p = 1$ or $W_r = 0$, our loss-minimization algorithm did not converge. For this reason, we restricted attention to values of $W_r \geq 0.05$ and values of $W_p \geq 0.05$.

the version of the Taylor rule in which the rate of interest is conditioned on current output, current inflation, and the lagged rate of interest and the coefficients are chosen to minimize loss (TS). EI is the best rule either when zero weight is assigned to stabilizing output or when very-substantial weight is assigned to interest rate smoothing. TS is the best rule when $W_y \geq 0.70$ no matter the distribution of weight across the other objectives. FS is the best rule when $0.25 \leq W_y \leq 0.35$ no matter the distribution of weights across other objectives. For other values of W_y, the optimal rule can be any of the three depending on the weight assigned to the other two objectives.

There are two interesting implications of our best rule findings. First, a simple rule in which the rate of interest is made a function only of the expected rate of inflation can be the best fixed-coefficient policy rule but only in the case where the central bank cares nothing about stabilizing output or greatly dislikes variability in the rate of interest. When even modest weight is assigned to output stability, FS produces lower loss than EI. Second, the advantage conferred upon the TS rule of conditioning the rate of interest on current rather than past values of output and inflation is valuable only when output stabilization is the dominant objective. In most nodes along the diagonal of the table, where interest rate stability is given little weight, FS performs better. If the Federal Reserve considers inflation stabilization to be its primary objective and output stabilization to be an important but secondary objective, it would be well advised to adopt an interest rate rule of the form of (14).

Figures 1–6 provide quantitative evidence on the relative performance of the rules. Figure 1 is a graph of the ratio of policy loss for the original Taylor rule to the policy loss for the full state rule. Given that Taylor assigned values to the coefficients on *a priori* grounds that did not include minimizing policy loss, it is not surprising that the ratio always exceeds one. What is surprising is how poor the relative performance of the original Taylor rule can be. Taylor-rule loss is much higher when W_y is small and when W_r is near zero. However, it is very interesting that the original Taylor rule performs almost as well as the full-state rule when $W_p = 0.80$ and $W_y = W_r = 0.10$ which in our view is not a bad guess about the preferences of the Federal Reserve since the end of the monetarist experiment.

Figure 2 plots the ratio of policy loss for the optimized Taylor rule to policy loss for the full state rule. Since this Taylor rule conditions the interest rate on current values of output and inflation, Figure 2 provides a referendum on the value of conditioning policy on current rather than lagged economic variables. The figure shows that the optimized Taylor rule performs slightly better when W_r is very small and when $W_y \geq 0.70$.

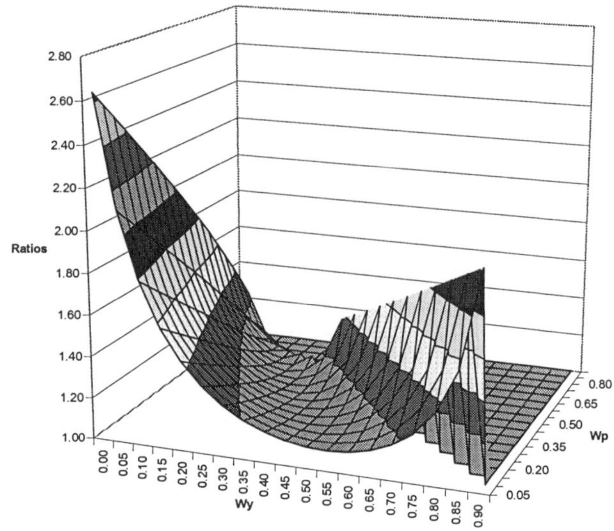

Figure 1: Policy Loss Ratio: Original Taylor Rule/Full-State Rule

On the other hand, the optimized Taylor rule performs relatively poorly when interest rate smoothing is important and when W_p is large. This latter finding is not surprising since the optimized Taylor rule does not allow the interest rate to be conditioned on its lagged value.

Figure 3 compares the performance of the full state rule to that of the version of the Taylor rule that allows for interest rate smoothing. Again, the coefficients of the Taylor rule are those that minimize loss. The most striking thing about the figure is that except for extreme values of W_y the performance of the two rules is quite close. This Taylor rule continues to have an advantage when W_r is very small; the full state rule has an advantage when $W_r \geq 0.10$. It appears that conditioning policy on current values of output and inflation involves a tradeoff between the benefits of more current information and the costs of a more volatile interest rate. Figure 4 compares the original Taylor rule to the Taylor rule with coefficients on output and inflation chosen to minimize loss. It confirms one of the conclusions supported by Figure 1. The optimized Taylor rule always performs better, but the performance of the two rules is nearly the same when W_p is large and W_y and W_r are of modest size.

Figure 5 compares the Goodhart rule with the full state rule. The Goodhart rule is the simplest interest rate rule we consider since it adjusts the nominal rate of interest only in response to departures of the

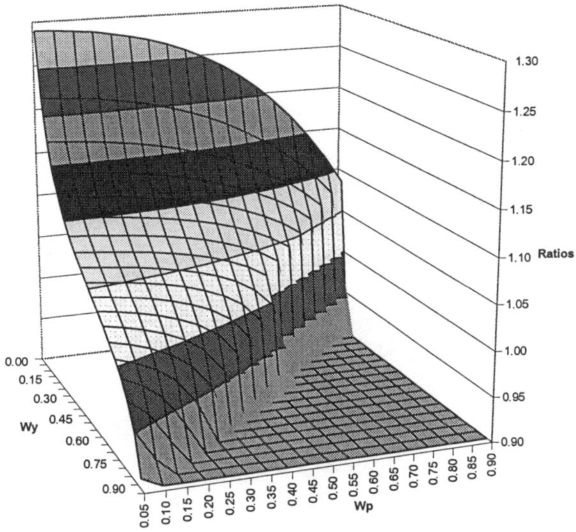

Figure 2: Policy Loss Ratio: Optimized Taylor Rule/Full-State Rule

current inflation rate from target values. The figure shows that the Goodhart rule never performs better than the full state rule despite its information advantage. The relative performance of the Goodhart rule is better when W_y is very small and, particularly, when W_p is very large. However, the full state rule performs much better for large values of W_y and for large values of W_p combined with modest values of W_y. We conclude that the central bank of an economy well described by our model ought not adopt a Goodhart rule. Figure 6 tells a similar story about the performance of the rule in which the nominal rate of interest responds only to changes in the current expectation of future inflation. The backward-looking full state rule outperforms this forward-looking rule unless a very high weight is placed on the interest rate stabilization objective. The full state rule performs better when W_p is sizeable even if W_y is very small. A central bank that cares mostly about stabilizing inflation and is not too concerned about interest rate stability would do better adopting the full state rule.

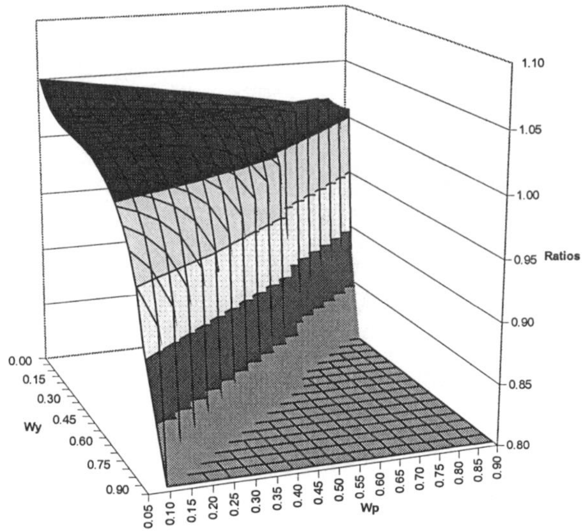

Figure 3: Policy Loss Ratio: Taylor-Smoothing Rule/Full-State Rule

4 Optimal Commitment and Discretion

In the previous section, we evaluated the economic performance of a set of fixed-coefficient policy rules. In this section, we compare the performance of our rules to that of two alternatives which Clarida, Gali, and Gertler (1999) call "unconstrained optimal commitment policy" and "discretionary policy."

The unconstrained optimal commitment (commitment) policy is fundamentally different from fixed-coefficient rules. Rules "live" in the space spanned by the current state vector for an economic model. The commitment policy depends on the entire history of the state vector dating back to time zero when policy is set. At time zero, the central bank evaluates all possible outcomes, decides how to react to each, and promises to stick with the chosen set of reactions.

To explain how we compute the commitment policy, we modify our notation to conform to that of Soderlind (1999) and write the constraint facing the central bank as:

$$\tilde{A}\begin{bmatrix} Z_{t+1} \\ E_t y_{t+1} \\ E_t p_{t+1} \end{bmatrix} = \tilde{B}\begin{bmatrix} Z_t \\ y_t \\ p_t \end{bmatrix} + \tilde{C} r_t \begin{bmatrix} S_{t+1} \\ 0 \end{bmatrix} \tag{18}$$

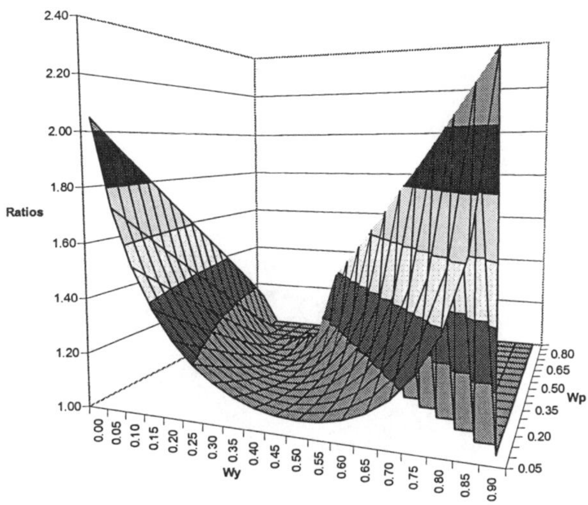

Figure 4: Policy Loss Ratio: Original Taylor Rule/Optimized Taylor Rule

where Z_t is redefined to include the structural errors from the IS equation and Phillips curve so that $Z_t = (u_t, v_t, y_{t-1}, p_{t-1}, r_{t-1}, y_{t-2})'$, where $S_t = (u_t, v_t)'$, and where the elements of $\tilde{A}, \tilde{B}$ and $\tilde{C}$ are obtained in a straightforward way by re-writing the structural equations in the above format. There are two essential differences between (15) and (18). First, the structural shocks are now considered to be part of the state vector permitting the interest rate under commitment to depend on current and past values of those shocks. Second, the interest rate is assumed to exactly equal the value specified by the commitment policy so that w_t, the interest rate shock, is assumed to be zero.

To characterize the commitment policy, we adopt the approach of Currie and Levine (1993) and formulate the Lagrangian function:

$$J_0 = E_0 \sum_{t=0}^{\infty} \delta^t \left[\begin{array}{c} W_p (p_t)^2 + W_y (y_t)^2 + W_r (r_t)^2 \\ +2\lambda_{t+1} \left(\tilde{B} X_t + \tilde{C} r_t + \varepsilon_t - \tilde{A} X_{t+1} \right) \end{array} \right] \tag{19}$$

where $X_t = (Z_t', E_t(y_{t+1}), E_t(p_{t+1}))'$ and where $\varepsilon_t = (S_t, 0)'$. We compute the commitment policy by using Klein's method to solve simultaneously a system of equations comprising (18) and the first-order conditions for the optimization problem. To compute the value of the loss function associated with the optimal policy we apply equation (4.15) of

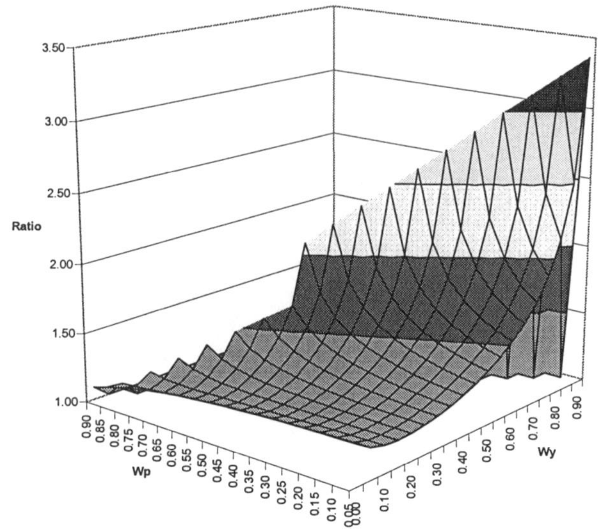

Figure 5: Policy Loss Ratio: Goodhart Rule/Full-State Rule

Ljungqvist and Sargent (2000).[5]

The second alternative policy design we consider is optimal discretion. What distinguishes discretion from commitment is that current and past policy decisions in no way constrain future decisions. Under discretion, the central bank re-optimizes its loss function (5) every period taking private sector expectations as exogenous. Under commitment, the central bank optimizes only in the inaugural period and treats private agent expectations as endogenous and changing with policy. Under commitment, the central bank simultaneously chooses paths for the interest rate and private sector expectations subject to the constraints imposed by the economic structure. Under discretion, the central bank lacks credibility and has no control over private agents expectations. An alert private sector adjusts expectations according to actual policy decisions. In the context of our model, private agents predict central bank decisions by solving the central bank loss minimization problem while recognizing that the bank is free to change policy. The outcome of the "game" played by the central bank and private agents is an equilibrium for which the central bank has no incentive to change policy although it

[5] For the detailed description of the algorithms used in these computations, see Givens (2002).

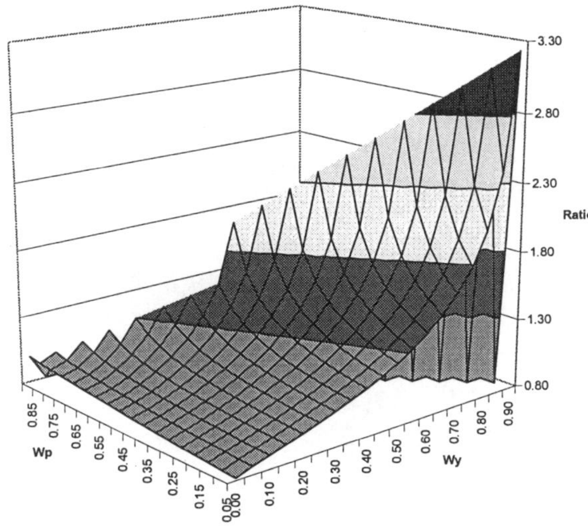

Figure 6: Policy Loss Ratio: Expected Inflation Rule/Full-State Rule

has the ability to do so.

To characterize discretion, we adopt the same notation used for commitment and formulate the following Bellman equation.

$$\Lambda_t = Z_t' V_t Z_t + d_t = W_p (p_t)^2 + W_y (y_t)^2 + W_r (r_t)^2 + \delta E_t \left(Z_{t+1}' V_{t+1} Z_{t+1} + d_{t+1} \right) \quad (20)$$

The solution under discretion involves minimizing (20) over choice of r_t, where V_t is a (6×6) positive definite, symmetric matrix and d_t is a scalar. Both values are initially undetermined and are found by solving for the fixed point of a particular system of equations. The equations we use are those explained in detail in Soderlind (1999).[6] The optimal policy is a fixed-coefficient feedback rule that relates the nominal interest rate to the current state of the economy. Unlike the commitment policy, the rule under discretion will depend only on the current state vector and not on its entire history.

Figure 7 reports the ratio of policy loss for discretion relative to optimal commitment. To compute loss, we use the parameter values from

[6] For the details, see Givens (2002).

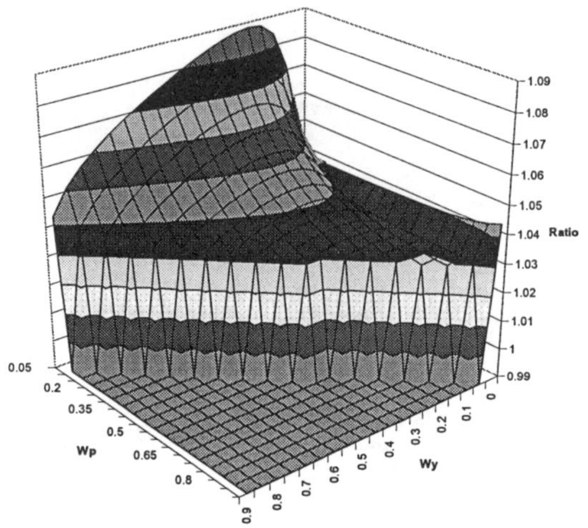

Figure 7: Policy Loss Ratio: Discretion/Commitment

Table 1, assume that variance of the error from the interest rate equation is zero, and then implement the programs described earlier in this section. Several conclusions are warranted. First, loss computed under discretion always exceeds loss computed under commitment. This is no surprise. Second, provided that W_r is very small, the loss ratio is about the same for all values of W_p. (Recall that $W_p + W_y + W_r = 1.0$.) We find this result surprising — we expected that commitment would do relatively better when inflation stabilization was the more important objective. Third, the relative performance of discretion worsens as more weight is placed on interest rate stability. This occurs because the interest rate is more volatile under discretion than under commitment. Fourth, for a given W_p, the relative loss ratio first rises and then falls with increases in W_y. For a given value of W_y, the loss ratio increases monotonically as W_r rises and W_p falls.

Figures 8 and 9 compare loss under optimal commitment and loss under discretion with loss under the full state fixed coefficient rule described in Section 3. We use the full state rule for comparison because it was the lowest-loss rule for a wide variety of policy objectives. In order to make a valid comparison across these three policy designs, we re-computed optimal full state coefficients and loss values under the assumption that σ_w^2, the variance of the error in the interest rate equation, is zero.

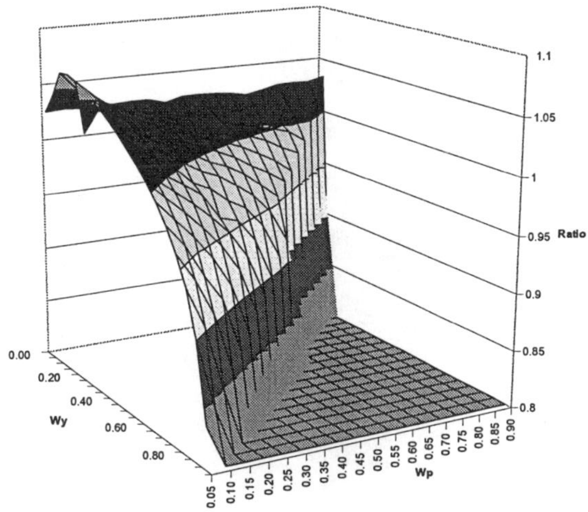

Figure 8: Policy Loss Ratio: Discretion/Full-State Rule

Figure 8 shows that loss associated with the full state rule exceeds loss associated with discretion whenever W_r is small so that interest rate stabilization is relatively unimportant. As W_r increases, the relative performance of the full state rule improves. The full state rule produces lower loss than discretion when $W_r > 0.35$. This is consistent with our earlier finding that the ratio of loss under discretion to loss under commitment is largest when interest rate stability is relatively important. Our finding that discretion can outperform the full state rule should be viewed in context. Discretion outperforms the full state rule for a subset of policy weights quite similar to the subset for which the optimized Taylor rule outperforms the full state rule.

Figure 9 confirms that loss associated with the full state rule always exceeds loss associated with optimal commitment. The full state rule falls furthest short of the commitment potential when W_r is small. For $W_r = 0.05$, the ratio of loss under commitment to loss under the full state rule is about 0.80 when W_y is 0.90 and falls steadily as W_p increases. The ratio is 0.99 when W_p is 0.90. Thus, as inflation stabilization becomes a more important objective, the full state rule, despite conditioning the rate of interest on lagged values of output and inflation, very nearly achieves the full commitment potential.

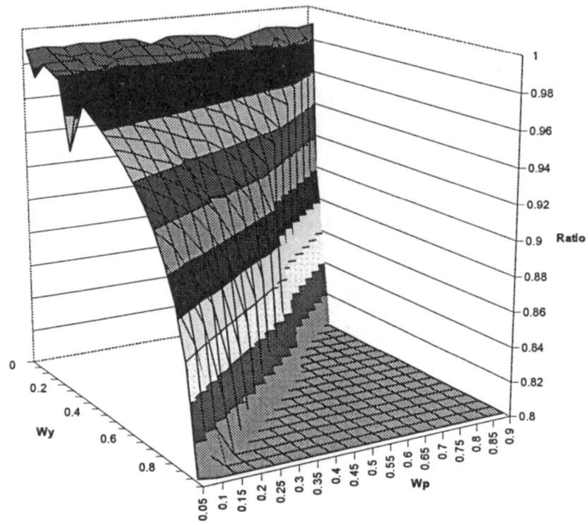

Figure 9: Policy Loss Ratio: Commitment/Full-State Rule

5 Concluding Remarks

We conclude by repeating our key findings. First, computation of optimal feedback parameters of a fixed-coefficient policy rule requires the researcher to account for the effects of changes in those coefficients on private agent expectations and reduced form parameters. We accomplish this complicated task with a Matlab program that marries Klein's solution algorithm with an iterative strategy for solving a Sylvester equation. Second, of the half dozen fixed coefficient rules we studied, one of three always performs best. The rule where the interest rate responds only to the current expectation of future inflation performs best when inflation and interest rate stability are the sole objectives of policy. We find it remarkable that a single-parameter rule could ever outperform all the other rules we consider. As output stabilization becomes a more important objective, one of two rules dominates. The full state rule, where the interest rate varies with lagged values of output and inflation, is the best rule for about half of the weight configurations that we consider, especially for those where $0.25 \leq W_y \leq 0.45$. The version of the Taylor rule that allows for interest rate smoothing and that has coefficients chosen to minimize loss is the best rule whenever $W_y \geq 0.70$. Third, the difference between policy loss under optimal commitment and policy loss under discretion ranges between three and nine per cent, with the greatest disparity observed when interest rate stability is relatively important. Fourth, discretion can result in lower loss than commitment with a fixed coefficient policy rule. Fifth, when inflation stability is the dominant objective of the central bank, loss under the full state rule is nearly as small as loss under optimal commitment and substantially lower than loss under discretion. When inflation stabilization is the primary objective of the central bank, fixed coefficient rules can nearly achieve the lowest loss possible.

BIBLIOGRAPHY

[1] Anderson, Evan, Lars P. Hansen, Ellen R. McGrattan, and Thomas J. Sargent, "Mechanics of forming and estimating dynamic linear economies," in Amman, Hans M., David A. Kendrick, and John Rust, eds., Handbook of Computational Economics 1, Handbooks in Economics 13, Elsevier Science, North-Holland, Amsterdam, 1996, 171–252.

[2] Batini, N. and A. Haldane, "Forward-looking rules for monetary policy," Presented at the NBER Conference on Monetary Policy Rules, 1998.

[3] Bernanke, Ben, Mark Gertler, and Simon Gilchrist, "The financial accelerator in a quantitative business cycle framework," NBER Working Paper 6455, March, 1998.

[4] Blanchard, Olivier J. and Charles M. Kahn, "The solution of linear difference models under rational expectations," Econometrica 48, 1980, 1305–1311.

[5] Calvo, Guillermo A., "Staggered prices in a utility-maximizing framework," Journal of Monetary Economics 12, 1983, 383–398.

[6] Clarida, Richard, Jordi Gali, and Mark Gertler, "Monetary policy rules and macroeconomic stability: Evidence and some theory," NBER Working Paper 6442, March, 1998.

[7] Clarida, Richard, Jordi Gali, and Mark Gertler, "The science of monetary policy: a new Keynesian perspective," Journal of Economic Literature XXXVII, 1999, 1661–1707.

[8] Currie, David and Paul Levine, Rules, Reputation, and Macroeconomic Policy Coordination, Cambridge University Press, 1993.

[9] Fuhrer, Jeffrey C., "Inflation/output variance trade-offs and optimal monetary policy," Journal of Money, Credit and Banking 29, 1997, 214–234.

[10] Fuhrer, Jeffrey C. and George R. Moore, "Monetary policy trade-offs and the correlation between nominal interest rates and real output," American Economic Review 85, 1995, 219–239.

[11] Gali, Jordi and Mark Gertler, "Inflation dynamics: a structural econometric analysis," Journal of Monetary Economics 44, 1999, 195–222.

[12] Givens, Gregory, "Optimal monetary policy design: solutions and comparisons of commitment and discretion," University of North Carolina mimeo, 2002.

[13] Hansen, Lars P. and Thomas J. Sargent, "Formulating and estimating dynamic linear rational expectations models," Journal of Economic Dynamics and Control 2, 1980, 7–46.

[14] Klein, Paul, "Using the generalized Schur form to solve a multivariate linear rational expectations model," Journal of Economic Dynamics and Control 24, 2000, 1405–1423.

[15] Kydland, Finn E. and Edward C. Prescott, "Rules rather than discretion: The inconsistency of optimal plans," Journal of Political Economy 85, 1977, 473–491.

[16] Ljungqvist, Lars and Thomas J. Sargent, Recursive macroeconomic theory, MIT Press, Cambridge, MA, 2000.

[17] McCallum, Bennett T., "Comment on Rotemberg and Woodford," Op. Cit., 1997, 355–361.

[18] McGrattan, Ellen R., "Solving the stochastic growth model by linear quadratic approximation," Journal of Business and Economic Statistics 8, 1990, 41–44.

[19] Salemi, Michael K., "Revealed preference of the Federal Reserve: using inverse-control theory to interpret the policy equation of a vector autoregression," Journal of Business and Economic Statistics 13, 1995, 419–433.

[20] Salemi, Michael K., "Econometric policy evaluation and inverse control," University of North Carolina, February, 2002.

[21] Sargent, Thomas J., Dynamic Macroeconomic Theory, Harvard University Press, Cambridge, MA, 1987.

[22] Soderlind, Paul, "Solution and estimation of RE macromodels with optimal policy," European Economic Review 43, 1999, 813–823.

[23] Svensson, Lars E.O., "Open-economy inflation targeting," Journal of International Economics 50, 2000, 155–183.

[24] Taylor, John B., "Discretion versus policy rules in practice," Carnegie-Rochester Conferences Series on Public Policy 39, 1993, 195–214.

[25] Taylor, John B., "Applying academic research on monetary policy rules: an exercise in translational economics," The Harry G. Johnston Lecture, Macro, Money, and Finance Research Group Conference, Durham University, Durham, England, revised February, 1998.

[26] Taylor, John B. (ed.), "Introduction," Monetary Policy Rules, The University of Chicago Press, Chicago, 1999.

[27] Woodford, Michael, "Control of the public debt: A requirement for price stability?," NBER Working Paper 5684, 1996.

[28] Woodford, Michael, "Interest and Prices," Princeton University Working Paper, 2002.

15 Policy Panel Contributions

1 Opening Panel on: 'Should the UK Join the Euro? The Monetary Issues'

(Edited account from the transcript by Patrick Minford)
Roger Mansfield, Director of the Business School, welcomed the participants warmly to the Panel which he invited Patrick Minford to chair.

Jacques Melitz: From a French point of view I think British entry would be wonderful: it would make the euro a bit more useful, covering a wider span of trade, and would improve the value of the currency. I think this is also the view of the other members of the European Monetary Union. From a British point of view I think entry is much more questionable, unfortunately. Three factors raise doubt about British entry from the British standpoint. One of them is that the UK gets a lot of the advantages of the euro without coming in. Now there is only one euro instead of 12 different monies when you travel on the continent. It means that you get a lot of the price transparencies also; and you get the benefits of a lot of the capital market integration without entry. Secondly, the recent change in the constitution in the Bank of England has removed the argument that monetary policy would become more responsible within the euro; the new Monetary Policy Committee has been a success. The third reason is the well-known one of the optimal currency area: that the UK would be unable to adapt the interest rate and exchange rate to its domestic conditions.

On the other hand, just very briefly I do think that there are some facts in the other direction: the evidence that monetary union does assist market integration. We have some surprisingly strong and robust results that there is remarkable impact on trade (I refer to the study by Andrew Rose of Berkeley); it's hard to understand how come the impact is as great as it is but it's got to have something to do with the fact that Monetary Union would remove a lot of uncertainty, would make it easier to make long term decisions and make it easier to trade. It is reasonable also to assume that accompanying this increase in trade comes an improvement in economic performance.

So, basically I think the issue is finely balanced form the UK viewpoint.

Casper de Vries: I would like to say that the topic of the forum is wrongly stated because there's no question but that the UK will enter the euro. The only remaining question is how. I guess the UK should therefore start by abolishing its monetary policy committee and quickly turn to targeting the monetary policy of the ECB as the Netherlands has done for 30 years. Then indeed in time we may hope that the UK can smoothly enter the Monetary Union without the disruptions we have seen in the past when the UK entered European monetary arrangements. So I would say that the discussion should focus on how we should pave the path towards entry and not do it overnight. From this perspective having an independent monetary policy for the UK is not beneficial.

Bernard Connolly: I have a quibble about the title too — this is not just about monetary issues. Looking around the room I think I am the only person here who was actually involved in the negotiations over British entry into the Exchange Rate Mechanism. And monetary issues were the only ones we were not allowed to talk about. Because the euro is not, never will be, an economic question; it's a political question, something perhaps we'll get the opportunity to come back to. It's worth making that point right from the beginning. Noone ever really thought that the euro would work or cared if it would work, it was a path towards a political unit. That's why it's there.

There are lots of monetary reasons for thinking that Britain should not abandon sterling and enter the euro. We have seen the problems on the downside clearly in a country like Argentina and we're going to see the same very soon in one of the European Union members — Portugal. When the downside begins you're in financial crisis, and it's very unlikely the EMU can cope with those financial crises without coming apart.

Let me say a little bit about trade and monetary union. The results of Rose *et al.* commented on by Jacques Melitz depend very heavily on the fact that most of the Monetary Unions studied consisted of a bunch of small island states entering into Monetary Union with a large, developed, economically and politically well-functioning, country. There is very little doubt that if you do that there are going to be favourable trade effects from that situation; including very probably the effects of the legal systems, the government systems and the political attitudes in the dependent countries. These have no relevance whatsoever to the question of whether Britain should enter the European Monetary Union.

Turning to broader political issues raised, I am in no doubt that Britain, if it joined the euro, would not end up losing just sterling but also the common law, a tremendously negative political factor for Britain.

If one looks a little bit further back to another sort of monetary union in the final third of the 19th century beginning of the 20th. The end of this monetary union — the Gold Standard — was associated with a war which was not only horrible in itself, but led to the destruction of globalisation for 50 years thereafter.

There are therefore massive risks involved in monetary union against what appear to be, even in the most favourable interpretation, very limited gains.

Michele Fratianni: I have been asked to present a mid-Atlantic position on whether the United Kingdom should join the European Monetary Union (Euroland). I interpret this position in a broad sense, that is to encompass the interests of outsiders who, while unable to vote on the euro referendum, may have an indirect influence on its outcome. In my presentation, I restrict the outsiders to three groups: owners of foreign direct investment, global investors and portfolio managers, and issuers of international currencies.

The United Kingdom is a magnet of foreign direct investment (FDI), especially from North America. Would the interests of these FDI owners be better served by the United Kingdom joining the euro or staying outside? Decisions about the location of FDI are partly microeconomic and partly strategic. Labor productivity, quality of the labor force, transportation costs, and unhampered access to a large and profitable market are among the key reasons for undertaking a project abroad. By investing in the United Kingdom a US company, among other things, buys a cheap option against the eventuality of a fortress EU. But there is more: FDI owners are also concerned that significant real appreciations of the local currency may translate into loss of competitiveness of their products. The stability of the pound relative to the euro must enter significantly into the calculus of FDI; in this sense, FDI owners' interests are aligned with those UK firms who export to the EU. Not only would FDI owners prefer the Euroization of the UK economy to the status quo, but they would want to see it take place at an exchange rate that is significantly lower than current levels (by several accounts the pound is suffering from a real appreciation, perhaps in the order of 20 per cent).

My second point relates to the benefit of using the British pound as a way to diversify portfolios. Global investors and portfolio managers would lose from the disappearance of the pound for the simple reason that opportunities for risk diversification would diminish. Since the inception of Euroland in 1999, the power of diversification using the pound and euro-denominated assets has increased. The simple correlation between the percentage changes of DM/$ and pound/$ from 1992 to 1998 was in the order of 0.50; in contrast, from 1999 to 2001, the correlation between the percentage changes of euro/$ and pound/$ has dropped to 0.10. Non-euro based investors, seeking international diversification, should have actually gained from this drop in correlation.

My final point relates to currency competition. Notwithstanding the very optimistic predictions of early euro enthusiasts — Richard Portes on this side of the Atlantic and Fred Bergsten on the other side — the euro has not nudged the dollar as the king of currencies in the world; at least not yet. A key currency like the dollar produces two distinct benefits to the issuing country. The first is seigniorage, resulting from widespread use of that currency around the world (estimates of dollars held outside the United States have ranged from 65 to 85 per cent of total currency outstanding). The second is the ability of the issuing country to consume over and above domestic production. The United States has been running current-account deficits for over 20 years; no country on earth could have duplicated this performance without the privilege of a key international currency. As the titular owner of this currency, the US government has no incentive to see a reversal of this environment. And a reversal may be more likely with the United Kingdom joining Euroland, for it would strengthen the most serious competitor to the US dollar in international transactions.

In sum, I have briefly considered the incentives of three non-UK groups in supporting the euroization of the UK economy. None of these groups can vote in the referendum; yet, they can influence its outcome. Of the three, only FDI owners would benefit from an expansion of Euroland. Global investors and the US government would gain more by the United Kingdom retaining monetary sovereignty.

Alan Walters: I'm not sure that I can add much but let me start with these estimates Jacques has mentioned that monetary union will double or triple trade. If that were true it would have had remarkable implications in particular cases. Take the splitting of the monetary union between Singapore and Malaysia in 1968; in fact Singapore's trade has far from collapsed, it has greatly increased both with the world as a whole and with Malaysia. There are many other examples; but plainly the estimates are statistical nonsense.

There's a presumption in all this discussion that EMU is here to stay. There's no sense in which anyone talks about it disappearing one way or another. Yet historically such unions have disappeared, typically lasting for some 5 or 7 years. Take Bretton Woods: it didn't really come into operation until 1960 when convertibility was re-established; by 1967 it had gone. It lasted 7 years. Not very long really. Then there was the Exchange Rate Mechanism: there are various views on when it started and finished. It began I think in 1987 and there is no doubt it finished in 1992 or certainly 1993. So I give EMU perhaps another 5 years.

There are much broader and more important issues involved. In joining EMU Britain would be joining a system which is dominated by Roman law, dominated by practices which are very different from those legal practices in the United States and Britain. EMU if we join is one step — a very big step in my book — towards the complete integration of Britain into Europe, a highly detrimental step for Britain. It seems likely that Anglo-Saxon law is far better for business than the Roman law; whether that's true or not I don't know, but one thing I am sure of. If you want to have a policy of growth and trade, there's a simple way of doing it: why don't we just unilaterally declare free trade? Leave the pound floating as now and retain our very successful monetary system, the Monetary Policy Committee and so forth. That's the way to go. Unilateral free trading is a proven system that's done very well; examples are Singapore and Hong Kong. Margaret Thatcher in her recent book comes very near to saying we should leave the EU. I think she should have gone the whole hog and said so. She's rather useful at going the whole hog and opening debate. Let the continentals make a mess of things at their will but keep Britain out of it.

1.1 Discussion:

The discussion from the floor that followed focused on

A) the political issues involved in the sort of union that had made the US single currency work well. There was general agreement that just having a monetary union was insufficient. Among the many potential sticking points in Europe that were mentioned were: language, housing (discussed by Gordon Pepper) and regulatory barriers to mobility, differences of law currently being addressed under the Corpus Juris proposals (and the recent general arrest provisions which will override habeas corpus), and the lack of a serious central fiscal authority. Bennett McCallum summarised the position succinctly in two propositions: 1. if the monetary union survives, there will be increasing integration in the direction of the US model

2. there must be considerable doubt whether the UK wants to be part of such a process. Laurence Copeland suggested that there could be a messy problem of break-up. Bernard Connolly quoted a high US official as saying: why did you people not have your monetary union like us after your civil war instead of before it?

B) the purely economic issues encapsulated in the optimal currency area literature. Here Harris Dellas, supported by Patrick Minford, suggested that the entry of the UK into EMU could be highly destabilising not only to the UK but also to the existing EMU members. Mobility on the huge scale regularly found in the US would simply cause massive political problems in Europe — indeed Bernard Connolly pointed out that it was the very fear of mobility that led to the many economic mistakes in German reunification. Dale Henderson stressed the helpful role of capital mobility in the integration and enrichment of poorer areas; nevertheless capital mobility cannot assist in the short-run stabilisation of shocks. Casper De Vries suggested that asymmetric shocks were largely the product of poor and asymmetric monetary policies; with a single money and fiscal discipline on the new state 'local authorities' there would be no serious problems of monetary asymmetry. However, as others noted, US evidence does not support the idea that asymmetric shocks wither once monetary union occurs; indeed they remain substantial, on a similar scale to existing inter-European asymmetries. Jacques Melitz stressed the Rose evidence as suggesting that with hugely higher inter-trade integration would be massively enhanced; however widespread doubts were expressed about this evidence, basically because Rose's methods cannot get around the problem of selection bias (a point made in discussion at greater length the following day by Michael Beenstock).

Bernard Connolly summed up the relative importance of politics and economics with the remark that previous single currencies had been the result of states deciding to unite and then issuing a currency rather than states issuing a joint currency and later deciding to unite. He added that while he struggled for twenty years in the Commission not to believe it, he had finally been forced to conclude that the main aim of the Commission's policies towards the UK had been to 'humiliate the nearest Anglo-Saxon nation'. The discussion was marked by an appreciation on the part of the trans-atlantic participants of the delicate politics of the UK's decision — in contrast to the traditional State Department line of 'why don't you Europeans get your act together and unite?' The idea put forward by the Labour government that the decision to join EMU should be governed by economic criteria does in the circumstances seem rather unrealistic.

2 Panel on: What Should Monetary Policy be Targeting?

2.1 Dale Henderson: What Should Monetary Policy be Targeting?[1]

2.1.1 Introduction

I interpret the question, "What should monetary policy be targeting?", to be equivalent to the somewhat less ambiguous question, "What variable should monetary policymakers choose as an intermediate target?" It is implicit in the question that the intermediate target variable should be kept 'close' to a target path, perhaps within a 'narrow' target range. Familiar examples of actual or proposed intermediate targets include measures of the money supply, nominal income, inflation, and the exchange rate. If my interpretation of the question is correct, my answer is 'nothing' or 'none'. My remarks are about what I think policymakers should do instead.

2.1.2 Target variables and target values

A discussion of policymakers' loss functions is the natural place to begin. Much effort has been expended in attempts to derive these loss functions directly from the utility functions of private agents. Considerable progress has been made, but there is still no generally agreed upon derivation nor is there likely to be anytime soon. Nonetheless, it is necessary to choose one formulation or at least a limited number of alternative formulations for policymakers' loss functions in order to rank alternative policies, including simple rules.

The period loss function of policymakers is often assumed to be a weighted sum of the squared deviations of target variables from their target values. Output and inflation are the target variables that receive

[1] These remarks were presented at a panel discussion on May 11, 2002, at the European Monetary Forum Conference in honor of Sir Alan Walters, sponsored by Cardiff University. The views expressed are solely the responsibility of the author and should not be interpreted as reflecting those of the Board of Governors of the Federal Reserve System or any other person associated with the Federal Reserve System.

the most attention.[2] The target values for these variables are potential output and a desired rate of inflation, respectively. It is supposed that the policymaker seeks to minimize the expected value of a discounted sum of period losses.

Many economists would agree that output gap variability should be in the policymakers' loss function, and, under reasonable assumptions, its inclusion can be justified by reference to the preferences of private agents. However, there is still considerable disagreement about how to define and measure potential output. The two definitions used most frequently are 'trend' output and 'flexible price' output. From today's vantage point, there have been significant errors in measuring potential output in the past. Estimation difficulties may be cause for responding less actively to changes in estimated potential output but not for making no response.

There is also wide agreement that inflation variability is undesirable, and its inclusion too can be justified by reference to the preferences of private agents. Some differences may remain among economists and policymakers regarding which measure of inflation should be stabilized. However, these differences may be more apparent than real. If what one really cares about is a measure of 'core' inflation, there are at least two possible strategies. One can choose the core inflation rate itself as the target variable and respond relatively aggressively to deviations from the target value or one can choose headline inflation as the target variable and respond less aggressively to changes in volatile prices which are not included in core inflation.

The question of what considerations should affect the choice of a target value for inflation has received more attention recently. At least over long periods, agents can anticipate that average inflation will be close to the target value. There is still considerable disagreement about what the costs of anticipated inflation really are, especially anticipated inflation no higher than five per cent. Shoe-leather costs are discounted by most analysts. More significant costs may be incurred when the tax system is not indexed, and this consideration has been incorporated in a few analyses. Also, there is the poorly understood empirical fact that the variance of inflation usually rises with its mean.

The benefits of keeping average inflation significantly above zero are now being take more seriously, partly because many countries have low inflation rates and partly because of the Japanese experience. Analysts have isolated at least two possible arguments for aiming for significantly

[2] Sometimes squared deviations of other target variables from target values or squared changes in policy instruments also appear in policymakers' loss functions, but I do not discuss these other terms here.

positive inflation. One is the old argument that a little inflation 'greases the wheels' because relative-price and real-wage changes can be made without lowering nominal prices or wages. The other, more recent argument is that the target nominal interest rate must be significantly above zero if policymakers are to have 'room' to lower the nominal interest rate, if necessary, in order to achieve their objectives.

Since the second argument may be less familiar, I discuss it in more detail. The target nominal interest rate is equal to the 'potential' real interest rate plus the target inflation rate. The potential real interest rate must be consistent with potential output, and it is well known that both are difficult to estimate. At least as difficult is estimating the response of the economy to changes in the policy instrument, which are transmitted through changes in real interest rates. If this response is relatively low, policymakers must choose a relatively high target inflation rate and associated target nominal interest rate in order to generate a given amount of stabilization potential.

The appropriate choice of an inflation target is considerably more difficult than picking a 'nice round number'. This task involves technical analysis. The best choice for a target rate of inflation may change over time both because estimates of the real interest and of the interest-rate responsiveness of the economy based on given data may change as methods improve and because these crucial magnitudes may change over time. It follows that policymakers should not make immutable commitments to particular target values. Rather, they should choose target values based on analysis, explain the general methodology used, and make clear that the same or improved methodology might lead to different choices in the future. Once these considerations are made clear, choosing an inflation target may not seem so much easier than arriving at an estimate of potential output.

2.1.3 Aggregation of preferences and forecasts

There are apparent differences among countries regarding how decisions are made. It is not yet clear whether these differences have important implications for which decisions get made. But it seems clear that they significantly affect how the reasons for decisions are communicated.

In most countries, decisions are made by a group, in a few by a very small group, in several by a medium-sized group, and in a few by a large group. The smaller the group, the easier it might be to get agreement not only on the value of the instrument but also on a group forecast and a group weighting of target variables, or to briefly summarize any remaining disagreements. The group can then decide how much it wants to reveal about how it reaches its decisions. A clear example of what is possible with a medium-sized group is the procedure followed by the nine-person Monetary Policy Committee in the UK. It has given some indication of the relative weight it places on output variability; it has stated that it intends to act so that its inflation forecast for eight quarters ahead is equal to the target value. It decides on a forecast and on an instrument value. Then it makes public this information and a record of its deliberations.

In contrast, when the group is large, getting agreement on a group forecast and a group weighting of targets might be more challenging. The group might choose to do no more than get agreement (sometimes not unanimous agreement) on the value of its instrument and a very general statement about the near-term prospects for the economy. Therefore, it might be more difficult to determine whether there are differences within the group on forecasts, on weighting, or on both, unless individual members are required to disclose their views.

It has been argued that an intermediate target variable is useful because policymakers are more likely to be able to hit such a target and can, therefore, be made accountable more easily. It is widely known that hitting an intermediate target is suboptimal in many circumstances. Having an intermediate target does not seem to be helpful no matter what the size of the group. The smaller the group, the more likely it is that its views about relationship between actual target variables and instrument settings can be made clear, making an intermediate target variable redundant. With a large group, members can vote for the same intermediate target value for different reasons making policy less transparent and true accountability more difficult.

Not much attention has been devoted to the question of what role independent staff forecasts should play in the policymaking process and when they should be made public, if at all. Some policymaking groups make all the major decisions regarding the forecast put together by the staff, so there are no independent staff forecasts. Others make use of the staff forecast as an input, perhaps the primary input, when constructing their own forecasts. Still others use an independent staff forecast as a starting point for their discussions and do not attempt to reach agreement on a group forecast of any variables. Some in the last group make public the forecasts of individual members for a few variables.

2.1.4 Instruments

In practice, the (primary) instrument of monetary policy in most countries is a short-term nominal interest rate or quantity variable that is kept very close to a particular value for at least the period between policy meetings.[3] It is important to study the implications of using an interest rate as the instrument because so many policymakers do so.

At one time the choice of monetary policy instrument was considered to be very important. The influential paper by Poole (1970) has 'choice of monetary policy instruments' in its title. Poole generalizes Bailey (1962) who concludes that if the policymakers must choose between keeping constant the money supply or 'the interest rate' that affects aggregate demand, they should keep the money supply constant when aggregate demand shocks are 'more important' than money demand shocks and *vice versa.* However, this prescription is better viewed as a prescription for the choice among intermediate targets rather than for the choice among instruments because the period being analyzed is long enough for the interest rate to have a significant effect on aggregate demand, at least a quarter and probably longer.

It has become standard to view the choice of instrument as the choice between, for example, an overnight interest rate and a quantity, such as non-borrowed reserves, which the policymaker can control quite closely and which affects short-term market rates. From this perspective it is clear that the choice of instrument is not nearly as important as the choice of how to change the instrument in response to changes in the economy.

However, the choice of instrument may not be completely inconsequential for at least two reasons. First, the policymaker might be concerned about variability in the short rate on non-meeting days. This variability is lower when the short rate is the instrument because shifts in reserve demand are accommodated. Second, the policymaker might be concerned about variability resulting from changes on meeting days. It has been argued that policymakers are more likely to be 'too concerned' about meeting-day interest variability when a rate rather than a quantity is the instrument. This concern has been suggested as one of the explanations for why the Federal Reserve switched to a quantity instrument for about two years after October 1979.

Policymakers affect aggregate demand by changing (expected) real interest rates for medium-run maturities. At times, policymakers may not have changed their instruments (interest rate or quantity) by enough to change real rates in the appropriate direction and by 'enough'. The exact consequences of the failure to do so depends on whether private

---

[3] Of course, in many, if not all countries, there are also secondary instruments, such as rates at special discount facilities, penalty borrowing rates, and reserve requirements, but these instruments are much less important and are not discussed in these remarks.

expectations are forward- or backward-looking, but they are undesirable in either case. Recently, Taylor (1993) and Henderson and McKibbin (1993) among others have emphasized the importance of changing the short rate by more than current inflation changes if current inflation is in the rule.

2.1.5 Roles for rules

Many have suggested the use of 'simple rules'. A few propose following a particular rule 'as closely as possible'. Others argue for what Bernanke and Mishkin (1997) call 'constrained discretion' under which policymakers must not deviate from a particular rule 'too far' or 'too long' except for 'good reason'. A third group, including Taylor (1993), believes in what I call 'rule-informed discretion' under which the implications of rules are treated as useful information but no rule need be taken as a constraint. Finally, there are some who argue for ignoring rules completely and for choosing instrument values so that forecasts of target variables conditional on available information and the instrument values minimize policymakers' losses.

Simple rules may be postulated or estimated. Some consider it to be a plus for a postulated rule if it is 'data-consistent', that is, if it 'approximates' actual policy. Estimated rules and 'data-consistent' postulated rules policy can be used to answer questions like what would happen if the economic 'structure' and the policymakers' rule stayed unchanged but the pattern of disturbances changed. It is not clear that they should be preferred to other rules on normative grounds. If these rules fit the data during a relatively long period in which the pattern of disturbances is considered to be 'typical' and outcomes are regarded as 'good' there might be some argument for urging their further use. However, the first question that arises is, "Good, relative to what?".

Some argue that so little is known about the economy that attempts to stabilize it using current information and forecasts are ineffective at best and may be counterproductive. Often they have suggested following one or another (simple) rule. Among the most familiar are rules involving possibly strict, but usually flexible, stabilization of a single intermediate target variable or a simple function of target variables that can be viewed as an intermediate target because it is not explicitly derived from a loss function.[4] Variables such as money growth, nominal income growth, or inflation are stabilized around a desired value, or variables such as the

[4] When the current values of intermediate target variables cannot be observed, forecasts are used instead. In these remarks, I do not discuss the many important issues that must be addressed when using forecasts.

money supply, nominal income, or the price level are stabilized around a desired growth path.[5] During the last decade, two-gap rules involving stabilization of a simple function of output and inflation gaps have become popular.[6] One possible reason is that such rules relate the actual policy instrument to the actual target variables, albeit to simple functions of them. It is well known that using intermediate targets puts possibly important limitations on the information that policymakers can use in choosing their instrument settings.

Few proponents argue for following rules slavishly. Some have proposed 'escape clauses' or called for 'constrained discretion'. Not all skeptics argue for ignoring rules completely. In my view, many favor what I call 'rule-informed discretion' under which the implications of some rules are regarded as useful information. These implications are compared with the policy under consideration, and attempts are made to understand any 'significant' differences. Then a decision is made about whether to make changes.

It seems clear that several simple rules would have yielded better outcomes than actual policy in some extreme situations like the Great Depression. However, Japanese monetary policy in the first half of the 90s suggests that rules are not always a cure all. Actual Japanese policy during that period was more expansionary than the policy implied by Taylor's parameterization of a two-gap rule.[7] However, it might have been better if policy had been even more expansionary. The lessons learned from extreme situations may make it less likely that they will recur whether or not a rule is being followed, the Japanese experience notwithstanding. The operational questions are, "Exactly which rules, if any, are worthy of attention and just how much weight should be placed on their implications?".

Of course, rules are plural. There have been many efforts to determine how rules measure up against one another and against policies based on more information, including optimal policy. A popular way to make such comparisons is to conduct simulations of econometric or cali-

[5] In the "Transparency" section below I argue that even policymakers who refer to themselves as money supply or inflation targeters put some weight on a measure of economic slack such as the output gap.

[6] See, for example, Bryant, Hooper, and Mann (1993), Henderson and McKibbin (1993), and Taylor (1993). Two-gap rules are called combination policies in the first two references. They are now usually referred to as Taylor rules, perhaps since Taylor suggested a set of (round number) parameters for which a two-gap rule 'closely' approximates actual policy during the period 1987-1992. Svensson (2002) critiques two-gap rules.

[7] See Ahearne *et al.* (2002).

brated models using disturbances implied by the models. It has become common to treat estimated or calibrated models as being 'structural', assuming either explicitly or implicitly that the Lucas critique can be ignored. Conclusions may differ across models, so analysts such as Bryant, Hooper, and Mann (1993) have considered several models. All models have shortcomings, but some have more than others. Therefore, it is useful to know not only how many models yield a given ranking but also which ones. Levin, Wieland, and Williams (1999) find that not much is lost by following simple rules rather than rules based on complete information. However, there is not wide agreement on either the ranking of simple rules or what is lost by following such rules rather than policies based on more information.

Rules are often compared with one another and to actual policy in historical periods like the Great Depression and the Great Inflation in the United States as, for example, in McCallum (2000). The rules may be postulated, optimal within a class of simple rules in econometric models of another period, or estimated using data from another period. They are evaluated on the basis either of how 'sensible' a policy they imply or of how they perform in one or more econometric models of the period. It has been conventional to use data that incorporates most, if not all, available revisions both for the historical period and for any estimation period. Recently, it has been shown that using 'real time' data, data available in the historical period, instead of revised data can significantly affect conclusions. Using 'vintage' data, as recommended by Orphanides (2003) in a series of papers, puts the rule and actual policy on the same footing as regards information and is now widely considered to be an important refinement.

2.1.6 Transparency

It is often argued that following simple rules increases transparency. Policymakers can state the intermediate target rule that they intend to follow. Whether they have followed this rule can be determined without much difficulty.

On the contrary, following simple rules may well decrease transparency. It is easy to make the case that even policymakers who say they are following simple rules, such as money-supply or inflation targeting, put some weight on a measure of economic slack such as the output gap. The Bundesbank often allowed German money growth to go outside its target range. Also, inflation targeters incorporate 'escape clauses' or promise to return inflation to its target value only over a medium-run period, sometimes of fixed length.

It is very difficult to communicate precisely relative concern about two target variables by choosing the parameters of a simple intermediate-target rule. Private agents are confronted with a formidable inference problem because the parameters must be chosen to reflect 'average' experience. Furthermore, attempting to communicate in this way puts a straitjacket on monetary policy. Some shocks may not be covered by escape clauses. The appropriate period over which to return money growth to its target range or inflation to its target value varies with the type and size of the shock. In addition, policymakers have less incentive to make clear their views about how their policy instruments affect their target variables.

In my view, transparency is increased not by following a simple rule but by providing a 'substantial' amount of information about the policymakers' objectives (their loss functions), their opinions about how the economy works, and their views about what shocks the economy has experienced or will soon experience. Of course, the benefits of increasing transparency in this way must be weighed against any costs that might be incurred if policymakers are not constrained by a simple rule. Over the last decade or so, policymakers have revealed much more information than had been expected. Most observers believe that this change has yielded net benefits and that revealing even more information would yield further gains.

2.1.7 Accounting for the unknown

The unknown comes in two flavors: what we know we do not know and what we do not know we do not know. If all disturbances had discoverable distributions, we could parameterize the unknown, reducing it to simply uncertainty. Then, under some other strong assumptions, we could discover exactly how the economy works, the true 'data generating process'. Under these unlikely circumstances, evaluating rules relative to one another and to policies based on more information would be a technically difficult but manageable task.

For many reasons, discovering exactly how the economy works is (almost certainly) impossible. The pattern of disturbances changes unpredictably over time, so there will never be a 'large sample' from which to make inferences. Also, economies are affected by unforeseen contingencies. One way of dealing with the unknown is the 'robust control' approach: if you know the worst situation but not the probability of its occurring, choose the policy that is best in the worst situation. The fact that we cannot know what we do not know weakens the case for commitment to a rule, even to one with escape clauses for foreseeable contingencies.

2.1.8 Summing up

It is probably best not to make any use of simple rules in monetary policymaking. At most there may be some case for 'rule-informed discretion' under which simple rules are considered, but, in contrast to 'constrained discretion', there is no commitment to any one rule, not even to one with escape clauses for foreseeable contingencies. Considering rules is one way to increase the chances of avoiding some of the big mistakes of the past. However, we are still far from a definitive answer to the key questions of which rules to credit and by how much.

BIBLIOGRAPHY

[1] Ahearne, Alan, Joseph Gagnon, Jane Haltmaier, and Steve Kamin, "Preventing Deflation: Lessons From Japan's Experience in the 1990s," International Finance Discussion Papers No. 729, Federal Reserve Board, 2002.

[2] Bailey, Martin J., National Income and the Price Level, 1st edition, McGraw-Hill, 1962.

[3] Bernanke, Ben, and Frederic Mishkin, "Inflation Targeting: A New Framework for Monetary Policy?", Journal of Economic Perspectives, 11 (Spring 1997), pp. 97–116.

[4] Bryant, Ralph C., Peter Hooper, and Catherine L. Mann, Evaluating Policy Regimes: New Research in Empirical Macroeconomics, Brookings Institution, 1993.

[5] Henderson, Dale W., and Warwick J. McKibbin, "A Comparison of Some Basic Monetary Policy Regimes for Open Economies: Implications of Different Degrees of Instrument Adjustment and Wage Persistence," Carnegie-Rochester Conference Series on Public Policy, 39 (November 1993), pp. 221–317.

[6] Levin, Andrew, Volker Wieland, and John C. Williams, "Robustness of Simple Monetary Rules under Model Uncertainty," in Monetary Policy Rules, J.B. Taylor, ed., University of Chicago Press for NBER, 1999.

[7] McCallum, Bennett T., "Alternative Monetary Policy Rules: A Comparison with Historical Settings for the United States, the

United Kingdom, and Japan." Federal Reserve Bank of Richmond Economic Quarterly, 86, 1 (Winter 2000), pp. 49–79.

[8] Orphanides, Athanasios, "The Quest for Prosperity Without Inflation," Journal of Monetary Economics, 2003, pp. 633–663.

[9] Poole, William, "Optimal Choice of Monetary Policy Instruments in a Simple Stochastic Macro Model," The Quarterly Journal of Economics, 84(2), pp. 197–216, 1970.

[10] Svensson, Lars E.O., "What is Wrong with Taylor Rules? Using Judgement in Monetary Policy through Targeting Rules," NBER Working Paper No. 9421, December 2002.

[11] Taylor, John B., "Discretion Versus Policy Rules in Practice," Carnegie-Rochester Conference Series on Public Policy, 39 (November 1993), pp. 195–214.

2.2 Bennett T. McCallum: What Should Monetary Policy be Targeting?

Unfortunately, I need to start with a word on terminology. What I am going to be talking about is the variables that enter on the right-hand side of a policy rule in the form of deviations from desired values — such as inflation and the output gap in a Taylor rule. This is not the way in which the word is used when speaking of "interest rate targeting" in the context of operating procedures. Furthermore, my terminology also differs from that of Lars Svensson (2002), who will only use the word "target" for variables that enter central bank (CB) objective functions. Lars has made many strong statements regarding the desirability of his terminology. I think it doesn't make much difference as long as one is clear about what he's doing, but in self-defense I'm working on a paper with Nelson in which we take up, and dispute, most of Lars' major claims in his recent 68-page paper on this and related subjects (Svensson, 2002), which is forthcoming in the *Journal of Economic Literature.*

The main contenders for target variables in my sense are inflation, the output gap, an average of the two as in the original Taylor rule (and previously promoted by Henderson and McKibbin (1993) and others), nominal income growth, nominal exchange rate depreciation, and level versions of the first, fourth, and fifth of these. I will show some results that pertain to the first four only. I am not going to present quarterly root-mean-square error values of the type that has been featured in the several papers that Edward Nelson and I, or I by myself, have been doing over the last 5 years (e.g., McCallum and Nelson, 1999). Instead I want to show some plots of actual instrument settings in comparison with rule-specified instrument settings over the period 1965–1998, the plots coming from McCallum (2000). This is the type of comparison that Taylor (1993, 1999) introduced and which was quickly picked up in the UK by Alison Stuart (1996). It has advantages and disadvantages; the advantages are that the comparisons are model-free and they focus on big, long-lasting policy errors, not the tiny departures from optimality that show up in the other type of study.

Let's start with a Taylor rule for the UK, specified as rule (1) in Table 1. The plot in Figure 1 indicates that policy was much too loose during the 1970s, but says that it was too tight over 1983–1987, and just about right ever since. Now I want to contrast that with the results of the rule (2) that I used to promote — e.g., McCallum (1993) — which uses a monetary base instrument and a nominal GDP growth target variable. Its plot in Figure 2, by sharp contrast, shows policy to have been much too loose during 1983–1989. Ex post, I think most would agree that this is the more correct conclusion since UK inflation rose much too high in the late 1980s and policy didn't really get straightened out until after inflation targeting was instituted in 1992. The point of this comparison is not to promote monetary base rules — I'm not concerned with that issue at present. But I am going to use comparisons across alternative target values that are embedded in base rules, rather than interest rate rules, because they seem much more reliable and there is not time for both.

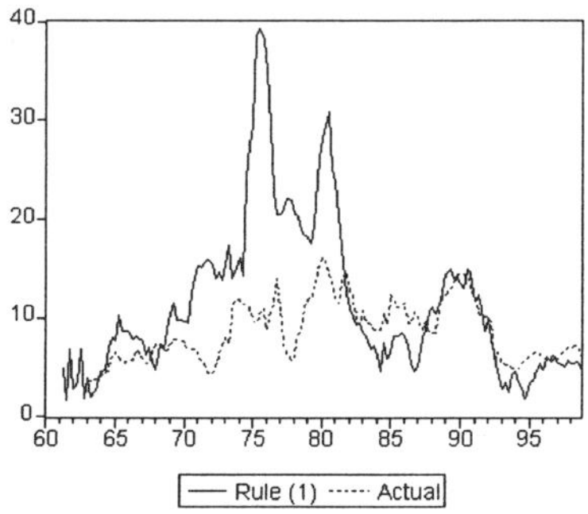

Figure 1: UK Interest Rate, Actual and Rule (1)

So let's compare base rules for (i) nominal GDP growth, (ii) the Henderson–McKibbon–Taylor hybrid target variable, and (iii) pure inflation targeting. There are three plots for the UK shown in Figures 2–4. They all tell the same story — policy much too loose before 1991,

1) (Taylor Rule)

$$R_t = \bar{r} + \Delta p_t^a + 0.5\,(\Delta p_t^a - \pi^*) + 0.5\tilde{y}_t$$

2) (McCallum Rule)

$$\Delta b_t = \Delta x^* - \Delta v_t^a + 0.5\,(\Delta x^* - \Delta x_{t-1})$$

3) (Interest Rate Instrument, GDP Growth Target)

$$R_t = \bar{r} + \Delta p_t^a + 0.5\,(\Delta x^* - \Delta x_{t-1})$$

4) (Hybrid Rule)

$$\Delta b_t = \Delta x^* - \Delta v_t^a - 0.5 h_t$$

$$h_t = (\Delta p_t^a - \pi^* + \tilde{y}_t)$$

5) (Inflation Target, Interest Instrument)

$$R_t = \bar{r} + \Delta p_t^a + 0.5\,(\Delta p_t^a - \pi^*)$$

6) (Inflation Target, Base Instrument)

$$\Delta b_t = \Delta x^* - \Delta v_t^a - 0.5\,(\Delta p_t^a - \pi^*)$$

Variable definitions, details reported in McCallum (2000):

R_t = nominal interest rate in period t

Δp_t = inflation rate (^{a} denotes average over previous 4 quarters)

π^* = target value of inflation rate

$\tilde{y}_t$ = output gap

x_t = log of nominal income

v_t = log of base velocity (^{a} denotes average of previous 4 years)

$\bar{r}$ = average real interest rate

Table 1: Specification of Alternative Monetary Policy Rules

just slightly too loose over 1991–1998. The main difference is that the nominal GDP growth target gives choppier signals, because it includes the growth rate of real GDP, which is itself quite choppy.

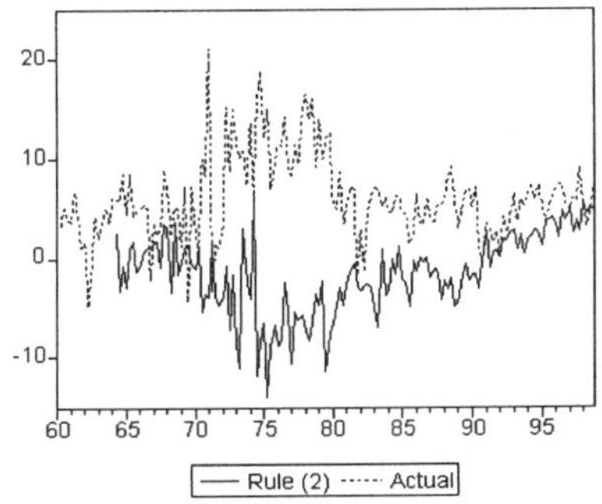

Figure 2: UK Base Growth, Actual and Rule (2)

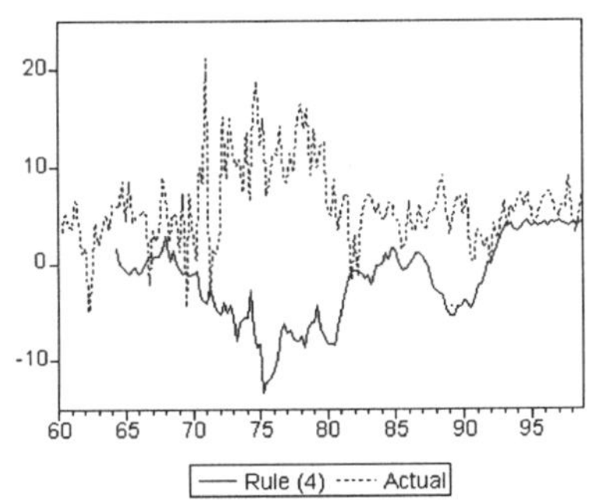

Figure 3: UK Base Growth, Actual and Rule (4)

For the US we have a similar situation: the rules plotted in Figures 5–7 yield the same principal conclusion: policy too loose over 1965–1987 and 1990–1993; too tight over 1994–1995.

For Japan, the hybrid rule in Figure 9 performs somewhat better than the other two (Figures 8 and 10) in the sense that it indicates more strongly that monetary policy has been too restrictive in recent years — since 1992 and most of the time since 1990. But the reason for this superiority is that my measure of the output gap gets quite large by 1998 — and would be huge today. There is, however, much dispute over that measure. And I think that this points to a significant disadvantage of

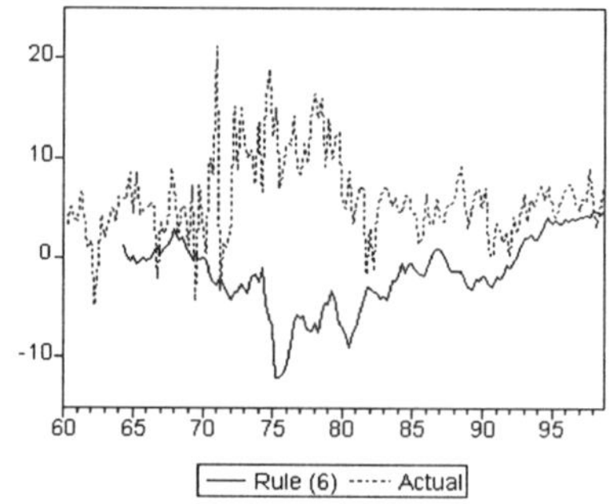

Figure 4: UK Base Growth, Actual and Rule (6)

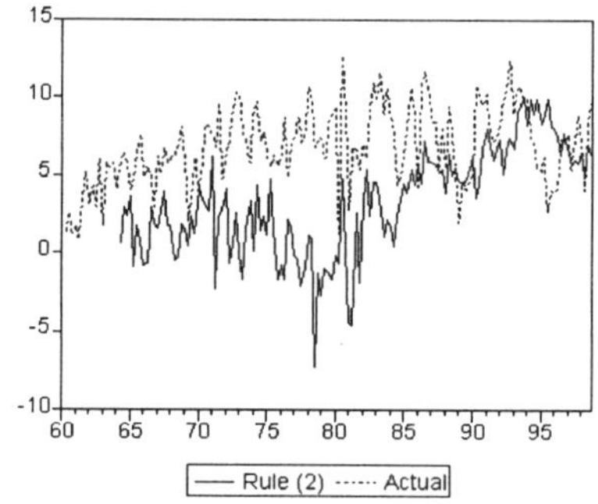

Figure 5: US Base Growth, Actual and Rule (2)

rules that respond to measured output gaps, namely, that there is not even any agreement as to what the correct concept of potential output is, much less how to measure it. One of my favorite lists is the variety of names that are used for this reference value: potential output, capacity output, NAIRU output, trend output, natural rate output, market clearing output, and flexible-price output. And there are dozens of "detrending" procedures. Now, if the CB uses the wrong concept it can make very big mistakes, as Orphanides (2000) has stressed. So I am inclined to stay away from rules that rely upon measures of the level of the gap.

As between nominal GDP growth and pure inflation targeting, I continue to slightly favor the former, as it represents a way to bring in real output considerations (with less danger than using the level of the output gap). The choppiness problem revealed in Figures 2, 5, and 8 can

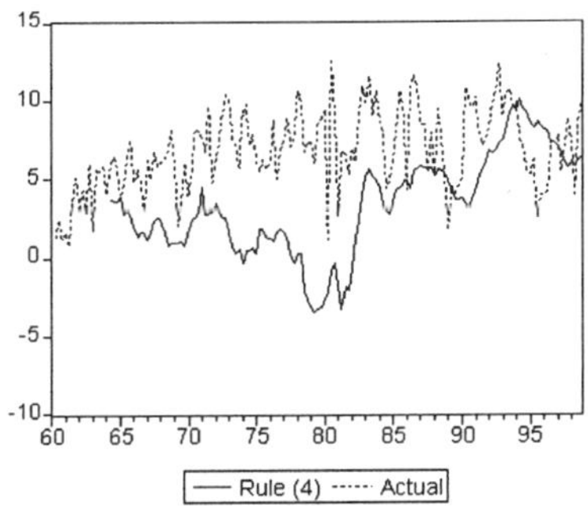

Figure 6: US Base Growth, Actual and Rule (4)

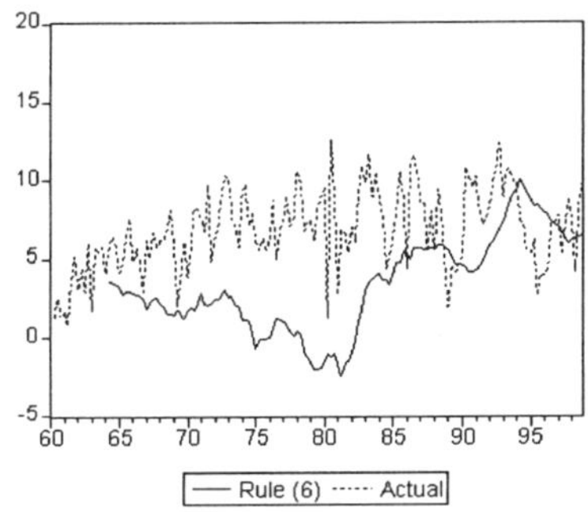

Figure 7: US Base Growth, Actual and Rule (6)

be overcome simply by averaging over four recent quarters — as is done for inflation with the Taylor rule. But I think inflation targeting is an attractive possibility, also.

What about exchange rates? I don't have pictures for rules with an exchange rate target variable — but I think that Figures 2–10 are relevant even to this issue. For the UK, the too-loose policy over the late 1980s can plausibly be attributed to the unofficial "shadowing of the Deutsche Mark" that was in place. [For a discussion of the period that emphasizes the mistake of this "shadowing" policy, see Walters (1990, pp. 102–113)]. And with respect to Japan, I believe that one significant reason why the Bank of Japan has been too restrictive ever since 1990 (up to a few months ago) was a desire to keep the yen from depreciating. That desire stemmed in part, of course, from a misguided wish not to offend the US Treasury (before the present administration).

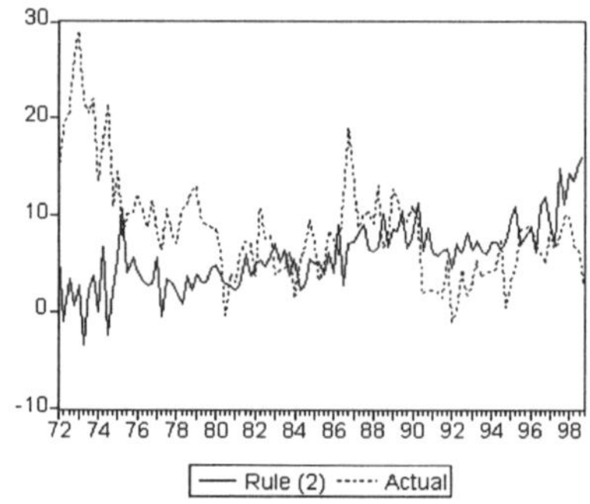

Figure 8: Japan Base Growth, Actual and Rule (2)

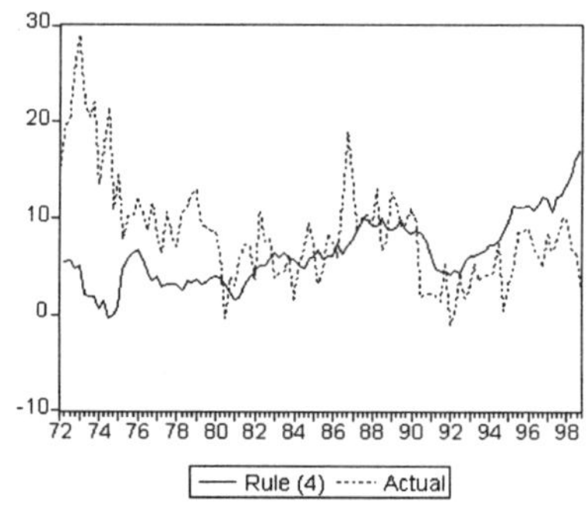

Figure 9: Japan Base Growth, Actual and Rule (4)

This experience seems to me to be typical of "international cooperation" in actual practice.

More objectively, my charts indicate that Japanese monetary policy was too loose over 1986–87, when the US government wanted Japanese demand to grow faster and wished to prevent the US dollar from depreciating. The resulting too-loose policy in Japan accommodated the asset price explosion that led to a sharp monetary tightening in 1990, which helped to start the slump that has gone on ever since. Basically, a combination of international experience and optimal-currency-area theory suggests that for some groups of countries it makes sense to have a common currency. For the rest, the exchange rate should float — i.e., should not be a target variable.

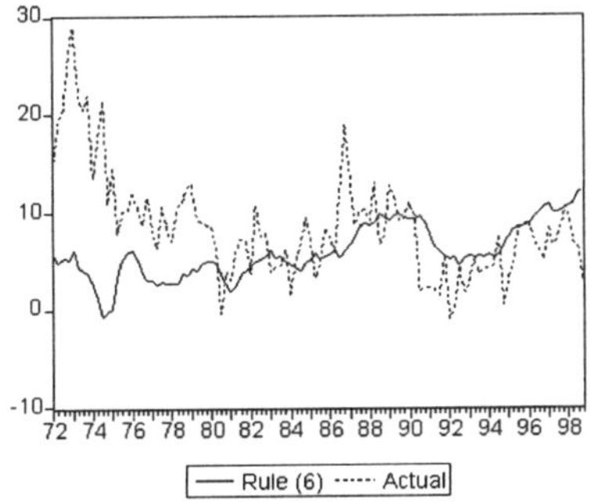

Figure 10: Japan Base Growth, Actual and Rule (6)

BIBLIOGRAPHY

[1] Henderson, Dale W., and Warwick J. McKibbin, "An Assessment of Some Basic Monetary Policy Regime Pairs: Analytical and Simulation Results from Simple Multiregion Macroeconomic Models," in *Evaluating Policy Regimes: New Research in Empirical Macroeconomics*, ed. by R.C. Bryant, P. Hooper, and C.L. Mann. Brookings Institution, 1993.

[2] McCallum, Bennett T., "Specification and Analysis of a Monetary Policy Rule for Japan," Bank of Japan *Monetary and Economic Studies* 11 (November 1993), 1–45.

[3] McCallum, Bennett T., "Alternative Monetary Policy Rules: A Comparison with Historical Settings for the United States, the United Kingdom, and Japan." Federal Reserve Bank of Richmond *Economic Quarterly*, 86, 1 (Winter 2000), 49–79.

[4] McCallum, Bennett T., and Edward Nelson, "Nominal Income Targeting in an Open-Economy Optimizing Model," *Journal of Monetary Economics* 43 (June 1999), 553–578.

[5] Orphanides, Athanasios, "The Quest for Prosperity Without Inflation," European Central Bank Working Paper No. 15, 2000.

[6] Stuart, Alison, "Simple Monetary Policy Rules," *Bank of England Quarterly Bulletin* 36 (August 1996), 281–287.

[7] Svensson, Lars E.O., "What is Wrong with Taylor Rules? Using Judgement in Monetary Policy through Targeting Rules," NBER Working Paper No. 9421, December 2002.

[8] Taylor, John B., "Discretion Versus Policy Rules in Practice," *Carnegie-Rochester Conference Series on Public Policy* 39 (November 1993), 195–214.

[9] Taylor, John B., "A Historical Analysis of Monetary Policy Rules," in *Monetary Policy Rules*, ed. by J.B. Taylor. University of Chicago Press for NBER, 1999.

[10] Walters, Alan, *Sterling in Danger: The Economic Consequences of Pegged Exchange Rates*. Fontana, 1990.

2.3 Michael Beenstock: What Should Monetary Policy be Targeting in Israel?

A great and heated debate is underway in Israel regarding the terms of reference of the Monetary Policy Committee, which is soon to be established. The "right" argue that the sole target should be price stability. The "left" say that unemployment and growth should be targeted too. I shall state my view at the end of these remarks. But first, we have to understand the specific context of the conduct of monetary policy in Israel. Indeed, I do not think that what works in one country or time period will necessarily work in another country or time period. The context matters.

In 1985 the Economic Stabilization Programme, designed by the late Michael Bruno,[8] reduced inflation from over 400 per cent to about 20 per cent. A fiscal deficit of 15 per cent of GDP was reduced to less than 5 per cent, and a fixed exchange rate was adopted in the belief that the exchange rate rather than the money supply is the relevant nominal anchor for Israel.[9] However, inflation remained stuck at 15–20 per cent and the shekel had to be devalued periodically.

In 1991 Jacob Frenkel replaced Michael Bruno as Governor at the Bank of Israel[10]. Frenkel too believed that the exchange rate should serve as a nominal anchor. However, he introduced a "diagonal" exchange rate mechanism in which the central peg crawled within pre-announced bounds. This was the beginning of informal inflation targeting in Israel because, according to PPP, the rate of crawl plus the rate of inflation

---

[8] See M. Bruno, Crisis, Stabilization and Economic Reform, Clarendon Press, Oxford, 1993.

[9] See M. Bruno, "High inflation and the nominal anchors of an open economy", in H. Barkai, S. Fischer and N. Liviatan (eds), Monetary Theory and Thought, Macmillan, London.

[10] He resigned in December 1999, when he was replaced by David Klein.

abroad should have determined the rate of inflation, if indeed the exchange rate served as a nominal anchor. But it didn't. In the meanwhile monetary aggregates suffered from benign neglect. Inflation continued to remain stuck at around 12 per cent despite the fact that the fiscal deficit as a percentage of GDP was persistently smaller than the rate of economic growth.

Many economists argued (me included) that the exchange rate in Israel is a poor nominal anchor. The main reason for this is that the equilibrium real exchange rate was not stable. This was especially the case during the 1990s when the economy absorbed a million immigrants from the former USSR on a population base of 4.8 million in 1989. The critics argued that because the demand for M1 in Israel is remarkably stable, M1 should serve as the nominal anchor instead of the exchange rate.

In 1994 Frenkel was finally persuaded by his monetarist critics. The exchange rate mechanism was made more flexible by progressively widening its bands, and the shekel began to float. Since 1997 it has floated freely. Money supply replaced the exchange rate as the nominal anchor. The BOI sets its rate of interest a month in advance in the light of monetary developments, inflation, and market based expectations of inflation[11] over the next 12 months.

Inflation began to fall during the second half of the 1990s. By 2001 it was almost zero.[12] The new monetary regime appears to have done the trick. Many leading Israeli economists[13] had claimed that Israel was endemically prone to inflation, and could not be cured. They were proven wrong.

Since 1992 the government took to announcing inflation targets for the following year. In 2000 the inflation target (band) was for 3 years ahead. There is no econometric evidence that these targets have made any direct difference to inflation. However, they have made an indirect difference. A recent study[14] shows that the BOI raises interest rates when expected inflation exceeds the target rate of inflation, which in turn

---

[11] Because of widespread indexation in the bond market, the implied expected inflation (which has a high profile in the daily press) can be estimated.

[12] In 2002 inflation has increased largely as a result of the deteriorating security situation.

[13] For example, N. Liviatan and R. Melnick, "Inflation and disinflation by steps in Israel", in L. Leiderman (ed.) Inflation and Disinflation in Israel, Bank of Israel, 2001, pp. 414–449.

[14] D. Elkayam, "A model of monetary policy under inflation targeting: the case of Israel", The Economic Quarterly, 49: 30–45, 2002 (Hebrew).

reduces inflation. Another study[15] shows that the BOI raises interest rates in response to expected inflation, actual inflation and the rate of exchange rate depreciation, but it lowers interest rates if unemployment increases.

Since 1994 the main preoccupation of BOI has been to eliminate inflation. The real economy was almost ignored. In the debate about the MPC's terms of reference the BOI is on the "right". My own view used to be with the "right". The elimination of inflation required single-mindedness. There was no room for the luxury of fine-tuning the real economy. However, once the inflation psychology has been eliminated the BOI can afford to be more flexible. Its main remit should be price stability, but it should consider, where possible, the real economy in pursuing this remit. Because monetary policy affects the economy with a lag, the BOI can allow some intertemporal trade-off between inflation and unemployment. I interpret the Fed's monetary policy in this way.

The inflationary psychology has not yet disappeared. We have only experienced two years of price stability. In fact, it is not surprising that after three decades of inflation we are still neurotic about inflation. Many contracts continue to be index-linked. It took almost a decade of inflation before indexation of commercial contracts became widespread towards the end of the 1970s. If price stability continues, the inflation psychology will disappear. We will know this when indexation spontaneously disappears. When it does, we will be able to behave like the Fed. In the meanwhile, the BOI must continue to be "right". However, the terms of reference of the MPC should be flexible enough to allow BOI to behave like the Fed, when the time is right.

2.4 Gordon Pepper: What Should UK Monetary Policy be Targeting?

First, whereas I am an advocate of monetary base control I am not in favour of targeting M0. A distinction must be made between supply-side control of the money stock and attempting demand-side control of M0 by administering alterations in interest rates.

If demand-side control is to be attempted, I am an advocate of attempting to control broad rather than narrow money. The stock of broad money can be different from people's demand for money. The disequilibrium has causal effects. In contrast, narrow money is very largely demand determined, because people can switch between sight and term

[15] G. Bufman and O. Bar-Efrat, "The Bank of Israel's reaction function: Can interest rate changes be predicted?" The Economic Quarterly, 49: 46-60, 2002 (Hebrew).

deposits. Narrow money is merely an indicator that is useful only some of the time. Buoyant growth of narrow money when interest rates are rising is powerful evidence that monetary policy has not been tightened sufficiently. Sluggish growth when interest rates are falling is evidence that monetary policy has not been eased sufficiently. At other times narrow money can be a misleading indicator.

Second, there can be serious problems with distortion to the data for monetary aggregates, for example from the Bank's chosen mechanism of control (for instance the 'corset' on the growth of banks' interest-bearing-eligible liabilities in the 1970s), and from financial innovation. If all the aggregates are behaving in the same way the message from them is clear. If they are not, careful analysis usually indicates which aggregate is reliable and which is not. Occasionally all of them may be distorted and reliance has to be placed on other factors. My overall conclusions from experience in the 1970s and 1980s are attached below.

A subject that is particularly topical at the moment is what attention should be paid to the behaviour of asset prices. When people expect asset prices to rise they borrow from banks to purchase the assets. Suppose, for example, that there has been a recession and an associated fall in the stock market. As the recession comes to an end, the stock market recovers. In these circumstances a company is quite likely to make a bid for another company and to finance the take-over by borrowing from a bank. The stock market rises when the bid is announced. When the bid goes through, holders of shares in the company being taken over receive bank deposits in exchange for their shares. They may well subsequently reinvest the proceeds in other shares. Such a reinvestment does not destroy the bank deposit, because the seller of the shares in which the reinvestment is being made receives the deposit in exchange for the shares. For example if someone switches out of a bank deposit into BP, the seller of BP receives the deposit. If this person reinvests the money in Marks & Spencer, the person who sells Marks & Spencer receives the deposit. And so on. Each time the reinvestment takes place the market tends to rise. The initial credit transaction has a one-off effect on the stock market whereas the consequential increase in the money supply has a continuing effect. The result of the buoyant monetary growth is asset-price inflation.

If the borrowing to acquire financial assets persists, the continuing monetary effects compound. The result of a borrowing boom can easily be a bubble in asset prices. Eventually the bubble bursts and asset prices fall.

Whilst a bubble is building up the rise in asset prices stimulates the economy, because of wealth and other effects, etc., and the process goes into reverse when asset prices fall. The economy is a little more unstable, because the boom is inflated and the recession is deepened. The position becomes serious when a downswing is no longer symmetrical with the preceding upswing. This happens when the value of collateral in general falls below the value of the loans secured. Forced selling of assets then occurs. The law of supply and demand reverses. Falling prices produces more rather than fewer sellers. The result is debt-deflation.

How can debt-deflation be avoided? Prevention is better than cure. The difficulty is that there is no easy solution once asset-price inflation has been allowed to gather momentum. This is because the real rate of interest for financial transactions can diverge sharply from that for transactions in goods and services. The real rate is the nominal rate less expectations of inflation. Real rates diverge if expectations of asset-price inflation differ from expectations of product-price inflation. This will be the case when financial markets are rising at a time when product-price inflation is muted. If nominal interest rates are set at a level appropriate for expenditure on goods and services, very low or negative real rates for financial transactions encourages further acquisition of assets. If nominal rates are set at the level needed to stop asset price-inflation and remain there for long the impact on the real economy will be severe.

I have two suggestions to make. The first is a plea for early action. The central bank must not raise interest rates by too little too late. Momentum must not be allowed to build up. Second, if momentum has been allowed to build up the remedy is shock treatment. Interest rates should be raised sharply until the stock market falls, and probably one more time. The aim should be to break expectations of a continuing rise in asset prices. After this has been done interest rates can be reduced. The real economy should suffer much less damage from a sharp rise in interest rates that is quickly reversed than from debt-deflation.

2.4.1 Overall conclusions from experience in the 1970s and 1980s[16]

2.4.1.1 Money supply policy

- The policy of announcing targets for the money supply with the aim of influencing expectations and for political purposes was a failure in the 1980s; reliance should not be placed on such a policy in the future.

- Monetary analysis in the 1970s and 1980s was reasonably efficient

[16]These conclusions are taken from my book, Inside Thatcher's Monetarist Revolution, Macmillan/IEA, 1998.

at predicting major events providing allowance was made for distortions to the aggregates but the precise timing of them was not forecast.

- The warnings were given in time for remedial action to be taken.
- The worst of the Barber and Lawson booms would have been avoided if the warnings from monetary analysis had been heeded.
- There were occasions when the monetary barometers were jammed; this should have been known at the time and the barometers should have been declared temporarily out of order.

2.4.1.2 Control of the money supply

There are various degrees in which the money supply can be used either as an indicator or as a factor to be controlled, for example:

- Discretionary measures can be based on warnings from monetary analysis. The danger of such a policy is that too little action may be taken too late, as in the past, in which case more powerful measures will be needed later on and the disruption to the economy will be worse.
- Direct action can be taken to rectify obviously excessive or inadequate monetary growth. This brings forward remedial action, in which case measures should not need to be so powerful and the disruption to the economy should be less. Providing allowance is made for distortions, this type of monetary control will act as a powerful self-stabiliser for the economy.

2.4.1.3 How quickly should the authorities react to undesirable monetary growth?

- The shorter is the reaction time, the greater is the chance that action turns out to be unnecessary and of needless disruption to the economy.
- Fluctuations in the money supply that last for less than six months should definitely be ignored.
- Assuming that the warning from the monetary aggregates is not a false alarm, the longer is the reaction time the more powerful need be the measures and the greater the consequential disruption to the economy.

- A balance needs to be struck between disruption from unnecessary measures and increased disruption because necessary measures have been delayed.

2.4.2 Optimum solution[17]

- The optimum solution is to leave the reaction time to discretion. Judgement should be based on how clear the situation is at the time.
- If the situation is clear, for example if the monetary aggregates are all behaving in a similar way, the reaction time might be as short as six months.
- If most of the aggregates are distorted but the message from them can nevertheless be discerned with a reasonable degree of confidence after analysis, the reaction time might be about a year.
- If the aggregates are all distorted, because for example of financial innovation, policy should be based on an overall judgement of the economic situation and not on the behaviour of the monetary aggregates until the message from the aggregates becomes clearer.

2.5 Alan Walters: Monetary Targets — the Fiscal Dimension

By March 1981, Margaret Thatcher had been in office, and arguably in power, for about 20 months — and according to opinion polls, it is widely thought, particularly among her party, that she would not survive much longer. Ever since her election in May 1979, the economy had degenerated further and further into a recession that certainly was the most severe since the 1930s. With a few exceptions, economists were of one mind: what was desperately needed was a policy of fiscal expansion — lower taxes and increased expenditure. In the 1981 budget, however, the Thatcher government pursed exactly the opposite policy, and no half measures either. It turned out to be the biggest budgetary squeeze in peacetime history. Yet, in the event, the economy did not nosedive into a black hole, as the majority of economists had so confidently predicted; instead, by mid-1981, the economy embarked on an expansion which persisted for more that nine years — the longest in statistical history.

---

[17] This assumes demand-side control of the money stock. The author has argued for supply-side control, that is, for control of the monetary base, providing adequate buffers are included in the chosen system of control.

All this is, of course, history, and might be thought to be of dubious relevance to the world some two decades later. But I do see some noteworthy parallels between Thatcher's Britain and contemporary Japan. Current doctrine in Japan is to fight the recession through fiscal expansionary 'packages' of tax reductions and, more important, public spending. In the light of Britain's experience in 1981 one may wonder whether this is the right policy. Would it not be better to do a "1981": reduce dramatically the budget deficit, now around 10 per cent of GNP, to a sustainable 3 per cent? No doubt any such suggestion will be treated as the ravings of a lunatic, as indeed was the case when I argued for a large retrenchment in Britain in 1981.

2.5.1 The budget of 1981

First let me remind you of the outline and peculiarities of the budget of 1981 (there was only one in the year). The PSBR had averaged around 7 per cent of GNP between 1973 and 1980. In our day we would view such figures with horror — banana republics and Russian roulette. (The three percent limit now imposed through the stability pact of the EU euroland seems very parsimonious). It is a matter of simple arithmetic to show that such deficits were unsustainable in an inflation-free environment. But, of course, the 1970s were anything but inflation-free: the average rate of inflation over 1973–1980 was about 15 per cent. Such inflation rates soon expropriated holders of non-indexed gilt edged, and the market value of the national debt, in spite of very large additions of new paper, fell substantially to about 35 per cent of GNP (compared with 86 per cent in 1976). All this expropriation of holders of gilts gave rise to periodic gilt strikes, a fall in market liquidity and soaring interest rates.

Such high interest rates across the spectrum of term structure, however, had already had an effect in tightening monetary policy. From 1979 to mid-1981, the rate of growth of M1 had fallen from about 15 per cent to virtually zero. Although the broad money indicators, on which government policy was based, had exhibited no such dramatic fall, from all the other indicators it was clear to me that there was a fierce monetary squeeze being imposed on the economy. (Many other monetarists in the Treasury, in the City and in academe quite reasonably held that since M3 was still roaring ahead, monetary policy, if anything, was too loose; and in evidence they pointed to the fact that it was still much larger than allowed for in the MTS.)

To assist in assessing the stance of monetary policy, I had suggested to (now Sir) Alfred Sherman that the Centre for Policy Studies ask Jurg

Niehans, a Swiss colleague and professor of economics at Johns Hopkins, to study the problem and report. In a convincing argument, Niehans demonstrated that there was a fierce monetary squeeze since mid 1979 and that this, rather than oil revenues, was largely responsible for the massive appreciation of sterling. I agreed — and after a little disputation, so did the Prime Minister. (The Treasury largely ignored Niehans' work; his name is not even mentioned in Nigel Lawson's somewhat restricted memoirs "... View from Number 11".)

What to advise on all this? From work done with my colleagues in Birmingham and from Friedman and Schwartz, I had long been of the opinion that the economy danced largely to the tune of monetary policy. The primary aim of policy should be to restore the growth of M1 and in operational terms this meant bringing down short term interest rates. But of course interest rates could not be reduced, at least for any length of time, and monetary growth could not appear, unless the PSBR were reduced substantially. Yet a reduction of the PSBR was the opposite to the Keynesian cure for a persistent recession. The Keynesians (or more strictly the anti-monetarists) firmly believed in the fact that only a fiscal expansion would restore economic growth and drag us out of the recession.

I eventually took the view that we must have a fierce cut of over £4 billion in the PSBR primarily through increases in taxes. (There was no time to pursue cuts in spending). It took a long while for the Prime Minister to be persuaded of the need for such draconian policies so far from the conventional wisdom. But, at last, under considerable pressure from her advisors at No. 10, she agreed to what was arguably the biggest fiscal squeeze in peacetime history. (In the event the forecast PSBR of £10.4 billion compared with an actual outcome of £8.6 billion, so the effective squeeze was much bigger than intended — amounting to roughly 3.6 per cent of GNP.)

The budget on March 10th was not well received. It had a rough passage through the morning cabinet and in the House. In financial circles, however, the general stance, and particularly the lower PSBR and 2 per cent cut in base rates, was quite widely welcomed, as was soon reflected in financial markets. British academic economists, with a few noteworthy exceptions, condemned it in the most extravagant language. On the 13th March in a round robin letter circulated to academic economists, Professors Frank Hahn and Robert Neild of Cambridge asked support for the following text:

> We who are all present or retired members of the economic staff of British universities, are convinced that:
>
> There is no basis in economic theory or supporting evi-

> dence for the Government's belief that by deflating demand they will bring inflation permanently under control and thereby introduce an automatic recovery in output and employment;
>
> Present policies will deepen the depression, erode the industrial base of our economy and threaten its social and political stability;
>
> There are alternative policies;
>
> The time has come to reject monetarists' policies and consider which alternative offers the best hope of sustained recovery.

No less than 364 economists signed it by the time the results were published in the Times on March 30th — and this was during the spring vacation! Included were all but one (Donald MacDougall) of past chief economic advisers to the Government, incipient Nobel Laureates, members of today's MPC, and a future "third-way" scholar and Director of the LSE.

The forecast of the 364 was soon discredited by the performance of the economy. By the time summer came it was perfectly clear that the economy had not merely slowed the decline but was exhibiting strong signs of healthy growth. Contrary to the 364 view, inflation soon started to slow from its ambient 15 per cent until, by the end of 1982, it was around 5 per cent — and, with one or two blips in 1985 and 1990, it has remained low to this day. Similarly the growth was no flash-in-the-pan. The budget of 1981 ushered in the longest period (almost nine years) of sustained growth in British economic history.

The other major change was in confidence and credibility. The many years of high borrowing requirements, expropriation of gilt holders, as well as the frequent financial crises, gilt strikes and emergency budgets, had eroded confidence in economic management. At least this Thatcher government was really getting to grips with the underlying problems. It was just credible that the policy would reduce inflation whereas with a large borrowing requirement any such forecast lacked any credibility. I would regard this sea-change in confidence as perhaps the biggest contributor to the turn-around.

One would have thought that such a massive discrediting of such a distinguished body of economists would have called forth a soul-searching to see what went wrong and to learn the lessons of the period. But that does not appear to have been the case. Those economists, such as Tim Congdon, Gordon Pepper and Patrick Minford, who were utterly opposed to the 364 did not flush out any explanation for the failure of the conventional wisdom. The only riposte I can recall is that of Frank

Hahn in the Times: there he claimed that all economies turn around sometime, and it just so happened that this was the occasion.

In "Britain's Economic Renaissance" (Oxford, 1986) I set out what I thought we had discovered about monetary and fiscal policy. In essence I would claim that the period showed that the economy, both in real and nominal terms, responded to the variations in the money supply. The response in the form of the traditional Keynesian fiscal multiplier was not merely weak but actually perverse. I conjectured that this was because of the persistently high borrowing of the 1970s; what was secularly needed was a reduction in borrowing; an increase, per contra, would have eroded confidence and almost certainly have led to yet another financial crisis.

Yet up to February 26th the Prime Minister, albeit with reservations, broadly accepted Howe's recommendation of a PSBR around £11.5 billion. Together with my fellow No. 10 advisers, John Hoskyns and David Wolfson, had been arguing for some weeks for a really large reduction in the PSBR, a far bigger cut than that contemplated by the Treasury. We even thought that an increase in the basic rate of income tax should be on the agenda — but generally we left the detailed measures to the highly competent Treasury team.

The many budget meetings on the extent of the fiscal squeeze are described with great accuracy in Margaret Thatcher's "Downing Street Years". The Prime Minister met with the Chancellor and Sir Douglas Wass, the Permanent Secretary, on 24th February — I was absent on other business. According to the account of the meeting, she had become more and more convinced of the case for a substantial reduction in the PSBR — but the Chancellor nevertheless stuck to his guns. But he agreed to think further about what could be done. (On 25th February, on being apprised of what had transpired at the meeting, I had written to Sir Douglas Wass stating that I had not changed my view and I urged him not to deliver the three or four per cent interest rate reductions that the markets were expecting and at most reduce them by 1 per cent).

As described in "Downing Street Years", the Prime Minister saw me early the following morning and told me that she had seen the Chancellor and 'insisted' on the lower PSBR. Shortly before she left for America, the Chancellor saw her and agreed that he could get very near to the PSBR we thought appropriate by not indexing for the 13 per cent inflation in the tax thresholds. Although highly undesirable in a microeconomic sense, there was a consensus that it would be politically better than raising the standard rate.

In retrospect the budget was clearly what the Prime Minister, albeit after much delay, wanted. She knew that it would encounter bitter opposition and controversy. It required immense moral courage to push through a budget which flouted the accepted canons of Keynesian fiscal policy. The Treasury team did wonders in getting the measures into the budget process. But the budget bore the unmistakable stamp of Margaret Thatcher.

2.5.2 What followed?

The role of the 1981 budget in paving the way for a relaxation of the severe monetary squeeze of 1979–80, the devaluation of sterling to somewhere near its appropriate level, the turn-around in output in mid-summer, the restoration of confidence in financial and other markets — all may be debated. My colleagues and I in No. 10 were of the firm opinion that the financial reform must be the basis of many other policies that were dear to the heart of the Prime Minister. The deregulation of the economy, privatisation etc. would have been difficult to achieve in an economy teetering always on the brink of financial crisis. So, I believe, the 1981 budget has earned its laurels as the foundation of Thatcherism.

And, in its way, Thatcherism — or at least what was said to be Thatcherism — spread throughout much of the world. Nowadays in political circles Thatcherism is being challenged by "The Third Way". But we stick to Thatcherism in next discussing the many trials and few tribulations of Japan in the nineties.

2.5.3 Some similarities UK 1980 and Japan 1990

- both were suffering from a persistent, verging on severe, recession in real output
- both had chronic problems of restructuring, with over-capacity in industry
- both had record levels of unemployment and problems of redeploying labour
- both had considerable government control of industry
- both had persistent, and growing, massive budget deficits, Britain at around 7 per cent of GNP and Japan heading for 10 per cent
- both had experienced an over-expansion of credit followed by a monetary and credit squeeze
- both found difficulties in funding these deficits and other covert obligations

- both experienced a massive real appreciation in their currencies and worsening of the current balance of payments
- both suffered from a lack of confidence in the authorities and in their leaders

The diligent will point out that there were marked differences in several aspects of the economies — probably the differences were greatest in the financial sector and in the forms of corporate governance and industrial ethos. But I think that these differences are rather like constants in economic policy: they do not insulate the economies from the fundamental forces of macroeconomics.

2.5.4 The propositions on policy

These similarities are worth bearing in mind when one examines the reaction of the economics profession and the nostrums of central bankers and treasury officials and their hangers on in the media. (Samuel Taylor Coleridge called these the "clerisy" — useful term I think.)

- both argued that there should be fiscal expansion (at least allowing the automatic stabilisers to work), an increase in public spending and reductions in taxes
- both thought that monetary policy should be 'accommodating'
- both recognised that structural reforms were needed but would take a long time

These are the traditional Keynesian measures to fight a recession so it is not surprising that they were the linchpin of policy.

2.5.5 A Thatcher policy for Japan?

In Thatcherite terms, what Japan needs is a sharp cut in its public sector deficit from 10 per cent of GNP to around 5 per cent. The best way to achieve this reduction is through attrition in public spending and particularly in notoriously wasteful infrastructure investment. (I would be much more chary about increasing tax rates.) A multiyear plan would anticipate eliminating the structural deficit in two or at most three years.

What would we expect such a plan to deliver? What we observed in Thatcher's Britain was a sea-change in credibility and confidence. The reaction in financial circles was one of astonishment — that this time "she really means it". For most of the 1970s, the government had been borrowing around 7 per cent of GNP every year with consequential frequent financial crisis and gilt strikes. After the 1981 March budget, it was clear that, at least as long as she was Prime Minister, this was no longer tolerated. Confidence in the government's courage increased apace. And with justification: there were no more gilt strikes or financial panics during the rest of the Thatcher era.

I do not think there is any doubt that credibility or confidence in their leaders has reached an all time low in Japan. Policy has drifted into the swamps. No political party leader has faced squarely the parlous state of the economy — and in particular the massive obligations of the government in recapitalising the financial sector, in dealing with the pension funds, and so on. As for the deficit, everyone knows that it must be dealt with sometime — and the longer the delay the greater the pain. At the very least it seems perverse to increase the deficit or the debt. The Japanese have been disappointed with the consequences of their successive attempts at fiscal stimulus. The results have been at most transitory (mainly subsidising the building and construction sector in putting up bridges to nowhere) and have left larger obligations and an increase in the debt. If fiscal stimulus could have lifted Japan out of the recession, then surely it would have done so already.

At the best, the fiscal squeeze from 10+ per cent of GNP to 5 per cent would generate a wave of confidence in the economy and in government. The deluge of bond issues would slow down. The old cliché of "light at the end of the tunnel" is wrong — but at least they could see the tunnel.

Would this two or three year fiscal squeeze produce the benign results we saw in Britain? Alas there is nothing sure in economics. But one can say with some confidence that the fate foretold by the 364 is virtually ruled out.

2.5.6 Monetary policy

The need for an expansionary monetary policy is widely accepted. Until recently the emphasis was on controlling short run interest rates. But as these have recently lapsed to zero the authorities have turned their attention to open market operations. The thrust is for the authorities to print yen and buy Japanese Government Bonds. The expectation is that eventually the flood of yen will erode the price declines and perhaps promote the expectation of some modest reflation.

Various gurus have made recommendations along these lines and I would not wish to disagree with them. In this context one must pay court to the writings of Paul Krugman, mainly because he has such a great following. Krugman has strongly supported the policy of monetary expansion and has been at most lukewarm about fiscal stimuli. However, he has recommended that the authorities aim to set negative real interest rates. I find this a difficult pill to swallow. If real rates become negative I would expect, not the stimulation of investment and activity which Krugman anticipates, but a grand flight of capital from Japan to more propitious environments where the Japanese saver could get something for his money. A target of negative real interest rates would, therefore, be entirely inappropriate.

There is some evidence that in recent weeks the authorities in Japan have changed their policies and are not maintaining target short interest rates but simply trying to increase the rate of growth of the money supply from its ambient (broad money) growth of 5 per cent. As with much Japanese policy, these measures are not yet clear cut and sustained; ambiguity still rules.

2.5.7 An aside — who to praise or blame?

The 1981 budget was widely perceived to be the foundation stone of Thatcherism. And of course it generated many claims by those who alleged paternity. One such was Geoffrey Howe in his IFS lecture in 1991:

> There has sprung up a myth about the paternity of those difficult Budget judgments, the implication being that the 1981 Budget was somehow 'made in No. 10' against Treasury advice. These budget judgments were in fact fashioned by the Chancellor of the Exchequer with the help of Treasury Ministers and on the strength of Treasury advice. (See Lawson, p98).

The truth, said Lawson, is "beyond dispute."(!) And in fact many of the budget judgments about particular taxes, within the fiscal guidelines, were made in the Treasury and, I would add, very well done. But, as Lady Thatcher's autobiography ("The Downing Street Years" June 1993) makes clear, she made the main decisions on overall stance of the budget and in particular on the size of the PSBR. (It is odd that, throughout their terms of office, Howe — and Lawson — complained bitterly about the 'bossiness' of the Prime Minister, yet Howe claimed to have fashioned the most important measure of her tenure without any of it 'made in No. 10'. So odd it beggars belief.)

Appendix: European Monetary Forum Conference in honour of Alan Walters

Held in Cardiff in May 2002, hosted by the Julian Hodge Institute of Applied Macroeconomics, Cardiff University

PARTICIPANTS

Ivo Arnold, Nijenrode University, Netherlands
Michael Beenstock, Hebrew University of Jerusalem
David Byers, Cardiff Business School
Bernard Connolly, AIG Trading Ltd., London
Matthew Canzoneri, Georgetown University, Washington DC
Laurence Copeland, Cardiff Business School
James Davidson, Cardiff Business School
Harris Dellas, University of Bern
Michele Fratianni, University of Indiana
Sugata Ghosh, Cardiff Business School
John Greenwood, Invesco
Jürgen von Hagen, University of Bonn, Institute of European Integration Studies
Dale Henderson, Federal Reserve Board, Washington DC
Andrew Hughes Hallett, University of Strathclyde/Cardiff Business School
Laurian Lungu, Cardiff Business School
Vidya Mahambare, Cardiff Business School
Su-Ling Marshall, Cardiff Business School
Kent Matthews, Cardiff Business School
Bennett McCallum, Carnegie-Mellon University
David Meenagh, Cardiff Business School

Jacques Melitz, University of Strathclyde
Patrick Minford, Cardiff Business School
Kris Naraidoo, Cardiff Business School
Edward Nelson, Federal Reserve Bank of St. Louis
Charles Nolan, University of Durham
Ivan Paya, Cardiff Business School
David A. Peel, Cardiff Business School
Gordon Pepper, Cass Business School, City of London
Francesco Perugini, Cardiff Business School
Michael Salemi, University of North Carolina, Chapel Hill
Mark Salmon, Cass Business School, City of London
Anne Sibert, Birkbeck College, London
Philipp Sibbertsen, University of Dortmund
David S. Smith, Williams de Broe
Peter N. Smith, University of York
Prakriti Sofat, Cardiff Business School
Naveen Srinivasan, Cardiff Business School
Casper de Vries, Erasmus University, Rotterdam
Sir Alan Walters, AIG Trading Ltd., Emeritus Professor, Johns Hopkins University, Baltimore
Peter Warburton, Economic Perspectives

The Julian Hodge Institute of Applied Macroeconomics

This Institute was launched in autumn 1999 in a new collaboration between the Cardiff Business School of Cardiff University and Julian Hodge Bank. The aim of the Institute is to carry out research into the behaviour of the UK economy, and to study in particular its relationship with the other economies of Europe. This research has been given added urgency by the ongoing discussions about the UK's adoption of the Euro in place of the Pound. The new Institute has aimed to develop research relevant to this important debate. The Institute's director since it was founded in 1999 has been Patrick Minford. Collaborators in the School are Laurence Copeland, James Davidson, Kent Matthews, David Peel, David Byers, and Sugata Ghosh. The Institute's staff of researchers is mainly based in Cardiff Business School, which is also the Institute's office.

Cardiff Business School:

http://www.cardiff.ac.uk/carbs/

The Julian Hodge Institute of Applied Macroeconomics:

http://www.cardiff.ac.uk/carbs/research/jhiam/

Index